Public Expenditure

Effective Management and Control

D. M. SHAPIRO

21 August 2004

Public Expenditure

Effective Management and Control

Edited by **Dan Corry**

Institute for Public Policy Research (IPPR)
London

The Dryden Press

Harcourt Brace & Company Limited KPMG

London Fort Worth New York Orlando
Philadelphia San Diego Toronto Sydney Tokyo

The Dryden Press
24/28 Oval Road,
London NW1 7DX

A catalogue record for this book is available from the British Library
ISBN 0–03–099064–5

Typeset by J&L Composition Ltd, Filey, North Yorkshire
Printed in Great Britain at WBC Book Manufacturers, Bridgend, Mid Glamorgan

Contents

List of Contributors

ALAN BAILEY was Permanent Secretary, Department of Transport, from 1986 to 1991, having previously been Second Permanent Secretary in charge of public expenditure at the Treasury from 1983, and Deputy Head CPRS, 1981–82. He is now Deputy Chairman, London Transport Buses.

MARTIN CAVE is Professor of Economics at Brunel University. He specializes in regulatory and public sector economics, and has written books and articles on output measurement in the public sector, performance indicators in higher education and methods for valuing public output.

YVETTE COOPER is an economics columnist and leader writer for the *Independent*. She has worked as an advisor on public expenditure to Labour's Shadow Chancellor of the Exchequer, the late John Smith MP, Harriet Harman MP, when she was Shadow Chief Secretary to the Treasury, and to Bill Clinton's 1992 Presidential Campaign.

DAN CORRY and **SEAN GRAY** have both worked as economists in government, including the Treasury, and for the Labour Party. Corry worked on the public expenditure side of the Treasury in the second half of the 1980s and then for the Labour Party Front Bench economics team from 1989–92. He is currently Senior Economist at the centre-left think-tank the Institute for Public Policy Research, and founding editor of its journal, *New Economy*.

JOHN FLEMMING is Warden of Wadham College, Oxford. He has written on public expenditure issues ever since 1965. From 1980–91 he was Chief Economist at the Bank of England. He has acted as a consultant to the Treasury on both public expenditure and macroeconomic issues as a member of its Academic Panel.

JOHN HALL, IAN PRESTON and **MICHAEL RIDGE** are all associated with the Institute for Fiscal Studies. Hall works there full time, while Preston and Ridge are Research Associates at IFS while being at University College London and Brunel University respectively. Until recently Michael Ridge was Economic Advisor at the Department of Environment providing advice on public spending trends and strategic policy issues.

DAVID HEALD is Professor of Accountancy at the University of Aberdeen, and acts as specialist adviser on public expenditure to the Treasury Committee of the House of Commons. In 1996/97, thanks to a Leverhulme Research Fellowship, he is studying the level and composition of public expenditure.

GEOFFREY HULME is a consultant on public expenditure to Chartered Institute of Finance and Accountancy (CIPFA) and former Director of the Public Expenditure Policy Unit. He was formerly Deputy Secretary and Principal Finance Officer of the Department of Health and Social Security.

PETER JACKSON is Professor of Economics and Director of the Management Centre at the University of Leicester. He was a Treasury economist 1969–71. He is the joint author (with C.V. Brown) of *Public Sector Economics* (4th edition 1990) and *Current Issues in Public Sector Economics* (1993) and has written on many aspects of the public sector, including particularly public expenditure and management.

JUNE PALLOT is Professor of Accountancy, Finance and Information Systems at the University of Canterbury, Christchurch, New Zealand. From 1993–95 she was seconded to the Office of the Controller and Auditor General with responsibility for accounting and financial management policy. **IAN BALL** is a Principal of Public Sector Performance (NZ) Ltd and Professor of Accounting and Public Policy at Victoria University of Wellington. Until December 1994 he was Central Financial Controller in the New Zealand Treasury.

PETER KELLNER is political commentator, and opinion poll analyst, for BBC Newsnight, *The Observer* and the *Evening Standard*. His books include *The Civil Servants: an Enquiry into Britain's Ruling Class.*

PAMELA MEADOWS is a Director of the Policy Studies Institute. She was previously Chief Economist and Head of Economics, Research and Evaluation Division at the Department of Employment. She is a Council Member of the UK Evaluation Society.

NICK MONCK worked in the Treasury from 1969 to 1992, becoming Second Permanent Secretary (Public Expenditure) in 1990. He was Permanent Secretary at the Employment Department from 1993 until April 1995. Since then he has acted as a consultant in Hungary, Mexico, and South Africa.

JON STERN is currently a Senior Consultant at NERA (National Economic Research Associates). Previously, he worked as an economist in the Treasury, the Department of Health and Social Security, and the Department of Employment. Much of his work was concerned with evaluation of public expenditure projects and programmes.

CHRIS TRINDER is Chief Economist at the Chartered Institute of Public Finance and Accountancy (CIPFA). Previous jobs include work at the National Institute of Economic and Social Research. He has specialized in issues concerning the public sector and especially pay for many years, contributing many articles on the subject.

SHEILA WATSON is Principal Economist at the Centre for Local Economic Strategies where she works on a range of public finance issues. Previously she was employed as a Research Officer at the Institute for Fiscal Studies, and as Economic Adviser to Labour's Shadow Chief Secretary to the Treasury and then Deputy Leader, Margaret Beckett MP.

GEOFF WHITE is with consultants Segal Quince Wicksteed where he specializes in aspects of local economic development. He has worked as an economist in both the DTI and on the public expenditure side of the Treasury and was involved in helping produce Treasury guidance on the appraisal and evaluation of projects.

Preface and Acknowledgements

The putting together of this book has been a rare pleasure. It covers a subject that I have spent many hours discussing over the years, both with colleagues in the Civil Service, the Labour Party and in academia. Particularly helpful have been discussions with Jon Stern, Helen Roberts, Sheila Watson, Yvette Cooper, Nick Pecorrelli and Henry Neuburger.

All the contributors in this book gave of their valuable time not only to write but to attend (long) seminars to discuss the draft papers. Several people – contributors and non-contributors – were especially helpful in discussing structure and in commenting on draft papers. These include Nick Monck, Michael Spackman and Elizabeth Ranson, Julian Laite and Neil Sherlock of KPMG. All chapters are, however, the opinions of those who wrote them. As the keen reader will discover, there are a number of important differences of opinion on various aspects of the public expenditure scene today.

Financial help to enable the book to be produced came from KPMG to whom we are very grateful, especially to Neil Sherlock. We are also grateful to Dryden Press for their help along the way, and in particular to Maggie Smith, the commissioning editor, and to Claire Bailey. From my side, help from Spencer Livermore, Helena Scott and particularly Robert Sierra was invaluable while James Sparling handled the graphics and Laura O'Leary helped with the sub-editing. My family, Joe, Elsa and Dinah, saw little of me for some time during the construction of this book. But they know that my obsession may now be put to rest.

Finally I would like to thank the Director of IPPR, Gerald Holtham, both for helpful comments on aspects of the book and for believing – like me – that this vital area must be part of the core work of a centre-left think-tank.

In a world in which the phrase 'the public sector' is so often used by the Right to conjure up pictures of inefficiency, strikes and tax hikes, I hope that this book helps open eyes to the fact that the public sector and public spending can be a positive force and so play a vital role in our economy and our society.

DAN CORRY

Introduction: Improving Public Expenditure

Dan Corry

Public expenditure concerns us all. We complain about the lack of it when the Tube breaks down or the schools are crumbling. We complain about too much of it when the tax bill arrives and we haven't got enough money left for a new car. We fume at the way it is wasted when we can't get through on the phone to the passport office or when the bureaucrats demand form-filling of us. And we hardly notice it at all when the train works perfectly.

All these things are important to everyday life, to the way we see ourselves, and to the kind of society we live in. In this book we look at the issues surrounding public spending from a variety of angles to give some answers to the question of whether public money could not be spent more effectively.

This book

There are many good and interesting books on this subject but this one is quite different from most of them. This is not a standard text book. In the first place, most (though not all) of the authors would probably describe themselves as centre or centre-left. The IPPR itself, from which this book originates, is a centre-left think-tank.

It is striking that, in the main, those who most deeply believe in the case for an active public sector have spent least time thinking about how public money is actually spent, how it could be spent more effectively and how the whole concept of public expenditure could be made more popular. Yet it is for this group that these issues should matter most. For *laissez faire* privatizers, critiques of the current system are often only ways of softening up the target for eventual closing down. For the authors in this book they are a prelude to making public action more effective.

Second, the contributors to this book come from a wide variety of backgrounds. Some of the authors are certainly academic students of the subject; but many gain their insights from having had experience of the actual processes involved in public expenditure, being former players in the game. Journalists, consultants and 'policy-wonks' are also represented. They bring a different perspective again to these issues. The differing backgrounds of the contributors come across clearly in their different approaches to the subject, both in subject matter and in style. The book thus gives a lively taste of the different perspectives on what is going right and wrong in our public realm.

Despite the intrinsic importance of the subject, it is sadly but understandably the case that most people find the issue of public expenditure offputting and tedious at best. And yet all the contributors are convinced that this is a very vital subject indeed. This book prides itself in trying to avoid getting lost in esoteric theory or innumerable acronyms: the aim is to explain how the current systems affect the everyday world. With luck, the book will not only be of interest to practitioners and the academic community but to anybody interested in the way that public money is spent and the way the relationship between the state and its citizens is evolving.

The UK system

The current UK system is well described elsewhere (see, for instance, Likierman (1988) and Brown and Jackson (1986)). Nevertheless, its basic outline needs to be set out here since it is the basis of what many contributions go on to discuss.

Broadly speaking, the Treasury is in charge of the process both of setting public expenditure targets and of trying to enforce them. This it does in addition to its responsibility for general economic management, an unusual combination – in most countries the two duties find homes in different departments. The Chief Secretary to the Treasury, a government minister of Cabinet rank, is the politician who spends most time worrying about these issues. But the Chancellor of the Exchequer also takes an interest, particularly in the setting of aggregate targets for spending, as these have crucial macroeconomic implications.

Each year the government carries out a Public Expenditure Survey (PES). The aim of this is to set budgetary targets for the next financial year and for the two after that. Naturally, plans for the forthcoming year are taken most seriously by all sides.

The survey involves many discussions between officials in the Treasury (the public expenditure divisions) and the relevant people in the departments (and agencies). These are primarily, but not only, to be found in the finance divisions. Discussions can and usually do involve the relevant minister at some stage. The results are announced in the Budget Statement at the end of November each year, with more detail on spending decisions given later in public expenditure White Papers (there is now one for each department: formerly they were issued as one). For several years now, the government has tried to put some order into this process by agreeing an aggregate total for spending before the survey round gets going fully in the summer.

There are often, of course, enormous conflicts about what should happen on public expenditure. Over the years governments have tried various methods to avoid this or at least to deal with them sensibly when they arise. The 'Star Chamber' was fashionable at one time. A minister in dispute with the Treasury would have to appear before this body, made up of various senior ministers chaired by a trusted member of the Cabinet (in actual fact this was Lord Whitelaw) to make their case. Fear of being shown to be indulging in special pleading was thought to be a great deterrent to spending ministers letting things go this far. Currently a Cabinet committee called EDX is used. This committee of senior ministers determines priorities after hearing evidence from spending ministers but without negotiating with them.

Public spending totals are agreed in cash terms. The agreements are broken down into different sections ('votes') and departments have only limited room to move moneys about between these different headings (although this may be beginning to change).

The Treasury, in fact, keeps a close eye on what goes on throughout the year: it is not just a budget setter. It is always pressing departments to prove they are achieving value for money. The Treasury also tries to ensure that departments appraise projects and schemes in consistent ways using guidance promulgated by itself. Departments can make their own final decisions below certain values of money ('delegated limits') but above this the Treasury can wade in (as it can with new schemes).

There has been much reform in recent years in the way that government operates. Much of this has been put in the context of bringing market forces more into the picture. A fair part of it is probably better characterized as attempts to improve performance through reforms which align the incentives facing public sector managers with those needed to provide high quality, efficient services.

Most reform to the marketization end of the spectrum has been the complete privatization of formerly publicly provided activities (most notably the utilities like gas, water and rail, but also research establishments and so on). Less dramatic but equally far-reaching has been the separation of the institution setting policy from the body that carries out that policy. Within the public sector, this has been done through the creation of executive agencies (usually known simply as 'agencies'). In many cases this idea has been taken further so that the private sector is used as the provider in an explicit contracting-out relationship. The use of private finance, via the Private Finance Initiative (PFI) can now also be added to the list of reforms to the structure of public service delivery.

These developments certainly change things in the public expenditure world. They aim to increase efficiency and effectiveness. To what extent they do, and what they imply for the control that the Treasury or the elected government has over what is happening to the public's money, is a major theme of the book.

On the whole, the Conservative years in office can be seen as years of centralization of decision making within the public sector, as local government has lost its power, public corporations have all but disappeared and agencies and so on have been kept to tight contracts drawn up from the centre. Yet at the same time it is certainly true that much power to make smaller management decisions has been decentralized (although to non-elected bodies or 'quangos'), following the general trend throughout the world.

Partly as a result of these changes the Treasury has in recent years been reorganized in what – to most – seems like an exercise in downsizing.

Looking forward

This is the basic situation. This book looks at all aspects of what is happening and what could be done. Although the views of authors differ on many issues, several main conclusions emerge.

Public spending is not 'bad'

The first point to come shining through is undoubtedly that public expenditure is not in any way a 'bad' thing. It can be spent inefficiently and on things that nobody really wants or that add nothing to either economic strength or social cohesion, but this is not a necessary feature of public expenditure or action, nor is it particularly the fact. Despite endless attacks, the public still values and rather likes the public services and the public sector even though it thinks they could be a lot better (Public Management Foundation, 1996; also see Chapter 6 by Kellner in this book).

The possibility of ineffectiveness has nevertheless rightly been recognized, and plenty of interesting and important solutions to it are being tried. These all amount to giving incentive structures to operators of public expenditure to act efficiently in accordance with the wishes of the citizens and users.

Nor is public spending spiralling out of control. There are, of course, pressures on the system. A lot of these at the moment stem from the size of the welfare budget. But this is mainly a result of economic failure, and few would argue that economic weakness is primarily a consequence of the size of the public sector itself.

Certainly it is arguable that the growing share of public spending in GDP since the 1960s in most OECD countries has had pretty marginal returns in terms of improved social or economic indicators (Tanzi and Schuknecht, 1995). That gives good grounds for scrutinizing spending carefully to see if all the things the state is doing are really necessary. But academic evidence that the scale of resources taken up by the public sector actually causes severe economic problems is very weak indeed (Atkinson, 1996; Bénabou, 1996).

To the extent that the public sector has negative effects, this is far more likely to be the consequence of inappropriate structures of many public services and benefits, given the changes happening in society. For instance, it is certainly arguable that the current structure of the welfare state discourages savings and effort. These are not trivial problems by any means but they require careful micro-change, not necessarily the taking of an undiscriminating axe to public budgets.

As Yvette Cooper explains, the pressures of the future are less likely to revolve around the problems of scale than of delivering the kind of services that those with rising income and aspirations want, without cutting off the service to those at the lower end of the spectrum. As Labour Party MP Alan Milburn has put it: 'If the middle classes opt out, problems emerge. The distancing of the middle class families from public services has profound implications. It weakens their commitment, as citizens and taxpayers, to services like the NHS and compromises its ability to survive as a comprehensive service' (Milburn, 1996). The attempt to buy off the middle classes through allowing choice and 'cherry-picking' within public services – for instance, by letting them have better (i.e. selective grant-maintained) state schools for themselves or by adding user charges for extra frills (e.g. for a TV in hospital) – may not be a long-term solution to this problem. More imaginative approaches will have to emerge.

Role of markets

It is an irony that the pressure on public spending, much of which comes from the paying out of welfare benefits, has been met largely by trying to squeeze a little more efficiency out of the system – often on things like the running costs. Conservative Social Security Minister Peter Lilley, for instance, has recently announced that he would like to privatize the delivery of child benefit (through contracting out) to reduce costs. This may well be worthwhile but it does not deal with the fundamental problems of child benefit expenditure: for instance, should it be a universal benefit and at what rate should it be paid? If running costs can be cut, all well and good. But they are comparatively small beer.

Nevertheless, where there is room to use markets and the private sector both to deliver and sometimes finance 'public' services, and this leads to increases in value for money, then this should be pursued. The delivery itself should not be stuck in some time warp. Many of the authors in this book argue very strongly on these points.

But that does not mean that we should naïvely bring in the market. There are serious questions about the nature of what is variously referred to as the 'new public sector management' and the 'contract state'. Does it make planning and efficient allocation of expenditure more or less easy? Does it cause problems for control or simply delegate them to different levels? Does it really increase efficiency of resource use in the longer term? Is accountability enhanced or trivialized in a contract relationship?

These are still early days for such an experiment. It is therefore not surprising to find that opinions vary as to the answer to these questions. Former Treasury official Nick Monck, for instance, believes that on the whole the new system is a better one. Peter Jackson, on the other hand, is at the forefront of those who doubt that the changes are getting us anywhere positive.

Several chapters in this book focus on the Private Finance Initiative (PFI) (Corry, Watson, Flemming and Heald among others). In the PFI the private sector builds and operates a facility in return for a contract that the public sector will pay an annual fee for it over the next 30 or 40 years. Although in its infancy, this could represent a very major change in the way public services are delivered and paid for. While offering potential advantages there is a suspicion that this policy, if handled wrongly, offers a little jam today but may cost future generations a lot.

There are other concerns about the use of market-type mechanisms to deliver public services. A deficit on a particular project or budget might be taken to imply inefficiency rather than a challenging client group; it is difficult with public services to punish bad management or give appropriate financial incentives without hurting the end-user; tying everything up in contracts leads to an inability to shuffle money around in response to changing priorities.

But more than this, there is a feeling that while each individual application of market-type mechanisms in one way or another seems to offer benefits, we are not exactly sure where this big shift will actually take us. The sum may not look as good as the parts.

This point has been well made by Robert Kuttner, commenting on the way that these debates have gone in the USA, a country that always had a smaller state sector than the UK and which is perhaps even more obsessed with cutting back the state and letting the market rip (and where a liberal is someone on the left and public schools really do mean state schools):

> The market is famous for jettisoning cost-centres – like sick people. Yet many liberals find this crusade seductive. The market is dynamic, efficient and modern. The state is archaic, bureaucratic and unfashionable. Why shouldn't institutions like schools, health plans and pension systems be run more like business? The modern neo-liberal to demonstrate his hipness, gamely rolls his eyes at the haplessness of public school bureaucrats, the self serving backwardness of teachers unions. Liberals can play this game. We can privatise just as well as conservatives . . .
>
> [The problem is that] Society is being systematically denuded of habitats that nurture an ethic of service rather than profit. These institutions took decades – sometimes centuries – to build and they will not easily be replaced (Kuttner, 1996.)

This is not a plea for status quoism, just a general warning that the public sphere is very important and must be handled with care. The never-ending search for efficiency must not cause us to forget this and we must not be seduced by what one Treasury insider has called the 'treadmill of change'.

Openness, transparency, democracy

Public expenditure is our money. Yet we seem to have little influence over exactly how it is spent, we have little information on why decisions are reached and even less on what the ultimate outcome of those decisions really is. It is hardly surprising, then, that many of these chapters cry out for more openness and transparency in the planning and control of public spending.

At the broad level, public opinion should be gauged more to find out what is actually wanted. There are two levels at which this is relevant. The first is that of the citizen. The chapters by Peter Kellner and John Hall, Ian Preston and Mick Ridge suggest that opinion polls can be used more intelligently in this area to discover what citizens want. Geoffrey Hulme puts forward more radical ideas where, for instance, citizens are consulted through 'juries', which could be televized. Hulme is also interested in getting MPs to vote on their priorities electronically. This may seem rather futuristic. But there is no reason why new technology should not give a boost to the democratic process just as it has to medical science.

It is certainly not legitimate for policy makers to take an elitist view here. I have heard officials say that it would be pointless to ask the public what they think about and want from the NHS, since it is too complex. It might however be OK to ask them what they think about the service they get in a particular hospital.

Clearly, the 'bureaucrat knows best' philosophy is still ingrained in some areas. Furthermore, this approach fails to see that the value of public services to the public they serve may well be in the system as a whole – in the whole NHS or education system – and not just the individual parts of the service, such as individual schools or hospitals.

More investigation of opinion can also be carried out at the consumer level. As Martin Cave discusses, important developments are being made here in terms of discovering preferences among different aspects of a service. It is crucial that in times of scarce resources, money and effort go into the right areas. Without the market to guide these choices, the methods Cave describes may be the missing link.

At a more technical level, we need to have adequate data to give us a better picture of what is really going on. The increasing use of performance indicators (PIs) is helpful in this respect. The dangers are well known – are the PIs appropriate; do they focus too much on the easily measurable; do they distort management priorities – but used intelligently they help open up the public sector to scrutiny.

Measures of real outcomes are, however, far more important than the intermediate indicators that PIs invariably are. After all, the public is most interested in results on broad things like health, education and crime than in the precise efficiency of day-to-day activity within particular public sector bodies. Such outcomes are the result of many programmes that cut across departmental or agency responsibilities and do so over many years. There have been improvements in data, including that on outputs and outcomes, as Corry and Gray outline, but these only whet the appetite for more.

The current system of accounts confuses so many things and brings out too few of the important ones. Moves to resource accounting will certainly help in adding to transparency and forward thinking just as they have in New Zealand, as Jane Pallot and Ian Ball show. However, the 'handle with care' notice is needed here as well. Used naïvely, private sector analogues can lead to managers getting rid of important assets to balance the books, as may have happened in NHS trusts and schools under LMS (Ryle, 1995).

In its assessment of the public sector's financial position, Britain has to start to move away from its exclusive focus on the PSBR, a point made strongly by Sheila Watson. This should be common ground by now between academics, practitioners, the Treasury and the financial markets. That it is not must be because it is suspected of being an excuse for going soft on public spending. Certainly the idea of looking for a system that suddenly allows all and any public corporation to borrow without it counting as public spending is not one that should be supported. As Vito Tanzi (1993) puts it: 'the argument has some validity for those public enterprises that are run on efficiency criteria and that may be as efficient as private enterprises, [but] it certainly has limitations when generalised to all enterprises'. If a body is not self-financing then, even if its social return is high, it is competing for funds with things like education and the accounts must reflect this fact.

Indeed, far from reform being a way of loosening up things, the real need at present is for a new framework of accounts to prevent the plethora of emerging quasi-public bodies escaping the public accounts net. Things like the future liabilities set up by the PFI and general loan guarantees are not picked up by the PSBR. Their implications need to be made far more explicit than they have been in recent years (see the chapters by Heald and Watson and also Radcliffe, Hawksworth and Glanville, 1996). Government has been weak in this area so far.

Finally, we need far more open and consistent appraisal and evaluation of projects. Geoff White makes the case at the micro-level that current systems of appraisal are not necessarily producing the best use of money; Pam Meadows makes a similar point very forcefully with respect to major programmes that happen to be in political favour or have been around for a long time.

In some countries, including the USA where the Congressional Budget Office has to be very open, and New Zealand, where now any proposal has to be published with an appraisal signed by a responsible civil servant, more openness has become a way of life. It is vital that this approach becomes the norm in this country too.

All these things are needed if public spending is to regain legitimacy. How can anyone expect people happily to pay their taxes when they have no clue what government is really doing with their money and why, and whether it is good value for money. Such accountability is crucial, as Labour leader Tony Blair has argued:

> Many different bodies make decisions that affect us vitally. Whether the decisions are taken well or badly makes a difference to our lives. Just as companies succeed or fail by the discipline of the market, so governments largely succeed or fail by the discipline of accountability. How government is made transparent, how we know what it is doing and why; how we complain; how we change it; how we influence it – this is the essence of democracy. (Blair, 1996.)

Treasury role needs reconsidering not weakening

Love it or hate it, the Treasury plays a dominant role in public spending issues in the UK. It has in its time been blamed for just about everything – from overspending to underspend; from squeezing investment to letting the public sector grow fat at the expense of enterprise; from hating the poor to discouraging the rich.

Someone has to be in charge of the budget and it is a difficult role. As the quotation from Wellington that opens Nick Monck's chapter reminds us, the conflict between the keeper of the budget and the people who feel that they are trying to achieve things with public money in the real world has always been with us.

One solution is to weaken the Treasury and give far more power to departments, agencies and so on. However, Jon Stern elegantly suggests why a weakened Treasury, which just handed out departmental totals and then went home, would lead to incoherent and contradictory policies. And while Alan Bailey, Nick Monck and Pam Meadows all have criticisms of it, the answer does not seem to be to go down this road too far. The broad message of the contributors to this book is that the role of the Treasury should be altered rather than weakened.

There is a leaning towards getting the Treasury to focus on the right things – the big things that eat up public spending. This also implies the Treasury getting the appraisal procedures right and popularizing them, rather than poking its nose into every decision. It means focusing on getting better measures of output into the public domain and the PES debates. It means clarifying and being open about the key trade-offs in expenditure priorities.

To some degree, the moves towards decentralization, which are generally supported by this book's contributors, do imply some shift in power downwards. However it seems unlikely that this reduces significantly the need for central control. Indeed, as Peter Jackson makes clear, since the principal in the new principal–agent relationship that decentralization brings is in most cases the provider of the finance rather than the end-consumer, the central government and Treasury have not really lost power at all. As Broadbent *et al.* put it: 'It follows from principal–agent theory that decentralised decision making in the public sector is simply a means of central government control over the management process' (Broadbent *et al.*, 1993). Some believe that performance indicators may take us this way as well (Smith, 1996).

This makes clear that this form of decentralization, at least, needs a strong Treasury. And probably a more democratic decentralization to a Scottish, Welsh and regional tier of government, and to local authorities, would also need the Treasury to play an important role.

What should an incoming government do?

A government coming into power in 1997 will face a difficult situation on public spending. It is well known that the government has been holding down spending in real terms at a rate fairly unprecedented even in its own time over the last few years (following the pre-1992 general election surge in spending). It is also clear that the government deficit is very large, partly due to lower growth and inflation than forecast, partly to a drop-off, below expectations, in revenues (although much of this expectation seems to have been ridiculous in the first place (Capel, 1996)). The net worth of the public sector is also very low (see Chapter 3 by Corry and Gray). Inappropriate tax reductions in the pre-election budget would clearly not help matters. In such a situation what should a new government do?

Of course, basic decisions need to be made about the scale of public spending wanted, the big priority areas and how to respond to the new pressures, both external and arising from the changing nature of the UK. It is readily apparent that there needs to be a shift away from expenditure on benefits and ameliorative expenditure and into investment. This will inevitably take time. But on matters more immediately within a new government's control, one can say a few things.

In general terms it should continue with moves to use the market and quasi-market mechanisms. The advantage of the purchaser–provider split in most areas appears to be large: and, where appropriate, and in a way that does not just lead to far worse conditions for the staff, the contracting-out approach seems to be able to offer rewards.

There should not be excessive haste in these areas. Proper evaluation of earlier uses of these approaches should be investigated, especially as the analysis here (Corry, Heald, Jackson) suggests that the gains are likely to be up-front, while any losses will only emerge further down the road.

What of the PFI? As the Director-General of the CBI recently put it: 'the PFI should not be a means simply of replacing capital spending now with current spending in the future' (Turner, 1996). Indeed it would be quite ridiculous to let policy be governed by the desire to shove things into PFI so as to reduce up-front capital costs, and become loose on thinking about where the money for recurrent expenditures is going to come from. Arguably this – the inverse of the old bias against capital investment – is starting to emerge. If a new government can open up the PFI process and its implications for future liabilities – at the same time as removing some of the bureaucratic blocks to PFI deals – then it will be a valuable tool. If not, it may be nothing but trouble.

The new honeypot of Lottery funding also has a bias towards capital projects. In addition, it is pressing strange priorities on the system. As one commentator has put it, we may come to wonder why 'money could be found for Covent Garden, the South Bank, the Tate, crackpot craft museums, Highland estates, ancient monuments, statesmen's old school reports and so on but not for roads, railways, council houses, health care or education' (Pawley, 1996). Making Lottery money better fit the government's and the public's priorities will be an important task.

A new government should move quickly to introduce a new openness to public expenditure. This involves consultation over priorities, more analyses of what the user wants, and a revamped set of accounts and output indicators. It would be sensible also to pencil in, in the parliamentary timetable, a debate on public expenditure for the spring, so that the subject has a focus – at least for parliamentarians and the media.

The Treasury will need changing. A new government with new ideas to think through may need to create a new body for longer-term strategic thinking on public spending, perhaps as part of the Prime Minister's office or the Cabinet Office, since the Treasury is much better at short-term thinking than long-term. Nevertheless, it may well need to increase that capacity in the Treasury: a capacity that, naturally, has been run down after having a government of the same colour for the best part of two decades.

Building up this capacity must not be at the expense of the short term. For a new government, a strong Treasury will be vital to deal with pressures for spending increases that inevitably emerge at the change of an administration, when priorities and approaches go through an upheaval.

It may also be worth thinking through the idea of splitting the Treasury into two and creating a finance department as well as an economic policy one. Although there are arguments on both sides of this debate, we must ask ourselves why we find ourselves alone in these arrangements. Are we really right and everyone else wrong? And, in the spirit of using assets efficiently, it might be sensible to use that opportunity to move the staff (permanently) to new offices that better reflect the realities of the 21st century rather than those of the 19th.

Public spending moves slowly, whatever the rhetoric of politicians. Governments that promise to slash spending as a share of GDP fast often disappoint their supporters. Governments that claim they will switch around the areas to which spending goes within a single spending round are equally unrealistic. But over time, decisions made in this area make an enormous difference to people's quality of life. It is vital to get these decisions right and we hope that this book will contribute to that task.

References

Atkinson, A. (1996). 'Growth and the welfare state', *New Economy*, **3**(3).

Bénabou, R. (1996). 'Inequality and growth'. In: *NBER Macroeconomics Annual 1996*, Cambridge, MA National Bureau of Economic Research (NBER).

Blair, T. (1996). John Smith Memorial Lecture, 7 February.

Broadbent, J., Dietrich, M. and Laughlin, R. (1993). *The Development of Principal Agent Contracting and Accountability Relationships in the Public Sector: Conceptual and Cultural Problems.* Sheffield University Management School, Accounting and Economics, Discussion Paper 93.34 (October).

Brown, C. and Jackson, P. (1986). *Public Sector Economics*, 3rd edn. London: Basil Blackwell.

Capel, J. (1996). 'Light at the end of the PSBR tunnel', *UK Economics Signals*, July, monthly briefing.

Kuttner, R. (1996), 'After solidarity', *The American Prospect*, May–June.

Likierman, A. (1988). *Public Expenditure: Who Really Controls It and How?* London: Penguin.

Milburn, A. (1996). '*Reforming public services*', Fabian Society lecture, June.

Pawley, M. (1996). 'Viewpoint', *Architects Journal*, 11 January.
Public Management Foundation (1996). *The Glue that Binds: the Public Value of Public Services*. March, Public Management Foundation/MORI.
Radcliffe, R., Hawksworth, J. and Glanville, J. (1996). *Consensus for Change*. Coopers and Lybrand/Chartered Institute for Housing.
Ryle, S. (1995). 'How public services are dying by numbers,' *The Guardian*, 14 August.
Smith, P. (ed.) (1996). *Measuring Outcome in the Public Sector*. London: Taylor and Francis.
Tanzi, V. (1993). 'Fiscal deficit measurement: basic issues'. In: Blejer, M. and Cheasty, A. (eds), *How to Measure the Fiscal Deficit*. IMF.
Tanzi, V. and Schuknecht, L. (1995). *The Growth of Government and the Reform of the State in Industrial Countries*. IMF Working Paper WP/95/130.
Turner, A. (1996). 'Please handle with skill', *Financial Times*, 12 July.

Part I
Why Do We Have Public Expenditure and What Do We Spend It On?

1

The Role of the Public Sector and Public Expenditure

Dan Corry

Contents

In the old days, people thought they knew what services the public sector should provide. The police, the post office, water and even swimming pools all seemed an integral part of the UK public sector, while clearly only the state could provide all that was needed for social welfare policies. However, recent experience in the UK has put a question-mark over all this. Services that were once regarded as part and parcel of the public realm have been privatized and the world has not ended.

One result is that many on the centre-left have become confused as to the proper role of the public sector. But if there is no clear conception of what government should do, a centre-left approach to public policy appears much less attractive. This hesitancy is unnecessary. There are certain goods and services that all sensible people regard as essential in a civilized society and which the private sector on its own will not deliver. There is still, therefore, a vital role for the public sector in many areas of life. What have changed are conceptions of exactly how that action should take place.

The first part of this chapter sets out some philosophical arguments for and against public action. At its root, the case for public sector activity is closely bound up with the concept of democracy. The libertarian arguments against public action, though important, are seen to be warnings about the way the power of the state is used, not against its existence *per se*.

We go on to describe the public sector's current functions and how its role has developed over time and why. This leads on to a discussion of one of the main technical reasons for public provision of services: market failure.

Public provision, however, appears to bring with it a number of practical problems, and some of these are discussed. Increasingly, the private sector is involved in the delivery of key public services, even where these continue to be financed (in the final analysis) by public funds. We look, in particular, at two such methods – contracting out and private sector financing initiatives. While there are potential gains from using the private sector in this way, there are also a number of disadvantages, including loss of democratic control of the service. An alternative, regulation of activity carried out and financed entirely by the private sector, suffers particularly from the hidden costs of regulation. The conclusion draws together the strands of what is a complicated, theoretical debate and suggests how a more consistent and open approach to public spending might be achieved. Such an approach would revitalize and re-legitimate the role of public action and expenditure.

Case for and against public action

The democratic case

Democracy requires an active public sector. Without the capability for public sector activity, democracy has given way and people collectively and individually have lost the ability to make decisions about how their society should run. That is why the concept of public action is so important.

The concept of a welfare state, for instance, evolved as people came to the view that it was their democratic right to be protected from the worst ravages of *laissez faire* capitalism. Their views were expressed through the democratic process and there was a clear demand that the power of the state should be used to do what the market clearly could and would not.

More generally, it is only through 'political' action that people can often influence their own lives. If something is going wrong, be it with a noisy neighbour, or in the local community or at a broader spatial level, action from government is frequently crucial to the solution.

Some argue that the market is the most practical application of genuine democracy. The only tolerable role for government, then, is to ensure that the market applies to all things. This, however, is a thin agenda. Sometimes people have political views about not wanting to use market mechanisms. This may be because there is a (correct) sense that the market-based approach would not work, but it is certainly not based on detailed analysis. There are also some areas in which, even if there is a view that the private sector could do things a bit better, we do not want them. This may be inefficient in the narrow economic sense – and one may want to try and influence opinions – but it is the democratic prerogative.

At a technical level, however, the call for public action can be – and often is – seen as a response to failures of the market. Here, there is an underlying assumption that, in an ideal world, the public sector would provide no services other than those judged desirable and which the market cannot deliver. The aim, therefore, would be to minimize the role of the public sector. Each public intervention would need to be justified strictly against the inability of the market to deliver.

Much of the opposition, in principle, to market-type solutions has now disappeared. However, even where a service is provided by the private sector, people still often want the potential for democratic control. This is particularly the case when there is danger of a monopolistic situation, as with many examples of privatization.

Delivery of a service by the private sector under contract to the public sector leads to a loss of day-to-day democratic control and of accountability to individual citizens. Direct accountability is considerably weakened if the public sector provides very little, and if everything is guided by legalistic controls or regulation. In this sense contracts do little for the democratic process. The role of the citizen as stakeholder has been reduced to the extent that the citizen only now has a say as a consumer.

On the other hand, the contract approach does have the advantage of keeping control over strategic decisions and focuses democratic control on these key policy issues. When direct public provision of public services was near universal, the producer interest – be it trade unions or the professionals – was often able to block the sensible exercise of democratic control let alone steps to increase efficiency. Producer capture was not only bad for consumers but also for citizens.

Putting aside efficiency arguments (which are considered later), there may be something intrinsically useful about public sector involvement in the provision of public services. A public sector as purchaser – or regulator – only, operates differently from one that also acts as a provider. A body that merely writes, signs and monitors contracts and regulates private sector behaviour, loses the ability to be flexible and to respond quickly to new situations. It no longer has direct responsibility for the pay and conditions of a large segment of the workforce. And, inevitably, the responsibility it takes for any mistakes and inefficiencies is diluted.

The public sector also has an important role to play in binding individuals together, in creating a sense of community and social cohesion. While often romanticized, the position of a local school in creating some sense of community is clear. A world in which one group of people within a local community used one type of school and another group another, would clearly lack this; a world with quasi-markets for schools or no state schools at all might tend to this situation (although this is not to deny the existence of geographical segregation by income). As Self (1989, p. 24) has put it: 'there is a certain intrinsic value in the public provision of some services for cementing common citizenship and a sharing of common values . . . ideals of solidarity and community are given some expression which otherwise would be lacking'.

Finding out what individuals want

Given that public activity should be governed and steered by the democratic will, we need to find out what society wants. Democracy is never perfect. Representative democracy is indirect, it often works with methods (first past the post) that fail to give power to the majority, and it is ill-equipped to discover what individuals think about particular issues (especially when individuals themselves are ill-informed). This is why, where there are no market failure or policy reasons to the contrary, using the market has so many attractions.

Nevertheless, however imperfect, discovering the democratic will must be our starting point. In general terms, elections tell us the broad strategy. For many years it seemed that this was all that was needed. Issues such as the type, quality and responsiveness of public services, let alone their value for money were not keenly debated. This is no longer acceptable.

However, some commentators are pessimistic as to whether it is ever possible to ascertain individuals' true preferences, for example regarding either the quantity or the quality of services they would like provided. In the early 1960s Walter Heller, chairman of the US President's Council of Economic Advisors, asked: 'how are preferences of voters for governmental services to be revealed, measured and appropriately financed' and concluded that while economists have done good work on the subject and 'have made some intriguing suggestions as to its solution . . . [they] . . . have concluded that it is next to insoluble'. Moreover, not only do the democratic processes have to be sophisticated to work any of this out, people may actually have incentives to give 'false signals' (Barnett, 1993).

Given these difficulties, there are those who conclude that it would be best, in almost all cases, to apply market-type mechanisms to the provision of public services. However, the market itself is not good at revealing true demands in many of the areas covered by public services. Indeed, this is one reason why the public sector became involved in the first place. Price signals do not necessarily reflect true costs and information problems may mean that perceived demands are not the 'true' ones. We are also talking about areas where we believe that the individual as citizen should have a say even if they are not actual users of the service. For instance, just because someone has no children does not mean that their views on the development of education locally should be discounted.

Currently, more sophisticated techniques are being developed that might enable policy makers to get a better handle on the quality and kind of public services that are wanted. Such methods include greater use of referenda and opinion polls, as well as citizens' juries and methodologies that use the willingness-to-pay approach (see chapters by Cave, Hulme in this book).

Case against public action

The philosophical case against public action is traditionally voiced by the libertarian right. This has much resonance nowadays, particularly for a new Left that has rediscovered individualism and shies away from paternalism. At its most basic, the belief is that publicly provided services – whether provided directly by the state or contracted out – offend against liberty because they give the citizen no choice. According to one commentator, when we provide, for example, free or subsidized housing we are 'in effect requiring the minority to accept services they might or might not have bought had they been handed an equivalent amount of cash. Perhaps they would have preferred to spend it on wine, women and song' (Heller, 1965, p. 156). A related argument is that free services will, in time, sap the will of individuals to run their lives, thus encouraging welfare dependency.

Both arguments are, however, confused and contradictory. Much of the case against state action is, in fact, against the provision of welfare defined in its widest sense. However, if the need for some kind of welfare provision is accepted, the key question is whether this is best done directly, or by cash hand-outs. There is no doubt that the former restricts choice, while benefit payments do not. As Phelps (1965) has pointed out: 'transfers raise many of the same issues raised by public expenditures . . . but they do not directly reallocate resources in the economy [between the private and public sectors]. Thus they do not interfere with consumer sovereignty, nor with free enterprise in any fundamental way' (p. xiii). On the other hand, cash payments are inevitably means-tested and this gives rise to major disincentive problems since they are withdrawn as income rises.

There are, however, possible solutions. For instance, provision in kind can be made more responsive to individual preference by providing choice within prescribed limits. Vouchers are one method of achieving this, although these are not without disadvantages of their own (Self, 1989, p. 25; OECD, 1995, p. 43).

Taken to its logical conclusion, the voucher approach leads to a world where the public sector does almost nothing in terms of services. Instead it redistributes income, either through issuing vouchers (that can be as progressive as it chooses) or directly through, for example, minimum wages and social security. Consumers are then left to make their own choices in the private market. However, these two aspects, no public sector activity and radical redistribution, are probably incompatible. In a world dominated totally by the private, market economy, the political conditions would not exist for anything but the most minor redistribution of income (Self, 1989, p. 21).

Finally, it is worth saying that while the maintenance of liberty is fundamental, one should not be over-obsessed about the need to protect the individual from encroachment from the state, but should be looking to a more 'positive' concept of freedom. If certain basic social goods such as health care, employment and education are necessary in order to give individuals the capacity to enjoy life, a case can be made for the state to provide these services universally (Dasgupta, 1989).

To recap: there is an enduring need for public action in many areas of life. While this does not need to involve direct provision by the public sector, there are drawbacks in the sector withdrawing entirely from such activity.

What the public sector provides

Over a third of all public sector spending is, in fact, on transfers (social security benefits); in other words, the distribution of resources from one set of individuals to another (Public Finance Trends, 1995, Table 1.4). Of the remainder, much is consumed by health, education and defence (see the chapters by Corry and Gray, and Cooper).

The combination of public services in which government plays a role, as purchaser and/or provider, may be categorized into four main types of activity.

- the core functions of law, order, income support and redistribution;
- defence and other public goods;
- merit goods; services that society believes individuals should have access to at uniform price and without the usual market constraints such as having the service cut off if payment is not made on time. The definition of these varies over time and across nations;
- services such as education and health.

It is difficult to envisage the core functions being performed by anyone other than government. However, it is not immediately obvious why government should have a major role to play in the provision of education and health services.

In practice it seems that public intervention goes far beyond providing the classic 'public goods'. These are goods that are non-rival (one person's use does not reduce their value to someone else) and non-excludable (where it is impossible to get anyone to pay). Education is an example of a good that is rival and could be excludable. However, government, reflecting public views, chooses to make it a 'publicly provided private good' (Barnett, 1993). One rationale for this is that such services are provided by professionals that society does not want to be guided by profit-maximizing considerations. The BBC also comes into this category.

There have been changes over time in the type of services provided by the public sector, in how much is spent and how. These have been the result of a number of factors, including:

- Changes in *ambitions or targets*. For instance, the growth in individualism has changed the nature of the products that people want and the degree to which they will accept uniform services. Beliefs about the appropriate degree of egalitarianism also change.

- Changes in *needs or circumstances*. Such exogenous changes include the collapse of the USSR which has reduced the need for defence spending. Demographic factors tend to affect expenditure on, for example, health, while changes in unemployment and inequality affect spending on social security and law enforcement.
- *The discovering of new ways of delivering an existing service*. This may result in the internal reorganization of the public sector, changes in planning and control procedures, or new forms of service delivery.

Criteria for public action

For the past decade and a half, UK governments have been mainly concerned with a strict and narrow definition of market failure (as defined in the neo-classical economic paradigm). Only where the market palpably fails is there a role for public action and, potentially, public expenditure. Given the requirement to identify a specific market failure, it is not surprising that there has been a concerted attempt to marketize and privatize as much as possible of what were generally regarded as 'publicly provided services'.

As we have argued, ultimate decision-making about what should and should not be done must rest with the democratic process. Analysis of market failure is useful in that it encourages vigorous examination of possible options (and likely cost-effective interventions). However, goals of fairness and equity also play an important role in determining public policy for most governments. It is undoubtedly the case that market provision of goods and services usually results in different outcomes for people with different incomes. Free marketeers either do not see this as central, or argue that any equity issues should be dealt with by the tax and social security systems (Dilnot, 1995), a solution with problems of its own (Corry, 1995b; Waterson, 1994).

Moral criteria

Using a broader approach to the concept of market failure than that of recent governments, what general criteria may be used to justify public action? First, there is the argument that some services, such as prisons, the army, the police and the judiciary, should not be provided by the market. Direct provision is therefore required. Furthermore, there appears still to be consensus within the UK that education and particularly health broadly come under this category of service where the profit motive would not be appropriate (even though the private sector is involved in the UK and, in some countries, such services are provided totally by the private sector).

In the UK, for example, most people object to the idea of paying for blood donations, or would find it unacceptable to allow a poor person to sell a spare kidney. The idea of someone being involved in providing health or primary school education primarily to make money is also met with disapproval. Many also believe that as people are in prison because of the coercive power of the state, it would be morally wrong to let the private sector play a role in any but the most peripheral aspects of prisons. As opinion polls carried out prior to privatizations show, similar views were held on issues such as water and (to a lesser extent) electricity.

Moral values are crucial and, as expressed in a democracy, cannot and should not be ridden over roughshod. Nevertheless, they should not be a barrier to innovative thinking.

Market failure criteria

There are some limited areas where the private sector would simply provide nothing if left unprompted. For instance, it is highly unlikely that the private sector would choose to produce driving licences. Here, there is clearly a need for government action to stimulate a market by bringing in a legal requirement that all drivers hold a licence. However, government need not necessarily deliver the service, rather its role is to put the appropriate legislation in place. This is also true of some policies that involve an element of redistribution (see Box 1.1 for a discussion of the role of the state in the provision of these services).

The main reason for government action, however, is where the market would not provide an appropriate service. Clearly, the market is capable of delivering some service when it comes to water, telephones, research establishments, hospitals, trains and so on. This does not mean, however, that the provision would always be of the desired quality (including price) or quantity. At the very least, public regulation is needed, especially where monopoly power may be an issue.

Markets only respond to the desires of individuals fed through their market demands. But the prices charged cannot capture the wider social benefits of, for example, an educated or healthy society. The market therefore provides too little of things with positive 'externalities' at the same time as it provides too much pollution – where the externalities are negative. Here, again, there is a role for government.

Public action is also required because of asymmetric information (where the user of a service has less information than the provider and so can be exploited). Moral hazard is also associated with markets, particularly insurance provision. Here, individuals have an incentive to adjust their behaviour once they are insured. Knowing this, the private sector may only provide cover at a very high price, if at all. Adverse selection is also a problem. Only those who are likely to become ill actually take up insurance, so that the insurer would not be able to spread risk in an efficient way. Finally, there is the much debated issue of short-termism that tends to bedevil the private sector in the UK. (See Helm (1989) for a good summary of the market failure rationale for public action.)

A related advantage of public sector action is that it is different from the private sector and therefore avoids some of its constraints. In particular, because of its size, the public sector is able to spread risk. It also has the unique possibility of raising money through taxation. As a consequence the public sector can borrow money more cheaply than any private sector organization. There are therefore intrinsic advantages in having it finance services and capital projects, whether or not it provides them itself. In addition and because of its ability to escape the constraint of short-term profit maximization, it can take on tasks that the private sector never would.

A final reason for the market's failure to provide the desired service is the issue of equity. If equal access to particular services and equal treatment by that service matter, then private provision may not deliver. If cherry picking and cream skimming occur, one may well find that the rich end up paying less than the poor for the same service (if the poor can get it at all) and that one region may get a poorer service than another. Fairness and social cohesion disappear. The voucher idea is one way of sidestepping this problem – so we all enter the market with the same 'income'. But this, of course, does not escape the need for public action and public expenditure.

Arguments for and against public provision

In addition to the reasons for public involvement in the delivery of services outlined in the previous two sections (democratic accountability and market failure), there are a number of advantages associated with public sector provision. They broadly fall into two categories: first, that certain problems associated with private sector provision are avoided. Second, that accountability and flexibility are easier to maintain. These may be briefly summarized as follows.

Avoiding the private sector problems

1. The public sector, at least in theory, is not vulnerable to short-term pressures from the financial markets or from the structure of private sector corporate governance.
2. Incentives to reduce quality or exploit workers in order to raise profits are absent.
3. The public sector is less likely to 'waste' money on advertising and PR.
4. Direct provision can deal more easily with imperfect and asymmetric information. There are for instance fewer market incentives for the experts (doctors) to give the users (the patients) expensive treatment that they do not really need.
5. The public sector can be more efficient than the private sector, at least for

How valid is the claim that social security/welfare expenditure has to be provided by the state? Some of this activity is redistributive across time, essentially for the same individual (ABI, 1995; Falkingham and Hills, 1995) and there is a case that government need not be involved: people could make their own provision and, it appears, increasingly are (Hills, 1995, p. 30–2). But aspects of the nature of insurance markets, like asymmetric information, moral hazard, myopia and so on, make a purely private solution problematic.

Alternatively, compulsory saving for things like pensions (with top-ups for the poor) could replace taxation and public expenditure. Although it is unclear that in the long run such a switch will lead to a lower PSBR, since 'traditional' taxes would have to go down as well, private provision carried out under compulsory regulation by the state (quasi-taxes) does seem to be increasing in areas like Child Support Act payments and firms paying maternity or sick pay for employees (Hills, 1995).

However, a certain degree of the social security system is undoubtedly redistributive between individuals. While the administration of such activity could in principle be done by the private sector, there seems to be no way of transferring this redistributive activity to the private sector. If the state does not help the poorest in society, no one else is likely to do so.

Since there are arguments that there are wider benefits from supporting the poor than those that go to the direct beneficiaries, and that some of these benefits are very intangible, it is right in principle too that government should assess their value and run the system.

Box 1.1. Social security/welfare.

some services. This is because the monopsony power that, for example, a national health service or education system gives to employers, allows wages to be held down.

6. The absence of a need to make a profit means that the break-even point is lower for the public sector. If efficiency were the same in both sectors, the public sector provider would always have the edge.

Flexibility/accountability

1. Direct provision is more flexible, being able to respond to new policy objectives faster than any arms' length, purely contractual relationship can.
2. The absence of rigid budget constraints may have beneficial effects on behaviour. When, for instance, hospital cleaners were directly employed they would have picked up a book dropped by a patient. Now, for fear of losing time, the contracted-out cleaner might not.

3. Publicly provided services ensure that national standards are met directly, especially those that encompass equality.
4. The public sector as provider is likely to be more responsible than one that just purchases since it has to answer for the consequences of its actions not just for its policy aims or contract-writing abilities.
5. Direct public sector provision of service delivery makes democratic accountability clear and obvious.

Disadvantages of public provision

Not everyone is convinced by the above arguments. Some commentators take the view that everything that government touches will turn to disaster. 'There are now considerable doubts about the capacity of governments necessarily to improve outcomes even when there is acknowledged to be some degree of market failure, lack of competition, or a particular concern about equity' (Keating, 1991, p. 235). These thoughts have dominated the academic literature for some time now.

In addition, the problems of using the private sector that are held to arise from the particular objectives and ethos of the private sector can to some extent be avoided by use of voluntary organizations and other not-for-profit organizations, if their motives are held to be more sound (Finley, 1989). The question then is whether the accusation of government failure is clinching or not.

There is no doubt that there are severe disadvantages associated with the public sector's involvement, particularly as the provider of public services. Decision makers, in the absence of both strict budget constraints and reasonable freedom to manage their own budgets, often act inefficiently. Ministers often want to involve themselves in operational decisions which they are poorly qualified to make. The political cycle causes short-term factors to dominate decision making. Vested interests often dominate at the expense of individual consumers. Large, bureaucratic structures can be slow to adapt, lack the thirst for innovation of the private sector and often seem obsessed with paperwork.

Recent efficiency gains and improvements in the quality of services following privatization and contracting out have drawn attention in some areas to previously low levels of efficiency, producer capture and a focus on everything but the user of the service. However, it is important not to exaggerate these supposed inefficiencies. The only major detailed work on this aspect of the public sector in the UK, carried out before many of the recent market-based reforms, strongly suggests that government departments carry out their business as efficiently as most private sector organizations. Levitt and Joyce (1987, p. 66) concluded: 'There is no overwhelming evidence that the government departments considered are markedly inferior in their performance to private institutions, despite significant differences in the financial incentives to the staff concerned'.

In any case, if we go down the private sector 'partnership' or contracting state routes to delivering public services we must believe that the public sector is good at writing contracts, setting regulations and so on. It is not obvious why this should be. If the public sector is inherently bad at things then it is likely to fail here too. Ending direct provision would not solve all the problems.

Clearly, we want to reduce incentives for inefficient decisions within the public sector. To some extent, recent reforms, particularly the introduction of agencies, means that there is now less short-term interference by politicians and reduced power for vested interests. Other positive changes include the proposed move to resource accounting; the relaxation of end-year spending restrictions; the delegating of running cost control to lower levels; the introduction of small teams working as business units with clear accountability to achieve certain performance measures; and the giving of tough personal contracts to senior managers, who become accountable, publicly as well as financially, for hitting targets set for them. One sees therefore that the scope to overcome many of the government failure problems does exist. However, two key questions need to be asked:

- Is the public sector capable of further reform?
- Should it abandon its role in the delivery of services?

These issues are considered in the next section, which describes the alternative methods of providing public services introduced in the UK over the past decade or so and examines the advantages and disadvantages associated with each.

Alternative ways of providing public services

If one wants to avoid public provision of services, various options are available (see Box 1.2) each with different implications for total public expenditure and spending priorities. One option continues to involve full state funding. It offers the possibility of the public sector defining the service wanted and contracting out its provision to the private sector. A second option, that has some strong links with the first approach, is the currently fashionable Private Finance Initiative (PFI), in which the private sector puts up the initial finance and also contracts to build and operate the infrastructure (for example, a hospital, a road, an IT system).

a. public provision, public payment (e.g. water pre-privatization; the army)
b. private provision, public payment (contracted-out swimming pool)
c. private provision (including the finance), public contract (PFI deal for a new bridge or a franchise to run a motorway service area)
d. private provision (including the finance), public regulation (e.g. water post-privatization)
e. private provision (e.g. bread)

Box 1.2. Options for the funding and provision of services to the public.

In principle, it should be possible to provide excellent public services through either option. If one believes that the private sector will be more efficient and innovative, partly because of the problems and dangers of public provision, then even if the public sector funds the project, the delivery should be private (Blankart, 1985, p. 196). However, such methods are not without costs and the key question that needs to be asked is whether the potential benefits are worthwhile.

Contracting out

In a contract relationship, the decision maker, or principal, has an objective but the work to achieve it is carried out by someone else, the agent. In the case of contracting-out in the public sector, there is a strong likelihood that the principal (in this case, the public sector) and the agent (the private sector) will have divergent objectives and incentives. Essentially then, the principal has to try to write down what it wants, monitor that it is getting it and enforce its desires. This process is not straightforward.

In practice, it may be impossible to draft contracts that deliver what is required from public services. One might, for example, want those providing a particular service to be polite or caring or even 'helpful' – such as dinner ladies helping out at playtime when a school is short of staff. In the case of a complex service such as education (where one objective might be to teach children the joy of learning as well as exam techniques) it would be difficult, if not impossible, to specify a sensible contract, let alone to monitor and enforce one.[1]

In addition, consumers seem to respond quite differently to a privatized provider, suspecting the motives of the company and not giving them the benefit of the doubt when things go wrong. One consequence may be that tight monitoring conditions are placed on the contracting company. The likelihood then is that it will act only to meet them and skip other things (Le Grand, 1996).

The conclusion, then, is that the absence of complex contractual arrangements and shareholder pressures that characterizes public sector provision, may, ironically, make it easier to achieve complex goals. Where transaction costs are likely to be high, delivering the service in-house may therefore make a lot of sense. According to Marchese (1985, p. 213) 'In a world where information is costly and people also pursue their interests by misrepresentation, transaction costs . . . may be higher than the organizations' costs of producing directly'. Furthermore, it goes without saying that, if the public sector's stringent conditions for greater efficiency are to be met, there needs to be a healthy, competitive and honest private sector. There are reasons to doubt that this is always the case in the UK (see, for example, Public Services Privatisation Research Unit (PSPRU), 1996).

Many of these issues have arisen clearly in the UK context from the application of Compulsory Competitive Tendering (CCT) in local government (see Box 1.3).

Although driven too much by ideology and dislike of public sector unions,

CCT is the name given to the legislative position where the UK government has insisted that local authorities put out to tender many of their services. Authorities are generally obliged to accept the lowest bid (although they have some room for manoeuvre on this). Thus in theory, the in-house provider can win the contract.

CCT began in services such as refuse collection and cleaning. It has since been applied more extensively to white-collar activities such as accountancy, information technology and architecture.

Box 1.3. CCT.

CCT has had some positive results. In particular, the need to specify a contract has made local authorities focus more on what they are trying to achieve and has encouraged thinking on efficiency and innovation (Szymanski, 1994). It is, however, difficult to say how much the improvements made in this area have been the result of CCT and how much the result of the tight financial controls under which local authorities have been operating. However, a number of disadvantages along the lines discussed above have also become apparent.

First, local authorities have lost a degree of flexibility. Typically, councils draw up a contract and put it out to tender. The contract the council signs usually runs for five years. This makes it difficult for service specifications to be changed in the interim, or for the nature of the relationship between the purchaser and provider to be refined. The result can be both costly and inconvenient. Although more flexible contracts could be agreed, the private sector would charge a much higher price.

This lack of flexibility can endanger efficiency objectives. Efficiency is not just a static concept. It must relate to the achievement of objectives which, due to changes in technology, prices, tastes and the democratic process, change over time.

Second, where a service is contracted out to a monopoly provider, there is no certainty that the service will be provided more efficiently. The reality is that competition for the contract is often partial at best (because there are few contractors in a position to bid). Where the private sector wins a contract, it is likely that any future capability to operate the service in-house disappears, removing another source of competition. Furthermore:

> Even if there is competition among suppliers before the contract is made, the supplier and the demander are locked in a bilateral monopoly position after the contract has been signed. Ex ante competition and ex post monopoly encourage opportunistic behaviour of the contractors, which is detrimental to efficiency. In order to avoid such difficulties it may be more advantageous to buy (Blankart, 1985, p.197).

Some of these disadvantages might be overcome by a more rigorous competition policy that encouraged a competitive private sector, by more flexibility in the contracting process itself and minimum standards of pay – since some of the much-vaunted efficiency gains may simply reflect pay cuts for workers and therefore not do much for overall welfare in society (Kerr and Radford, 1995). However, it has to be remembered that many of these services were taken on by the public sector in the first place because it was generally felt that the private sector was oligopolistic, inefficient and exploited its workforce. (See IPPR (1996) for more discussion of these issues.)

All the available evidence suggests that CCT works best in a number of limited circumstances: where a market existed previously (e.g. catering and cleaning); where there is scope for the private sector to be truly innovative and add extra services (e.g. breakfasts in schools); where the contracts are big so that the costs of bidding and so on are a small percentage of the contract price; and where there is potential to casualize the workforce.

This is not to say that contracting out is never worth it. Far from it. But the conditions for it to be a real success and to really save major amounts of money are limited. Indeed, one notices that despite massive amounts of contracting out and claims of savings, government spending has not obviously declined.

Private finance

There is a great deal of interest currently in the concept of using the private sector not only to construct and operate major infrastructure projects but to finance them as well. This also involves a contracting relationship between state and private company, but this time the contract includes the financing factor.

The immediate attraction of the private finance approach is that it appears to offer the prospect of someone other than the public sector paying for public projects and services (see Box 1.4).[2] In this way, the public expenditure constraint on delivering public services is avoided. As we discuss below, this view is mistaken. Nevertheless, there may be some advantages to such an approach. In particular, it is argued that the full benefits of private sector expertise cannot be secured without them putting their money in (although the All Party Treasury Select Committee's report of 1996 argued that 'many of the assumed benefits of PFI would appear to be available to . . . conventional procurement'. See also Chapter 14 by Flemming).

There are, however, four main disadvantages associated with using private finance in this way (Corry 1995a and 1996; Chapter 2 by Watson and Chapter 9 by Heald in this volume).

First, using private sector finance for public sector projects delivers no free lunch. Unless the private sector is able to raise capital that the state could not, then private finance does not ease any macroeconomic constraints on the resources available for public services (unless it increases the efficiency of resource use) (Heald, 1996; Treasury Committee, 1996). For example, where the public sector pays for the service, the private sector finances, builds and often operates the facility in return for a contract with the public sector that specifies payments for the use of that facility for a number of years (up to 60 in some recent PFI negotiations). The state (taxpayer) still pays, all that has happened is that the time profile of payments has changed.

Second, the costs of borrowing are higher for the private than for the public sector. This means that there would need to be strong efficiency reasons for involving private sector finance in the first place. One estimate of the cost of a PFI approach to a road project assessed it at more than 80 per cent higher than the conventional approach (Metropolitan Transport Research Unit, 1996).

Third, it is not clear what advantages there are where the end-user is made to pay. For example, if the private sector is to be allowed to charge for the service it provides (for example, road or bridge tolls), why could not the public sector itself have applied tolls in the first place? This would have had the effect of reducing the PSBR without the need for recourse to the PFI. Furthermore, charging in this way does qualitatively affect the service provided. What is being provided is no longer a 'free' road, but a 'toll' road.[3] And if one is searching for self-financing projects, there may well be a downgrading of the importance of non-financial benefits, or externality gains. This is true even when additional spending in one area – for example, roads – reduces spending in another area such as health. In a 'privatized' system, the incentives do not allow for these spill-overs.

Fourth, it is difficult to negotiate a fair PFI contract because of the problem of allocating risk. The private sector will be looking to minimize the risk it takes on – often by looking for guarantees (to provide a higher expected return). For instance, a private sector firm may not want to build a tube line, even if it could have all the receipts, because it would not know for certain that demand would continue or that fares would not be altered by the state. It will be looking for clauses to protect it from such events.

It is arguable, however, that the government cannot avoid taking on, at the very least, the risk associated with the project collapsing completely. Will government actually stand by if and when a project fails or when a purchaser like a major NHS trust or a grant-maintained school goes bankrupt? In reality, in any major project the state guarantees and takes on all the project risk. This means that a whole host of contingent liabilities are being built up. Furthermore, private lenders are, in effect, being underwritten by the taxpayer, and there is no incentive for the private sector to monitor the project. There is also an asymmetry in the distribution of risks, for if the project goes well the private sector gets all the rewards (unless complex clawback deals are arranged and enforced). Joint ventures can avoid some of this (as well as other problems) and are probably a more fruitful line of progress.

If risk is not transferred to the private sector, there are no efficiency gains and it is unclear what gains there are for the public sector.[4] The present government's attempts to encourage private sector finance for large-scale projects have been riddled with difficulties of allocating risk and designing contracts that are fair to the public sector and do not discourage private investors. In practice, the private sector has been demanding a high price for taking on any of the risk involved (knowing that the government is committed to bringing in private finance). The Treasury has been criticized for the slow pace of the PFI. While some of the criticism may be valid, the danger is that a 'more relaxed' Treasury may just be a euphemism for less insistence on value for money.

The danger then with PFI is that it is being pushed primarily because of the political attraction that it appears to provide investment in public services without public spending and increased PSBR. Out goes a great lump of spending which makes the financial markets scream. In comes some kind of commitment to a stream of payments over 30 or so years. The danger, however, is that reducing the PSBR in the short term is merely piling up massive liabilities in the future. If the PFI is in fact mainly being used as a way to evade tough public spending decisions, then at some point the financial markets will cotton on to the fact. It will then collapse in a heap with severe consequences for the private sector, for the public sector and for the citizens of this country.

One way of avoiding this would be the introduction of more transparent, balance-sheet accounting (Smith, 1996). In particular, more information must be provided on the efficiency gains that are expected to be and are being achieved and the additional financing costs that are involved. In this way the public can check that value for money is being achieved.

To sum up: there is nothing wrong with the PFI *per se* and it may produce extra efficiency gains that we cannot secure in other ways. But we need proof of this because PFI is not 'costless' to the public. A PFI-driven deal will be

1. *Financially free-standing*, when a bridge is financed by tolls paid to the private sector provider.
2. *Services sold to the public sector*, where the public sector agrees to 'rent' a new hospital (and its services) to be built and financed by the private sector, for a period of time.
3. *Leasing*, when a private company supplies an asset to a public body (for instance, trains to the Northern Line), in return for a stream of payments over time. In other words, the private sector buys the train in the first place and is so taking on some of the risk.
4. *Joint ventures* between public and private sector, so that returns (as well as finance) are shared, are another way of using private finance. Examples of these include housing associations and urban development corporations. There are also increasing numbers of 'GoCos' (government owned, contractor-operated companies) where the private sector takes over a public asset and runs it (and makes incremental investments) on commercial lines. Finally, 'corporatization' is where public managers have more freedom to borrow on private markets. (OXERA, 1996; Watson, 1995, London Economics, 1996).

Box 1.4. Types of private finance arrangement.

different from a conventionally financed project. The way that the service is delivered, the way management behaves, even the projects that are started, will change and so the PFI will start to determine the shape of our public services. Over the long run, this may have important implications both for the Exchequer and for the public.

User charges

Charges for users is another way of introducing the disciplines of the market to public services and of reducing the need to raise money for public spending. These are only feasible when the service is not totally a 'public' good (for example, entry to a museum), and it is not widely used at present. The OECD estimated that charges represented only around five per cent of total government revenue in member countries (Oxley *et al.*, 1990, p. 20).

Proponents of charging argue that people resist these less than they do taxes because payment is linked to specific services. It is also argued that charges reduce 'fiscal illusion' and so reduce the demand for services that individuals are not willing to pay for. A further argument in favour of charges is that services become more tailored to what consumers want. This is especially true if the public agency that provides the service is allowed to keep the revenues raised through charging. Finally, charges provide an incentive to new suppliers to enter the market (Marchese, 1985, p. 224).

As with the other forms of public service delivery discussed above, charging raises a number of issues. One might ask why if one is prepared to charge more than a token amount, one pulls back from privatizing fully? In fact, the costs of a particular service are usually only partially met by user charges. This raises concerns about equity without eliminating the funding issue.

Consequences of market-type mechanisms

Do they ease the public sector size problem?

Market-type mechanisms (MTMs) now apply to large areas of the public sector. When used appropriately, they have the potential to improve cost effectiveness and to make services more responsive to user requirements. Such mechanisms also have the potential to ease the role of the public sector as provider and, possibly, as payer. If all goes well, then, they may reduce the pressure on public spending. However, there are also a number of disadvantages, including loss of control and the costs of regulation.

First, however, what of the view that the public sector in the UK is too big? Are MTMs a way out of this problem?

In the first place, we have seen that contracting out probably only offers marginal changes to public spending overall. Second, we have found that the

PFI does not really alter the scale of the public spending over the long term. MTMs therefore should not really be addressed at the size issue but at the efficiency one.

In any case the major critique of the bloated public sector is essentially that public sector activities are using too many of the resources of the economy, not that public spending (however this is defined) is too high. The old criticism of 'too few producers' (Bacon and Eltis, 1976) does not go away if private money is being diverted into what are essentially public sector projects. In this sense, just looking at spending/GDP ratios is misleading (see also the discussion of regulation below).

Furthermore, attempts to twist the rules and structure of organizations, either to reduce the need for public money or to make it seem legitimate to exclude their spending and borrowing from the PSBR (Heald, this volume) may result in important and unintended changes to the services being produced.

In the case of housing, for example, the government has insisted that housing associations raise more and more of their money from the private sector. This has led associations to squeeze unit costs and to build on large, greenfield sites. These are likely to be the problem estates of the next decades. Rents being charged are also higher, to pay for the private finance with major implications for housing benefit bills, poverty traps and future public expenditure.

It is now being suggested that arm's-length local housing companies take over existing council housing stock (Institute of Housing, 1993). These would have only a small percentage of council representatives on the board and the hope is that their spending would not count as public expenditure. But this too would undoubtedly lead to a different type of housing service being provided.

There are also suggestions that the Post Office be restructured within the public sector, such that its borrowing would no longer count as public spending. The idea is that the restructured body would have no guarantee from government to secure its lending and would be run by a board of directors made up of business people, with no interference from politicians (London Economics, 1994). If adopted, these proposals would result in a very different Post Office. Indeed, it is difficult to see what the advantages of such a system would be over a fully privatized and regulated Post Office.

Public policy must focus on the desired outcome. Playing about with the structure of the organization for financial reasons may well lead one to take one's eyes off this. This suggests that MTMs and other changes to the organization of public services are no short-cut to reducing the spending/GDP ratio.

Loss of control

There are other more general problems associated with the use of MTMs. In the case of leasing and the PFI, both involve long, binding contracts that have implications for the scale and flexible use of public spending in the future. Future governments may find their hands tied on policy issues, particularly if contracts give compensation to the private sector in the event of major policy changes. This raises interesting constitutional issues with risk implications. A government today effectively signs up future parliaments to contracts. Is this democratic? Will they hold if a government 20 years later prefers to spend on something else?

There is also a problem arising from the fact that the PFI seems to be intended by the current government as a replacement and not a supplement to existing resources. This means that there is a danger that the investment decision itself has become 'privatized', with private sector interests coming to dominate public welfare ones.

PFI deals offer another possibility of 'losing control'. Some are attracted by the idea of PFI only for the basics, like the construction of hospitals. But it is difficult to see the benefits of the PFI when used for construction-only contracts over a straightforward contracting-out approach. The real gains in involving the private sector (innovation and so on) will only result if the sector runs and operates a large proportion of the service. Then, for instance, they look at how to design the hospital so as to reduce the costs of delivering the other services they run.

This is also true of other services. A recent study on social housing, for example, pointed out that 'a firm that is interested in development only may not be as concerned about the long-term implications of building standards for the maintenance and management of the property as one which sees the provision of social housing as a long-term enterprise' (Day and Klein, 1996).

If, however, the private sector is allowed to take over the running of, for example, clinical services, there is a danger that it will manipulate demand for these services (as many commentators believe happened with Medicare in the US).

Overall, then, MTMs must not be introduced simply to reduce public expenditure. It is their potential to improve cost effectiveness that matters, and this too should be considered with an open mind. As the market-orientated OECD has concluded: 'the notion that market arrangements are inherently more efficient than non-market arrangements has been shown to be rather naive' (OECD, 1995, p. 112.[5] See also Martin (1993) for a critique of the move to privatization and market-type mechanisms in general).

Regulation

Public provision and contracting out involve public expenditure. So too in most cases, does the PFI. In addition we have seen that there are problems with all of them.

There are several other approaches to delivering 'public' services through public action that have only minor public expenditure implications. We can use revenue neutral changes in subsidies and/or taxes to shift the private sector in the way we want.[6] We can use industry levies to try and alter behaviour. Or we can try and change the objectives of a private sector firm, perhaps by altering corporate governance arrangements. The most important idea, however, is of using regulation, instead of ownership or funding of any kind, to help deliver required services.

It is difficult to put in place a regulatory system to deal with the private sector that delivers public sector objectives (including accountability) and also provides the private sector with the right incentives to deliver services efficiently. For these reasons, the privatization/regulation approach needs to be motivated by the belief that it can help to achieve public policy objectives more easily than other measures.

Outside the utilities, regulation is often a response to information asymmetries (hence restrictions on the behaviour of insurance companies, health and safety legislation and so on) or because of externalities (for example, control of polluting emissions from industry). In the case of the utilities, issues of natural monopoly and social policy objectives are often as important.

In theory, the regulation of a private sector monopoly would appear to be fairly straightforward. Left alone, the monopoly would restrict output and raise prices. The regulator therefore places restrictions upon its behaviour. In the UK, restrictions imposed by the regulators on the utilities have taken the form of ceilings on the prices that can be charged to consumers.

In practice, the regulator does not have perfect information on crucial aspects of a utility's business – for example, its cost structure. This makes it difficult for the regulator to put appropriate restrictions in place. As recent events in the electricity industry show, the regulator often only has the information that the monopoly wants it to have. This has resulted in outcomes (particularly in terms of very high profit levels) that many consumers have found intolerable.

There is also the difficulty that regulation will often have multiple public policy objectives. In the utilities, for example, there are concerns over equity, quality, shareholder interests, potential new entrants, management, workers, prices, possible strategic interests specific to that industry (such as diversity of energy sources) and environmental objectives. This means that regulation has to try to balance the conflicting interests in a way that is both open and accountable. Where this turns out to be difficult, the question that has to be asked is whether public provision would have been better.[7] (See Corry, 1995b, for more discussion.)

A more general point is that a 'desire to comply' or 'trust' may be essential if regulation is to work. Day and Klein (1996), for instance, note that the Housing Corporation can focus on efficiency while regulating essentially non-profit-making housing associations, assuming that the ethos of the housing associations will take care of quality. However, the opposite will hold if and when for-profit organizations are brought into the social housing field (Day and Klein, 1996, p.12).

A very important argument against regulation is that it involves costs that do not appear in the accounts. Some estimates of the total cost of regulation, especially made by those on the right of the political spectrum, are enormous (Stein, 1995). The aggregate cost of all regulation in the US has been put as high as 10 per cent of GDP (OECD, 1995, p. 69). Although these figures are open to debate, there is no doubt that regulation of the private sector often hides the true costs of delivering either a service or a particular standard. Regulation may, in fact, be a mechanism for government spending through indirect taxation. This means that policy makers and the electorate cannot judge whether the cost of providing a service is worthwhile. As the OECD rightly says, 'if governments are finding it difficult to control fiscal costs, which are highly visible, how much more difficult will it be to control the invisible costs of regulation?' (*ibid*., p. 70).

Some use this as a reason not to regulate at all: however bad the private sector, at least it is clear and transparent. However, if one is trying to achieve a policy objective, then if the cost of regulating in some cases seems too high we should reject the privatize-and-regulate approach in favour either of a contracting approach or, if that is deemed to be a problem, direct provision.

Conclusions

Policy makers starting with a clean sheet of paper at the end of the 20th century might well devise a public sector that did things differently from our present arrangements. But while there is always a case for thinking from first principles, of performing fundamental expenditure reviews and zero-based budgeting, we have to take where we are as a starting point and focus on several key issues in guiding our decision making.

There will always be a need for public action in order to make the world a better place in which to live. It is right that we constantly debate how wide this remit should go and how best to do this. In the long run, value for money will never be as important as the fundamental reasons for public action discussed at the beginning of this chapter. This does not mean that the current expenditure constraints, which are likely to persist for the next few decades, can be ignored. All future governments, in an attempt to reduce public expenditure, are likely to look to the private sector. The result will be more market-type mechanisms, either of the contracting-out or PFI type, 'corporatization', or privatization with regulation.

What must not happen is that an unjustified bias in favour of public provision is replaced with an unrigorous bias towards market-based solutions. The semi-privatized world creates a strong lobby for increases in government activity since the private sector values highly these safe and reliable contracts (Bosanquet, 1995). Add to this the attraction of keeping spending off the books and, from the new Left, a desire to look fashionably pro-market and the dangers are clear.

The ideal is probably a continuation of a 'mixed economy' of public service delivery. This will enable learning from trying different approaches, testing the public sector to be as efficient as the private, keeping in-house provision as a way of providing competition to the private sector (de Fraja, 1995) as well as coping with situations where transaction costs are high and keeping flexibility is essential.

Above all, we must be rigorous in demanding a consistent, clear and open approach to public spending decisions, where accountability and effectiveness are the watchwords. Openness is important because the knowledge that the decision-making process and analysis of public policy decisions – both in a technical and political sense – are subject to public scrutiny would help ensure that decisions were carefully thought through and evaluated properly. It would also help to ensure that resources were devoted to services that individuals valued most. Rational decision-making might be forced on politicians and the electorate might come to trust its politicians more. When they picked a particular delivery mechanism it would be because it was the best option available.

For any public project, the following sort of details should be discussed in the public domain:

- the degree to which public good and equity issues are raised;
- the value for money of the project, and different ways of delivering the service, to include specific estimates of the alternative costs (including financing costs) and (assumed) benefit and efficiency gains of each option;
- the degree to which any arrangement incurs future and contingent liabilities (massively aided if one had real resource accounting and budgeting – see Chapter 13 by Pallot and Ball);
- an assessment of the long- and short-run risk in using the private sector;
- an analysis of the likely disadvantages involved in using or continuing to use the public sector as a provider;
- evaluation to see if the assumptions were correct.

Finally, it is worth noting that no 'expert' really knows what the long-run consequences of letting the private sector genii out of the bottle will be. Public scepticism with regard to many of these issues may reflect a sensible risk aversion rather than just a blind defence of the status quo.

Christopher Hood (1989) has suggested that the limits to the contract and subsidiarity state will lie 'in terms of transactional convenience and constitutional answerability'. To these might be added value for money, given ever-changing needs and desires of the electorate, as well as the capability of the private sector. In exploring these issues an open mind must be the starting point.

Notes

1. Barrow *et al.* (1996) talk of the importance of 'atmosphere', the idea that 'social networks and non-price competition may be more important than conventional incentives' and the belief that institutional form may lead to more altruistic behaviour (p. 4).
2. In fact all finance is ultimately private, be it funded through general borrowing by the public sector or via taxation raised from private firms and individuals.

3. Much the same applies in 'partnership' deals that involve transfer of assets, development rights, planning gain, exemption from tough regulation and so on (see Brown *et al.*, 1994). None of these are a case of something for nothing: the public sector is in essence paying the private sector in kind. Some of these issues would become clearer if the public sector had proper accounts.
4. Of course exactly what risk is transferred has to be clearly assessed. There may be little point in transferring risk to the private sector that they can do little about. On the other hand, there are dangers that the public sector isolates the private sector to too great an extent. Under pressure from the private sector the Conservative government has gone some way to underwriting private sector involvement in PFI in hospital trusts (see e.g. *Health Service Journal*, 7.3.96), and has also had to amend ideas for regulating private finance in housing associations (Roof, 1996).
5. The OECD (1995) points out that in theory at least it is better to add in lots of elements that mimic a competitive market rather than just one or two. 'Market outcomes are predictable, generally speaking, but not when isolated elements of private practices are incorporated into large public organizations' (p.113). In other words, go the whole hog or not at all.
6. However, tax reliefs have costs which are essentially the same as public expenditure so we do not really relax the spending constraint by switching from grants, for example, to tax breaks. They also have efficiency and distributional consequences that are too rarely examined (Kvist and Sinfield, 1996).
7. This of course is not to say that one avoids the need for regulation within the public sector. Many of the answers to traditional government failure may well lie in this sort of approach.

References

ABI (1995). *Risk, Insurance and Welfare: the Changing Balance between Public and Private Protection*. Association of British Insurers.

Bacon, R. and Eltis, W. (1976). *Britain's Economic Problem: Too Few Producers*. London: Macmillan.

Barnett, R. (1993). 'Preference revelation and public goods'. In: Jackson, P. (ed.), *Current Issues in Public Sector Economics*. Macmillan.

Barrow, M., Johnson, P., Smith, P. and Taylor, J. (1996). *Targeting and Control in the Finance of Local Governance*. Paper presented at ESRC Local Governance Seminar held at the Dept of Environment, 12 March.

Blankart, C. (1985). 'Market and non-market alternative in the supply of public goods: general issues'. In: Forte, F. and Peacock, A. (eds), *Public Expenditure and Government Growth*. London: Basil Blackwell.

Bosanquet, N. (1995). 'Public Spending into the Millennium'. Social Market Foundation).

Brown, G., Cook, R. and Prescott, J. (1994). *Financing Infrastructure Investment*. February, Labour Party.

Corry, D. (1995a). 'Public and private partnerships', *Renewal*, **3** (2).

Corry, D. (1995b). 'Why should we regulate and why is it so complicated?' In: Corry, D. (ed.), *Regulating in the Public Interest: Looking to the Future*. IPPR.

Corry, D. (1996). 'Making the PFI honest', *Private Finance Initiative Journal*.

Dasgupta, P. (1989). 'Positive freedom, markets and the welfare state'. In: Helm, D. (ed.), *The Economic Borders of the State*. Oxford: OUP.

Day, P. and Klein, R. (1996). *The Regulation of Social Housing*. National Federation of Housing Associations.

de Fraja, G. (1995). In praise of public firms, *New Economy*, **2** (3).

Dilnot, A. (1995). *What Role for the State in the Economy*? ESRC State of Britain Seminars, Economic and Social Research Council (ESRC).

Falkingham, J. and Hills, J. (eds) (1995). *The Dynamic of Welfare: the Welfare State and the Life Cycle*. Prentice-Hall/Harvester Wheatsheaf.

Finley, L. (1989). 'Alternative service delivery, privatisation and competition'. In: Finley,

L. (ed.), *Public Sector Privatisation: Alternative Approaches to Service Delivery*. New York: Quorm Books.

Forte, F. and Peacock, A. (1985). *Public Expenditure and Government Growth* London: Basil Blackwell.

Heald, D. (1996). *Privately Financed Capital in Public Services*. Paper for the Local Governance Programme of the Economic and Social Research Council, March.

Heller, W. (1965). 'Reflections on public expenditure theory'. In Phelps, E. (ed.), *Private Wants and Public Needs*. New York: Norton.

Helm, D. (1989). 'The economic borders of the state'. In Helm, D. (ed.) The Economic Borders of the State. Oxford: Oxford University Press.

Hills, J. (1995). 'Funding the welfare state'. *Oxford Review of Economic Policy*, **11**(3).

Hood, C. (1989). 'Rolling back the state or moving to a contract and subsidiarity state?' In Coldrake, P. and Nethercote, J. R. (eds) *What Should Government Do?* Sydney: Hale and Ironmonger.

Institute of Housing (1993). *Local Housing Companies: New Opportunities for Council Housing*. Joseph Rowntree Trust.

IPPR (1996). Submission to the House of Lords enquiry into relations between central and local government, February, IPPR.

Keating, M. (1991). 'Management of the public sector' in Llewellyn, J. and Potter, S. (eds) *Economic Policies for the 1990s*. London: Blackwell.

Kerr, A. and Radford, M. (1995). 'CCT challenged', *New Economy* (2)1.

Kvist, J. and Sinfield, A. (1996). *Comparing Tax Routes in Denmark and the United Kingdom*. Danish National Institute of Social Research.

Le Grand, J. (1996). 'The thinkable', *Prospect*, July.

Levitt, M. and Joyce, M. (1987). *The Growth and Efficiency of Public Spending*. NIESR, Cambridge University Press.

London Economics (1994). 'The future of postal services: A critique of the Government's Green Paper', *London Economics*.

London Economics (1996). 'What price commercial freedom? Economics in action'. *London Economics Newsletter*, Issue 3.

Marchese, C. (1985). 'Market and nonmarket alternatives in the public supply of public services: some empirical evidence'. In: Forte and Peacock, *op. cit.*

Martin, B. (1993). *In the Public Interest? Privatisation and Public Sector Reform*. Zed Books in association with PSI.

Metropolitan Transport Research Unit (1996) 'For whom the shadow tolls: The effects of design, build, finance and operate on the A36 Salisbury Bypass', *Transport 2000*.

OECD (1994). *New Ways of Managing Infrastructure Provision*. Public Management (PUMA) Occasional Papers No. 6. OECD.

OECD (1995). *Governance in Transition: Public Management Reforms in OECD Countries*. OECD.

OXERA (1996). *Infrastructure in the UK: Public Projects and Private Money*. The OXERA Press, Oxford Economic Research Ass. Ltd.

Oxley, H., Maher, M., Martin, J. P. and Nicoletti, G. (1990). *The Public Sector: Issues for the 1990s*. Dept. of Economics and Statistics Working Paper No. 90. OECD.

Phelps, E. (1965). Introduction to Phelps, E. (ed.) *Private Wants and Public Needs*. New York: Norton.

Public Finance Trends (1995). HMSO.

Public Services Privatisation Research Unit (1996).

Radcliffe, R., Hawksworth, J. and Glanville, G. (1996). *Consensus for Change; Public Borrowing, Housing Investment and the City*. Coopers and Lybrand and Chartered Institute of Housing.

Roof (1996). 'Private Finance warnings', *Roof Briefing* April.

Self, P. (1989). 'Redefining the role of government'. In Coldrake, P. and Nethercote, J. R. (eds) '*What Should Government Do?*' Sydney: Hale and Ironmonger.

Smith, A. (1996). *The State of the Public Finances; Labour's Approach*. Speech to the Opening Plenary Session of CIPFA Conference, 11 June, Labour Party.
Stein, P. (1995). 'Measuring the costs of regulation' in Stein, P., Hopkins, T. and Vaubel, R. (eds) *The Hidden Cost of Regulation in Europe*. London: European Policy Forum.
Szymanski, S. (1994). 'CCT: a clean solution?'. *New Economy*, **1**(2).
Treasury Committee (1996) *The Private Finance Initiative*. HC 146, HMSO.
Waterson, M. (1994). 'The future of utility regulation: economic aspects'. In: Corry, D. (ed) *Regulating our Utilities*. IPPR.
Watson, S. (1995). 'Innovative approaches to the financing of infrastructure and public service projects'. *Local Work*. Manchester: Centre for Local Economic Strategies.

2

What Should Count as Public Expenditure?

Sheila Watson

Contents

Introduction

In principle, it should be relatively straightforward to say what should count as public expenditure. If what we mean is *what should be included in the public sector account?* then the answer is simply everything that is currently spent in the government's name, as well as all its future obligations and liabilities. In fact, it is more complicated than that, and the reason that the issue is so often debated is because it is as much a theoretical argument about the real scope of the public sector as it is about accountancy.

There is, in fact, no universally accepted notion of what the public sector is, and no perfect model against which the current process can be measured or indeed towards which we could aim. Moreover, the definition of public expenditure in the UK has changed and developed and is now 'contestable terrain' (Mullard, 1993). It is generally acknowledged that most of the definitions of total public expenditure are biased, in one way or another, to suit the objectives of those who seek to promote them. There are few objective truths, therefore, in this area which is value laden and subjective in nature.

This might be due, at least in part, to the place which the concept of the 'public sector' has in modern political debate. Public expenditure policy bridges the divide between politics, economics and social policy. It links the extent of government's involvement in 'social policies' with the resource cost of this approach, as well as indicating the wider 'cost' to the economy. Public expenditure is also relevant at both micro- and macroeconomic levels (Heald, 1996; Mullard, 1993).

All governments, when faced with a difficulty or with pressure in any one policy area, very often seek escape through a manipulation of public expenditure. They may decide to increase the level of spending in an existing budget (for example, buy more school books) or extend the scope of the public sector and, thereby, incur new costs (for example, introduce a new service such as free eye tests). These policy decisions may involve no increase in total spending, if resources are switched from one service to another. Another way of avoiding problems in politically sensitive areas is for the government to swop between different 'forms' of expenditure, for example from capital to current, rather than just between different services.

Accounting for the activities of government in purely financial terms is also complicated by the fact that its role goes beyond spending. Government also acts as a regulator, raises taxes and provides tax reliefs. It owns property and other assets, from trading companies to houses and buildings. In spite of these complexities, it is important that the public accounts be defined in such a way that they accurately reflect all the activities of government.

This chapter discusses, first, the purposes of the public accounts. The current methods used for controlling and measuring public spending have developed for a number of reasons and these are briefly outlined. The way in which public expenditure is currently calculated in the UK – in particular, the definition used in the construction of the public sector borrowing requirement (PSBR) – has a number of limitations. This matters because there are implications for the wider economy. Several approaches which might improve the way in which public spending is measured are considered. Finally, we discuss how resistance to change might be overcome.

Purpose of the public accounts

As with any private company, or even any household, financial accounts are intended as a source of information about the true financial position of the concern: its size, the state of its trading balance and the debts it might have incurred. This will enable an outsider to take a view on the relative strength of the organization based on certain key indicators. For example, a potential investor might examine a company's debt-to-equity ratio because that would give a sense of its longer-term strength. It could also act as a basis for comparison with other potential investments.

In the case of the public sector, information of this kind is also important, for additional reasons as well. In the mixed economy an assessment of the size and scope of the public sector is also a summary of the public sector demand within the economy, and therefore where resources are limited, the space which is left for the private sector. For example, some believe that public sector borrowing for investment purposes may force up interest rates and, thus, restrict the ability of the private sector to invest (Brown and Jackson, 1986). This makes it all the more important to distinguish between government activities – for example, consumption and investment – which make a claim on the real resources in the economy, and transfer payments or subsidies, which merely involve transferring resources around (Buiter, 1985).

Of equal importance to the total of overall government spending is the balance between what government spends and what it funds itself through taxation, charges and rents. This balance, allowing for some accounting adjustments, is the PSBR. This has itself come to be considered a key economic indicator because it is assumed that it is a valid reflection of the government's wider fiscal stance or its net use of resources in the economy over and above what it funds itself. Successive Chancellors of the Exchequer have in recent years been gripped by the importance of this measure and have focused upon it as a key indicator of their financial rectitude. Clearly with such focus on this measure it is critically important not only that the total sums which are being raised through taxation are properly identified but that the other side of the coin, namely the amount which is being spent, is similarly well and properly documented. Otherwise, the PSBR will become increasingly meaningless. The limitations of the PSBR are discussed further below.

It is unlikely, however, that any one indicator is capable of summarizing all the activities of government. A cash measure of total current spending – broadly the current system – would ignore its role as an investor, an owner of property and a regulator. Such a measure might include spending by other groups on behalf of government over which it has little control compared with what it spends directly itself. For wider economic considerations, a range of separate but interrelated measures may be needed, including total spending on transfers; total deficits; total investment and total debt. Searching for a way to reconcile all of this in one measure may simply be an impossible and fruitless task.

Why is it so difficult to count public spending?

A simple analogy might serve to exemplify the difficulties inherent in using a financial measure to establish what resources the public sector is using. My bank statement tells me what part of my income I have spent either in cash or through direct debit on clothes, rent, books, fuel and so on, and also what I have left. My salary cheque and some interest on the money I may have deposited in a savings account is the income against which I spend. The balance – whether positive or negative – is some indication of my overall financial position and also reveals whether I need to borrow to fund my spending. By the same token the revenues which the government raises, whether from taxes, or charges, should be balanced against its spending on goods and services. The resulting balance, which can also be positive or negative, will also give an indication of the degree to which it is 'living beyond its means'.

But this does not convey the whole story. We would not consider our spending to be only that which we took from our current account in any one month. There might also have been payments direct from our wages into pension funds, we might have spent monies withdrawn from savings accounts, and of course we may have bought on credit, either through loans, credit arrangements or credit cards. Thus, just as the picture of our spending pattern is not complete without reference to other credit statements, so too we need to know what the government has spent on account to get the full picture of its activities. That means that we have to look carefully at the goods and services which governments supply and in particular analyse the time profile of its spending allowing for the fact that it will very often be spending now on projects which do not have any benefit until the future, and that it may be entering into agreements where the commitment to pay is similarly far away.

The analogy with a personal bank account is already too simplistic, for a number of reasons. While it is possible to draw a line around the spending of any individual and to be clear where it ends and where someone else's spending begins, the core problem for the public sector is that the boundary of its activities is far less clear, and is open to interpretation. In part this is because there are many agencies acting and spending on its behalf. However it is also due to the very nature of the activities which the public sector undertakes – many of which are really not recognizable as spending at all. For example, the government regulates and this imposes a direct cost on the activities of the private sector. It also gives implicit subsidies, for example, in tax reliefs which is more like foregone revenue than direct spending but ultimately impacts upon the PSBR in exactly the same way. It also acts as guarantor on the loans of such bodies and offers cheap finance for investment projects. It begins to be clear, therefore, that spending really means something rather different when applied to government than it does when applied to the individual, and clearly it is impossible to calculate a total for all spending without a very clear definition of what the public sector is.

Yet if we accept the idea that we do need to know what government is spending we must address these problems and at the very least incorporate these differences and difficulties within some meaningful measure or range of measures which are generally understood. We need now to examine where the line is drawn around the public sector currently and to identify more explicitly what the problem areas are.

How the current methods have developed

The current methods for controlling and measuring public spending in the UK have developed for a number of reasons:

- a desire to control the size of the public sector and fear of fiscal imprudence;
- changes in the way in which the public sector has operated (for example, the provision of more sophisticated services);
- ad hoc development of new rules and regulations.

The desire to control the size of the public sector and fear of fiscal imprudence are relatively new phenomena which gained impetus following the oil price shock of the early 1970s. This resulted in the intervention of the International Monetary Fund which made substantial demands on the UK's freedom to spend and, in particular, on the use of spending as a Keynesian demand management tool (Mullard, 1993). Thus, while there are stark differences in terms of the individual spending choices which different governments make, the consistent approach towards public spending has been one of the centre exerting control over the other arms of government.

Traditionally, the Treasury has promoted a restrictive approach to the level of spending. One aspect of this control has been its approach to future liabilities incurred in the name of government, whether directly by government department or indirectly by quangos and semi-autonomous bodies. At the heart of the current Treasury approach is the view that 'clever games', which secure benefits now but defer costs to future taxpayers, must be avoided. As Rose and Peters (1978) observe, 'the bad news is that unlike an individual citizen a government cannot go bankrupt and be discharged from responsibility for its past liabilities. A government carries its past commitments forwards into the future.'

This desire to control and to be clear about the real commitments of government, and to account for those commitments in as complete a way as possible is an understandable and even laudable approach. However, sensible rules may become excessively resistant to natural change and evolution and may impose costs on the economy (Ashworth *et al.*, 1984).

Second, the way in which the public sector itself operates has developed over time. The scope and form of government spending has changed and increased responsibilities have brought increased spending. It has moved from the collective provision of defence and roads, through safety net expenditures such as education, which could be bought privately but which not everyone could afford, to insurance spending on services such as health and unemployment benefits which were only introduced in the earlier part of the century. These developments meant that things became increasingly complex in an accounting sense. Where taxes were raised for collective goods such as defence it was easy to see how monies came in and were spent directly on services which were 'enjoyed' almost immediately. As public spending became more sophisticated, governments began taxing not only to spend on services now but also to invest in services which might not be delivered until some point in the future, and to 'store up' resources for the delivery of insurance or safety net type expenditures, where those paying currently may not benefit until some future date. A good example of this is the current 'pay as you go' approach to pensions. And, as the range of public spending expanded, governments not only increased the scope and rate of taxation to generate income but also began to levy charges for their services and to borrow money. The way in which services are delivered has also changed. More recently, there has been the development of arm's-length spending through agencies, public corporations and quangos. These raise important new issues for measuring public expenditure.

Third, and a direct result of the above, a number of ad hoc rules and regulations that govern the detail of public spending have developed over many years. Between 1977 and 1983, for example, there were 26 changes in definition and coverage of the public finances (Likierman, 1988), including the redefinition of nationalized industry spending on capital items which took this item out of public spending. Because the revenues involved are substantial, this change meant that the headline figure on public spending (as a percentage of GDP) was reduced. This ad hoc approach to the definition and scope of public spending may well be partly to blame for a series of inconsistencies in approach which are examined later.

How public expenditure is calculated

The types of expenditure of the different layers of government – central government departments, local government, public corporations, quangos and trusts – vary widely (see Box 2.1, p. 52). Essentially, these may be divided into spending on services with an immediate benefit (current spending), spending on goods where there is a longer time horizon involved (capital expenditure), and direct transfers of money to individuals in the form of benefits (transfer payments) (Bean and Buiter, 1987). However, in terms of accounting for the total amounts spent, they are all treated in the same way. For example, the £100 million spent on a capital project is judged to be exactly the same as £100 million spent on unemployment benefits. This is in spite of the fact that capital spending makes a positive contribution to the infrastructure, and consequently the potential earning capacity, of the economy, while spending on unemployment benefits merely involves moving money between people.

The government's overall plans for public expenditure are set in terms of a Control Total. This comprises all central government expenditure (excluding cyclical social security spending), all local authority expenditure, the financing requirements of nationalized industries and any amount drawn down from the national reserves. It accounts for around 85 per cent of total government spending, the remaining 15 per cent being made up of cyclical social security spending – that is, spending on unemployment benefit and income support to people of working age – and debt interest, which are not included in the control total because these are the two areas 'most affected by the economic cycle' (HM Treasury, 1995).

If these missing elements are added back in, and in 1994/95 they totalled a substantial £41 billion, a new higher total is generated which is defined as General Government Expenditure (X) GGE(X). GGE(X) is then reduced by the level of privatization receipts, counted here as negative expenditure, then increased by a series of other adjustments, including National Lottery-financed expenditure and interest and dividend receipts. This final total, general government expenditure (GGE), is set against general government receipts, including taxes, duties, rates and social security contributions, to generate the general government borrowing requirement. The latter can be either positive or negative. After allowing for the borrowing of public corporations, the balance is the PSBR. Money raised through the Lottery – even though it is spent on public sector projects – is not included in GGE(X) or the control total.

As mentioned earlier the particular way that the total of public expenditure is calculated and accounted for matters not only in itself but because it is a crucial element in the calculation of the PSBR. As Table 2.1 shows, the total used to calculate the PSBR is not even the same as the GGE (with all its imperfections).

Table 2.1. Public spending (1994/95: £bn).

	Central Government spending (excluding cyclical social security)	174.1
+	LA spending (self financed and Central Government funded)	73.4
+	public corps EFLs	1.0
+	drawing down reserves	–
=	**Control Total**	**248.5**
+	cyclical social security	14.2
+	Central Government debt interest	17.5
–	public corps market and overseas borrowing (PCMOB)	1.6
–	LA debt interest to central Government and other debt interest and receipts	−4.2
+	other accounting adjustments	11.9
=	**GGE(X)**	**289.7**
–	privatization proceeds	6.8
+	other adjustments (Government interest and National Lottery)	5.1
=	**GGE**	**288**
–	general Government receipts	250
=	**General Government Borrowing Requirement (GGBR)**	37.8
+	PCMOB	−1.9
=	**PSBR**	**35.9**

Source: *Public Expenditure Statistical Analysis* (1996/97); Tables B1, 1.3, 2.1; *Financial Statement and Budget Report* (1996/97); Table 4.1, 4.5.

The PSBR is now considered a key economic indicator. It is also among the most keenly watched of statistics in the modern UK economy. Not even inflation, and certainly not the rate of unemployment unless it is rising, are more central to the political debate then the question asked of every policy suggestion in recent years 'will it add to the PSBR?' There are two related reasons for it to be considered a key indicator. First, there is a belief that the PSBR gives an indication of the fiscal stance of the government of the day (Blejer and Chu, 1988). Second, the PSBR has implications for the financial markets because it indicates the degree to which the public sector is raising funds through gilts and other financial instruments (Radcliffe *et al.*, 1996). In fact, the PSBR as an economic measure is inherently flawed in both of these regards. Because of the attention paid to the PSBR (not least by recent Chancellors of the Exchequer who have considered it a key indicator of their financial rectitude) our discussion below focuses very much on the PSBR rather than GGE itself.

Limitations of the current system

Cash and capital

As we discussed above, GGE is almost entirely a cash concept in that it concentrates on the actual cash transactions between the public sector and the rest of the economy. The PSBR derived from it is not comparable to any other measure of the public finances in the rest of the world, and is a measure of the balance of public finances in just one year on a cash basis (Hawksworth and Wilcox, 1995).

The cash approach has particular implications for the treatment of capital spending. Although they have different impacts on the economy, in the current method used to account for current and capital spending both are treated as if they were exactly the same (Ashworth *et al.*, 1984; Likierman, 1988; Buiter, 1985). This has made it possible for successive governments to reduce spending on capital investment (claiming that this slows their fiscal rectitude) at times when there have been overall pressures on current spending, particularly caused by increases in transfer payments. They have done this without taking into account fully the true costs to the economy of reduced capital investment (Ashworth *et al.*, 1984; Watson, 1996). While borrowing to pay for spending involves payment in the future, cuts in capital investment are a drain on the future earning capacity of the nation. As Heald (1995) observes: 'the justification for cuts in capital spending must be in terms of current economic policy alone, not in appeals to notions of prudent regard for future taxpayers' (p. 8).

The way in which capital goods – or assets owned by government – are treated in the public accounts is also flawed (Likierman, 1988). Unlike in the private sector, where there is allowance for deterioration of those assets, there is no similar allowance in the public sector. This is by no means an easy issue to resolve. However, resource accounting, which is increasingly being adopted in the internal accounting of government departments (Heald, 1995), and which includes an evaluation of asset values, is one way to proceed (see Chapter 13 by Pallot and Ball).

An alternative measure, the General Government Financial Deficit (GGFD), is used in the European Union to measure the deficits of member countries. The GGFD excludes privatization receipts as well as the borrowing of public corporations. According to the Chartered Institute of Housing, a growing number of economists see the validity of moving towards a GGFD approach in the near future, particularly as Europe moves closer towards monetary union (Radcliffe *et al.*, 1996).

Privatization

Furthermore, many commentators have drawn attention to the way in which the current PSBR system deals with privatization receipts, treating them not as extra income but as negative expenditure (Ashworth *et al.*, 1984; Likierman, 1988; Bean and Buiter, 1987 and Blejer and Chu, 1988). Privatization receipts in 1995/96 are projected to be around £3 billion. While substantially lower than in some of the peak years of the mid to late 1980s, when privatization proceeds exceeded £8 billion in some years, it is still sufficient to have a sizeable impact on the headline PSBR figure. Clearly, the sale at a fair price of a nationalized industry which was previously in receipt of subsidies may result in savings for the public spending total. What is not obvious is why the income received from the sale of assets should count as negative spending. This practice has been roundly condemned as little more than an attempt by the government to reduce the level of the PSBR in any one year (Likierman, 1988; Hansard, 1984). It has certainly given an incentive to reduce the headline PSBR total by selling off assets too cheaply and, thus, diminishing the stock upon which future wealth can be created. This has had a detrimental effect on the government's long-term budgetary position (Tanzi, 1993). Moreover, as Blejer and Chu (1988) point out, if privatization proceeds are treated as negative expenditure, account should also be taken of the consequent reduction in income flows from the asset which has been sold.

Some commentators have also argued that privatization merely reflects a change of ownership and does not alter the level of goods and services commanded in the economy by the public sector, although it appears to have reduced the level of government borrowing (Bean and Buiter, 1987). As Ashworth *et al.* (1984) note: 'In effect when assets are sold the public and private sectors exchange existing companies for financial assets. It is not clear that there is necessarily any effect on real demand for current production, and yet the PSBR reduction implies a tightening of the government's fiscal stance'.

Public corporations

Another flaw in the current accounting system is the extent to which borrowing by public corporations and other bodies are included within spending totals. Where such bodies receive permission from central government to take out loans, the full amount of the loan is included as the potential loss in the spending total. This is true even when the real risk of default is slight. For example, even if a public corporation borrows to invest in an asset which has a guaranteed revenue stream or where the corporation may be in a position to pay back that loan quite quickly, because it is in a healthy financial position, the full extent of the liability is included as 'spending' that has been discharged. The implicit reasoning behind this is that if the government could be called upon to cover any debts then it must fully account for that possibility. However, in a situation where there are limits on the total amount of public spending in any one year, this unrealistic treatment of the risk involved may be 'crowding out' other public investment.

PFI and other future liabilities

The role which private finance should play in the development of public sector projects has always been the subject of differing opinion. In June 1981 the National Economic Development Council set up a working party under the chairmanship of Sir William Ryrie, then Permanent Secretary to the Treasury. This working party was instructed to review the investment rules for nationalized industries and to devise a set of criteria which became known as the Ryrie rules, under which private finance might be introduced into public sector projects. The working party concluded that any attempt to introduce private finance into a public sector project should be on the basis of there being no special advantage, such as a guarantee, which would make this project more advantageous than any other in the private sector. It also concluded that the extra cost of the finance coming from the private sector would have to be balanced by the gains in efficiency to the public sector from having the project take place. As a result private funds could only really be used if they were proved to be the most cost effective way of proceeding. Given the unique position of the government in terms of the collateral which it offers and therefore the rate at which it can 'borrow' money, it was virtually impossible to achieve these objectives.

The Private Finance Initiative (PFI) which ultimately replaced a reformed set of Ryrie rules was introduced in 1992 and sought to 'remove unnecessary obstacles to private sector investment in Britain's infrastructure' (HMSO, 1992). This initiative modified and relaxed the constraints on private money, although still very much in the context of overall control of public spending.

After a range of modifications in the three and a half years for which it has existed, the PFI in essence requires local authorities, government departments and other semi-autonomous bodies to view capital projects less as physical things and more as a bundle of services to be made available over a period of time. This is an important concept because it automatically challenges the requirement that a capital asset should be owned by the public sector. For example, if a local health trust needs the use of a new hospital, it does not need to own the building to have full access to the range of services which it might provide. It needs only to guarantee that it will use the hospital building if one were to exist, and to develop a clear specification of what the 'hospital service' should look like, and then hand over to the private sector to build, design and pay for the hospital which the health trust could then use – at a price.

Thus PFI money need not be additional to public sector capital investment funds. Indeed it seems that it is replacing those funds, while the capital sum is not itself being counted as public expenditure, even though in most cases the contracts by which these projects are set in place are predicated on a guarantee from the public sector that the service will be bought over a period of time – thus the scope of the 'public sector' is extended.

So, while private money might be going into building a school which is almost entirely used by the public education service, spending on education – insofar as the charge for using the facility comes from the existing current budget – would not increase and certainly the capital element would stay the same, even though potentially the public sector is taking up more resources.

There is therefore a clear difference between controlling public spending and controlling the size of the public sector, and this is a good example of where the current means of accounting for public spending does not actually reflect the current scope and scale of the public sector. Thus the PFI, the latest 'creative means of hiding the PSBR' (Ashworth *et al.*, 1984), might help to bring down the spending total, but if private resources are going on public projects, the public sector is at 'best' the same size and at 'worst' even bigger.

That still leaves less room for the private sector to access funds for its own investment. This automatically generates questions of definition: when is a privately funded project a public sector project? Just because the school is used on a regular basis by the public sector and owned totally by the private sector need not necessarily mean it is a public sector resource unless the decision to build it remained in the public sector. Moreover, the way in which the PFI is developing suggests that in fact the decision to build or to become involved in such public infrastructure projects on the part of the private sector is far more driven by them and far less by the public authorities (Treasury and Civil Service Select Committee, 1996).

Just as investments can bring benefits in the longer term, so too other Government activities are in some sense liabilities for the future. This applies in particular to the issues of pension and social security payments. While most people who hand over National Insurance payments from their wages believe that this money enters a fund from which they will be paid a range of benefits when they need them, the process is far more 'pay as you go' with unfunded liabilities building up for the future. This has clear implications for the

Central government departments

Total spending by central government is disaggregated in a number of ways in official publications – for example, by geographic area, by general purpose and by activity. However, the most common subdivision is into departmental totals, such as education and employment, trade and industry, or health. These are also the basis upon which total annual spending is allocated.

Within these totals resources from the control total allocated to the department will be deployed in a range of ways, from capital investment to service delivery. Moreover, they will increasingly be delivered through a range of other agencies such as health trusts, or Training and Enterprise Councils, under the direction of, or in contract to government officials. Only 'cash' spending, whether on capital or current or transfer payments, is included, unless public corporations within the department's remit wish to pursue capital investment through loans, in which case special arrangements to endorse that borrowing are required. Increasingly, while the total spending levels are centrally determined and allocated, the actual process of service delivery is in the hands of semi-autonomous bodies.

Local authorities

Local authorities are responsible for setting their own spending budgets, which are financed indirectly by support provided by central government and directly from local authorities' own resources such as rent, charges and other income. This does not mean, however, that a local authority can simply plan to spend as much as it feels is appropriate so long as it can raise the extra income over government grants to cover that spending. Indeed, central government has developed powers to cap local authority budgets by establishing a total standard spending – or an amount of spending deemed appropriate by central government – for general revenue expenditure.

Local authority capital expenditure is an inherently more complicated process. Housing used to be the main programme in which local authorities had a role as capital investors. Over the past 15 years, however, there has been a clear redirection of resources from capital to transfer payments. Capital investment made up 68 per cent of the total spent on housing in 1979/80, with housing benefit payments taking just 10 per cent. By 1994/95, housing benefit made up 49 per cent of the total, with capital spending a long way behind at 27 per cent. At the same time, the monies available to local government have been directed towards an increasing number of competitive capital spending funds ('challenge funding'). Furthermore, central government ruled that local authorities which sold off capital stock were not allowed to reinvest the capital receipts although there has been some recent relaxation on this point. Very interestingly HM Treasury does not include receipts from the sale of council houses as negative spending for local authorities, although it does include all of the proceeds of privatization at a national level as negative spending in the accounts of central government.

Local authority spending is a component part of total public spending in the UK. Total local authority expenditure, which is made up of that part that is self-financed, as well as a far larger proportion which comes through revenue support grant, the distribution of the non-domestic rate revenues and other specific grants, is all included within the control total of public spending. This means that it is subject to constraint, particularly in times of economic difficulties.

Public corporations, quangos and trusts

Spending by semi-autonomous government bodies and public corporations makes up a growing proportion of all public spending. Yet, the way this spending is reflected in the accounts is becoming increasingly confused. For some of these bodies, all spending comes within the control total of the central government department with ultimate responsibility for its activities. It therefore counts towards total government spending in the same way as any other departmental spending would. For other bodies defined as public corporations, separate accounts are available, and the balance of those accounts is declared in the annual Financial Statement and Budget Report (the Budget 'Red' book). For others, which operate through local authority control, the regulations on local government apply. However, even then not all public corporations are treated in exactly the same way by the Treasury. As Likierman (1988) pointed out, 'their transactions with central government are classified in a variety of ways reflecting a different degree of integration into government finances'. Since then, the situation has become even more complex.

The sustained period of privatization of the nationalized industries and public corporations over the past 15 years means that very few remain, and those that do tend to be relatively profitable and fly in the face of the traditional image of heavy industries requiring extensive subsidy. Public corporations which require funds for investment purposes face limits on the amount which they can borrow, constrained through external financing limits (EFL) to which would count any government subsidies, loans or market or overseas borrowing as well as the capital value of any newly leased assets. The EFL is what determines the contribution of nationalized industries and public corporations to public spending. The assumption is that any liability taken on by a nationalized industry, which relies on security offered by the government, is a potential loss which would have to be covered were the corporation to fail.

Box 2.1. Different layers of public spending.

government's fiscal stance, as its net worth is potentially gradually diminished because its net liabilities are constantly increasing, particularly in a period of an ageing population. This would not however be reflected in the measure which is thought to reflect the government's fiscal stance, namely the PSBR, because the spending totals to which it relates do not reflect these future liabilities, even though the income which is generated from payments in social security funds is included in the total receipts. This is a very important point because as we have seen, there are a range of other liabilities which *are* included in public spending, in particular the liabilities incurred by the public corporations who take on borrowing on the private market even where the actual risk of them not being covered by the corporation in question are small. This inconsistency needs to be addressed.

Tax expenditure

Public expenditure is regarded as the spending by the government on goods and services, transfer payments and investments in pursuit of its policy objectives. What this definition excludes, however, is the implicit spending, often running into billions of pounds, involved in foregone revenues, for example, tax relief on mortgage interest. Insofar as these reduce the amount of revenues generated and, therefore, cannot be offset against spending, they also make a direct contribution to the PSBR. Yet they are not commonly counted as expenditure.

This is not a clear-cut issue. In part, it depends on how a neutral tax base is defined (Wildavsky, 1985) and, therefore, what is considered foregone revenue as opposed to taxes that were never levied in the first place. Similarly, implicit subsidies such as reduced rate of cheap loans are not reflected in the cash-based PSBR (Blejer and Chu, 1988). A number of other countries – including France, Austria and the US – have developed accounting mechanisms that identify these tax expenditures, thus giving a fuller picture of the government's fiscal stance (Hogwood, 1992).

Effects on the economy of the current system

It is generally accepted that the UK economy suffers from a lack of investment. In the public sector, severe problems are found in housing and the environment, but also in education, health and roads (Mullard, 1993). Yet capital expenditure by government is regularly 'deferred, deferred and deferred again' (Barnett 1982; Bean and Buiter, 1987; Pliatzky, 1982). The public accounts system has certainly had a role to play in this, due to its treatment of investment. Since the PSBR system was introduced in the mid-1970s, overall investment by central government has fallen steadily, to its present rate of around two per cent of GDP. Over the same period, investment by public corporations has also fallen and was less than one per cent of GDP in 1994 (Radcliffe *et al.*, 1996). This is particularly disturbing given growing levels of homelessness, the existence of housing stock in need of renovation, and the huge cost of unemployment in terms of benefit payments, and forgone tax revenues of which a large component is unemployed construction workers (House of Commons Employment Select Committee 1996). The PFI was introduced by the government as a means of providing additional funding for capital investment in the public sector. However, according to the most recent assessment, the initiative is likely simply to replace current public capital expenditure (Treasury and Civil Service Select Committee, 1996, p. 5). Restrictions on investment together with the ease in which cuts in capital spending can be and have been made is having a very real impact on the UK economy.

The PSBR system also leads to other inefficiencies regarding investment. For example, in a period of high unemployment and increased spending on transfer payments, an investment programme is far less likely to be approved because of constraints on the size of the PSBR. Ironically, this may in fact be the best time to carry it out both for 'Keynesian' reasons and because the 'price' of investment goods falls in recessions. Macro-economic constraints make a mockery of any rules on the rates of return which a capital project must fulfil, or the requirement that a public corporation be faring well to be able to sustain a loan.

This implicit investment bias affects the activities and future profitability of those public and quasi-public sector bodies that remain in the public sector (for an example of how investment in local authority airports is affected see Box 2.2). Given that public corporations have the potential to create profits and put money back into the public finances, this could have detrimental effects on those finances in future.

One alternative would be to adopt a *Golden Rule* and simply refuse to borrow unless it is for investment purposes. This is the likely approach of a future Labour administration. This policy is likely to be difficult to sustain, however, in a period of continuing pressure on social security budgets and falling receipts.

The way forward

Opinions differ as to what the ideal government accounts should look like. Buiter (1985) describes his ideal, 'comprehensive, consolidated public sector balance sheet at current market or implicit prices' as including all assets, financial, real, capital, land and mineral; the present value of future tax programmes; the imputed present value of seigniorage; together with liabilities which should include government debt, the stock of high powered money, the present value of social insurance and other entitlements and guarantees. The balancing item would then represent government net worth.

While the above makes sense at a conceptual level, it would be difficult to operate (Blejer and Cheasty, 1993). As discussed already, it is difficult to capitalize the values of tax and spending programmes, or to value assets in the public sector. And while it would be possible to improve on some of the worst

Local authority airports in the UK (these include Manchester, Teeside and Birmingham) are in direct competition with privately owned and commercial companies such as the privatized BAA airports at Heathrow and Gatwick, as well as with publicly owned airports elsewhere in Europe. Moreover, they are operating in an environment which is subject to high levels of regulatory control and which has expensive and extensive safety and security requirements. However, the current investment rules that affect local authority airports severely constrain their investment possibilities. For example, where such a corporation might seek to invest in additional capacity, it is constrained by the extent to which central government offers the lending capacity through local government, which the airport can then take up.

The airport can, of course, decide to fund its investment in other ways. However, this involves additional costs:

- In missing the opportunity to make the investment at the correct time in the demand cycle for its product, any company runs the risk of losing market share. In the case of the UK airports, for example, profitable long-haul flights out of Europe can be transferred relatively easily to other airports if capacity or service is lacking.
- While new investment devices such as the PFI exist, these are more expensive options given the increased expense of private finance. Furthermore, the corporation will be paying a premium rate to use facilities which, in all likelihood, will revert back to public sector ownership at the end of the contract period.
- While the most profitable airports have the capacity to fund investment from their own resources, this means diverting resources from other uses, resulting in an opportunity cost for the corporation.

Controls on local authority airports in terms of capital allocation are determined by the Department of Transport. Airports are, first, required to use their internal funds before they receive permission to borrow from public sector sources or the commercial market. In the past, airports were able to use leasing to avoid capital allocations. Changes in the 1989 Local Government and Housing Act, introduced to prevent local authorities from avoiding other financial controls and financing their capital expenditure through revenue accounts, has ruled out leasing. It is ironic that this transfer from capital to revenue spending is exactly what the government aims to promote with the PFI.

The rules place local authority airports in a very different position to the private companies they compete with, insofar as they are required to risk short-term problems with funding in order to fund long-term projects where private companies would simply choose long-term debt as a means of financing its investments.

The degree to which the management of local authority airports are therefore in some senses not in control of their own destiny; the short-term nature of funding approvals which are made; and the involvement of political considerations which simply would not impinge on a private company are all a cause for great concern given the lack of similar controls on many of the European airports.

While the rules on investment which affect local authority airports are slightly different from those that apply to other public corporations, the principle is the same. Any freedom to borrow must be bid for on an annual basis. This means that the airports are competing in the usual spending round against nurses' pay and investment in schools, even though the impact and effects of their investment programmes are quite different.

Similar constraints apply, for example, to the Post Office and local authorities' housing investment. However in these cases there is no competition for exactly the same services. The Post Office still enjoys a monopoly on standard postal services even though it has to compete with commercial organizations in the growing market for courier and express delivery services. In housing, investment itself is not obviously self-financing since much of the rent in the social rented sector is paid for by government – in the form of housing benefit. Local housing companies may get around this.

Box 2.2. Local authority airports.

excesses of the current PSBR system, any solution would bring new limitations of its own. There are, however, three approaches that are worth exploring.

First, to give some measure of central government's 'non-obligatory' spending, including only that part of spending over which government has some 'control', a variation on the present 'control total' approach, might be most appropriate. Such a measure would exclude cyclical social security benefits and related payments, such as housing benefit, income support and child benefit, as well as interest charged on debts and self-financed spending by local authorities. This would continue to be a cash-based concept, but would give a sense of the extent of the 'positive involvement' of government in the economy. It would be as much as 30 per cent below the measure of government expenditure (measured in cash).

Second, to get a wider sense of the activities of central government, allowing not only for the cash which departments are spending, but also for their 'use' and 'stock' of assets, something more akin to resource accounting which includes a value for asset depreciation might be more appropriate. This approach, which is beginning to be established for internal accounting in government departments, would have a profound effect on the 'spending' levels of departments, identifying the resource-rich departments, such as Defence which has a lot of assets that are depreciating in value.

Third, to give a sense of what activities the government is involved in, a mixture of these approaches, disaggregated not on a departmental or sectoral basis, but by the form of spending undertaken, would be more useful. Thus if spending totals were made up of current spending on ameliorative measures (such as unemployment-related benefits), current spending on general services, investment spending on capital and infrastructure, investment spending in other areas (e.g. education and training) plus asset deterioration or accumulation, not only would a fuller picture be provided, but the 'building block' approach would enable all government activities to be clearly identified.

If adopted, the approaches outlined above would have knock-on implications for the calculation of revenues, as well as for the financial balance. Their adoption would need careful examination based on experience in other countries. Less ambitious, but also worth considering, are two other specific proposals that still work with the grain of the current approach.

First, it should be possible to reconsider the position of certain public sector organizations to reflect more fully their role in the quasi-public sector. Clearly there is some room for movement here. The proof of this comes in the fact that the government has in the past employed a differential approach to public corporations based on some concept of the strategic importance of their activities. British Nuclear Fuels Ltd (BNFL) was for a time allowed to borrow outside of the PSBR when British Rail was not, even though both were wholly owned by the government.

Moreover, if it is possible to allow finance raised through the Private Finance Initiative to exist outside of the public accounts, on the basis that the services delivered are coming through the private sector with an assumption of improved efficiency, greater attention should be paid to alternative ideas which might enable existing profitable public sector structures to invest more freely. As Stella (1993) points out, it would be sensible in the case of a profitable public enterprise to treat its capital expenditure as likely to increase the value of the firm and, therefore, not to record this as current expenditure.

Thus even with the current system, a corporation with a proven track record in terms of profitability, past revenue streams and sales, and which had a solid projected business plan, should be allowed to develop a portfolio of borrowing outside of the public sector on the basis of being able to finance that borrowing from a future revenue stream. Clearly, it would be important to maintain strict controls on the extent to which such organizations could gear up extra borrowing or to ensure that the capital investment programme had some strategy for dealing with debt preference. Such a scheme would have the advantage of enabling expansion to take place without the requirement that the corporation give over a resource to a private concern as would occur with the PFI only to have to take it back at some point in the future. It would also be advantageous in strategically important corporations where ownership of the capital asset is important in itself because it brings with it control. Airports, for instance, could be considered to fall within this context particularly because of their importance in defence terms and their role as centres for regeneration. Similarly, those corporations with assets should be allowed to mortgage these, subject to restrictions, to raise funds for additional investment (as happens with Channel Four television currently). Another idea being examined is the establishment of 'halfway house' public investment companies, in which the government would hold a minority, 49 per cent equity. These would be free to borrow more cheaply without coming up against PSBR constraints.

Second, it is time to reconsider the means by which the public sector financial balance is drawn up. As discussed above, there are differences between accounting in cash terms through the PSBR and accounting in accrual terms through GGFD. A move towards GGFD would exclude the borrowing of public corporations. This would enable such bodies to have access to funds in a more open and imaginative way, while still maintaining public control over their activities. It would have the added advantage of making it easier for a range of other public investments to take place, for example, housing. Use of the GGFD would also bring the UK into line with practice in most other countries.

Overcoming resistance to change

There has been growing resistance in recent years to any suggestion that the current PSBR system – widely flawed as we have seen – be reformed. This resistance is found in both political and financial circles.

One of the most commonly heard criticisms in the House of Commons and elsewhere of any new policy suggestion or any change to existing policy is 'how much will it cost?' There has never been a time in electoral history when the focus of debate has been so closely attached to the issues of public spending. Moreover, and perhaps more importantly, this issue seems to have pervaded every area of the media and is therefore relatively well understood in its simplest terms by the voting public. In particular, the PSBR, which has been linked very closely to levels of taxation, is viewed as a clear indicator of a government's or opposition's position on fiscal rectitude. There are a range of reasons for a rise in the PSBR, from falling tax revenues – as is currently the case – to increases in 'ameliorative' spending, to increases in capital investment. While no increase can be countenanced regardless of the reason behind it, real investment opportunities will be lost. Moreover this is paradoxical given that the current Conservative government has run and continues to run very high levels of the PSBR at the same time as cutting income tax rates and being viewed as a party of low taxation.

Recent electoral politics have been dominated by the need to reduce public spending – often defined by a low PSBR – and commitments to avoid increase to taxes. The Labour Party's election manifesto in 1992 was the final output of a process of careful control of any potential, 'costable' commitments (Jones, 1992). The broad message of the Labour's election campaign was: 'we will not spend nor will we promise to spend more than Britain can afford' (Butler and Kavanagh, 1992, p. 94).

There is every indication that the current general election campaign is building up a similar head of steam. Indeed, it could be argued that the Labour party is following an even tougher line on public spending in 1996/97 than it did during 1992. Against this background, any suggestion of revamping the public accounts or making any necessary change to them will be viewed as a means of fiddling the books, which might be politically damaging. This is in spite of the fact that, as we discussed above, there are good reasons for re-vamping the PSBR and other public spending definitions, regardless of whether one wants to cut, increase or re-balance public expenditure.

Within financial circles, there are concerns that any changes would merely be a disguise for increasing government profligacy or for extending the tentacles of the public sector. However, it is worth noting that public account definitions are not carved in stone: there is not a definitively right or wrong way to treat many expenditures. They have already been subject to many changes. As we have seen, BNFL has had its treatment altered. Other public statistics have also been changed, with little concern expressed (for example, the definition of unemployment has been changed 31 times over the past 15 years or so). Finally, recent research (Radcliffe *et al.*, 1996) suggests that there is scope to address the concerns expressed by the financial sector while, at the same time, improving the public accounts along the lines suggested above.

Conclusions

This chapter has identified a number of flaws in the way in which public spending is accounted for in the UK. Two main issues have been highlighted: what should count as public spending; and what measure of public sector expenditure that implies. Clearly, there will never be consensus on the true scope of the public sector and it is difficult to imagine any conclusions being reached on how to account for such a fluid concept. It should, however, be possible to remedy some of the weaknesses in the current PSBR system along the lines outlined above.

Any new approach to the public accounts needs to consider the growing impact of Europe on the UK economy. The UK is now the only European country that uses a fiscal deficit definition such as the PSBR. The most common measure of budget deficits used by our European partners, the GGFD, does not include the activities of public corporations or privatization receipts. Furthermore, the Maastricht criteria are framed in terms of the GGFD. On a national accounts basis, the GGFD was £6 billion higher than the PSBR in 1994/95 and, at 6.25 per cent of national income, well above the Maastricht convergence criteria of 3 per cent. The GGFD is already identified in the Red Book accounts, and is calculated on the same basis as the national accounts. It would not, therefore, be difficult to move over to such an approach.

Finally, a more extensive examination of the public accounts should be the subject of a Royal Commission. As long as all spending ‘counts’ in the same way, investment or capital projects which have paybacks in the longer term will continue to be set aside. It is inappropriate that excess current spending, particularly ameliorative spending on benefits, should restrict investment. Only by opening up the process of accounting, and working to remedy its worst excesses, can progress be made.

Bibliography

Ashworth, M., Hills, J. and Morris, N. (1984). *Public Finances in Perspective*, IFS Report Series No. 8.

Barnett, J. (1982). *Inside the Treasury*. Andre Deutsch.

Bean, C. and Buiter, W. (1987). *The Plain Man's Guide to Fiscal and Financial Policy*. Employment Institute.

Blejer, M. and Cheasty, A. (eds) (1993). *How to Measure the Fiscal Deficit*. IMF.

Blejer, M. and Chu, K. (1988). *Measurement of Fiscal Impact: Methodological Issues*. IMF.

Brown, C.V. and Jackson, P.M. (1986). *Public Sector Economics*, 3rd edn. Oxford: Basil Blackwell.

Buiter, W. (1985). 'A guide to public sector debts and deficits', *Economic Policy*, November: 14–75.

Butler, D. and Kavanagh, D. (1992). *The British General Election of 1992*, Macmillan Press Ltd.

Hansard (1984). Comments by Terence Higgins MP (6.12), column 541.

Hawksworth, J. and Wilcox, S. (1995) *Challenging the conventions: public borrowing and housing investment*. Chartered Institute of Housing/Coopers and Lybrand.

Heald, D. (1995). An evaluation of French concession accounting', *The European Accounting Review*, **4**(2): 325–349.

Heald, D. (1997). Privately Financed Capital in Public Services. *Manchester School* (in press).

HM Treasury (1995). *Financial Statement and Budget Report 1996–97*, House of Commons No. 30, November.

HMSO (1992). *Autumn Statement*. London: HMSO.

Hogwood, B. (1992). *Trends in British Public Policy*, Open University Press.

House of Commons Employment Select Committee (1996). *The Right To Work, Workfare*, 2nd Report, London HMSO (Feb.) HC82.

Jones, N. (1992). *Election 92: The inside story of the campaign*, BBC Books.

Likierman, A. (1988). *Public Expenditure*, Penguin.

Mullard, M. (1993). *The Politics of Public Expenditure*, Routledge.

Pliatzky, L. (1982). *Getting and Spending*, Blackwell.

Radcliffe, R. Hawksworth, J. and Glanville, J. (1996). *Consensus for Change*, Coopers and Lybrand and the Chartered Institute of Housing.

Rose, R. and Peters, G. (1978). *Can Government go Broke?* Basic Books, New York.

Stella, P. (1993). Towards defining and measuring the fiscal impact of public enterprises'. In: Blejer and Cheasty (eds), *op. cit.*

Tanzi, V. (1993). 'Fiscal deficit measurement: basic issues'. In: Blejer and Cheasty (eds), *op. cit.*

Treasury and Civil Service Select Committee (1996). *The Private Finance Initiative*, HMSO.

Watson, S. (1996). *Innovative Approaches to the Financing of Infrastructure and Public Service Projects*, Local Work.

Wildavsky, A. (1985). 'Keeping kosher: the epistomology of tax expenditures', *Journal of Public Policy*, **5**: 413–31.

3

Recent History of Public Spending

Dan Corry and Sean Gray

Contents

Telling the story of public spending is not simple. The figures are disputed and suspect; even the terms used are controversial. Public services are not sold in a market but are commissioned by the political process. They cannot be measured in the same way as, or easily compared with, the output of commercial products. No one has yet managed to develop successful measures of what most public services are supposed to achieve. Even where, as in the case of parts of the health service, it is possible to produce an index of the activity of the service, this is a poor proxy for the real objective, the amount of health achieved. In part, this is because the state of people's health depends on a range of factors and public services, of which the NHS is only one.

Nevertheless, if we care about the public sector and believe that it can play a useful and important role in a modern economy and society, we must try to understand what has happened over the past few decades. This chapter covers most of the areas usually touched upon by a standard analysis of the public expenditure record and also widens the debate by painting a broader picture of the public sector and its context. We start by looking at how public spending is measured. We go on to examine the limited data that is available on output and achievements. The pressures that public spending places on the country's resources, including effects on taxation levels, are then discussed. Finally, the impact of public spending on the stability and freedom of manoeuvre of government is assessed.

Measuring public spending

At first sight, it might be useful to use internationally developed measures of public spending. This would avoid difficulties that arise from changes of definition (that sometimes look like short-term political manipulation) that bedevil national UK measures. One set of international measures, those associated with the Maastricht convergence criteria for membership of European economic and monetary union, have some advantages over the UK's own definition (see Chapter 2 by Watson) and they may be free of short-term political manipulation. However, the Maastricht measures do not get us much closer to addressing the key issues of what public spending is and what it is for. In what follows we will use a mixture of UK and 'international' definitions (see Box 3.1).

Figures 3.1 and 3.2 (p. 66 and p. 67) describe what has happened to overall expenditure, both in real terms and as a proportion of GDP, using GGE(X) which excludes privatization receipts.

In real terms, there has been a constant and inexorable rise in expenditure, with the only 'blip' being in the mid-1970s, a consequence of fiscal restraint and high inflation. Perhaps more surprisingly, government spending as a percentage of GDP has remained remarkably stable at a level of around 40 per cent. This ratio has however shown considerable variation between the peaks and troughs of the economic cycle. Expenditure as a percentage of GDP increased rapidly in the midst of the mid-1970s OPEC-induced recession, and remained high during the first Thatcher recession. Spending fell sharply during the Lawson boom of the mid-1980s and subsequently rose again during the recession that followed.

Quite a lot of this story is rather surprising in view of the fact that the government and the opposition constantly talk about cuts in public expenditure. The government wants to achieve cuts in what it regards as wasteful bureaucracy; the opposition accuses the government of making cuts in vital public services. In fact, the statistics indicate that, for most of its life, the present government has failed to deliver the promised cuts in spending. As a percentage of GDP, public spending is now the same as it was in 1979. After a sharp initial rise to 1981/2, spending fell in the years to 1986, rose between then and 1993 and is now on a downward path (or at least is forecast to be).

Why is this? There are those within the present government who tend to believe that public spending could be brought under control and taxes cut were it not for the subversive attitude of treacherous bureaucrats. On this view, all that is needed is someone who is prepared to exercise firm discipline and the waste will disappear. However, the idea that a lack of political will or bureaucratic inertia lie behind the failure to control public spending is likely to

Levels

The international definition of public expenditure (general government expenditure (GGE)) includes the spending of central government, of local authorities, and in the case of most countries, regional governments, *but not spending by nationalized industries*. The public sector also includes a range of companies known as public corporations. For most of its post-war history, *most of* this sector in the UK comprised nationalized industries, and in most countries it still does. While most countries exclude the spending of public corporations from their measures of public spending, the UK often includes their borrowing for capital spending in its public spending definitions (in particular, it is included in the Control total – see below). The definitions change from time to time.

Categories

Spending is divided into three categories depending on whether it is used to buy something only for immediate use, like childcare, something which will last, like a hospital, or a financial claim like a mortgage. These are known respectively as current spending, capital spending and lending. These correspond to three levels of accounts. The first looks at current spending and revenue with the balance being 'savings'. The next looks at savings and investment with the balance being the financial deficit. The third account looks at how the financial deficit is financed by borrowing. The UK pays a great deal more attention to the last of these accounts than do most other countries (although borrowing in most cases leads to debt which is given attention in many countries and is one of the Maastricht convergence criteria). (See Hawksworth and Wilcox, 1995.)

Current spending

This is divided into five categories. The first two – pay of government employees and procurement of equipment or supplies from the commercial sector – are combined and called government consumption. The other three are transfers, subsidies and debt interest. Transfers are income given to people, not because of the work they do, but because of who they are – for instance, pensioners or parents. The main function of transfers is, therefore, to redistribute income to those who need or deserve it, often by virtue of their age or poverty. Subsidies, like the money used to keep down prescription charges, are paid to keep prices down. Debt interest is the payment for borrowing to service the national debt.

Capital spending

This involves expenditure on items that have a return that goes beyond the current year – often referred to as investment spending. In the UK, this is generally held to consist of machines, buildings, vehicles and so on. Maintenance expenditure, which extends the normal life of an asset, is also included. Capital spending can be defined either as a gross amount or, with the cost of depreciation deducted, net capital expenditure.

Real terms spending

The amount of cash spent is not a true indicator of what can be bought, because of the effects of inflation. In simple terms, inflation can be taken out to give a volume, or real terms assessment of trends. However, inflation is not the same across sectors. For instance, where there are high levels of labour input (for example, in schools) spending is affected more by general wage increases than are more capital intensive areas. To take account of this, it is possible to calculate sector-specific price deflators and this is often done with health.

Keeping up with need

In addition, if a service is faced by new demands (for example, an ageing population) it may need more money just to keep the level of service constant. This, plus the points made above, helps explain why people often feel a service is being cut, when the 'real terms' figures show this not to be the case.

The control total

The UK measure of public spending used for Treasury purposes, the Control Total, combines genuine resource use, current transfers and some financial transactions. The control total is derived from the administrative process of planning and controlling departmental spending. In assessing the true economic significance and scale of public expenditure, it has only limited relevance.

Box 3.1. Definitions.

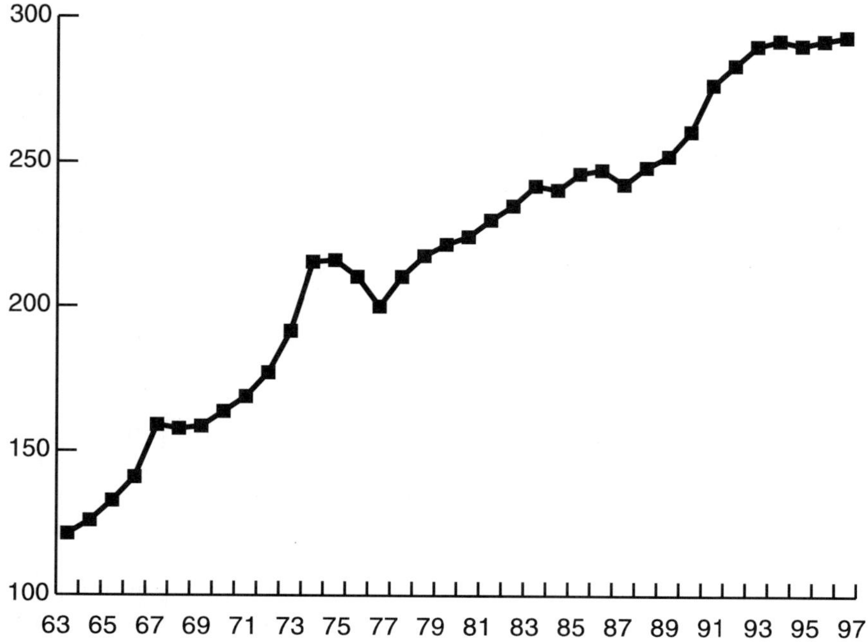

Figure 3.1. Public spending in real terms: GGE(X) (£bn/financial year).
Source: Public Expenditure Statistical Analyses (PESA) (HMT, 1996), Table 1.1.

be only part of the explanation. In practice, spending is driven by enormous demographic and social forces that are largely beyond the control of government.

There is a lot of confusion in this area. One question is whether central government has improved the way in which it controls the overall budget – in other words, hitting the targets that have been set. In judging this, underspending would clearly be as bad as overspending. In spite of the many reforms of the control systems introduced over the past two decades, the degree of success in hitting the stated targets appears to be little better in the 1980s and 1990s than it was in the 1970s (see Chapters 9 and 12 by Heald and Jackson respectively).

A rather different question is whether or not the government has managed to cut public spending. While we have drawn attention to the present governments failure to cut spending as a proportion of GDP, others might want to compare its performance relative to that of other countries. Its performance then looks 'better' (see Chapter 16 by Monck). This, of course, begs the question whether cutting spending makes sense. If it does not really deliver efficiency or macroeconomic gains, and is against the democratic will, one might question such a strategy.

Much of the continued growth in public spending has, in fact, been the result of economic, rather than administrative, factors. The impact of the economic cycle on such items as unemployment benefit or income tax revenue is well known. However, there has been far less recognition of the effects of increased use of means testing and linking of different means tests, bringing in additional items

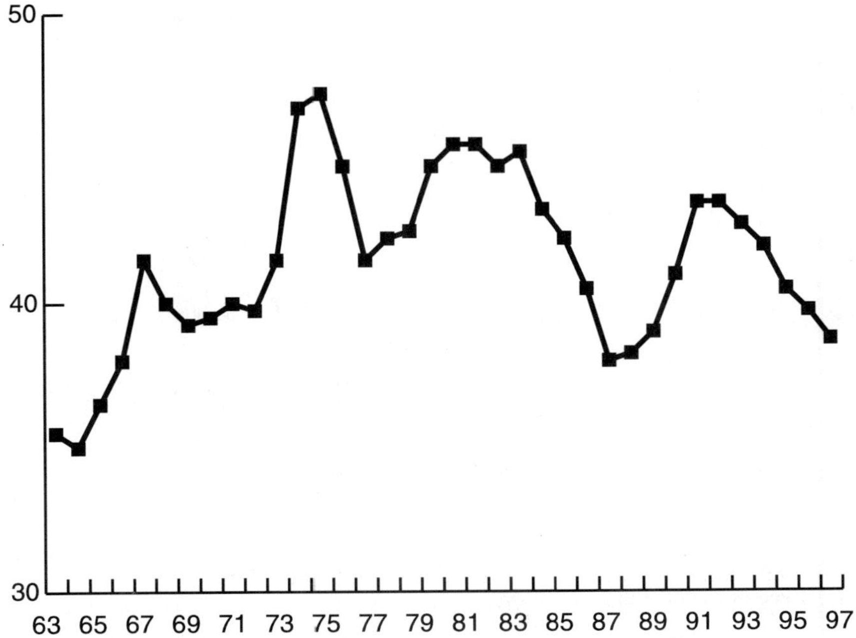

Figure 3.2. Public spending as a share of GDP
GGE(X) as percentage of GDP (%/financial year).
Source: PESA (HMT, 1996), Table 1.1.

such as housing benefit and legal aid, and the widening of the income distribution. The result has been to put more people into the kind of poverty which qualifies them for benefits. This may have made public spending more sensitive to the state of the economy. It is also true that in the core areas of health and education the present government has only introduced sporadic cuts in spending, and has often deliberately increased spending. Once spending has been increased in these areas, it is hard to reverse its expansion.

A little more insight into what has happened is provided by analysing how spending has changed over time in various areas. Figure 3.3 shows the general evolution of government spending as a proportion of GDP. The main shifts have been an increase in spending on social security and a decline in defence spending. Both health and education spending have remained relatively constant, with education stuck at around 5.5 per cent and health rising over the period from 4.6 per cent to 5.8 per cent. Meanwhile, combined spending on housing, recreation, and agriculture has declined relatively sharply.

The four graphs in Figure 3.4 look at spending by functional areas as a proportion of total government spending over a longer time period. This shows us how government divided up its expenditure, abstracting from the way that the total of spending altered over time.

In the financial year 1964–65, social security was the largest spending area, representing a fifth of total spending. It was closely followed by defence,

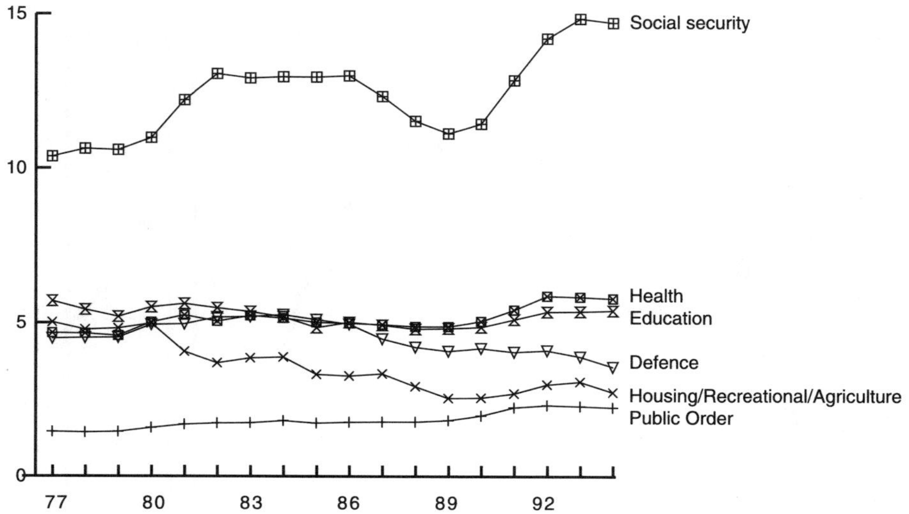

Figure 3.3. General Government spending as a proportion of GDP on selected functions (% GDP), all measured in current market prices).
Source: Office of National Statistics (ONS).

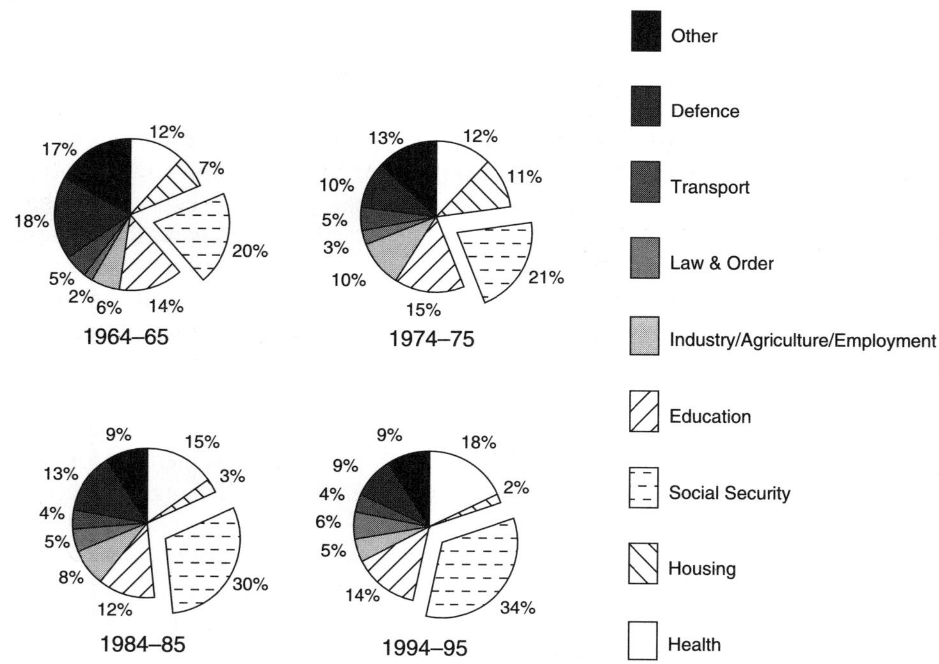

Figure 3.4. Spending share in four periods (as percentage of total public spending).
Source: Treasury.

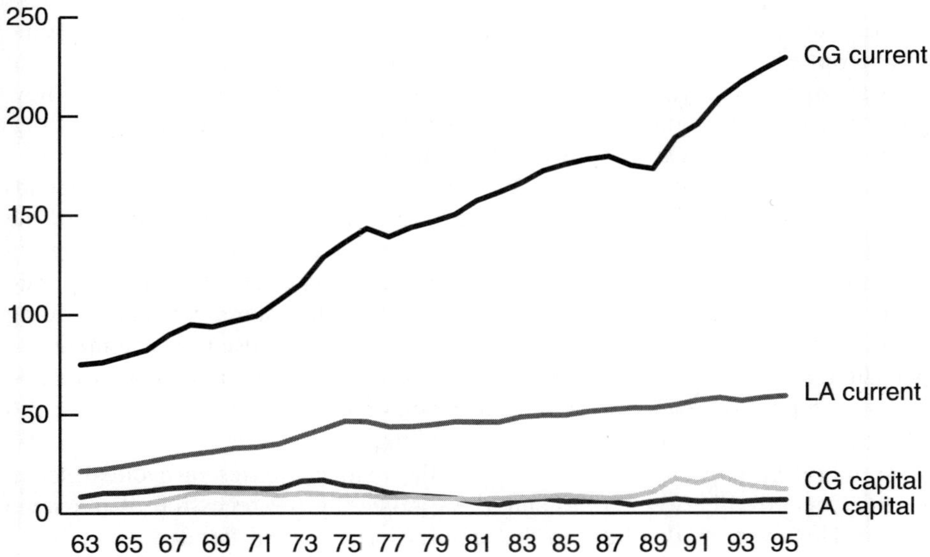

Figure 3.5. Local authority and central government spending (1990 prices, £bn). *Source*: ONS.

education and health. By 1974–75 spending on social security had grown, as had education; but health remained constant, and defence spending had been sharply reduced. Other areas of growth over this period included housing and employment. By 1984–85 there had been a dramatic increase in social security spending. It now represented £3 of every £10 of public spending. There was also an increase in health spending, and a reversal of some of the decline in defence spending. These increases were compensated by decreases in spending on education, employment and housing. Finally, by 1994–95 social security spending had grown to one third of all spending, while the defence share resumed its downward trend, along with housing and employment. Over the period as a whole, the three biggest spending areas, education, health and social security, grew from 46 per cent to 65 per cent of all government spending.

We can also look at the differences between central government and local government. Figure 3.5 shows that the vast bulk of spending is central rather than local. Despite the high profile given to local authority spending when out-of-control spending is discussed, it is clear that the action is mainly at the central level. Local authorities attract so much attention because often their out-turn spending differs from what the government had planned. But since central government only has few instruments to control their spending and there are often political divergences between central and local government, it would be surprising if there were not divergence between plans and out-turn expenditures.

As the analysis above indicates, much of the increase in public spending over the past decades may have been in areas where expenditure is demand led and, to some extent, outside the short-run administrative control of government. It is difficult to separate discretionary from non-discretionary expenditure. The government now publishes separate figures for what it terms cyclical social security spending. This is largely made up of social security benefits which, because they cannot be controlled easily, have been excluded from the official target for public spending, the control total. A long time-series is not available, which makes the measure difficult to analyse. However, it is a weak measure, even of spending that is cyclical, because it excludes many elements that move with the economic cycle (for example, crime, health and legal aid). Furthermore, cyclical spending is not entirely beyond government control; indeed, the present government has persistently cut the value of benefits. Despite these reservations, it gives some feel for impact of external factors on expenditure. It is shown in Figure 3.6 alongside growth in total government spending.

As might be expected, this shows that the main increases in cyclical social security occurred between 1990 and 1993, reflecting the recession of the same period. However, it adds little to the explanation of recent trends in spending.

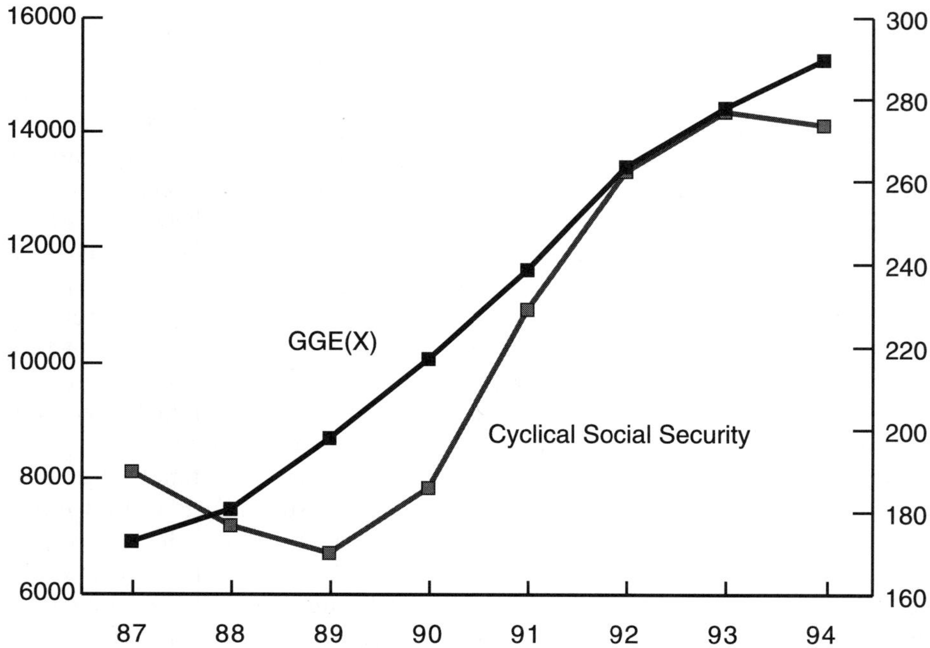

Figure 3.6. Spending and the cycle: cyclical social security and total government spending.
Left axis: cyclical social security (£m, financial years); right axis: GGE(X) (£bn, financial years).
Source: Public Finance Trends (PFT) (CSO, 1995b), Table 10.25, PESA (HMT, 1996), Table 1.1.

Beyond expenditure measures

Expenditure, of course, is simply a measure of input – what the government spends and not what it achieves. There are also a number of other important factors that we want expenditure measures to tell us about, including:

- What does spending achieve – and how responsive is it to need?
- What pressure does spending place on the nation's resources?
- How much tax is required to finance spending?
- How does it interfere with freedom?
- How efficiently does it operate?
- What impact does it have on the stability and freedom of manoeuvre of the government?

The efficiency point is dealt with in other chapters. We go on to look at what the available data tells us about achievement in terms of these measures.

Outputs and outcomes

In recent years, the government has tried to introduce more and more measures of both the output and outcome of public services. There has probably been a range of motives behind this trend. There has been a suspicion that such measures were designed to divert people's attention from the cuts in spending that the government was trying to make. The suspicion is based partly on the observation that so much of the Conservative government's rhetoric is hostile to public spending. In addition, output and outcome figures are clearly not taken that seriously internally: they are rarely used for planning and monitoring, still less as currency in the negotiation of plans in the annual public spending round.

But while this diversionary motive may be a factor, it is also likely that the government wants to be able to measure the efficiency of the public sector in order to compare it with the private sector; and for this it needs a measure of output. Such measures are at the heart of what any government will want to know about its activities if it is to monitor and control public spending. Given the enormous range of objectives which any government will want to achieve with its public spending, and the scarcity of resources, setting and sticking to priorities to achieve certain outputs is essential. Indeed, good output measures are arguably more important for a government that wants to achieve a set of policy objectives through public spending, rather than for a government that merely wants to reduce it.

It is necessary to distinguish between outcomes and outputs. The former measures the results of an activity, while the latter measures the scale of the activity. Neither is easy to measure. The ultimate desired outcome of a successful defence strategy must be peace. However, even if this could be measured by the number of people killed in wars, it would be difficult to isolate the UK's contribution to this outcome. And peace for instance in Northern Ireland, may be as much a consequence of economic and political measures as of defence ones. Outcome might also be measured in terms of levels of defence preparedness in different potential theatres of conflict. Data on this does not exist and it is hard to think how it could be produced. This illustrates the problems of valuing some of the most important things that the public sector does. In the absence of such measures one must make do with what is available. But one must make sure that one keeps an eye on the ultimate objectives on outcomes.

Few output measures are available over a long time-series and the data must be treated with care. Here, we concentrate on four major areas of public sector activity – law and order, health, education, and the reduction of poverty. These cover a large section of public expenditure and illustrate the main points.

Law and order

Spending on law and order has a clear outcome – less law-breaking and criminal activity. The statistics do not suggest that increased spending has led to any great improvement in either. The measurement of police activity and output is complicated and controversial, particularly as we do not know what would have happened to the trends without increased spending. The measures are also weakened by the fact that these statistics are reported by, and form the basis for funding of, police authorities.

Figure 3.7 nevertheless shows a generally deteriorating situation.

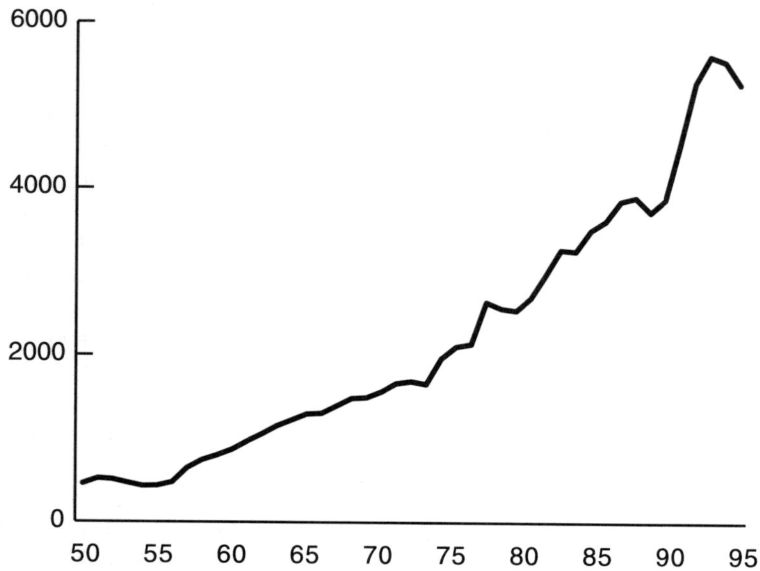

Figure 3.7. Criminal offences: notifiable offences recorded by the police (thousands). *Source*: ONS.

The number of criminal offences has been rising for several decades, although the increases appear to be cyclical around this rising trend. Following a steep rise between 1988–92, the level is currently showing a slight fall. Some of this pattern is undoubtedly attributable to factors such as the state of the economy and other government policies (Dickinson, 1995). However, there is no reliable way to separate out these factors. This illustrates the need to consider different government policies as they affect our ultimate outcome aims.

Health

Statistics on health outcomes, on the other hand, show that there has been a general improvement in the state of people's health. There is a far from complete picture, especially for morbidity, but for instance, perinatal and infant mortality both show substantial improvements (Figure 3.8).

Of course, health status is reliant on a great deal more than the activity of the NHS. Other factors, such the state of the economy and the impact of other government policies, play a more important role. Even more so than in the case of crime, measures to reduce poverty may have an impact on health status. In addition the impacts of investment in health care are long lasting. This year's health is the product of many years of health care. This offers further challenges to measurement.

We can also look at two other kinds of measures – activity and pressure.

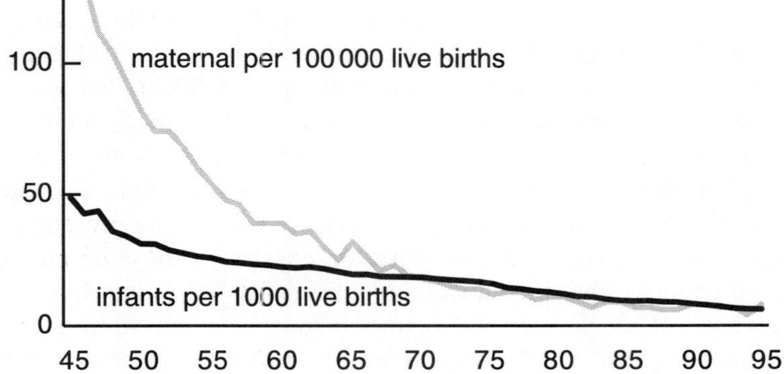

Figure 3.8. Falls in deaths associated with birth
(Deaths per live birth, infants under one year of age. Maternal deaths include those in pregnancy and childbirth).
Source: ONS.

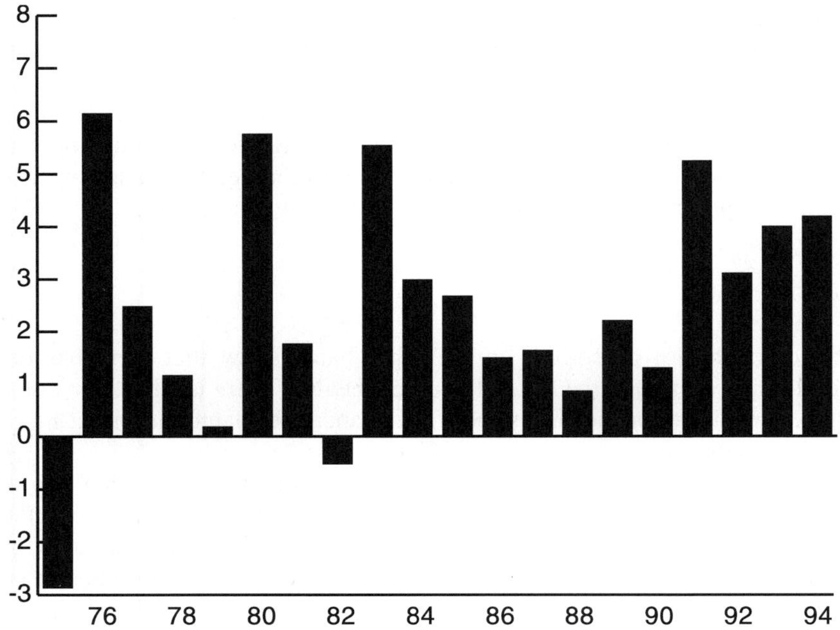

Figure 3.9. Annual percentage change in the Hospital Services cost-weighted activity index.
Source: Department of Health.

Changes in activity are shown for hospital services in the cost-weighted activity index illustrated in Figure 3.9. The index is designed to combine a range of activities like operations and courses of treatment. Figure 3.10 shows annual spending growth in the hospital service after allowing for changes in NHS costs. There are risks in interpeting this data, especially if increased 'throughput' of patients has been achieved at the cost of the quality of care. Nonetheless, the evidence in the two graphs is consistent with the conclusion that the government has increased spending on health and that this has produced improved results.

The most commonly used measures of pressure on resources in the health service relate to waiting lists, the statistics on which frequently appear in the media. Statistics on waiting lists have been altered by the present government more often than any other official indicator, except for those on unemployment. As usual the motives have been a combination of trying to improve the precision and relevance of the figures and opportunism. However, waiting lists on their own are meaningless: it may be that waiting times are more relevant. Waiting lists are, however, an indicator of the extent to which health care provision is keeping up with rising expectations and changing technology. As with the crime figures, such statistics have to be treated with caution because they are used as measures of performance and are, therefore, subject to reporting bias. This

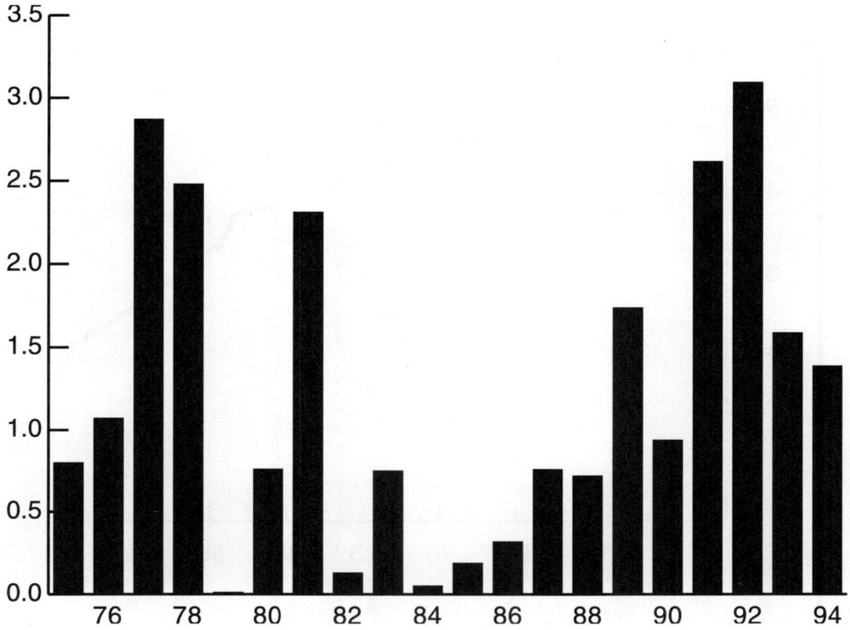

Figure 3.10. Annual percentage change in NHS expenditure (adjusted for NHS inflation). *Source*: Department of Health.

displacement of effort into hitting the target set may explain to some degree the improved performance on waiting lists.

As well as the direct use of services, individuals derive a benefit from the assurance that health care is available. People value the idea that their GP may have time to see them or that the nearest available emergency bed is reasonably close to where they live. Figure 3.11 shows that the number of available hospital beds has declined considerably over the 1980s and 1990s. The decline in the number of beds is much steeper than in earlier periods. At the same time, the number of patients treated on a day-care basis has risen sharply. On the other hand, the number of doctors and dentists rose (Figure 3.12).

Of course, these figures can also be used to tell different stories. 'Productivity' may have improved, reducing the number of hospital beds that are needed. Certainly, over the period cases treated per day went up. It could also be true that more doctors indicates over-supply. Again, the data must be treated with care and the focus must be on desired outcomes.

Education

Conflicts over the basic objectives of education are less common than they once were. There is now a much broader consensus that a useful output of education is

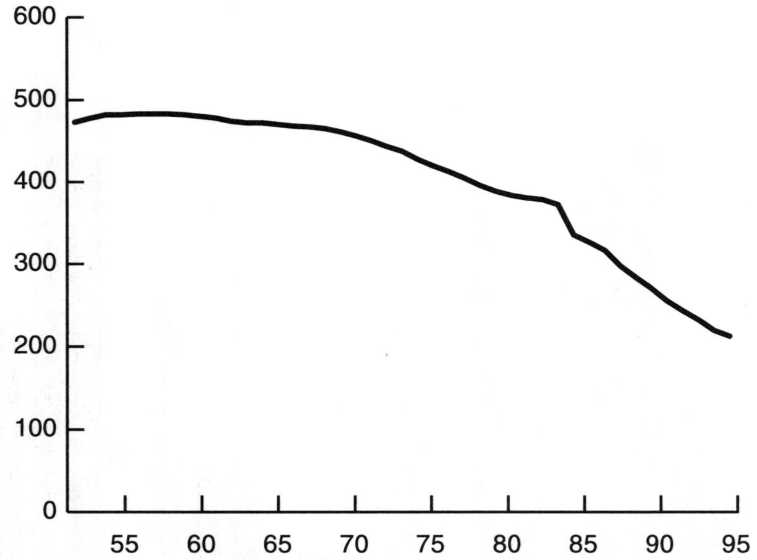

Figure 3.11. Hospital beds available per day (thousands).
Source: ONS.

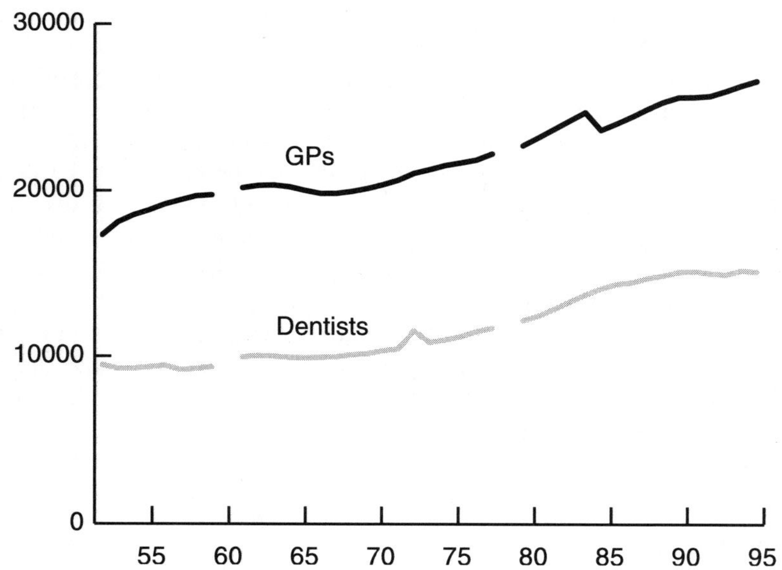

Figure 3.12. Numbers of GPs and dentists employed in the Family Health Service.
Source: ONS.

people with wider capacities. While there are doubts as to whether educational qualifications on their own adequately measure these capacities, they are the simplest measurable proxy. Clearly, the number of qualified people as a proportion of the population will continue to rise long after an improvement takes place in the level of education services. For this reason, an outcome measure based on the number of new qualifications may be a better indicator of current effectiveness of education (even though it takes many years to develop a person's ability to acquire new capacities and qualifications).

Throughout the period since 1980, the number of pupils who achieved either five or more GCSE A to C grades or one or more A grade at A-level remains remarkably constant. However, as a proportion of the school age population, the number achieving 'good' GCSE results grew steadily (Figure 3.13). It is interesting that there was a marked decline in pupils per teacher between 1978 and 1990, although a clear reversal of this trend thereafter. This suggests, at the very least, that small class sizes help to improve results.

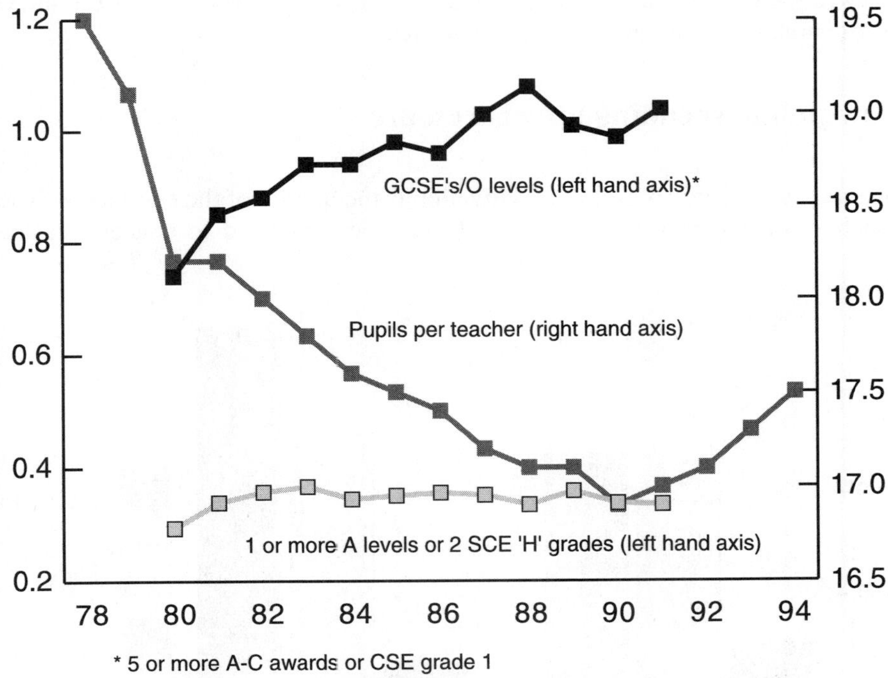

Figure 3.13. Pupils per teacher (UK) and children getting certain grades as percentage of all pupils in school (GB).
Note: Exam success has been divided by total pupils in schools (rather than totals taking the exams) to avoid the problem of variable drop-out over time and the fact that increased focusing on test results may have led schools to stop those likely to do badly in exams from taking them. In addition the published series we use on exam passes is unreliable after 1992 so we have not shown more recent dates (i.e. it jumps from 96 000 achieving five or more GCSE A–C awards in 1991/2 to 262 000 a year later!).
Source: CSO, 1996a, Table 5.3 and 5.5: ONS for earlier periods.

Poverty

Indicators of poverty are controversial. The government's own publication, *Households Below Average Income* (DSS, 1994), clearly suggests that there has been an increase in poverty, as do most other measures. Figure 3.14 shows that there was an absolute decline in income (after housing costs) of the poorest 10 per cent of the population between 1979 and 1993. Furthermore, the middle decile of the population has shown a small increase in income, while the total population shows a marked increase. This must indicate that, while the poorest have become poorer, the richest sections of the population have become substantially better off.

As with other objectives of government spending, poverty is the result of much more than direct government activity. In this case, however, there is general agreement that government has an obligation to offset these factors at least to some extent. It could also be argued that government must bear some responsibility for factors which may have increased levels of poverty, such as the state of the economy and deregulation of labour markets.

How public spending affects resources

One measure of the progress of civilization is the quality of the common services which a society provides for itself. Poorer societies need to concentrate their

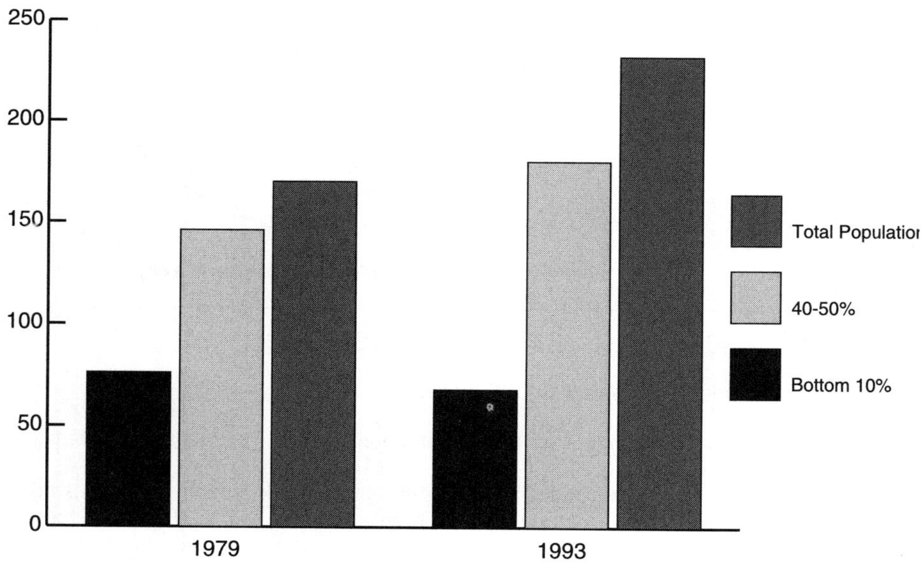

Figure 3.14. Changes in income 1979–1993 for households in different income deciles (after housing costs) (£ per week equivalised, March 1995 prices).
Source: Households Below Average Incomes (DSS, 1995).

limited resources on survival. It is only as countries become richer that they can spare resources for the common good of both present and future generations. As a nation becomes richer, its capacity to pay taxes also rises. Of course, the fact that more could be afforded does not mean that citizens will want to pay more. This is especially true when there is a move to private consumption and away from consumption of 'public' goods. In any case, government needs to monitor the extent to which its activities put pressure on the living standards of its citizens. A common proxy for the pressure of public spending on resources is the share of taxes in GDP, as shown in Figure 3.15.

This shows that tax as a share of national income in the UK fluctuated but is now at 36 per cent, not very different from what it was in 1979. This percentage is lower than in some OECD countries but higher than in Japan and the USA (CSO (1995b), Table 7.3). Following tax increases between 1992 and 1994, the proportion has, in fact, risen strongly since 1992 and is forecast to rise further.

We also want to look at how much of the nations resources are devoted to public sector activities of one sort or another. One element of this is the ratio of public spending to GDP (see Figure 3.2).

For this, it is important to use GGE(X), which excludes privatizations, rather than a measure which deducts privatization receipts. These financial transactions

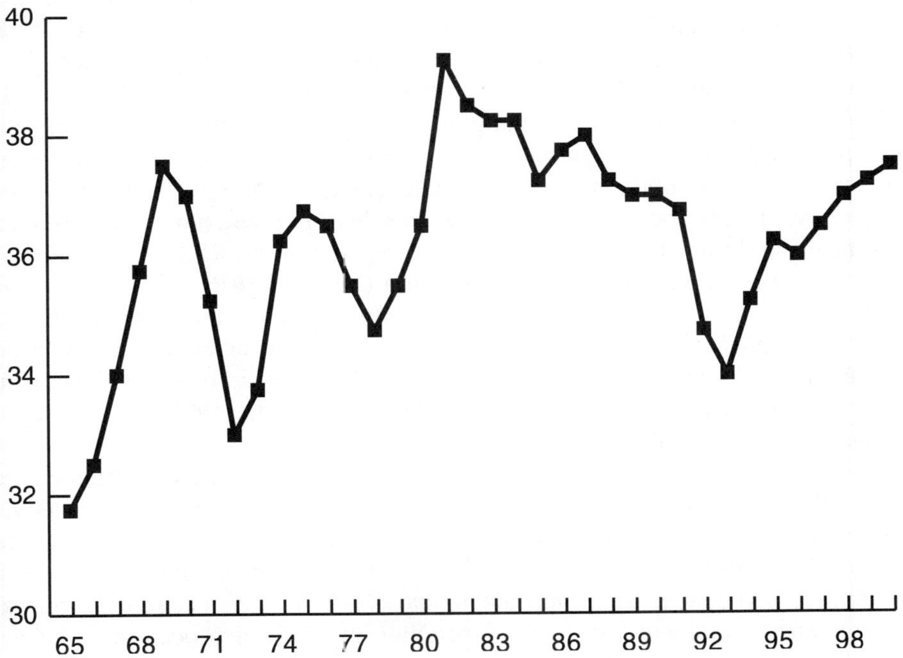

Figure 3.15. Taxes as a share of national income (non-North Sea, NICs included as part of tax).
Source: Budget Red Book (1995), Table A4.9.

have little to do with resources. They are concerned with financing the gap between expenditure and revenue. Privatization involves relinquishing a stream of future profits and dividends from the assets privatized in exchange for reduced current debt. Whether it is a good deal for the government depends on the price obtained. However, this has little direct impact on the pressure on resources; it involves no more than the transfer of ownership.

The other major difficulty with the usual measure of public spending used in the UK as a measure of resource use by the public sector is that it includes borrowing for capital spending by public corporations (although such borrowing has been treated in different ways at different times over the past 50 years). With the privatization of the last of the major nationalized industries, this sector is no longer as significant as it was. Investment by the public corporations fell from 2.8 per cent in 1983 to 0.6 per cent in 1994 (CSO, 1995b, Table 10.53). By comparison, and following the government's reorganization of the public service sector, the capital expenditure of hospital trusts was £1750m in 1994/5, of which £613m was included in the control total (HMT, 1996, Table 3.10).

Public corporations such as opted-out schools and hospitals supply services to government only. At present, these are commercial organizations only in a limited sense and their transactions should be regarded as part of public spending. It could however be argued that because they are fundamentally commercial operations, true public corporations' fixed capital formation and its financing are better regarded as part of the overall balance in the commercial sector between current and capital spending. The pressure on resources they represent is a general one and not one specific to the public sector.

In fact not all government spending puts the same pressure on resources. For example, transfers do not use resources but shift them between individuals, as do, for example, council house sales. Investment spending, which should be creating value for the future, arguably puts less pressure on resources than current expenditure. For these reasons, we need to consider how spending is divided between investment and consumption (Figure 3.16).

One of the most striking facts to emerge from the data is the enormous fall in public investment (and the linked increase in the share of public spending on consumption). Figure 3.16 shows that compared with a ratio of some 12 per cent from the mid-1960s to the mid-1970s, investment in the 1980s has averaged around 4–5 per cent of total spending (GGE(X)).

This is not a consequence of privatizations, since the public corporations are excluded from the definitions of general government spending. Neither, as we can see from the lower line in Figure 3.16, is the reduced investment entirely due to the sharp fall in net housing expenditure – although this is important. Indeed, the falling investment trend appears to have begun as a reaction by central government to the local government spending 'boom' which occurred between 1971 and 1973.

The importance of the pressure placed by the public sector's use of resources depends on the pressure coming from other sectors. If there is serious underemployment of resources in the wider economy, it makes sense for these to be

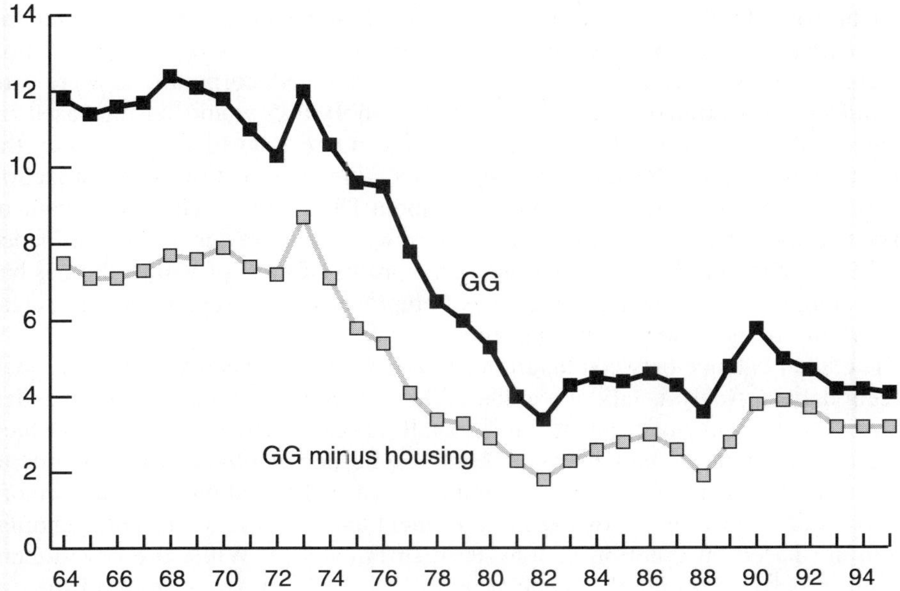

Figure 3.16. Public sector investment trends: General Government (GDFCF) with and without housing (% of GGE (X)).
Source: Blue Book (1995), Table 9.2, CSO (1995a) Table 1.8; PESA (HMT, 1996), 1.1.

used by the public sector. Keynesian stabilization policies, which suggested that public spending be used to keep up resource use, are no longer fashionable. Nevertheless, it must be that the more resources are available in the economy, the less stressful public sector use of them is. In fact, often, there are links between the degree of pressure on resources and public sector policies.

For example, the payment of unemployment benefit is a good example of what is called an automatic stabilizer. As unemployment rises, public spending rises. Automatic stabilizers are not usually big enough to keep resource use constant, although they are often very powerful. They give rise to a strong response of government finances to economic conditions and the stage of the economic cycle. According to a recent study by the UK Treasury, the effects of the cycle on the PSBR are ('marginally') higher that those reported in 1990 (Virley and Hurst, 1995). Since the Treasury also says that the tax elasticity has been revised downwards, this must mean that the reaction of spending to the cycle has been revised upwards.

Effect on taxation levels

A key purpose of taxation is to finance public spending. Taxation, however, is not the only method of finance, since governments can receive other income and can borrow. In the case of the UK, its once substantial revenues from the nationalized industries have mostly been used up and there are few remaining assets left to sell. If all the profits of the privatized corporations were still included in government income, its revenue in 1994/5 would be increased by some £12bn (source FT500). By contrast, the interest saved on the money the government received for these assets is about £4bn. The cost of the privatization in terms of extra burden on taxpayers is about £8bn a year. Those in favour of privatization argue that increased efficiency will yield greater profits and hence higher tax revenue. But since the rise in the profits of most privatized bodies has been achieved, in the main, at the cost of employees or consumers, it is not clear yet where the government has gained.

The ideal balance between taxation and borrowing has been a subject of much recent debate. Analysts talk of a golden rule. In fact, there are at least two golden rules. The present government tends to talk about borrowing at a level which would ensure that, in the long run, the interest burden would be financed without increasing the share of borrowing in public finance. The Labour party talks more in terms of allocating borrowing to investment and taxation to current spending. Both are based on a notion of long-term sustainability. While the government criterion is based on purely financial notions, Labour's takes account of the use to which the money is put.

The Maastricht Treaty focuses attention on two relevant criteria, the share of general government deficit in GNP and the ratio of outstanding debt to GNP. These are illustrated for the UK in Figures 3.17 and 3.18.

The ratio of the general government deficit to GNP shows how much government needs to finance its activities by borrowing or other financial transactions. In 1994–95, several years into an economic recovery, the PSBR was almost exactly the same (5.3 per cent) as in 1980–81, when Britain was in a very deep recession. The equivalent measure for Labour's 'golden rule' is the ratio of government saving to GNP shown in Figure 3.17. As the figures show, the government has been breaking its own 'golden rule' for several years; in other words, it has been borrowing to fund current spending. This is a major departure from the practice in most of the post-War period when governments largely stuck to the golden rule. The golden rules in both cases also need to be compared with interest rates and inflation (see Corry and Holtham (1995) for a fuller explanation of this).

This takes us to perhaps the truest guide to the health of the public finances – the underlying government balance sheet in terms of public sector assets and liabilities (although even this does not take account of all future contingent liabilities). As Figure 3.19 shows, following many years when these were built up (alongside a fairly steady balance in financial assets), public sector assets have been seriously run down over recent years.

As Figure 3.20 shows, the overall result of these trends is that the net wealth or net worth of the public sector has gone into serious decline in recent years. (See also Pain, Young and Westaway (1993).) This mainly concerns the central government and public corporation side of the sector. Perhaps surprisingly, given

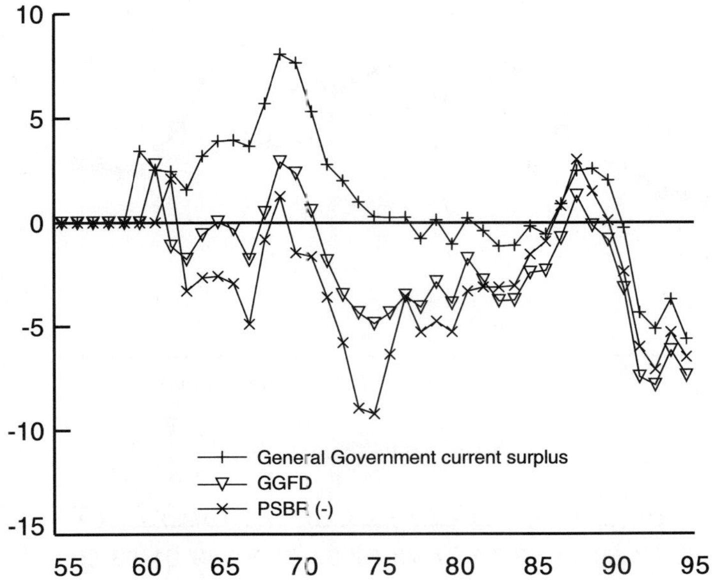

Figure 3.17. Different measures of the government deficit (% of GDP).
Source: ONS.

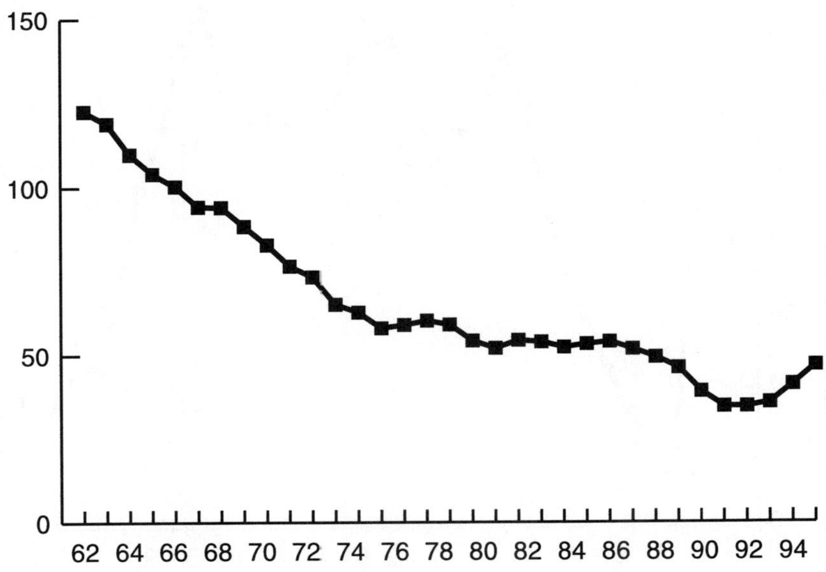

Figure 3.18. Ratio of government debt to GDP.
Source: ONS.

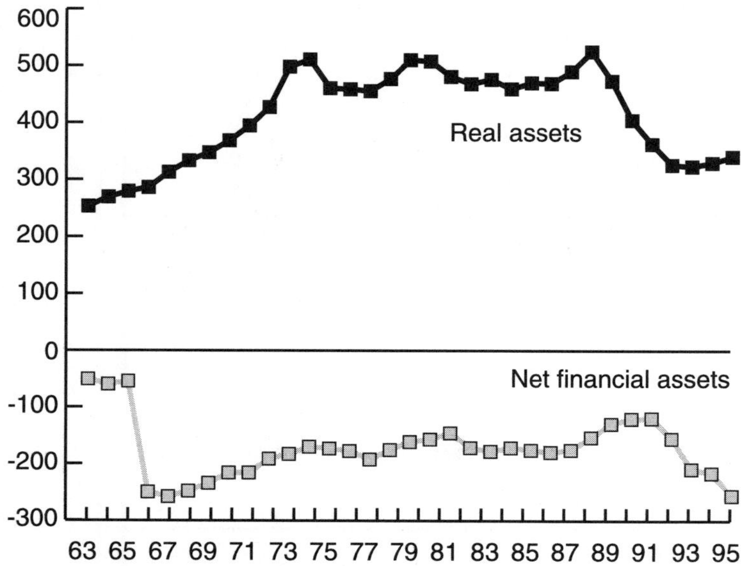

Figure 3.19. Public sector assets and liabilities, real and financial (1990 prices, £bn).
Source: ONS and CSO (1996b).

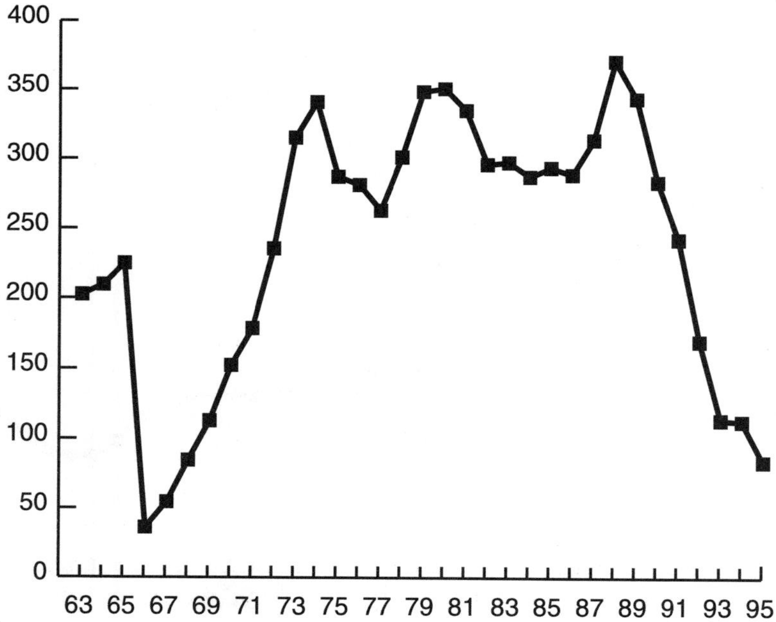

Figure 3.20. Net worth of the public sector (1990 prices, £bn).
Source: ONS and CSO (1996b).

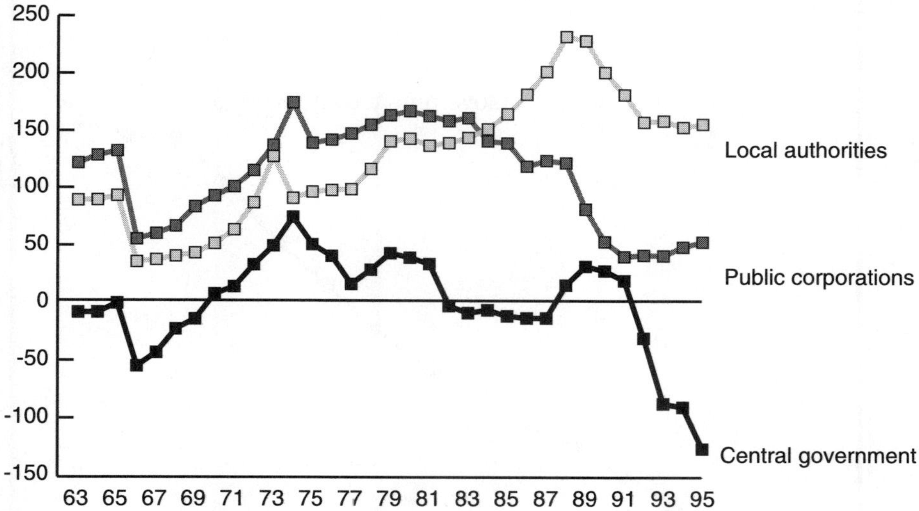

Figure 3.21. Net worth by sector (1990 prices, £bn).
Source: ONS and Blue Book (1996).

all the fuss made about it, the only sector with positive net worth is the local authority sector (Figure 3.21).

Effect on liberty

Politicians from all political parties have often claimed that the concentration of power implied by a large share of public spending may pose a threat to liberty. The concentration of power, however, depends on the structure of government. The UK has always had a peculiarly centralized structure but increased centralization has occurred very rapidly in recent years.

There is no simple measure of this concentration. But one useful measure is the loss of control by local authorities over their revenue. Figure 3.22 shows how much of their revenue local authorities raise themselves and how much central government does. The proportion of local authorities' revenue raised by themselves has fallen and the proportion raised by central government on their behalf has increased sharply.

As with resource pressure, concentration of power needs to be put into context. A large and highly centralized government is more threatening in a nation of small traders and isolated citizens than it would be in a nation with large powerful multinationals. One way of assessing this is to look at the ratio of public spending to the turnover of, say, the ten largest companies. Although the figures could be debated, Figure 3.23 suggests that the UK has a high concentration ratio compared with most other major countries. This suggests that it is perhaps important

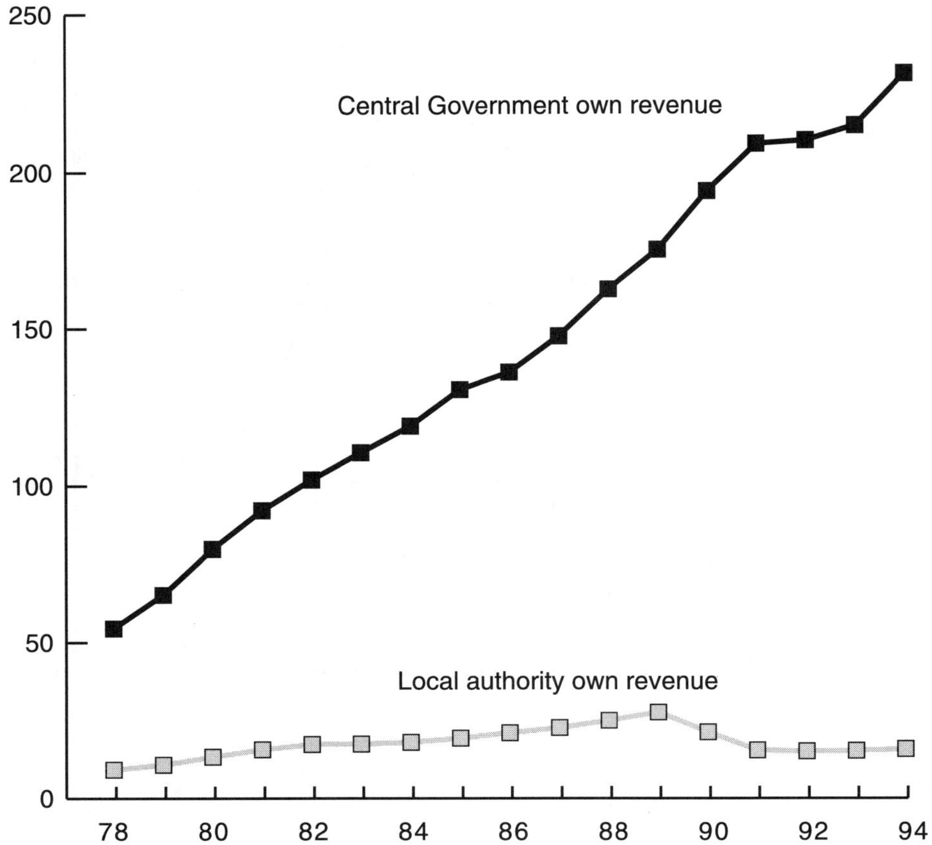

Figure 3.22. The relative revenue-raising power of central and local government (£bn).
Source: ONS.

to have the countervailing power of a relatively powerful public sector. The US, by comparison, appears to be closer to the model of perfect competition and, here, it may be appropriate that there is a more limited state sector.

Effect on autonomy

How valid is the widespread assumption that high levels of public debt threaten the stability both of a country's finances and its government? This is a different debate from that concerning the potential threat to a nation's finances of high levels of borrowing and the consequent upward pressure on interest rates, an argument which is, in any event, rather confused (see Box 3.2). The argument is more that the long-term stability of governments is threatened by borrowing.

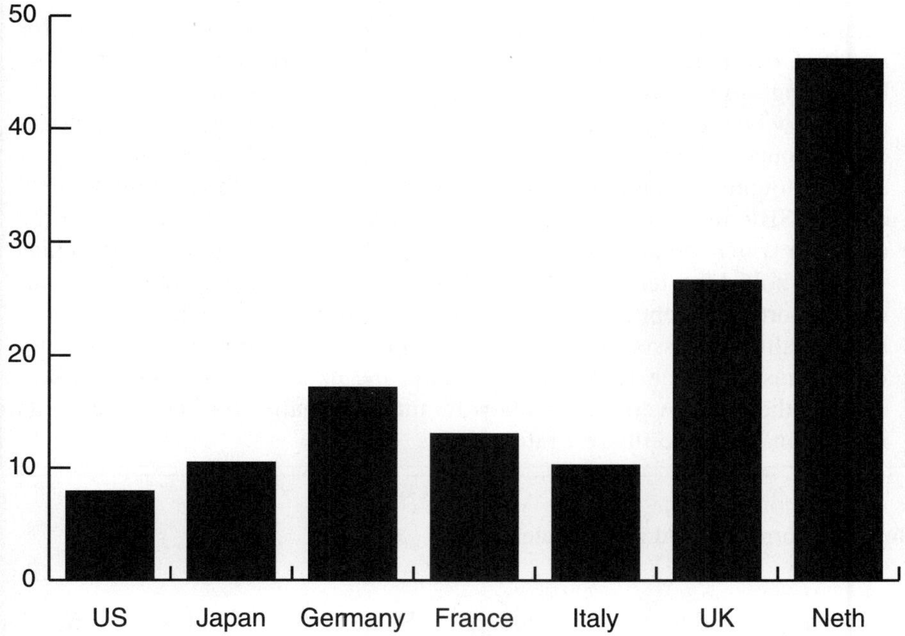

Figure 3.23. Share of turnover of top 10 companies GDP (%).
Source: FT500 (1996).

Experience suggests that the major financial collapses of recent years have rarely been the result of the build-up of large amounts of debt. This is as true of the collapse of UK merchant bank Barings as it is of the crisis that affected Mexico in 1994/5. We have already discussed the sustainability of any level of debt in the context of golden rules. Provided borrowing is used to invest in the economy, either in terms of directly used government equipment or in the productive capacity of skills or equipment used in the private sector, the debt will be sustained by increased tax revenue from a more productive economy. Devising a true golden rule which assesses the productivity of government investment, and the extent to which this improved capacity translates into greater tax revenue, would require a more complex model of the economy than is possible here.

Conclusions

Three main trends emerge from the analysis of public expenditure in the UK over the past two decades. First, there have been some switches in expenditure categories over time with social security, in particular, taking a bigger and bigger slice of public spending. Second, the share of spending as a proportion

Interest rates reflect the balance of supply and demand in the market for credit. Government is the largest user of long-term credit. Most of its borrowing comprises long-term loans on the financial markets, known as gilts. New borrowing normally represents only a fraction of the total amount of debt outstanding. In 1994 for example, market holdings of government stock amounted to about £275 billion, seven times even the inordinate level of the PSBR in 1994–5. Interest rates will depend more, therefore, on the extent to which wealth holders like pension funds and insurance companies want to hold long-term fixed interest debt instead of, say, company securities, short-term debt or real assets such as land. It will also depend on their total wealth. The issue of new debt through increased government borrowing is thus only one factor. Furthermore, the existence of global markets enables the UK government to borrow internationally, further reducing its impact on domestic interest rates.

Box 3.2. Borrowing and interest rates.

of GDP has moved very little (although as Monck explains in Chapter 16, it has moved closer to the OECD trends and away from the higher trends in the EU). Third, there has been a major switch from capital to current spending. What is striking, however, is that successive Conservative governments have failed to achieve cuts in the overall level of public expenditure in core areas of the public sector. It appears that aside from the decimation of public sector housing and sharp cuts in defence, the trends observed in the core of the public sector were little different from the earlier period.

Conservative governments did, however, successfully change the way in which the public sector is structured. This may well have been in an attempt to secure efficiency savings and, in this way, to reduce spending. It is, however, difficult to assess from the available data whether any gains in efficiency were achieved (except, as we discussed above, in the case of health care) nor whether the changes are likely to lead to lower public exenditure in the future. If there were any productivity gains overall (and this is difficult to establish), it seems they have not allowed room for expenditure cuts so far.

It may also be the case that other reforms were introduced in order to undermine the case for public provision. The NHS dental service, for instance, has been so undermined that most people now have to pay for private dental treatment. The problem from a Conservative 'cutter' viewpoint, was that some of the reforms, although aimed at trying to undermine the public sector ideology, did not lead to lower spending: indeed some, like NHS trusts and GP fundholding, have an element of the whimsical about them and may push up spending in the longer run. It is true that some government policies – for example, the social security reforms – have been directed very consciously at saving money. These may have some impact on public spending in the long term, although there is little evidence of this so far. But the main consequence of the shift to more means testing seems to have been to make spending on social security more cyclical and unpredictable in the short term.

One interpretation of recent events might go as follows. The government began to shift the social security system toward more means testing. This had the effect of making underlying spending much more cyclical. However, the economic boom of the second half of the 1980s, which created negative PSBRs for some years, led the government to believe that the underlying problem had been solved. This led to a continuation and intensification of such policies. When the recession began in the early 1990s, the public sector deficit quickly surged and it has taken a long time to come down.

People sometimes talk about inexorable trends in public spending patterns and scale. This is nonsense. However, recent history suggests that it takes an exceptionally determined government to change spending trends. The Thatcher government tried its best and did not get very far. It could be argued that much of its failure was the result of a lack of understanding and sympathy with the overall aims of public spending. By contrast, the same government succeeded in cutting spending in an area of public spending it did understand, defence. A future government that was committed to the aims of public spending stands a far greater chance of both reducing waste and targeting services more effectively.

References

Corry, D. and Holtham, G. (1995). *Growth with stability: progressive macroeconomic policy*. IPPR.

CSO (1991). *United Kingdom National Accounts* ('The Blue Book'). HMSO.

CSO (1995a). *Economic Trends Annual Supplement*. HMSO.

CSO (1995b). *Public Finance Trends*. HMSO.

CSO (1995c). *United Kingdom National Accounts* ('The Blue Book'). HMSO.

CSO (1996a). *Annual Abstract of Statistics*. HMSO.

DSS (1995). *Households Below Average Income (HBAI), 1979–1992/3*. London: Department of Social Security.

Dickinson, D. (1995). 'Crime and unemployment', *New Economy*, **2**: 4.

Hawksworth, J. and Wilcox, S. (1995). *Challenging the Conventions*. Chartered Institute of Housing/Coopers and Lybrand.

HMT (1995). *Financial Statement and Budget Report, 1996–97*, (The 'Red' Book). London: Her Majesty's Treasury.

HMT (1996). *Public Expenditure Statistical Analyses*. London: Her Majesty's Treasury.

ONS (Office of National Statistics) (1996b). *United Kingdom National Accounts* ('The Blue Book').

Pain, N., Young, G. and Westaway, P. (1993). 'The state of the public finances', *NIESR Review*, August.

Virley, S. and Hurst, M. (1995). *Public Finances and the Cycle*, HMT Working Paper.

4

The Key Public Expenditure Issues of the Future

Yvette Cooper

Contents

Introduction

> 'Most Western societies are already at or beyond the limit of their taxable capacity'
> (Robert Skidelsky, *Prospect*, 1996)

> 'The countries that are going to make it . . . have brought their spend well under 40 per cent. We have to join the leading group or we will be in trouble.'
> (William Waldegrave, Chief Secretary to the Treasury, 1996)

> 'I would like to get it down to 35 per cent.'
> (John Major, January 1996)

To hear the politicians and pundits lament you would think that the state was about to explode as a result of its own internal contradictions. It would seem that the big questions to be resolved over public spending concern just how much we can really afford to spend. Forget accounting methods, forget decision-making procedures, forget, in fact, half the topics covered in this book. According to the alarmists about public spending, there are much bigger issues to be resolved.

The taxpayer – so this consensus goes – cannot afford to pay any more. Moreover global competitive pressures mean that it is economically damaging for so much of our income and wealth to be absorbed by the public sector. Just as in other countries, Britain must face up to the need to curtail public spending and taxation. Quite how severe people think the curtailing or the cutting need to be depends on their ideology, but many on left and right agree that all important pressures on how much the state can spend go in only one direction: downward.

But what turns this into a crisis, according to these public-spending alarmists, is the fact that other pressures are pushing state spending ever onwards and upwards. Be it the ageing population, families in poverty or crumbling hospitals, everything seems to need more money. Meanwhile, politicians stumble their way through the minefield of competing pressures and priorities: what to cut, what to privatize, what to ration, what to charge for and how to persuade voters that their simultaneous demand for lower taxes and better services are incompatible.

This all sounds very persuasive and depressing. It certainly provides a plausible explanation for the unpopularity of Conservative politicians; they have tried and failed to cut total spending for 18 years. At the same time it explains Labour's caution: if spending pressures are rising and taxes cannot go up, it is not possible to promise an expensive programme of reform.

But is it true? Only in part. There are indeed limits on how much the state can tax and spend without the economy suffering and those limits may well have been affected by global competition. However, the limits remain broad and leave nations with considerable freedom to manoeuvre. Whether we look at domestic family budgets or international comparisons, it is clear that the 42 per cent of national income spent by the British government in 1995/6 is perfectly affordable.

There are, however, genuine and binding political constraints on how much the state can tax and spend; many people do not want to pay so much towards certain kinds of state activity. The supply of public spending – the proceeds from taxation – is therefore heavily constrained. But it is constrained by political legitimacy rather than by any law of economics.

This constraint makes the changing demands on public spending ever more difficult to deal with. But there is no cause for panic. Despite the rhetoric from the right, neither the welfare state nor the public sector as a whole are veering beyond our control.

However, there are two serious areas for concern. First, the composition of spending, both in the public and private sectors is unbalanced: we are consuming too much and investing too little. Whether it be in human capital or in infrastructure, we are under-investing in our future, and it will cost us a lot of money if we don't do something about it. Similarly, we should be investing public money in making people more employable rather than paying out large sums of money on benefits.

The second problem is more intractable. Economic and social changes (in particular rising wage inequality) are placing new demands on public spending – demands that the taxpayer is unhappy about supporting. For example, the middle classes are starting to demand higher quality and wider choice from their public services. While the better-off are probably willing to pay the extra price of such luxuries for themselves, either in taxes or charges, it is not clear that they are prepared to stump up for the less well-off. If the net result is that they start to opt out of public services in large numbers, our universal public services may start to lose the legitimacy that has kept them thriving for so long.

Resolving these problems will not be easy. Switching the balance of spending will upset people in the short run. And steering a path between accommodating the self-interested demands of the better-off, and carrying out policies of redistribution will be difficult. New schemes which explore different ways of paying for public services (including top-up vouchers, charges and hypothecated taxes) are bound to rise up the agenda.

But sooner or later politicians and the public will have to confront the ethical issue of the kind of society they want in the future. Disguising these kinds of debates under broad claims about global trends in taxing and spending is just a way of dodging difficult choices. The middle classes have to decide to what extent they have an obligation to subsidize those who are less fortunate than themselves. And politicians have to face up to the fact that while they spend badly and secretly, no one will want them to spend at all.

Are there constraints on the supply of public spending?

The economic constraints

After almost two decades of Conservative government in Britain the economic arguments in favour of cutting the size of the state are well rehearsed. They are as fashionable as ever. In fact, as global competition increasingly brings the success of the East Asian economies to our attention we should expect the issue to get hotter. No doubt others will follow the former Conservative minister and Governor of Hong Kong, Chris Patten, in his claim that the key to the Tiger economies' success is the low proportion of national income absorbed by the state.

Yet much of this debate is nonsense. Neither economics nor 'globalization' justifies this growing obsession with the size of Britain's public sector. In the first place, while there are strong economic arguments against the state taxing and spending too much of a nation's income, there is very little evidence that Britain has reached that critical damaging point – with our tax representing 38 per cent of GDP and public spending 42 per cent of GDP (HMT, 1995).

Extremely high levels of tax do risk distorting normal market incentives and making the economy less efficient. Many economists suggest that high levels of income tax drive a wedge between the wage the company pays out, and the cash the worker takes home; as a result they are bad for employment (Feldstein, 1994). Others argue that income tax is a disincentive to hard work – but the evidence on this is mixed and inconclusive. And high marginal tax rates can be counterproductive if they encourage the rich to flee to tax havens, while the poor join the informal economy instead.

However, many of these arguments concern the optimal structure and distribution of taxation, rather than the overall level of revenue raised by the state. Moreover they ignore the fact that state action and spending can also be extremely good for the economy and for national well-being (Oppenheimer and Flemming, 1996).

Plenty of services (particularly those involving insurance) can be more effectively and efficiently delivered by the state. Government investment in people and infrastructure can be good for the market and for growth. Intervention for the sake of social justice is morally essential and need not be at the expense of efficiency either.

So where should the balance lie? Conservative politicians often seem content to respond by picking numbers out of thin air. Ken Clarke thinks spending cannot realistically fall far below 40 per cent of GDP (*Financial Times*, 31.1.96). John Major wants to go significantly further (*Sunday Telegraph*, 28.1.96), and Chris Patten regales us with the virtues of Hong Kong, which takes only 16 per cent of GDP (*Independent*, 25.10.95).

However, there is no convincing evidence that countries with a public sector share of, say, 50 per cent of national income necessarily have a worse economic performance than those with a state with a 30 per cent share. In an IMF working paper, economists Vito Tanzi and Ludger Schuknecht (1995) find that there is no substantial difference between high and low spending nations in terms of growth, investment and inflation. They conclude that bigger government was associated with higher unemployment. However their evidence does not show whether countries with high unemployment (for other reasons) therefore have higher public spending or whether the higher spending causes the higher unemployment.

Could globalization make the size of the state more important? Increasing global competition would seem to make these international comparisons more important. Companies will surely take into account corporate tax regimes when deciding where to locate new plants. Highly skilled mobile individuals will also be able to pick a tax haven of their choice to work from and avoid high rates of personal tax.

These kinds of effects remain limited, however. Labour markets are still largely national; few people have the flexibility or the inclination to switch countries at will. Also there are trade-offs to be made. Slightly higher rates of corporation tax are bearable if there is a good-quality infrastructure and a highly skilled workforce nearby. Moreover well-qualified Britons, contemplating a move to the US, for example, trade lower income tax levels for health insurance premiums and college fees for their children.

Countries with lower shares of tax, and spend, pay for things in different ways. US citizens pay privately for health care, and they spend far more money on it as a result: 14 per cent of national income, compared to only 7 per cent in the UK. The 'burden' on the productive economy remains, despite the fact that it is born directly by employers rather than paid through taxes. While he was still optimistic about health care reform in 1992, President Clinton argued, 'Businesses now pay as much in health care as they earn in after tax profits. Health care costs have resulted in a loss of up to 2.5 million jobs since 1989 . . . They add almost $1100 to the cost of every American car, undermining our global competitiveness' (*American Journal of Medical Health*, October 1992).

Similarly, in Singapore individuals are compelled to pay contributions into a private pension fund. It is not state spending but its impact on individuals is little different to that of National Insurance contributions for a state retirement pension. So while Britain could certainly decide to emulate Singapore or the US and privatize sections of the welfare state, its citizens would not be financially better off.

So long as Britain remains roughly within the broad range of tax and spending of our international competitors there is little to worry about. As John Hills (1996) argues in the book *Options for Britain*, the range of feasible taxing and spending levels among our closest international competitors is extremely broad: from 29 per cent in the USA to 57 per cent in Sweden. Historically the range of the tax burden in Britain since 1968 has been far more limited than that, oscillating between 33 per cent and 39.25 per cent. It appears then that there is little reason for Britain to worry about hitting against any international economic buffers.

But regardless of our foreign neighbours, can British families afford to pay so much? The claim that ordinary British households are now vastly over-taxed, and unable to afford to support the welfare state, is hard to substantiate. We are richer in Britain than ever before. The idea that most of us cannot afford to pay our taxes or to pay any more tax should circumstances demand it, is absurd. The tax burden on the average family is still between 34 per cent and 39 per cent – just as it has been for the last 20 years (Hills, 1996). Real earnings have risen considerably over the same period, so after tax we are still better off.

However, those on low income are indeed heavily taxed. The high effective marginal tax rates people face as they move off benefits and into low wage jobs discourages the unemployed from finding work. But by historical and international standards, most of the rest of us get off rather lightly in Britain today.

Political constraints

What politicians really mean when they say that families cannot afford to pay more is that families do not want to pay more. Given the other things we want to spend our money on (ranging from mortgages through foreign holidays to private school fees), we do not want to pay more in tax.

We must not underestimate this. In a democratic country, if voters want lower taxes governments who cannot find spending cuts to pay for it will be punished. Political limits on acceptable taxing and spending can be fierce and binding. However, estimating where those political limits lie is even more fraught and controversial than trying to calculate economic limits. Everyone has their own – and different – opinion on whether voters have the stomach for more taxing and spending in Britain today.

Many people who themselves want higher taxes and spending cite the survey, *British Social Attitudes*, to bolster their case. At first sight it does seem to show a growing appetite for higher levels of public spending (Taylor-Gooby, 1995). The proportion of respondents answering that the government should 'increase taxes and spend more on health, education and social benefits' has risen from 32 per cent in 1983 to 63 per cent in 1993, before falling again to 58 per cent in 1994 (see Chapter 6 by Peter Kellner for a development of this case). But we should beware of relying too much on these results.

Certainly the politicians don't trust the results, and they are the people who have most to win and lose by miscalculating public opinion on such matters. The Labour Party clearly takes seriously the charge that it lost the 1992 election on the issue of spending and taxation (Radice, 1993). Labour has taken great care to avoid making careless commitments in the run-up to the 1997 election. Meanwhile the Conservatives seem still to believe that pre-election tax cuts win votes.

People who tell pollsters they would happily be taxed more to pay for higher spending on schools and hospitals may still be furiously opposed to paying new taxes imposed in a Chancellor's Budget. They may be prepared to pay for better health care and education for their own families but not for the cost of providing such services for everyone. And they may be hoping that someone else – the vaguely defined 'rich' – will be the ones to pay the higher taxes anyway. Cynics suggest they may even be telling pollsters one story and then voting for a completely different one.

Most plausible of all is the idea that voters may believe that any money raised in extra taxes will just be thrown away. Heath, Curtice and Jowell (1994) in their analysis of the 1992 election, argue that Labour lost votes not on tax itself, but on its failure to convince people that the money would be well spent. They claim that 'it is of no conceivable value to be seen as a high tax party unless voters are convinced that the high taxes will yield effective returns'.

Voters have even less reason to trust politicians now. In 1992 they were told by the Conservative government that they could have tax cuts at the same time as public spending increases. In 1993 and 1994 that same government imposed £17bn of tax increases and few have seen any improvement in their public services as a result. No wonder politicians are distrusted on tax and spending and that voters think public money is wasted.

So if politicians want to carry on spending they will have to justify it and themselves to a sceptical public. Making spending more transparent would help. So would a little bit of integrity and promise-keeping. Until they can build up voters' trust, their freedom to manoeuvre on tax and spending will be seriously constrained.

Is there rising demand for public spending?

Handling future pressures on public spending given these political constraints will require difficult choices. The Conservatives tell us their government has been making these choices. Faced with ever-increasing demands for more money they have, we are told, been resolute in defending the interests of the taxpayer and keeping spending under control.

There is some truth in this. Public spending (GGE(X)) in Britain has remained roughly stable since 1979, oscillating between a high of 45.5 per cent (1982/3) and a low of 38 per cent (1988/9) depending on the state of the economy at the time. In many other EU countries, on the other hand, the trend has definitely been upwards.

Of course this does not tell us that existing Conservative policies for containing spending are sustainable or sensible. Nor does it imply that there are overwhelming pressures for higher spending in the UK, that the government has successfully struggled to fend off.

In fact, there are two important areas of concern for the future, where changing demands for more spending will clash with constraints on the supply of cash. Both will require voters and politicians to confront difficult moral choices about the kinds of society they want to live in.

Some myths

Popular debate about pressures on public spending are often shrouded in myths. One of the most often cited demands on future spending – the ageing of the population – is a case in point. It is true that the proportion of the population over 65 is set to rise over the next 50 years; from 16 per cent in 1991 to 24 per cent in 2041. However, the demographic changes will not be as substantial as in other countries (Germany and Japan in particular) in part because our baby boom was smaller.

In addition, our financial commitment towards pensioners is lower than in other countries – especially since benefits were linked to prices rather than earnings and the state earnings related pensions schemes (SERPs) was reformed. John Hills (1993) has calculated that even if we spent exactly the same amount on each pensioner in the future as we do today (in pensions, benefits, health care, etc.) spending would only increase by 3.8 per cent of GDP.

Julian Le Grand (1996) suggests the burden on the NHS as the population ages could be less than we expect too. Although we spend a lot more NHS money on the over-70s, that could be because more of them are dying, rather than because they are old. People tend to need most health care in the last year of their life. In which case, estimates for health care spending which look at how old people are rather than the overall death rate may be exaggerating the cost. Le Grand argues too that as we increasingly allow people to die with dignity, we will need to spend less on expensive treatments to drag life out as long as possible.

Even the much vaunted advances in medical technology need not break the bank in the future. It is true that medical advances have made it possible to carry out expensive treatments for cancer (now 7 per cent of the NHS budget) or organ transplants. However there is no reason in principle why technological change on its own should always push the bill upward. For example, new drugs which are costly when they first hit the market can become extremely cheap several years down the road; the anti-rejection drug which cost Dulwich Hospital £350 000 over ten months in 1980, is 80 per cent cheaper today (Timmins, 1995). Similarly, kidney transplants are actually cheaper at £10 000 than endless dialysis at £18 000. So technological developments which make transplants easier (including pig organs for example) could save the NHS money in the future. The story that the NHS is in deep financial crisis is, at least, overplayed (Wordsworth *et al.*, 1996).

Too much consumption, too little investment?

If there are overblown stories, there are genuine problems that have been underplayed. The first area for concern is the growing demands on public spending which have been generated by short-termist policy decisions in the past – and which could be averted if appropriate reforms were instituted.

The composition of public spending has changed in 20 years, even though the overall level of spending has not. We are spending far less on investment (only in part because privatization has reduced the need for it) and far more on current consumption. And we are spending more on benefits, and less on education. In 1978/9 we spent 6 per cent of GDP on education and training and 2.5 per cent on income-related benefits. In 1996 the figures are 5.6 per cent and 5.5 per cent respectively.

Such low levels of investment (in both public and private sectors) are brewing up problems in the long term. Across the board from physical infrastructure to teenagers, from council houses to social insurance, money that could have been invested to give a return has been diverted to current expenditure instead. Sooner or later that was bound to cost us more.

Look at the way privatization was carried out, or as Harold MacMillan described it, the sale of the family silver. Getting rid of those rusting dinner plates wasn't so much the problem. Many are doubtless better polished in the private sector. But when the assets were sold income streams were lost too, yet the money raised was not invested. Privatization proceeds were used for tax cuts and to meet current spending bills instead. The gap between the value of the state's physical assets and its financial liabilities (things like pensions and debt interest) has deteriorated badly as a result; from 99 per cent of GDP in 1979, to 45 per cent of GDP today (Hills, 1996).

No wonder then that several years down the road, when the cupboard is almost bare of things to privatize, Britain has trouble meeting its bills. Taxes on North Sea oil revenues and privatization receipts between them raised around 4 per cent of GDP in income for the government between 1984 and 1989. Now we raise only around 1 per cent of GDP in this way. It is hardly surprising that the Conservatives were forced to raise taxes instead.

The Private Finance Initiative (PFI) may prove to be another damaging way to cut and delay investment while raising future spending too. In theory the PFI is a way of levering in private skills for public projects and giving them incentives (because their own capital is at stake) to implement those projects efficiently. This means that investment expenditure for the government today is being exchanged for higher current spending in future as, for example, government agencies rent premises that the private sector has built. Switching the spending profile like this is fine so long as no one pretends that it is a free lunch and that those future rents do not exist. Even more important, there is a serious risk that insisting on private finance even where the government could borrow and build more cheaply, will make future taxpayers much worse off.

We have also failed to invest enough or at least to invest wisely enough, in people. The market value of human capital is increasing with technological change. Yet Britain has a badly educated population. Better (not necessarily more) spending on educating the current generation of disaffected youth might have saved us in unemployment benefit expenditure today and even raised national income in the future.

Without some kind of action the problem is likely to get worse as the need for human capital in the economy increases. Moreover, investing in skills is a prudent strategy; the social and individual returns from education are considerable. Those in managerial and professional occupations earn two and a half times as much as their unskilled peers. This means that in the long term there is plenty of scope for recouping the costs of higher-level education from the individuals who benefit.

Across the board we need to shift the balance of public spending away from consumption and towards investment in our future – whether it be investing in the education of the young, the employment chances of the working population, the pensions and long-term care needs of the middle-aged, or even straightforward physical infrastructure.

The politics of such a shift are not easy. The current generation of young taxpayers will have less to spend than they expected – whether they have to save more themselves, pay more in tax, or receive less in current services (such as student grants). They will not take the news well.

However, the goal of increasing investment need not be torpedoed by the political constraints on taxation. For a start, government could try to reallocate cash within the public sector or find less politically sensitive ways to raise cash to boost investment at the start (including, for example, Labour's proposed windfall tax on the unpopular utilities.) Alternatively people could be encouraged (or forced) to do the saving and investing themselves – perhaps by saving more for their own retirement, or insuring themselves for long-term care.

The impact of rising inequality

The other major pressure on public spending arises from changes in the labour market and in income distribution.The changing distribution of wages alongside rising unemployment and inactivity have meant that the number of people dependent on benefits to mitigate their poverty has grown. One in three people now live in households containing someone who receives a means-tested benefit. Not surprisingly the burden on the taxpayer to support them has risen. The Conservative government's response to the problem has been to cut benefits. This is not sustainable.

A better approach, as most people now acknowledge, is to tackle the causes of inequality, rather than just administering palliatives. The attempt to redesign benefits, often known as the 'welfare-to-work' agenda, is aimed at turning the support the State gives into a springboard, not a safety net. Providing people with education, and with job subsidies rather than unemployment subsidies, would generate savings in benefits over time.

Pressures from the new labour market

The 'modernized' welfare state will indeed, as all the politicians say, have to deal with the economic circumstances and the labour market of the next century, rather than that of 50 years ago when Beveridge proposed the modern British welfare state. The trouble is that the new kinds of demands on their pockets may not appeal to today's taxpayers in the way the universal welfare state did to taxpayers in Beveridge's day.

The losers in tomorrow's labour market may be just as much in need as the losers in the 1950s, but they may excite less compassion or duty among the winners. In a 'meritocracy' it is easier for the successful to blame the poor for not trying hard enough. But just as the welfare state of the past supported the weak who could not work in a world that depended on brawn, so the good community of the future will need to support those who cannot earn much in a world that depends on brain. Wider education opportunities will clearly help, but the chances are that, through no fault of their own, some people will struggle to get employment.

The cost may be different in future too. The 'weak' who commanded less power in yesterday's labour market included women who could be supported privately by their husbands; redistribution took place within the family. Those who are not valued by tomorrow's market are less likely to have high-earning spouses to support them and will need state support instead. At this stage we have no way of knowing whether the labour market of the future will generate more or less demand for state spending on balance.

The demands of the growing middle class

Rising inequality has a further, more troubling consequence for the future of public spending. The taxpayer does not just provide benefits for the poor; wealthier taxpayers also subsidize the public services of those who cannot afford to pay much tax themselves. However, as the middle classes grow richer, they naturally want the kind of luxury and choice in their public services that they get as consumers in other areas of their lives. Unfortunately, it is not clear that they are willing to pay to provide the same high quality and choice for everyone else.

The trouble is that those universal services that lie at the core of the welfare state – health, education and social insurance – are also luxury goods; the richer we get, the more we want of them, and the more we are prepared to pay. But it does not seem certain that we are prepared to pay for them for others too.

Many people are already prepared to fork out to buy extra luxury in the private sector. Fourteen per cent of British households now have private health insurance. The Institute of Fiscal Studies found that people who had private insurance were less likely to favour increased spending (and taxes) on the NHS (Besley *et al.*, 1996). In education, some of the middle classes are clearly prepared to pay the £4000 or more annual private school fees to purchase class sizes of 25 or less for their own children. Only £2300 is spent each year by the taxpayer on children in state schools according to the Department for Education and Employment (DfEE). Providing every child in state secondary schools with the kind of educational resources that some are able to give their own children in the private sector would cost an extra £6bn; that is equivalent to about 4p on the basic rate of tax. It seems highly unlikely that those opting out of the public sector will be keen to pay for the same high quality in the state system for everyone.

If public services cannot accommodate new demands for greater luxury and choice, those who can afford to may well opt out of our public services altogether. The risk, however, is that this will threaten the entire legitimacy of the welfare state. Peter Taylor-Gooby (1995), in his analysis of the 1995 British Attitudes Survey, argues that 'popular support for "old welfare" has proved to be robust because it is rooted in the self interest of Britain's contented majority'. He finds considerably more support for higher spending on universal services such as health and education, than for services which predominantly help the poor (such as housing and benefits). (See also Chapter 7 by Hall *et al.*).

For 50 years, the middle classes received high quality health care and education provided free at the point of use, in exchange for funding redistribution to others. If they start opting out of our universal public services, will they stop wanting to pay for them for everyone else too? Certainly in the US where most people pay privately for health care, public financing of the health care of the poor is widely resented. And it seems the privately insured in Britain may be going the same way.

The universal welfare state has lain at the heart of social cohesion and fairness in the UK for decades. No wonder people are worried that it is being undermined.

What is to be done?

There remains no cause for panic. The total amount of spending is not about to bring the country down and some of the fears about public spending are very much exaggerated. However, it is clear that there are real challenges that need to be met at a time when political room for manoeuvre is limited. The public are deeply suspicious of public spending and certainly of any new demands for tax increases. Yet at the same time we need to increase the resources devoted to saving and investment, in the public as well as the private sector. Moreover, rising inequality is putting new strains on public spending too. Some of the pressures may be eased by shifting people off welfare and into work, but others will remain. Most important, the middle classes appear to be imposing new, loud demands for higher quality and choice in public services, without being prepared to finance such improvements for everyone. The problems for public spending in future are predominantly political rather than economic, but they remain very real problems nevertheless.

So what should we do?

For a start we have to make taxing and spending decisions more transparent. Gimmicks such as hypothecating the revenue from a particular tax to a specific spending project may irritate the Treasury, but they may appeal to voters. Anything which can show a sceptical public how their money is being spent may increase their willingness to contribute. So, when a family buys a washing machine for £400, perhaps they should be informed that £60 goes to the government in tax. Buying a washing machine therefore contributes £6.50 to the NHS, £2.70 to education and so on. Similarly anything which makes obvious exactly how much they personally stand to lose from spending cuts may appease a little their appetite for tax cuts.

As for increasing saving and investment, much of that may be politically more acceptable if done on an individualized basis. People may be more willing to save for their own personal education and re-skilling than for schools in general. Compulsory savings accounts too (along Singapore lines) may be more politically attractive than higher taxes to pay for higher state pensions.

Julian Le Grand (1996) suggests that what he calls 'legal welfare' could be an increasingly popular option. We already have several ways to force people to look after themselves and others in the private sector; for example the Child Support Agency makes absent fathers pay up for their children. Other countries go further: minimum wages to stop employers exploiting their workers and reduce poverty; *obligation alimentaires* compel people to support their ageing relatives.

To accommodate rising demands for luxury and choice in public services, politicians are bound to start contemplating ways to allow the middle classes to spend extra resources on their own health and education. Vouchers for schools and colleges have been touted by many, allowing the middle classes to top up their value as they see fit. Localized contributions are another option so that families can be sure it is their own local school or hospital that benefits from increased resources.

The IMF research suggests that providing services in the private sector need not be disastrous for social welfare. Tanzi and Schuknecht (1995) found that small state countries (often where more welfare services are privately provided) do not have any lower life expectancy or higher infant mortality than high spending countries. And they only have slightly higher inequality; countries with big government allocate 24 per cent of their income to the poorest 40 per cent of the population, while countries with small government allocate 21 per cent.

However, country-to-country comparisons can be misleading here. Even putting aside issues of causation and cultural differences across the high and low spending nations, death rates and income distributions are not the only things that contribute to social justice and a good society.

But politicians and voters who want to privatize sections of the welfare state will have to face up to a few difficult problems. Providing services in the private sector need not be disastrous where the framework and the regulation works well. Some services, however (the NHS for example), depend for their legitimacy and support on the fact that the public can see that their service providers (doctors and nurses) are insulated from the pursuit of profit.

But even where services can be privately provided, problems arise when they are privately paid for too. It may seem harmless to use private money to queue-jump several months to cure ailments which are not life threatening, or to enjoy the comfort of a private room and tasty food while convalescing. But when health care itself is distributed according to money rather than need, and when the educational opportunities of children depend on their parents' income rather than their own merit, social justice is badly compromised.

Politicians can dodge difficult decisions for a while by spinning myths about the direction of public spending or the demand for tax cuts. Meanwhile the public can stick their heads in the sand and kid themselves that better public services, more social cohesion and lower taxes are all compatible. But in the end, the future of public spending will depend on a difficult moral debate about the kind of society we wish to live in, and our obligations to support those who are less well-off than ourselves. We cannot duck such questions for very long.

References

Besley, T., Hall, J. and Preston, I. (1996). *Private Health Insurance and the State of the NHS*. Institute for Fiscal Studies.

Clinton, W. (1992). *The American Journal of Medical Health*, October.

Feldstein, M. (1994). *American Economic Policy in the 1980s*. NBER Conference Papers, University of Chicago.

Heath, A., Curtice, J. and Jowell, R. (eds) (1994). *Labour's Last Chance: the 1992 Election and Beyond*. Aldershot: Dartmouth.

Hills, J. (1993). *The Future of Welfare*. Joseph Rowntree Commission.

Hills, J. (1996). 'Tax policy: are there still choices?' In: Halpern, D. *et al*. (eds), *Options for Britain*, Oxford: Nuffield College.

HMT (1995). *Budget Report November 1995*, ('Red Book'). London: HM Treasury.
Jowell, R., Curtice, J., Park, A., Brook, L. and Ahrendt, D. (eds) (1995). *British Social Attitudes*, 12th Report 1995/6.
Le Grand, J. (1996). *Prospect Magazine*, July.
Oppenheimer, P. and Flemming, J. (1996). National Institute for Economic and Social Research. Review Summer 1996
Radice, G. (1993). 'More Southern Comfort'.
Skidelsky, R. (1996). 'Welfare without the State,' *Prospect Magazine*, January.
Social Justice Commission (1994). IPPR/Random House
Tanzi, V. and Schuknecht, L. (1995). *The Growth of Government and the Reform of the State in Industrialised Countries*. IMF Working Paper, December.
Taylor-Gooby, P. (1995). 'Comfortable, marginal and excluded: who should pay higher taxes for a better welfare state?' In: Jowell, R., Curtice, J., Park, A., Brook, L. and Ahrendt, D. (eds), *British Social Attitudes*, 12th Report.
Timmins, N. (1995). 'Can we afford the Welfare state?' *The Independent* 24 September.
Wordsworth, S., Donaldson, C. and Scott, A., (1996). 'Can we afford the NHS?', IPPR.

Part II
How Much Public Expenditure Should There Be?

5

How Public Expenditure Priorities Are Determined

Geoffrey Hulme

Contents

Priority-setting in government involves finding the best answers to two kinds of questions. First, there are questions that relate to value and preference which, for large-scale collective choices, require political decisions. Included in this category are decisions on, for example, how much should be spent on health and education; how much income redistribution should there be; how much current consumption should be forgone to secure adequate income in retirement and unemployment. Typically judgements have to be made between variables which cannot even be valued in the same way: is another submarine worth more than rebuilding Covent Garden Opera House?

There is no simple technique available to help politicians to make these kinds of decisions (although political judgment can sometimes be helped by decision-analysis techniques such as those discussed by Neuburger and Fraser (1993)).

Second, there are questions relating to what economists call technical efficiency – in other words, what inputs of resources and processes produce what outputs. Into this category come questions that are subject to scientific analysis, as well as managerial questions of what a given set of people can be motivated to achieve at a given cost.

Both kinds of questions are, of course, interrelated. Success in answering the technical efficiency questions affects what is available to meet value choices. Since the evidence on these questions is often inconclusive, particularly when one is looking into an uncertain future, value judgments are involved in who or what should have the benefit of doubt. Decisions on things like EMU and global warming are often ultimately informed gambles on an uncertain future. In the case of BSE, for example, a judgment has to be taken as to how far public safety, as opposed to farming and economic interests, should affect the decisions being taken.

Other chapters in this book describe the present system for deciding levels of public spending. Here, we look in more detail at how spending priorities are determined. We look, first, at the current priority-setting process, its strengths and weaknesses. We go on to consider how the process might be improved such that it reflects more closely what the public wants and is willing to pay for in taxes and charges.

How the current system works

The main priority-setting process in central government is the annual *Public Expenditure Survey*. This results in decisions being taken in the autumn on firm cash plans for the year ahead and less firm plans for a further two years. These figures then become the starting point for the following year's survey. In local government, the main priority-setting process revolves around budgets for one year ahead. These are accompanied by different forms of longer-term strategic review – for example, reviews of expenditure totals over three or four years, priorities for developments to be financed and savings to be made over those periods.

Box 5.1 outlines the various levels of decision-taking involved in spending by central government, government agencies and other bodies (such as health authorities) that derive their authority and finance from central government. Box 5.2 outlines the decision-taking levels for the quarter or more of total spending for which local authorities are responsible.

The essence of the process is iterative interaction between budget setters and budget or programme managers at different levels of the expenditure hierarchy shown in Boxes 5.1 and 5.2. Typically, the process begins with budget guidelines provided by the centre, leading to spending proposals from the periphery, followed by a process of collective decision taking, which may be preceded by bilateral negotiations. In the centre the interaction is between Treasury ministers and other ministers with overarching strategic responsibilities, whose primary concern is with overall objectives, and 'service' ministers and their departments, who have to assess and respond to pressures and demands within their fields of responsibilities. Within departments, the interaction is between the strategic centre (Secretary of State, Permanent Secretary and central finance and policy review staff) and junior ministers and staff with programme responsibilities, who in turn interact with budget holders down the line. (There is a different set of interactions with local authority services, where elected members are in theory head of the local decision hierarchy but are heavily constrained by central policy and a variety of controls which confuse responsibilities and public understanding.)

Location	*Sets of priority decisions*	*Expressed in*
A Centre of government (Cabinet, Treasury, ministers)	1. Between public and private spending, saving, borrowing	Budget; UK expenditure totals
	2. Between departmental programmes	Departmental allocations, budgets and key objectives
B Centre of departments (senior minister(s))	Between sub-programmes, management groups and agencies	Group and agency budgets and policy priorities
C Top management of departmental groups and agencies	Between operational management and/or purchasing units	Budgets (including objectives) of operational and purchasing units)
D Operational management	Between service delivery units (including professional groups, individual professionals)	Service delivery budgets, contracts, guidelines, etc.
E Service delivery units	Between service needs of individuals, projects, etc.	Allocation of time and other resources to individuals, projects, etc.

Box 5.1. Hierarchy of priority decisions (central government).

The approach needs to be interactive because the centre tends not to have enough information to assess what is practically and politically feasible within detailed expenditure fields. It has to be iterative (try, try again) because of the difficulty of getting the balance right and because of uncertain changes in the constraints such as economic variables and in spending on 'demand-determined programmes'. As a government gains experience it can reduce the iterations and adopt a more top-down approach, in which spending proposals closely follow initial guidelines. This has been the position in the last spending reviews, when a Cabinet committee of senior ministers (EDX) has determined priorities after presentations from spending ministers but without negotiation with them. There are, in any event, practical limits to how much analysis and discussion can take place within the time-scale of the annual survey. Decisions within it tend to be

Location	Sets of priority decisions	Expressed in
A Central government (Cabinet, Treasury, ministers with local government responsibilities)	Between central and local spending, saving, borrowing Between LA programmes Between LAs	Central Government grant totals Spending controls and guidelines Grant distribution rules and controls
B Centre of LA (council, policy/ resources committee, corporate team)	Between local spending, saving, borrowing Between LA departments and programmes	Total local spending, borrowing Council tax rates Committee budgets
C Council committees and chief officers	Between operational and/ or purchasing units	Budgets (inc. objectives of operational and purchasing units)
D Operational management	Between service delivery units (including professional groups, individual professionals and external suppliers)	Service delivery budgets, contracts, guidelines, etc.
E Service delivery units	Between service needs of individuals	Allocation of time and other resources to individuals, projects, etc.

Box 5.2. Hierarchy of priority decisions (local government).

incremental (on how much should be added to or taken from inherited plans). They need to be backed by longer-term strategic reviews, currently referred to as fundamental expenditure reviews.

The decision-takers at the various levels of the hierarchy shown in Box 5.1 depends not only on the system but on the interaction of individuals within it (see various ministerial memoirs and Thain and Wright, 1995). The responsibility at the top of the central hierarchy rests with ministers, who are accountable to the Prime Minister and their colleagues in Cabinet, to Parliament and in the longer run to the electorate. They come under a wide range of pressures and constraints, and have to assess which are beneficial and which should or can be resisted or circumvented. With the help of advisers, ministers need to carry out their own analysis of strengths, weaknesses, opportunities and threats in their field of responsibility and decide how to position themselves and their departments to achieve beneficial change, counter threats and enhance their own reputation. Success or otherwise often depends on the personality of the individual minister.

For A1 (in Box 5.1), the lead rests with the Chancellor of the Exchequer; for A2 with the Chief Secretary; for B with the Cabinet minister responsible for the Department. Consultation with Cabinet colleagues is usually through Cabinet committees or direct discussions, with Cabinet agreeing guidelines at the beginning of the process and approving its outcome. Since no individual is likely to have all the skills or knowledge needed, ministers supported by the permanent secretaries have to establish a team of people with complementary skills (political, analytical and technical) who have access to relevant information and expertise. Teams typically comprise members of the department's ministerial team supported, when necessary, by political advisers and parliamentary private secretaries: the permanent secretary and principal finance officer (or their representatives); and senior officials with programme and management responsibilities.

How effective?

Experience of working within the system and discussion with those currently operating it suggest conclusions very similar to those of Thain and Wright (1996). These may be summarized as follows:

- it is responsive to political leadership;
- it is effective in ensuring that budgets are agreed in time;
- it provides sufficient control over public expenditure to contribute to the government's principal economic objective of containing inflation;
- it has enabled UK governments to move further and faster than other EU in containing public spending as a share of GDP (see Chapter 16 by Monck);
- there has been a high degree of public acquiescence in the decisions taken;
- there has been increasing commitment by programme managers and other professionals to increased efficiency and value for money.

The present system also has a number of weaknesses, including:

- government has frequently failed to meet its explicit public expenditure targets;
- there has been too much emphasis on short-term factors, such as spending in the year ahead;
- there have been considerable fluctuations in the planned growth rate even for 'priority' programmes such as health and education;
- a *lack of transparency* about the underlying facts may have contributed to public acquiescence but has also contributed to increasing cynicism about government;
- a lack of parliamentary and public debate on the choices involved in public spending has reinforced this cynicism about the political process;

- there is confusion as to responsibilities between central and local government, leading to weakening of the latter and a continuing shift of responsibility to the centre, which is often less well-placed to assess local preferences and priorities;
- a lack of objective evaluation of policies and initiatives to which the government has been politically committed (for example, its education and health reforms).

What have the priorities been?

What have been the effects of these strengths and weaknesses on the political and technical decisions taken by recent governments? Any judgement on the quality of political decisions is, of course, itself political. This is a judgement made by the electorate when it assesses whether the available alternatives could have done better, or will do in future. However, the choice that faces electors is an extraordinarily crude one, between vaguely defined and uncertainly priced bundles of public goods. In the final analysis, electors are primarily influenced by their views on the qualities of the political teams that present the various alternatives. In the absence of improved public debate and/or political market research into what the public wants and is ready to pay for, it is impossible to offer more than subjective views on how good the political judgements have been.

The evidence on the quality of technical decision-making is often inconclusive. However, we can look at the way that UK priorities in public spending have shifted over time, and see whether they appear – broadly – to accord with what people would want to have had the money spent on. Table 5.1 (p. 113) shows that the highest percentage growth over the whole period has been in spending on law and order (and other Home Office protective services), which has consistently grown at above the rate of growth of GDP. Its share of GDP (at 2.2 per cent) is now greater than that of the economic departments (Agriculture, Trade, Industry, Energy, Employment) at 1.9. In 1978 these were at 1.8 and 3.5 per cent respectively. Public spending on infrastructure and environment has also declined over most of the period, mainly because of the reduction in spending on public housing. Spending on Defence and overseas services increased during the first two parliaments and has since declined, giving a small overall reduction.

Broadly speaking, then, we might think that the changes in priorities do make some sense. However it is unlikely that anyone wanted to see social security eating up more and more of the budget (see Chapter 3 by Corry and Gray). And while the increase in the ratio to GDP of health spending would be welcomed, the fact that the ratio to GDP of spending on education has not increased would perhaps not gain great favour.

One cannot easily deduce from these figures what decisions on priorities were being made. The extent and pattern of need may change, for example, due to demography (more old people needing health services, fewer children needing

Table 5.1. Changing priorities: growth rates, 1978 to 1995 (% pa in real terms).

Function	*1978–1982*	*1982–1986*	*1986–1990*	*1990–1995*	*1978–1995*
Law, order, protection	5.9	3.8	5.5	3.2	4.5
Social security	5.0	3.9	−0.5	5.8	3.6
Health, social services	3.6	2.0	3.5	4.4	3.4
Education, heritage	0.4	1.1	2.4	2.4	1.6
Central services	−3.2	−1.8	5.3	2.6	0.8
Defence, overseas	3.6	1.3	−2.0	−2.9	−0.2
Economic	5.3	−3.7	−4.3	−0.5	−0.8
Infrastructure, environment	−4.7	−2.1	1.5	−0.6	−1.4
Total	2.3	1.4	0.9	3.1	1.9

Source: CIPFA derived from Treasury (1996) (Tables 1.1 and 1.3).

education), or social and economic change (more poor people) or external circumstances (end of the Cold War).

Comparing spending in the UK with that of other countries can shed some light on the question since to some extent all countries are faced with the same problems (although here, too, the evidence is difficult to interpret). Table 5.2 (p. 114) sets out expenditure as a percentage of GDP in a number of EU countries with broadly comparable data in 1992.

It shows that the UK spent:

- 40 per cent more than the EU average on defence (1.8 percentage points more of GDP);
- 33 per cent more than the EU average on public order (0.5 per cent of GDP);
- around the EU average on health: but 10 per cent (0.6 per cent of GDP) less compared with the four largest EU countries – Germany, Spain, France and Italy;
- 20 per cent less on social security than the EU average;
- 50 per cent less on general public services;
- 10 per cent less on education (about the same as in the four largest EU countries).

Some of these differences may be explained by greater use of private spending in the UK. For example, lower UK spending on social security is, in part, the result of greater private spending on pensions. Total spending on health is lower in the UK than in the rest of Europe, because the UK has less private spending (including charges for public services).

There are obvious difficulties of comparing like with like. Even where progress has been made with input comparisons (such as those provided for health

Table 5.2. Expenditure as % of GDP in EU countries with broadly comparable data (1992 or nearest year).

Country	*General*	*Public order*	*Defence*	*Education*	*Social*	*Health*
Belgium	3.3		2.7	7.3	22.4	
Denmark	4.0	1.1	2.1	7.2	26.0	5.6
Germany	4.8	1.6	2.2	4.1	19.7	5.9
Spain	1.8	1.3	1.6	4.2	18.4	5.1
France	3.9	0.9	3.2	5.4	23.5	7.5
Italy	4.2	1.8	1.9	5.4	18.7	6.5
Netherlands	na	na	2.7	5.3	na	na
UK	1.9	2.0	4.2	4.9	15.8	5.9
EU Median	3.9	1.5	2.5	5.4	19.7	5.9
UK−EU	−2.0	0.5	1.7	−0.5	−3.9	0.0
Big 4 EU*	4.1	1.5	2.1	4.8	19.2	6.5
UK−Big 4	−2.2	0.5	2.1	0.1	−3.4	−0.6

Source: EC (1996).
* The ‘Big 4’ are Germany, Spain, France, Italy. The figure given is the median.

by the OECD), there is a long way to go before reliable conclusions can be reached on service outputs. This means that we cannot assess what the UK gains as a result of spending more on public order or what it loses through spending less on health than, for example, France. There is a strong case for supporting the development of objective comparative analysis in the OECD and EU and presenting the latest results annually to ministers (rather than data simply being used by Treasury or spending ministers when it suits their case).

Table 5.2 also tells us something about successive Conservative governments’ priorities for growth and reductions in public spending over the period. In particular the figures reveal important features of Conservative policy including:

- scepticism about government intervention and preference for market solutions as reflected in reduced spending by economic departments and lower levels of social insurance spending than in other EU countries;
- social spending increasingly focused on safety net provision for the poor and vulnerable as reflected in increased targeting of social security spending and the switch in housing policy from large-scale provision of subsidized housing to support for poor tenants through housing benefit;
- strong commitment to spending on defence and public order;
- ambivalence towards public spending on education, training and health (with growth rates fluctuating according to the view that was taken on the extent to which unmet needs could be met through increased efficiency).

As time has gone on, the weaknesses in these policies have tended to be more prominent than the strengths.

Improving the present system

The discussion above has highlighted a number of weaknesses in the present system for setting public spending priorities. The weaknesses are not, in the main, of the kind that can be remedied quickly. Nevertheless, it is worth considering a number of areas in which both technical decision taking and political decision taking can be improved.

Technical decision-taking

It will not be easy to improve the efficiency with which technical decisions are made. Successful organizations are those that combine a high degree of continuity with innovation and challenge (Kay, 1995). They maintain and develop systems and relationships that are successful in adding value, while challenging those that are not and testing out new approaches. An incoming Labour government would need to identify and build on what is relatively successful.

It can and where necessary should replace people in key positions. In the main however, it will need to work with the professionals it inherits and there are practical limits to the initiatives that can be successfully carried forward in a single parliament.

Among key actions to be considered should be the following:

- *Filling evaluation gaps* with regard to the present government's main policy initiatives and management innovations – for example, in education and training, health and law and order. While conclusive evidence will not always be available, there is scope for the kind of reviews that have successfully been undertaken in the past by Royal Commission-type bodies, as well as by impartial observers such as Griffiths and Dearing (see e.g. Dearing, 1994 and Griffiths 1984, 1988).
- *Improvements in the way in which information is collected and used.* The proposed development of resource accounting and budgeting should provide a valuable framework for evaluation and planning, as well as allowing independent analysis. However, whereas there are relatively simple techniques of accrual accounting that can be adapted from commercial practice to help measure resource inputs, they do not solve the crucial and more difficult problems of measuring and valuing processes and outputs such as education and health and social care. Progress is being made in assessing the effectiveness of these, mainly through improved sampling of complex domains of knowledge and fields of data and potential data. Examples include improved testing to sample the knowledge and skills acquired through education; inspections to sample the quality of teaching; collecting sample or 'sentinel' data of patients' experience of health services through surveys, follow-up studies and data on avoidable deaths.
- *Improvements in the identification of relative success.* This could involve using

performance indicators to identify units which should have resource priority; service performance indicators to help identify effective school and hospital management; and giving those who have led successful change the opportunities and incentives to increase the effectiveness of the less successful.

- *Testing new approaches through evaluated innovation.* This could be done by centrally planned pilot projects but also through wider learning-by-doing and a variety of local initiatives. These could include projects promoted by challenge funding, in which extra resources go to those who produce the best response to a competition. Monitoring should be used to identify projects and developments which merit selective evaluation in greater depth.
- *Increased devolution to regional and local levels.* This will lead to different views being taken as to what works best and, hence, offer different approaches which can be evaluated.
- Establishing *relations of trust between budget-setters and budget-managers*, based on shared objectives, so that unproductive budgetary gamesmanship is minimized. Budget-managers need to present vigorously the case for resources. However, they need to do this fairly and with commitment to continuing increases in efficiency.

Improved political decision-taking

The quality of political decision-taking depends ultimately on the quality of the ministerial team, its capacity to develop and carry forward coherent strategies adapted to the country's capabilities and preferences and to give leadership to the professionals who carry through the work of government. There are, however, several initiatives that could improve the quality of political decision-taking.

Setting of objectives

It is conventional management wisdom that politicians define objectives and managers implement them. This does not fit well with the traditional UK approach, which tends to start with specific cases and infer principles from them inductively. Neither does it fit with the uncertainty of events and the desire of politicians to avoid giving hostages to fortune in future adversarial debate. Statements of objectives tend to be inferred from specific decisions after the event, and little public or parliamentary attention tends to be paid to them. Those that have been produced and are reported in departmental reports do, however, have potential value both as tools of accountability and of departmental and inter-departmental coordination. They should be particularly useful to new ministers in understanding the current direction of their departments and deciding where it should be changed.

Clarification of responsibilities

There has been some progress in clarifying the responsibilities of ministers and their departments and agencies. However, this is not true of the relationship between central and local government. Local authorities are legally responsible for a wide range of services. However, key decisions that relate to those services are largely determined by central government through legislation, inspectorates and financial control. When things go wrong, each can blame the other. Furthermore, excessive attention is paid to decisions relating to grant levels and distribution and there are perverse incentives for local authorities to conceal potential efficiency gains.

An alternative model would involve central government being responsible for setting and financing basic national standards in services considered of national interest – such as education, police and social services – and providing the necessary finance from national taxation. Local authorities would then be responsible for financing and commissioning or providing purely local services – for example, local economic development, leisure and environmental programmes – as well as additions to national services to meet local needs and preferences. They would have power (e.g. through supplementary contracts) to finance local improvements to services for which they are not, at present, responsible such as health and employment services (see also Holtham and Kay, 1994).

It should now be feasible to define minimum cost standards *de facto* by answering the question: who is providing nationally acceptable standards at the lowest cost per head (after allowance for relative need). Grants for national services would be set initially at or just below that level; they would periodically be adjusted upwards to take account of unavoidable costs (with an allowance for efficiency gains). As and when national resources become available for improvement of services, government would decide what should be spent on national initiatives to improve basic standards and how much should be allocated for initiatives by local government; it would increase the national grant to enable even minimum spenders to achieve defined objectives; money would not be formally hypothecated, for the reasons outlined below, but there would be greater transparency nationally and locally. Authorities and inspectorates would report on whether objectives were being achieved and how spending compared with other comparable authorities.

Such proposals would increase the power of local authorities to do what they are, or should be, best suited for: assessing local needs, preferences and readiness to pay and developing strategies across service boundaries. Central government would also do what it is or could be better suited for: assessing and responding to national needs and pressures and providing political leadership to powerful national professions (political leadership being taken to include stimulating and organizing professional leadership through national inspectorates and promotion of peer-review and self-audit). Proposals of this kind were put forward in the Day minority report to the Layfield report, the last independent comprehensive review of local government finance (Layfield, 1976) which correctly forecast the consequences of confusion of responsibilities.

Greater transparency and objectivity

In recent years the amount of information provided on government spending plans and performance has been substantially increased. As many as 18 individual departmental reports are now produced in the place of one section of the former public expenditure White Paper. Further improvements are planned as part of the resource accounting and budgeting initiative.

The government is sometimes suspected of information overkill but the expanded reports mainly reflect legitimate demand for more information from parliament and elsewhere. The volume of accessible information needs in fact to be increased but it needs to be structured in layers of progressively increasing detail, with short summaries at the top and detailed research documentation at the bottom and clear signposting between the layers (IT should facilitate this).

There needs, however, to be increased information on outputs, outcomes and quality standards. Furthermore, the way in which it is presented could also be improved to make it more accessible. For example, the Treasury's annual 'Grey Book' on Public Expenditure (Treasury, 1996) should include, in addition to the present statistical summaries of past and planned spending, a well-signposted summary of the key factors that influence each department's plans, including efficiency gains achieved and planned and key spending needs and pressures. Data on plans and past performance could be brought together on CD-ROM. In the longer term, it should be possible to develop a widely accessible information network on public expenditure and taxation.

There is also greater need for more objective analysis of the standards of public services (as opposed to special pleading by interest groups for unrealistically high standards). The current departmental reports tend to select good news and to gloss over shortcomings. Inspectorates need to develop the kind of approach adopted by Ofsted of sampling activities and providing an assessment of the percentage that reach acceptable standards. Surveys of customer satisfaction also need to be undertaken on a consistent basis over successive years to find out what progress has been made.

Greater openness and transparency should not only make for greater public confidence in decision-taking but should also increase the efficiency of decision-making by exposing the technical rationale for decisions to public comment and scrutiny. Openness needs to be accompanied by strong political leadership and public recognition that decisions often have to be taken on the basis of imperfect analysis.

Strengthened audit

Presentation of information in a digestible form means that it has to be summarized and selected. This carries with it risks of biased and misleading presentation. There is a need for audit processes to be strengthened and for its role to be extended to include checks on whether departmental accounts give a true and fair view of operations and to develop methods of validating their performance data. Traditionally, the National Audit Office and Public Accounts Committee have been excluded from review of policy issues. However, the technical analysis carried out within departments, and which feeds into policy reviews, should be open to both audit and review by parliamentary select committees.

Better informed political debate

At present, the budget debate in the House of Commons provides the only opportunity for public discussion of the government's expenditure priorities. This discussion is usually based on sketchy analysis of the budget's spending plans and on selective departmental press notices. As a result, most emphasis is placed on economic and taxation issues.

There needs to be a focus for debate and media comment in the spring (or early summer), when fuller information is available on departmental spending performance and plans. Such a debate would provide an opportunity for the government to be held publicly to account for its previous review of spending and taxation. This could be done by developing the annual Treasury Grey Book, the present supplement to the Budget report, in the way we have suggested as a summary review of the government's performance and plans, which would be the focus of parliamentary discussion in spring or early summer and would feed into the government's next review of spending plans.

In addition to the present financial tables, the revised Grey Book might also include the key points in the separate departmental reports on performance and plans, together with an account of what were considered marginal spending issues at the time of the previous review. It might also include information, currently published separately by the Office for National Statistics, on how much average households in different income bands contribute to national taxation and what they receive in services. Select committees would have the opportunity to comment on whether the statements of performance, plans and issues at the margin needed to be amended or amplified, whether there were new factors to take into account and their views on how the balance of priorities should be changed.

In providing public analysis of its marginal spending options along the lines suggested above, government would be publishing key elements of the dialogue between central government (Treasury and/or EDX) and spending departments. This would be a bold step, but government does now publish an account of discussions on inflation between the Chancellor and the Governor of the Bank of England which, at one time, would have seemed equally unthinkable. Admittedly the latter is to reassure international financiers but reassuring the British public might also be a worthwhile benefit.

A basic difficulty of involving parliament is that the adversarial procedures of motion, counter-motion and amendment are poorly adapted to bringing together points of view on numerical issues and developing consensus positions. There is scope for *experimenting with numerical electronic voting* to enable MPs to present their views in numerical terms and where appropriate accommodate them to those of colleagues. For example, after listening to an analysis of spending pressures, MPs could record electronically their preferred priorities in terms of how much should be added to or taken away from each main programme (as a percentage or in £million, with computer conversion from one to the other). Rapid feedback could be provided to show the distribution of priority scores and average and median scores. Preference scores of each electronic voter could, if necessary, be proportionately scaled down so that the total net addition did not exceed an agreed amount. There could be further discussion of what the effects would be of adopting the average or median position, followed by a further round of voting and feedback.

The government could usefully experiment with this approach to help build up its own consensus on what the priorities should be across government and within departmental fields. It could for example be used at an away-day conference of ministers and senior officials at which initial guidelines for the spending review were discussed and at similar conferences led by departmental ministers. Once the gadgetry had been installed and experience gained in its use, the approach could be extended to consultation with backbench MPs and be offered to select committees. Variants could be developed for use by local authorities and the citizens' juries we discuss below. There could be valuable exchanges of views with local authorities, some of which have already experimented with decision-conferencing techniques.

Greater public involvement

Finally, there is the key question of whether and how the electorate should be given a greater say in how its money is being spent. The difficulty here is that the choices are complex, few people have the time, energy or motivation to understand them; those that have are not representative of the public as a whole and they tend to focus on their own sectional interests. Detailed decisions have to be left to elected representatives. However, they could be made more sensitive to public preferences if there is greater devolution to local authorities, alongside greater clarification of their responsibilities.

Increasingly, doubts are being expressed about how effectively local authority members represent local preferences. Furthermore, there is the difficulty of assessing how much weight should be given to the views of those who may be in a minority locally but are in a majority at a national level. In the commercial sector answers to similar problems are found through market research and there is a need to develop political market research, going beyond the relatively crude surveys of spending preferences which have been adopted so far and which produce results that correlate poorly with voting patterns.

Experimentation with citizens' juries (Stewart *et al.*, 1994) should be on the agenda. Such ideas have already been adopted by a number of local authorities and health authorities to look at various difficult policy issues. Small groups of citizens (randomly chosen in the case of citizens' juries, but they could also be from particular sub-groups of the population) would be given the opportunity to be briefed on public expenditure issues and to discuss and vote on numerical choices concerning public expenditure choices (for example, relative growth rates of blocks of expenditure). Their conclusions would, to a certain extent, be representative of what people might think if they were better informed and had the time to consider the issues. Such discussions would therefore help to highlight issues on which it was worthwhile to hold more general surveys and, possibly, where there were particularly controversial and clear-cut issues, local referendums. But in any case they would certainly extend the degree to which debate became public, particularly since they may be attractive to the media (Channel 4 has already organized and televized groups of this type).

Some may argue that elected political leaders are so well in touch with what the public wants and is ready to pay for that citizens' juries would not add value. This could and should be tested by putting the same sets of questions to citizens' juries and sample groups of elected representatives and analysing the differences. If they really added nothing to the judgements of politicians, they could be discontinued save as an occasional check. In any case, the confirmation that political leaders were in touch with public preferences would give useful reassurance about the political process. In practice, public feedback of this kind is likely to lead to better decision-taking and better understanding of the decisions taken.

Conversely it may be argued that the populist answer emerging from citizens' juries would not necessarily be best or right and that elected politicians might still need to take different decisions. There will certainly be times when it is right for government and parliament to differ from the popular view, as they have over capital punishment. But cases where there are overriding moral or technical arguments are likely to be the exception and, where there are good reasons for not accepting a majority view, these should be explicitly debated.

Politicians may, of course, be concerned that citizens' juries and the like would diminish their power. However, the final decisions would still rest with elected representatives. Better information about public preferences would no more reduce the power of politicians than market research does that of commercial management.

But not hypothecation of taxes

One proposal often made to better 'connect' citizens to the tax and spending decisions made, is to use hypothecated taxes. Here, specific taxes are hypothecated (i.e. earmarked) to particular services. The former Road Fund Tax was earmarked for road-building and at present national insurance contributions are earmarked for pensions and other benefits that are conditional on such contributions. Some suggest that pollution taxes should be used only for energy efficiency measures, tobacco taxes only for health. The Liberal Democrats are prominent in arguing for an extra penny on income tax to go exclusively to fund increased education spending.

The argument is that people who were interested would have more and clearer information on who was paying what for what and what the options for change were; and the public would have more opportunity to influence the choices on those options. But there are serious disadvantages of hypothecation (Wilkinson, 1994). These may be summarized as:

- reduced flexibility and increased cost in managing public spending to cope with changing circumstances (since tax revenues are tied to particular expenditures);
- perverse incentives to spend to the limit of the hypothecated total and hence disincentives to seek efficiency savings;
- increased complexity because the amount raised from a hypothecated tax will seldom, if ever, match the spending needs of a particular programme (separate reserves become necessary, as does funding from different sources);
- reduced transparency and the likely confusion of the public (e.g. the widespread misapprehension that the NHS was entirely financed by the hypothecated weekly contribution – the 'NHS stamp').

In any case, the other measures we have suggested would offer most of the benefits claimed for earmarked (or hypothecated) taxes, while avoiding their serious disadvantages.

Conclusions

What opportunities would a Labour government have for improving the current system for determining public expenditure priorities? In the first place it would have the advantage that it can radically review policies and practices to which its predecessors were committed. Second, it is likely to have a breathing space in which deficiencies can be blamed on predecessors. On the other hand, a new Labour government would face high expectations for an improvement of public services which will make things highly charged in this area.

As we have discussed, the weaknesses in the present system are not of the kind that can be quickly remedied. Moreover, changes seem unlikely to be of the highest priority for an incoming government, given both the high degree of public acquiescence and the likelihood that there will be little financial room for manoeuvre. This implies that there would necessarily be a period when the existing systems would continue to be used and inherited spending plans would continue, except where these conflicted with firm election commitments.

However, new ministerial teams would be able to correct the imbalance that has resulted from the ideological bias of the present government. Departments would set up the supporting teams to provide the analysis of spending needs and pressures and the opportunities for savings that new ministers will need if they are to decide, for example, how the part of the reserve that is allocated in the spending round should be spent. In addition, Labour would need to build on the strengths of the present system, address the weaknesses outlined above, while delivering some results in a first parliament and offering prospects for reform in a subsequent parliament.

References

Dearing, R. (1994). *National Curriculum and its Assessment*. London: DFE.
EC (1996). *Eurostat*. Brussels: European Commission.
Griffiths, R. (1984). *Management of the NHS*. London: HMSO.
Griffiths, R. (1988). *Community Care: Agenda for Action*. London: HMSO.
Holtham, G. and Kay, J. (1994). 'The assessment: institutions of policy', *Oxford Review of Economic Policy*, **10**(3).
Kay, J. (1995). *Foundations of Corporate Success*. Oxford: OUP.
Layfield, F. (1976). *Local Government Finance*, Cmd 6453. London: HMSO.
Neuburger, H. and Fraser, N. (1993). *Economic Policy Analysis: A Rights-based Approach* (Avebury, Aldershot).
Stewart, J., Kendall, E. and Coote, A. (1994). *Citizens' Juries*. London: IPPR.
Thain, C. and Wright, M. (1995). *Treasury in Whitehall: the planning of public expenditure 1976 to 1993.*
Treasury (1996). Public Expenditure: Statistical Analyses 1996–97, Cm 3201. London: HM Treasury.
Wilkinson M (1994) 'Paying for public spending: is there a role for earmarked taxes?' *Fiscal Studies*, **15**(4).

6

What Does the Public Think?

Peter Kellner

Contents

Some things in politics are 'known' even if not proven. Currently the leaderships of the Labour and Conservative parties 'know' that they will suffer badly in electoral terms if they say they will raise taxes to pay for better public services. In this chapter we analyse whether they are right in this supposition. Or is what they 'know' a fallacy?

We first examine how public opinion on this issue has evolved. Then we go on to look at current attitudes and how robust the evidence on it is. Next we analyse why those proposing higher taxes have done badly in terms of votes in recent years, with specific attention to the 1992 election. Finally we look at the way the trends are going and the dilemmas this poses for the future.

How opinion has changed since the late Seventies

The longest continuous series of polling data comes from Gallup. In October 1978, during the final months of the Labour government headed by James Callaghan, Gallup asked people to choose from three options:

- cutting taxes, 'even if it means some reduction in government services, such as health, education and welfare';
- leaving things as they are;
- spending more on 'Government services such as health, education and welfare . . . even if it means some increases in taxes'.

The biggest single group, 45 per cent, chose the third option. But if we add the first two groups together, they were outnumbered by the 55 per cent who opposed higher spending. It was against this background that Margaret Thatcher committed the Conservatives in their 1979 manifesto to reduce both tax and public spending as a share of Britain's national income. At the time of the 1979 election, the public verdict was more emphatic. The public divided evenly between the lower and higher tax-and-spend options; when those who wanted 'no change' were added in, Gallup found a clear 63–37 per cent majority against higher tax-and-spend.

That majority soon evaporated, as Table 6.1 shows. By March 1980 it had declined to 52–47 per cent against higher tax-and-spend. A year later, as

Table 6.1. Views on reducing taxes/increasing government spending (% of respondents).

Date	*Cut taxes*	*No change*	*Extend services*
Oct 78	29	26	45
May 79	37	26	37
Mar 80	25	27	47
Mar 81	22	25	53
Feb 82	22	27	52
Feb 83	24	23	52
Oct 83	18	23	53
May 84	15	27	58
Nov 84	13	26	62
Feb 85	17	19	63
Feb 86	17	20	63
June 86	17	14	64
Sept 86	9	18	68
May 87	12	21	61
Oct 87	11	19	66
Nov 88	10	15	71
Dec 89	13	18	64
Feb 90	11	16	66
Aug 90	13	14	69
Dec 90	10	16	69
May 91	11	13	72
Aug 91	10	20	64
Mar 92	10	20	66
Apr 93	10	13	69
July 93	8	15	75
Feb 95	8	16	69
Mar 96	9	13	71

Source: Gallup

unemployment increased sharply and Conservative popularity plummeted, the figures had reversed. Now 53 per cent wanted higher taxes to pay for higher spending. The two other options – lower tax-and-spend (22 per cent) and no change (25 per cent) could muster only 47 per cent between them.

As Table 6.1 shows, those figures did not change much during the rest of the 1979–83 Parliament. But during the mid-1980s – the critical years of the Thatcher revolution, and also the years of Nigel Lawson's economic boom when the standard rate of income tax was reduced from 30 to 25 per cent – public opinion did move sharply. By November 1988, 71 per cent favoured the higher tax-and-spend option, outnumbering by almost three-to-one the combined support for the other two options. Just 10 per cent favoured lower tax-and-spend policies, while 15 per cent favoured the new status quo. Since 1988, the figures have shown no consistent trend up or down; they have fluctuated around the same level.

How robust is the evidence?

Gallup's question, it must be said, is not perfect. It does not specify who should pay higher taxes. It could for instance be that a large number of lower- and middle-income people want the rich to pay higher taxes so that everyone can enjoy better schools and hospitals. Nor does it test the proposition that it may be possible through faster economic growth and better management of the public sector to enjoy both tax cuts and improved public services.

However, whatever the defects of Gallup's question wording, they are *constant* defects. The wording has not changed over almost 20 years. The *level* of support for each option may be influenced by the way the question is worded, but the *trend* through time represents a real shift in public attitudes. Public sentiment altered significantly between the late 1970s and the late 1980s, and has remained fairly constant ever since. And even if Gallup's wording is flawed, the fact that as many as 66–75 per cent regularly say they want higher taxes to pay for higher spending should at least cast doubt on the view that the only way to win elections is to promise lower taxes and squeeze public spending.

What is more, other questions have produced broadly similar answers. The public's views on taxes and public spending seem to be fairly robust, and not particularly prone to be distorted by particular question wordings. For example:

- In November 1991, shortly before the 1992 general election, NOP asked: 'If extra money becomes available as a result of economic growth, which of these options do you think would be best for the country?' To this, 71 per cent replied: 'The Government spending more on public services and keeping taxes at the present level'; just 25 per cent replied: 'The government keeping public services at their present level and cutting taxes'.

  NOP then asked which of the same two options 'would be best for you and your family'. The margin narrowed, but still favoured higher public spending over tax cuts by 55–36 per cent (*Independent*, 7 January 1992).

- In March 1992, during the general election campaign, NOP tested six policy proposals that different parties had put forward in their manifestos. As Table 6.2 shows, not only was the 'raise-taxes-to-pay-for-education' popular; this policy – put forward by the Liberal Democrats – was the *most* popular of the six policies tested by NOP (*Independent*, 26 March 1992).
- During the Conservative Party leadership contest in 1995, NOP polled people who had voted Conservative in 1992. They were asked: 'If there is money available to the government in the next budget, which of these would help you and your family most?' The answers were:
  - Spend more on services such as health and education' – 51 per cent;
  - 'Reduce income tax' – 30 per cent;
  - 'Give more tax relief to mortgage payers' – 17 per cent (*Sunday Times*, 25 June 1995).
- Immediately after the 1995 Budget, when Kenneth Clarke, the Chancellor of the Exchequer, announced restrictions on public spending and a 1p cut in the standard rate of income tax, MORI asked: 'On balance do you support or oppose the government reducing spending in order to reduce levels of taxation?' Opponents outnumbered supporters by 54 to 30 per cent. In other words there was a majority of almost two-to-one against tax cuts even though (a) the survey was conducted immediately after such cuts had been offered, and (b) when the question referred only to 'spending' in general terms, without specifically mentioning services such as health, education or welfare (*British Public Opinion*, January 1996).

Table 6.2. Reaction to policy proposals (%).

Proposed policy	*Approve*	*Disapprove*	*Neither*
Raise the standard rate of income tax by 1p to 26p and spend the money on education	78	15	7
Make it illegal for employers to pay their workers less than £3.40 an hour	66	23	11
Stop the recent changes to the way the health service is run	56	30	14
Scrap the present first-past-the-post system for electing MPs and introduce proportional representation	47	20	33
Help more schools to opt out of control by their local education authorities	37	43	20
Privatize Britain's railways	26	54	20

Source: NOP.
Fieldwork: 24–25 March 1992.

Do the polls reveal what people really think?

The polling evidence, then, is clear. Faced with an opinion-poll choice between lower taxes and higher public spending, the British public consistently opts by large majorities for higher public spending – however the choice is phrased.

Could it be, however, that the problem lies not with the wording of specific questions, but with the phenomenon of opinion polls themselves? Do people tell pollsters one thing, and then do another when faced with the real choice of voting for a tax-raising or tax-cutting party? This view gained currency after the 1992 general election, when the polls wrongly predicted that the Conservatives would lose their majority.

The answer to this comes in two parts. First, there is no evidence that respondents lied in statistically significant numbers to the pollsters. On average, the eve-of-election polls overstated Labour's support by four percentage points, and understated Conservative support by the same amount. Post-election research, most of it conducted under the auspices of the Market Research Society, shows that this error was the result of a number of small, cumulative mistakes by the polling organizations: their samples contained too few middle-class and too many working-class respondents; a small number of Conservative voters replied either 'don't know' to the voting intention or refused to divulge their intentions; there was a slight swing to the Tories during the final 24 hours of the campaign, after the last polls were conducted; and there was a slightly higher turnout of Tory supporters than Labour supporters on election day.

These mistakes completely explain the four-point error in the eve-of-election polls. Were we to rewind the clock and redesign the polls to ensure fully accurate surveys during the run-up to the 1992 election, we would still find large majorities favouring public spending over tax cuts.

The second part of the answer to the 'why-trust-the-polls' question comes from the large-scale academic study of the election conducted directly after the Conservative victory by the Centre for Research into Elections and Social Trends. This study, financed by the Government's Economic and Social Research Council, looked specifically at the impact of taxation on the 1992 general election. Its conclusions are clear:

> When we looked at those of our panel respondents who said they would vote Labour before polling day but in fact failed to do so, there is no evidence that they were people who were particularly averse to high taxation; rather they seemed to be people who had relatively little faith in Labour's ability to improve services like health and education.
>
> Nor is there any evidence that the Conservatives' focus on taxation in the run-up to the election campaign cost Labour votes compared with 1987 . . . We find that taxation may actually have cost some votes between 1987 and 1992. On the other hand it may well be that the Labour Party's general image as a high tax party consistently depresses their electoral performance.

The authors go on to ask whether Labour could 'make electoral gains by a further policy review which tried to get rid of its image as a high tax and high spending party?' They argue that this would not work; their main reason is that

> Labour's current commitments to the national health and education services are popular both with Labour voters and with the electorate in a way that disarmament and nationalisation never were. Labour would risk losing many more supporters by dropping its commitment to the welfare state than it risked by ditching nationalisation or unilateral disarmament.
>
> (Heath *et al.*, 1994, pp 292–3)

The evidence, then, is that opinion polls do reflect, fairly accurately, a real public preference for better public services over tax cuts. As NOP's survey in November 1991 indicated, there are some people who believe that tax cuts would be better for them personally than for the country as a whole. All this does, however, is to reduce the majority in favour of public spending – it does not create a majority for tax cuts.

Competence matters more than taxes

Nevertheless, the Conservatives have won the last four general elections, each time promising lower taxes than the Labour Party. And much of the Tory *un*popularity since 1992 has been caused by tax increases. How can we square the opinion poll evidence with actual electoral behaviour? Three reasons may be advanced.

First, Britain's voting system worked to the advantage of the one low-tax party. Fourteen million people voted Conservative – but 18.4 million voted for parties more committed to spending on the public services: Labour (11.6 million), the Liberal Democrats (6.0 million) and the Welsh and Scottish Nationalists (0.8 million). The Tories won the last election by winning a majority of seats, not because they won a majority of votes.

Second, tax and public spending were not the only election issues. Values, traditional loyalties, trust, fear, suspicion, law and order, defence, the trade unions, the personalities of the party leaders and so on: these all played their part. It is dangerous to pluck out one topic, however important, and conclude without direct and specific evidence that it was the sole, or dominant, cause of victory and defeat.

Third and most important, there is evidence that voters did warm to Labour's priorities for health and education – but that these sentiments were trumped by a fear that Labour would run the economy badly. NOP's exit poll for the BBC, conducted among voters as they left polling stations on the day of the 1992 general election, found that 53 per cent trusted the Conservatives most to take the right decisions about the economy; only 33 per cent trusted Labour most (BBC, 1992, p. 13). A Gallup poll, taken during the final 48 hours of the campaign, found that only 38 per cent thought 'Britain as a whole would be better off under a Labour government'; 42 per cent thought Britain would be worse off (*Gallup Political Index*, April 1992). And, as we have seen, Heath Jowell and Curtice found that Labour lost support during the campaign not because of its tax policies, but because worried voters had little faith that Labour would actually improve public services such as health and competence.

In addition, 63 per cent of voters believed that Labour would increase the standard rate of income tax, while 51 per cent thought prices would rise more rapidly under Labour (BBC, 1992, p. 11). Most voters evidently disbelieved Labour's protestations to the contrary.

These findings counter the view that voters made a conscious choice in 1992 to favour tax cuts over public spending increases. In truth, too many people believed that Labour would make such a mess of the economy that taxes would rise but public services would *not* improve. It was not Labour's tax-and-spend values that cost the party votes, but its poor reputation for economic competence.

What happened after 1992

Since 1992, the competence shoe has been on the other political foot. The Conservatives' reputation has suffered, while Labour's has recovered. It has been the Tories' turn to be blamed as the party that puts up taxes without improving public services. NOP's polls for the *Sunday Times* since July 1995 have recorded Labour leads of 20–25 points when people are asked who they trust more to make them and their families better off – the Conservatives under John Major, or Labour under Tony Blair.

It is, though, worth noting that Labour has secured this advantage without persuading voters that the party would be any more successful than the Tories at keeping taxes down. In October 1995, NOP found that 50 per cent expected their own taxes to rise if Labour won the next election, and only 16 per cent expected their taxes to go down. The figures for the Tories were similar: 47 per cent expected taxes to rise if they won again, while 15 per cent expected them to fall (*Sunday Times*, 22 October 1995).

The conclusion is clear: perceived economic competence is what matters, not promises to reduce taxes. On the contrary, voters are wary of parties that offer tax cuts paid for by squeezing public services. The Conservatives won in 1992 *despite* their priorities on the tax-and-spend issue; subsequently Labour sustained huge leads while convincing only a minority of the electorate that it would bring their taxes down.

The polling evidence suggests that the way for a political party to sweep the country is to show that it will both run the economy well and find the money to pay for decent public services. Indeed, it may well be that this sentiment has played a part in sustaining Labour's huge opinion poll leads: rightly or wrongly, millions of voters think that Labour would put more money into schools, hospitals and welfare, and give them precedence over tax cuts. If the electorate really did come to believe that Labour would hold the public sector purse strings as tightly as the Tories, Labour's support might start to melt away.

It might be argued – indeed, has been argued – that this data can be looked at another way. Labour was perceived to be a tax-raising party in 1992; it lost the election. The Conservatives have increased taxes since 1992; they have plunged to their worst-ever poll ratings. Surely this shows that when voters focus their minds on taxes, they punish high-tax parties – whatever they tell pollsters about their hypothetical preferences for public spending?

The problem with this argument is that tax and general economic competence became intertwined both during the 1992 election and afterwards. The evidence is strongly supportive, not of the self-evidently ludicrous view that millions of voters like to pay high taxes for their own sake, but that they are willing to pay higher taxes *if they believe that these will lead to better public services.* That belief was not present when voters looked at Labour in 1992 or the Conservatives after Black Wednesday. What the data from the past five years shows is that most voters resent paying higher taxes to pay for political incompetence. This should surprise nobody, and does nothing to undermine the proposition that a party would win more votes than it lost if it (a) were perceived to be competent, and (b) offered a higher-tax-for-better-services package.

Why voters prefer better public services to tax cuts

Why is it that such a large majority of British people consistently say that they prefer better-resourced public services to tax cuts? More specifically, why are most voters dissatisfied with levels of public spending that have continued to increase, as a percentage of GDP, in most areas even under the Conservatives?

For a start, most people do not believe that spending has risen. An NOP survey in July 1995 found that 61 per cent agreed that 'this government is spending less on the National Health Service than it did two years ago'. Only 22 per cent disagreed. Even among Conservative supporters – the people most likely to recognize the truth of ministerial claims that spending had risen – only 38 per cent believed that it had in fact done so; 43 per cent thought spending had fallen (*Sunday Times*, 23 July 1995).

This might suggest that the appetite for tax cuts would revive, if only people were persuaded to recognize the truth about public spending. If they truly believed that more is being spent than ever before on schools, hospitals and social security, then their clamour for yet more to be spent might start to subside.

On the other hand, the 'mistake' made by the majority could reflect a more profound sentiment which will be harder to change. It is the everyday experience of parents and patients alike that school and health budgets are constantly being squeezed. Large (and true) statements about the aggregate level of national funding are at odds with personal experience. It is in the gulf between those two trends – increasing national spending, but squeezed local budgets – that the clue is to be found to the public response to the whole tax and spending debate.

The long-term shift from basic consumption to social provision

To explain this point, a brief historical excursion is necessary. In the mid-Sixties, around 16 per cent of Britain's gross domestic product was devoted to health, education and welfare; almost all of this was spent by the state; only one per cent or so was spent on school fees, private health, and occupational pension schemes. In contrast, twice as much – 32 per cent of GDP – was spent on food, fuel, clothing and tobacco. Almost all of this was spent out of after-tax income.

Over the past 30 years those figures have almost reversed. In 1995 we spent around 28 per cent of GDP on health, education and welfare (divided roughly 24–4 between state and private spending), and just 20 per cent on food, fuel, clothing and tobacco. (Those figures are estimates distilled from various sources; there is some room for debate about the precise percentages, but these do not alter the thrust of the argument.)

This does not mean that we spent less in absolute terms on food, fuel and so on. On the contrary, spending rose (by about 20 per cent in real terms). But it rose less fast than GDP, which doubled during those 30 years. However, spending on health, education and welfare more than trebled in real terms. Some of this is the consequence of higher unemployment, leading to higher social security bills. But even without that, the shift from basic consumption to social provision would have been huge. Overall, the 12-point switch between 1965 and 1995 is equivalent to £80 billion a year at today's prices.

The basic reason for this switch is not hard to fathom. We do not (or, perhaps more accurately, *should* not) eat more calories than we used to. We do not need to keep any warmer, or wear any more clothes. To be sure, we have traded up: to central heating, better clothes, more exotic food, and so on; but these relatively modest changes have been partly offset by reductions in the real price of energy, the more efficient production of food and clothing, and an absolute decline in the consumption of tobacco. The overall result – not just in Britain but in every developed country – has been a steady reduction in the proportion of national income devoted to basic consumer needs.

On the other hand, spending on health, education and welfare has grown enormously everywhere. Teenagers stay in full-time education longer. More adults need to retrain. Older people retire earlier and live longer: so there are more elderly people who need pensions and health care. New, more expensive drugs and medical equipment have been developed; and they treat more people of all ages – often people (especially babies) who would have died in the past for the lack of today's medical knowledge. And so on.

To some degree the expansion of social provision has been privately financed

– for example by the rapid growth of private pension schemes. To some extent the state has sought to offset rising costs through current or deferred charges such as prescription charges and student loans. Yet these developments have only affected the figures at the margins. In general, there has been a huge shift from privately financed basic consumption to publicly financed social provision.

This inexorable trend helps to explain the paradox that more than ever before is spent on health, education and welfare – yet the public perception is that public services are badly underfunded. It is possible that both are right. That is, the expansion of social provision has not kept pace with the rising costs of meeting the growing demands that are placed on it.

That also helps to explain why such a persistent majority of voters say they would prefer extra public spending rather than tax cuts. Their essential consumption needs have been met; their essential social needs, in contrast, have not.

Dilemmas for the future

In the short term, this underlines the potential electoral advantages that could accrue from promising extra resources for health, education and welfare. In the longer term, however, a more fundamental dilemma arises. It seems certain that demand for these services will continue to grow; it is almost as certain that a limit will be reached at some point to the willingness of the electorate to fund this growth through higher taxes.

This means that sometime in the nearish future (the first decade of the 21st century, during the second Blair administration?) a party committed to the adequate provision of such services will need to find alternative – that is, private – ways to attract extra funding. Put bluntly, the long-term choice for the centre-left is either, arrange for the state to do less; or force taxes up beyond the level that voters are prepared to support; or curb social provision and disappoint its own most needy supporters.

The essential message from the opinion polls, and from the underlying social and economic trends that underpin public attitudes, is that there is more room in the short-to-medium term than many centre-left politicians suppose to provide better-funded public services. In the longer term, however, large and difficult strategic choices must be made. The good news for the centre-left is that there is time to plan those changes and introduce them gradually. The bad news is that such changes cannot be avoided for ever.

References

BBC (1992). *Vacher's Guide to the New House of Commons*. London.
Heath, A., Jowell, R. and Curtice, J. (1994). *Labour's Last Chance*. Dartmouth.

7

How Public Attitudes to Expenditure Differ[1]

John Hall, Ian Preston and Michael Ridge

Contents

Introduction

In the previous chapter Peter Kellner discusses evidence from Gallup surveys since the late 1970s which show that the public's support for increased taxes to finance higher public spending on health, education and welfare has grown significantly over the period. This pattern in attitudes towards public spending is repeated in a number of regular opinion polls and surveys. An example is the British Social Attitudes survey (BSA) which asks its respondents a very similar question to that in the Gallup poll. The BSA survey indicates that between 1985 and 1994 those favouring higher spending on health, education and social benefits, while at the same time accepting that taxes will rise, increased from 48 per cent to 61 per cent. Moreover, those respondents preferring less taxation and less spent on the three services has remained relatively constant at around the 5 per cent level.

In this chapter we explore the attitudes of the public towards public spending in a little more detail. We investigate the relative popularity of a range of public spending programmes. Some items of expenditure, such as health and education, appear to attract far more public support than others, such as defence or culture and the arts. We also consider whether support for higher expenditure is spread evenly throughout the population or whether it is concentrated among particular groups categorized either by incomes, age, housing tenure or political beliefs. This chapter also discusses whether the promotion and development of an alternative sphere of private provision alongside the state sector has any implications for the future popularity of the welfare state.

In the first section we look at how the attitudes to public spending of respondents to the British Social Attitudes survey have developed between 1985 and 1994. Next, we attempt to identify 'who wants what'. This section splits the survey respondents into various demographic groupings, thus allowing us to examine whether attitudes to spending differ between individuals of different ages, genders or incomes. The following section explores how the growth in the private provision of health since the early 1980s may have impacted on attitudes to public provision of health. Finally, we present a summary of our conclusions and discuss some of the implications for policy.

Attitudes to government spending

The British Social Attitudes survey asks questions on a variety of economic, political and social issues on a regular basis to a large sample of British adults. Among these questions are a number concerning support for public spending. These allow the evolution in attitudes to public spending to be traced (Bosanquet, 1986; Taylor-Gooby, 1991, 1995; Lipsey, 1994). In this chapter we concentrate on the responses to questions of this type included in the 1985, 1990 and 1994 surveys. The number asked these questions in each survey varied: 900 in 1994, over 1500 in 1984 and over 3000 in 1990.

A majority of the respondents to the British Social Attitudes survey in 1994 wished to see a higher level of public expenditure on health, education and social benefits, taken together, even if this were to require an increase in taxation. The percentage of respondents who want higher spending has increased by 13 percentage points to 61 per cent since the mid 1980s, leaving nearly twice as many people wanting more spending compared to those who are happy as things currently are, and 15 times as many wanting more as compared to those who want less.

Over this period, the growth of public expenditure has not been evenly spread across the various spending programmes. Relative to other components of the nation's spending, real spending on health, education and social benefits has increased significantly since the early 1980s although the paths of health and education spending have been rather different. In the early and mid-1980s, education and health expenditure accounted for close to 5 per cent of GDP each. While the share of national income devoted to education has remained roughly constant since, the share devoted to health spending has increased to over 6 per cent.

Social security spending remains the largest component of General Government

Expenditure (GGE). In 1994 it accounted for 34 per cent of government spending, compared with health at 13.5 per cent and education at 12.6 per cent.

Knowing that the majority of citizens would prefer additional tax-financed public spending is not necessarily that helpful to politicians attempting to formulate public spending priorities. For example, it could be that the public strongly prefer spending on health but are indifferent to additional spending on education and social benefits. In the following, therefore, we examine the BSA respondents' attitudes to public spending in slightly more detail by concentrating on eight individual areas of government spending. These are shown in Table 7.1.

Respondents were asked to consider whether they would like to see:

- much more
- more
- the same
- less, or
- much less

government spending in each area. Respondents are warned that if they say 'much more' it might require a tax increase to pay for it. Table 7.1 ranks public expenditure programmes in order of proportion of the population preferring 'much more' spending. It also shows the percentage of respondents who answered that they would prefer merely 'more' spending.

However, this question poses a number of problems of interpretation. First, the question does not specify which tax would be raised or whether this tax change would affect the respondent personally. Individuals might be far more willing to enjoy the benefits of higher public spending if they think that somebody else will have to pay for it than if they think they will have to foot the bill themselves. Second, 'more' spending appears to have no tax cost associated with it. Third, the question does not make it explicit to the respondent that 'much less' spending might allow tax cuts.

Nevertheless, the format of the question is common to each spending programme in each year so we can make useful comparisons of the relative popularity of each component of public spending at one point in time, and how

Table 7.1. Relative popularity of each spending programme in 1994.

	Percentage that want to spend more	*Percentage that want to spend much more*
Health	50	38
Education	45	30
Pensions	48	29
Police and law enforcement	48	26
The environment	41	10
Unemployment benefits	28	10
Military and defence	16	6
Culture and the arts	9	4

the popularity of each type of spending programme varies over time. We now examine each of the spending programmes in turn to examine how much popular support exists for higher spending on that programme, and how individual attitudes have changed over time.

Health

Health spending remained the most popular public spending programme throughout the period. In 1994 close to 90 per cent of respondents said they would prefer a higher level of spending ('much more' or 'more') on health, roughly the same proportion as in 1985. Thirty-eight per cent of respondents said they wanted much more spent. Nearly all of the 10 per cent not wanting more spending preferred health spending to remain the same. Attitudes to health spending appears to have changed little over the last ten years.

Education

There has been a significant increase in the proportion of respondents wanting more spent on education over the last ten years. While only 23 per cent of respondents wanted 'much more' spending in 1985, this proportion had increased to 30 per cent by 1994. A further 45 per cent of respondents said they would prefer to see more spending on education in 1995.

Social benefits

The BSA survey asks questions about two major social benefits: unemployment benefits and old age pensions. Higher spending on pensions was supported by a far larger share of respondents than higher spending on benefits to the unemployed. The relative popularity of these two aspects of the welfare state has been more or less constant over time. Higher spending on pensions received support from nearly 80 per cent of respondents in 1995, a similar proportion to that found in 1985. Less than 1 per cent would like to see less or much less spending on pensions. In contrast to their views on pensions, in 1994, a majority of respondents (62 per cent), wanted unemployment benefits kept at the same level or reduced while only 10 per cent preferred 'much more' spending on them.

Various explanations could be offered to explain the stark differences we have found in the relative popularity of different social security benefits. It may be that individuals' perceptions of the merits of the welfare state are largely coloured by self-interest rather than broader notions of the public good. Thus, since all individuals can reasonably expect to receive a state pension at some stage of their lives, but many individuals may not expect ever to be dependent on unemployment benefits, individuals may see a more direct (even if rather long-term) advantage from higher levels of pension spending. As Lipsey (1994, p. 8) notes,

'People are, it seems, much more likely to favour the benefits from which they or their families expect to gain directly than those from which they perceive little immediate self-advantage.' An alternative explanation could be a distinction between notions of the 'deserving' and 'undeserving' poor.

Military and defence

Compared to the other major spending programmes, defence expenditure is relatively unpopular. In 1994, only 22 per cent of respondents wanted higher defence spending compared to nearly 47 per cent who were happy for defence expenditure to remain at current levels. Despite this, it is interesting to note that defence expenditure has become relatively more popular between 1990 and 1994. For example, the percentage of respondents not wanting a higher level of spending on defence dropped from 87 per cent in 1990 to 78 per cent in 1994. In addition, while nearly half of all respondents in 1990 wanted to see a reduction in spending, this proportion had fallen to 30 per cent by 1994. These changes in attitudes have occurred at a time when the share of national income devoted to defence expenditure has been falling.

Police and law enforcement

Increased spending on law and order has become significantly more popular since 1985. The 40 per cent of respondents who would have preferred a higher level of law and order spending in 1985 had increased to almost half of the BSA sample in 1990, and to 75 per cent in 1994. The proportion who would prefer to have 'much more' spending increased from 9 per cent in 1985 to 26 per cent in 1994.

The environment

The popularity of higher spending on the environment, which grew during the 1980s, appears to have fallen off slightly during the 1990s, from 63 per cent of respondents in 1990 to 51 per cent in 1994. At the same time, lowering the level of expenditure on the environment does not attract any significant public support, appealing to only 3 per cent of respondents in 1994.

Culture and the arts

Spending on culture and the arts is relatively unpopular. In 1994 only 13 per cent of respondents wanted to see more spending in this area, while 44 per cent were happy with the status quo, 43 per cent wanted to see less spending and nearly 13 per cent much less spending on culture and the arts. Support for higher levels of spending increased slightly between 1985 and 1990 but has remained roughly constant since. It is possible, of course, that the widespread publicity given to spending on the arts from Lottery revenues will have diminished the attraction of this sort of spending.

Other areas

Although the spending functions listed above account for a significant amount of public spending there are no questions that touch on attitudes to spending areas such as transport, inner-city regeneration or housing. To take account of these omissions we report results from an additional question in the BSA survey which asks respondents to prioritize spending functions. Respondents were asked which of a number of items of government spending would be their highest priority for extra spending. The items, with the responses in brackets, were: health (44 per cent), education (30.4 per cent), housing (5.5 per cent), police and prisons (5.2 per cent), help for industry (5.1 per cent), social security benefits (4.7 per cent), defence (1.6 per cent), roads (1.4 per cent), transport (1 per cent), others (1.2 per cent). The survey responses show that even when items such as housing and spending on roads are taken into account it is clear that respondents do not class them as high priorities when compared with health and education.

Attitudes to spending across different groups

Individual spending programmes appear to vary considerably in their popularity with the general public. Support for each programme may also differ considerably between individuals, according to their own views as to which particular types of spending would be most beneficial to either themselves or the country as a whole, or some combination of the two. The information on households available in the British Social Attitudes survey then gives us an insight into which spending programmes are popular with which segments of the population and which factors may exert an important influence over the determination of individual attitudes towards each public expenditure programme. In this section we examine how spending priorities vary according to houshold income, gender, housing tenure, political views and age.

We should expect income to have a major influence on people's willingness to pay for expansion of public services. Richer households have greater resources and therefore greater ability to pay. But at the same time they may bear more of any tax increase given the progressive structure of taxes. The affordability of higher quality private substitutes may also be greater for better-off households. The way in which these considerations balance out in determining the correlation between incomes and support for public spending can only be assessed by looking at data. Demographic attributes, like age and the presence of children, will also matter, both through their impact on the likely use of public services and through their effect on the households' other expenses. Other attitudes, including party political affiliation, will also impact on preferences and opinions regarding public spending.

Understanding the complexities of these relationships is important. Any evaluation of the costs and benefits of increasing public spending needs to take account of to whom the perceived advantages accrue and needs to make allowance for the varying circumstances of different groups. Electorally, particular sub-groups may also be of importance so that no political strategist can afford to ignore the distribution of opinion on these matters.

Health

In the 1994 BSA survey, we saw that 88 per cent of respondents wanted higher health spending. This popularity appears to be evenly spread across segments of the population. For example, if we divided respondents into five groups according to their household income, we find that increased health spending is supported by roughly similar proportions of each group. Figure 7.1 splits the BSA sample into approximate income quintiles and shows the percentage in each of the five income groups that would like to see more spending on health. The 'poor' are those with incomes in the bottom 20 per cent. The 'rich' are the top 20 per cent of income earners. Figure 7.1 shows the remarkably flat distribution of attitudes to health spending across the groups.

The uniformity of the support given to increased health spending across different groups of individuals is borne out if we divide the population in other ways. Owner occupiers appear to be just as strongly in favour of increased health

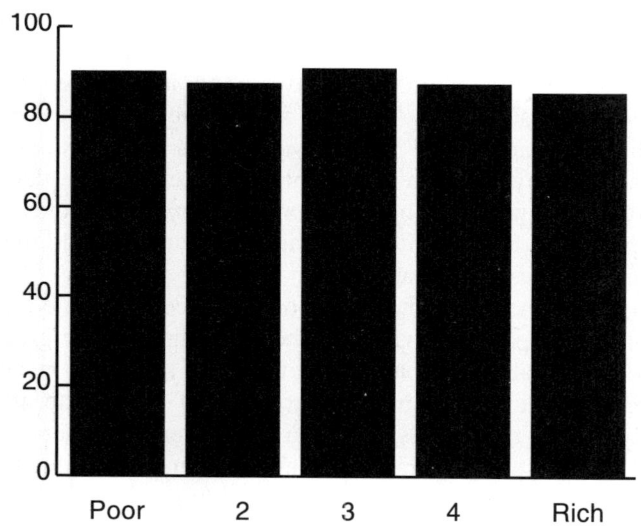

Figure 7.1. Percentage of people who want more spending on health by income quintile. *Source*: BSA Survey (1994).

Table 7.2. Attitudes to increased spending on health by political affiliation (%).

	Conservative	*Liberal*	*Labour*
More spending	77	94	95
Same	21	6	4
Less spending	2	0	1

spending as tenants in public housing. There is also very little variation in attitudes between the sexes and across the age spectrum. Only slightly more women (90 per cent) than men (86 per cent) supported higher health spending and while 93 per cent of young adults under the age of 25 would prefer higher health spending this was also true of 85 per cent of the elderly.

The major source of variation in attitudes towards health spending appears to be related to individual's political views. While hardly any individuals desire lower levels of spending on health, whatever their political affiliation, Table 7.2 shows that those that identified themselves with the Labour Party or the Liberal Democrats were more liable to desire higher health spending than those who identified themselves with the Conservative Party. Even so, 77 per cent of Conservatives still desired more spending in this area.

Education

Education spending also appears to attract support from similar proportions of respondents in different segments of the population. It is very difficult to discern a difference in attitudes to more education spending across the income profile. Figure 7.2 shows low income earners are just as likely to want more spent on education as those in the higher income groups. The same is true across individuals with different types of housing tenure and between males and females.

However, as with health spending attitudes, political attitudes appear to exert some influence on attitudes towards education spending. Labour and Liberal Democrat voters have similar attitudes to education spending with 83 per cent wanting more spending. A majority of Conservative voters also want to see higher levels of spending on education but the majority is smaller at only 65 per cent.

In examining attitudes towards health spending, we saw that there was a slight tendency for the young to be more supportive of spending increases compared with the older generations. This difference is understandably more stark when we consider attitudes to education spending. Table 7.3 below shows the relative support for more education spending across the age groups. It can be seen that support for increased education spending is greater among the under-45 age group, with the lowest levels of support being found among the over-65s.

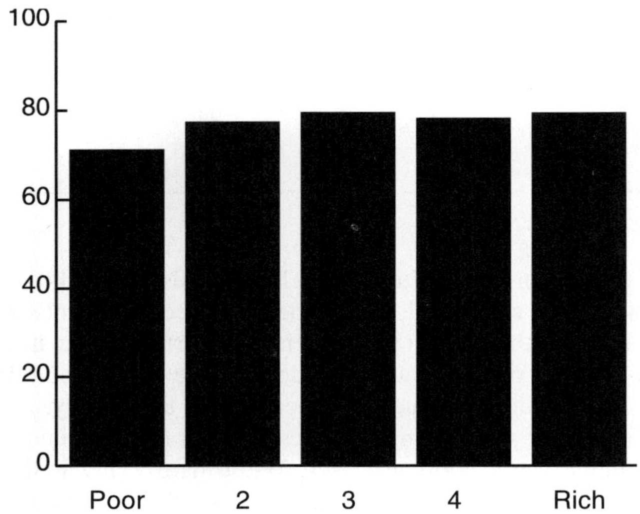

Figure 7.2. Percentage of people who want more spending on education by income quintile.
Source: BSA Survey (1994).

Table 7.3. Attitudes to increased expenditure on education by age (%).

	18–24	*25–34*	*35–44*	*45–54*	*55–64*	*65+*
More spending	84	82	82	72	71	64
Same	15	17	17	26	27	34
Less spending	1	1	1	2	3	3

Social benefits

Pensions

In contrast to the broad consensus among population groups in the support given to higher spending on health and education, different groups in the population appear to have rather distinct attitudes towards pension provision. There is, for instance, a clear divergence in attitudes across the generations, as one would expect. While 65 per cent of young adults wanted to see more money spent on pensions, this proportion increased to 75 per cent of those between the ages of 35 and 65 and reached 80 per cent among those respondents who were aged over 65.

The popularity of higher spending on pensions declines gradually as household income rises (Figure 7.3a). As a result, there is a relatively sharp distinction between the popularity of higher spending on pensions among the richest and poorest quintiles in the sample with the support for higher pensions spending

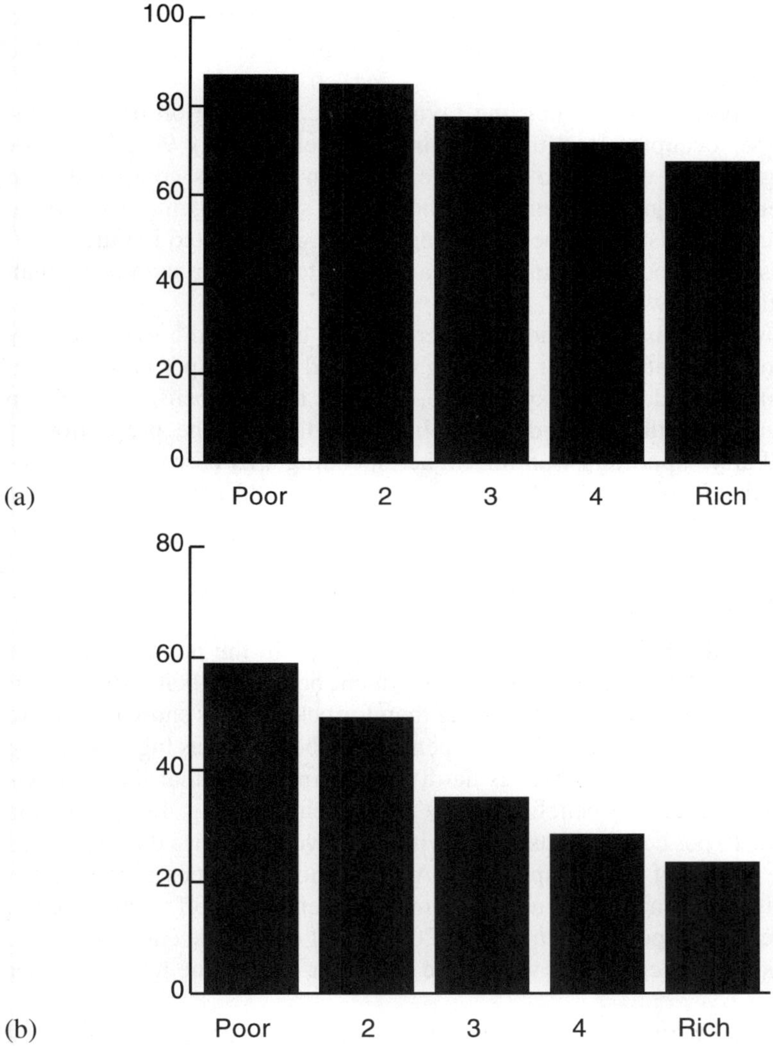

Figure 7.3. Percentage of people who want more spending (a) on pensions, and (b) on benefits, by income quintile.
Source: BSA Survey (1994).

differing by almost 20 percentage points between the richest and poorest groups in the sample (although a majority of each group still support higher spending).

This distinction may, of course, be related to the income levels of those individuals who are retired. While it is certainly not the case that all senior citizens are poor, there is a concentration of the elderly in the lower two income quintiles, and these individuals would benefit directly from higher spending on pensions. In addition, richer households may have access to alternative forms of support in their old age such as company pensions, personal pensions and savings, and hence be less dependent on an adequate level of provision of the basic state pension.

Respondents living in social housing favour public spending on pensions far more than owner occupiers and those renting privately. Nearly 90 per cent of social housing tenants wanted to see more spent on pensions compared with close to 75 per cent owning or renting in the private sector. Again, this may be related to the characteristics of social housing tenants. As reported in Giles *et al.* (1996), tenants in the social housing sector are likely to be older and poorer than in the population as a whole.

Attitudes towards pension spending differ slightly between the sexes. Eighty per cent of women wanted higher spending compared with 75 per cent of men.

As with health and education expenditure, attitudes towards pension provision differed according to the respondent's political affiliation. The proportion of Conservative Party supporters wanting higher spending was 65 per cent, markedly less than the 79 per cent of Liberal Democrats and 85 per cent of Labour supporters who wanted more.

Unemployment benefits

There are similar differences between different groups in the population in the support for increased expenditure on unemployment benefits, albeit with a lower overall level of support for higher spending than for pensions, as shown in Figure 7.3b. As for pensions, support for higher spending on benefits was highest among those on the lowest incomes, which is hardly surprising given that these individuals are the most likely to benefit directly from such spending. Indeed, it was only among the 20 per cent of households with the lowest incomes that there was a majority in favour of higher spending. As household incomes increase, the support for higher spending on unemployment benefit falls off quite rapidly. Only 24 per cent of respondents in the top 20 per cent of income earners wanted to see higher spending compared with close to 60 per cent in the bottom 20 per cent.

Given that tenants in social housing are more likely to be unemployed and on relatively low incomes it is unsurprising that this group has a far greater proportion who would like to see more spent on unemployment benefits. Over 60 per cent of tenants in social housing would like to see more spending, compared to only 30 per cent of owner occupiers. There is some gender difference with 40 per cent of women prefering higher spending compared to 35 per cent of men. Across the age groups, there was a relatively higher level of support for higher spending among individuals below the age of 35, the group which is most likely to benefit directly from such spending, than among older age groups.

Unsurprisingly there are very different attitudes when political affiliation is considered, although in this case the attitudes of supporters of the Liberal Democrats are far more attuned to those of Conservative supporters than to

Labour supporters. This is in contrast to the pattern of attitudes towards health and education spending. While 54 per cent of Labour supporters are keen to see higher spending on unemployment benefits, this is true of only 15 per cent of Liberal Democrat supporters, broadly the same proportion as among Conservative supporters.

Military and defence spending

Support for higher levels of defence expenditure is much higher among the lowest two quintiles in the income distribution than among richer households, as shown in Figure 7.4. While nearly 32 per cent of respondents in the bottom quintile of the income distribution supported higher spending, this falls to less than 15 per cent in the top income group. This pattern is also reflected across the tenure types. Thirty per cent of respondents in social housing wanted to see higher defence spending compared with 19 per cent of owner occupiers. There was little difference between the attitudes of men and women.

Somewhat surprisingly, there was very little difference in attitudes towards higher defence spending between Labour and Conservative supporters (both close to 24 per cent), although only 18 per cent of Liberal Democrats supported higher expenditure. Attitudes to defence spending across the age groups differed substantially. Table 7.4 shows that only 8 per cent of those between the ages of 18 and 24 want to see more spent on defence. Those in the older age groups are

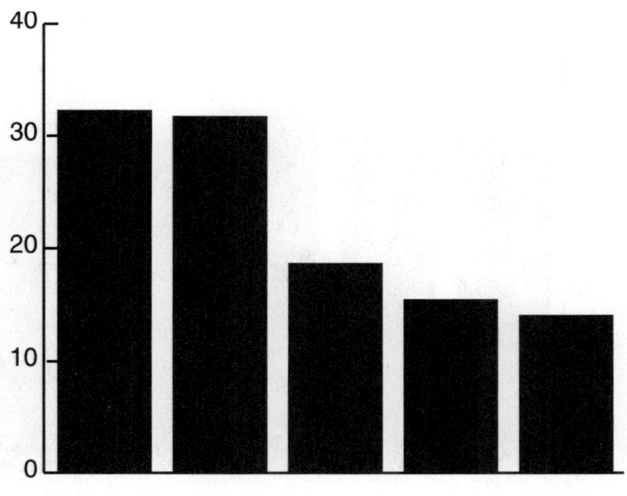

Figure 7.4. Percentage of people who want more spending on defence by income quintile.
Source: BSA Survey (1994).

Table 7.4. Attitudes towards spending on the military and defence by age (%).

	18–24	*25–34*	*35–44*	*45–54*	*55–64*	*65+*
More spending	8	16	15	21	30	36
Same	52	47	46	51	46	45
Less spending	39	37	39	27	24	18

much more favourable to defence spending, although none of the age groups have a majority in favour of higher defence spending.

The police and law enforcement

Support for higher levels of expenditure on the police and law enforcement was spread fairly evenly across respondents grouped by income, with roughly 75 per cent of individuals in each income quintile expressing a preference for higher expenditure (Figure 7.5). Attitudes to spending were also remarkably similar when individuals were grouped according to their housing tenure or political affiliation. Higher spending on law and order was supported by 77 per cent of Conservative supporters, 75 per cent of Labour supporters and 74 per cent of Liberal Democrat supporters.

By contrast, there is a clear divergence of attitudes towards spending on law and order between the generations. Older respondents are far more likely to support spending increases than younger respondents, as shown in Table 7.5.

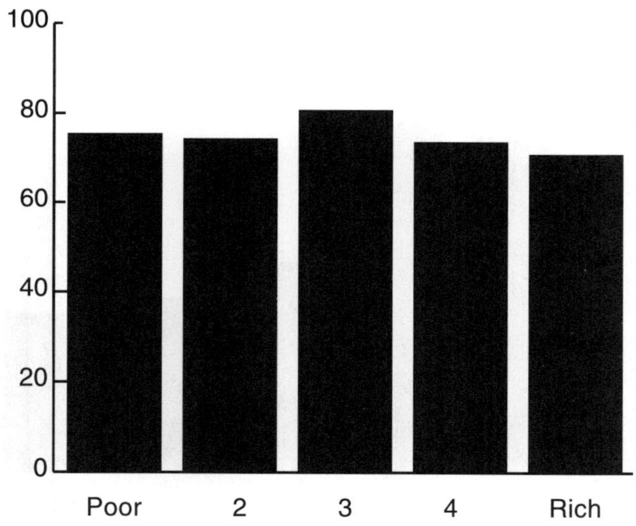

Figure 7.5. Percentage of people who want more spending on law and order by income quintile.
Source: BSA Survey (1994).

Table 7.5. Attitudes to expenditure on the police and law enforcement by age (%).

	18–24	*25–34*	*35–44*	*45–54*	*55–64*	*65+*
More spending	65	71	69	76	78	83
Same	31	26	28	23	21	17
Less spending	4	2	3	1	1	0

The environment

While spending on the environment was relatively popular among respondents to the 1994 British Social Attitudes survey, an interesting pattern emerges once we group respondents according to their household incomes. As shown by Figure 7.6, support for higher spending on the environment is greatest among those in the highest income quintile and those in the lowest income quintile. It is least among the middle income quintile.

The popularity of higher spending on the environment varies according to gender, age and political affiliation. While 55 per cent of men claimed they wanted more environmental spending, this was true of only 48 per cent of women. Clear political differences also emerged with 57 per cent of both Labour and Liberal Democrat supporters favouring higher expenditure, compared to only 46 per cent of Conservative supporters. Young people are also more likely to favour higher environmental spending, with a majority of those between the

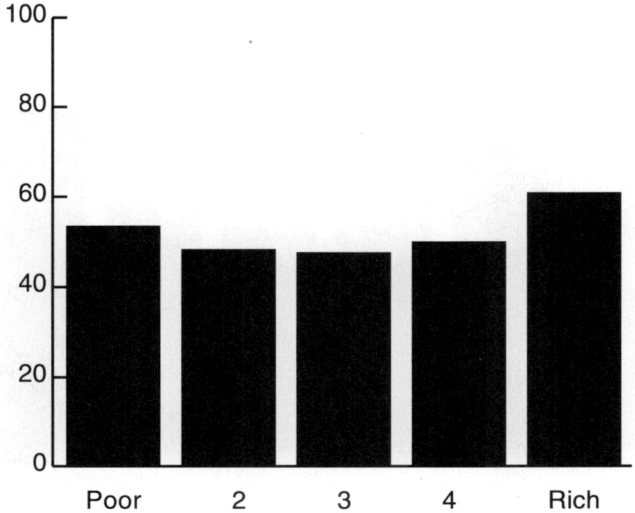

Figure 7.6. Percentage of people who want more spending on the environment by income quintile.
Source: BSA Survey (1994).

ages of 18 and 55 favouring higher spending compared to only 40 per cent of the over-65s.

Culture and the arts

While no particular groups in the population appear to be strongly in favour of higher spending on culture and the arts, this spending programme is less unpopular among some groups of respondents than others. A complex relationship appears to exist between attitudes to cultural spending and household income. As with spending on the environment, it is those in the lowest and highest income quintiles who are most supportive of higher spending on culture, although even among those with the highest incomes, less than 20 per cent of respondents support higher levels of expenditure, as shown in Figure 7.7.

Once respondents are grouped according to their housing tenure, it appears that tenants in the private rented sector are more disposed towards this type of spending than other groups, although even within this group, spending increases are only supported by 25 per cent of respondents. While attitudes to cultural spending do not appear to vary much between men and women, Labour supporters are more likely to favour higher spending than their Conservative or Liberal Democrat counterparts. The pattern of attitudes across the age profile is particularly uneven, as shown in Table 7.6.

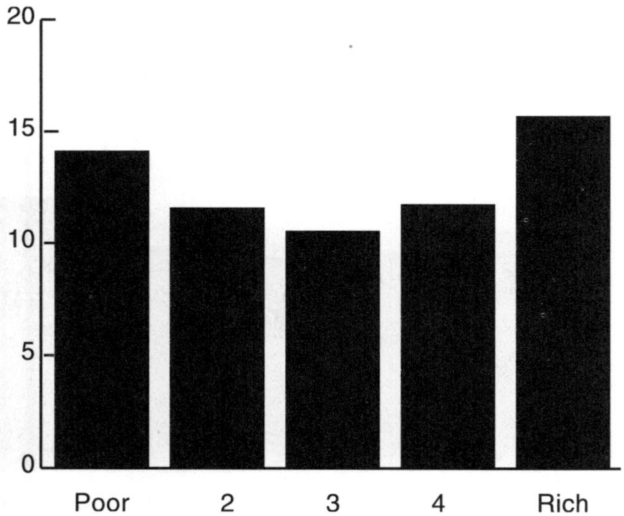

Figure 7.7. Percentage of people who want more spending on culture and the arts by income quintile.
Source: BSA Survey (1994).

Table 7.6. Attitudes towards expenditure on culture and the arts by age (%).

	18–24	*25–34*	*35–44*	*45–54*	*55–64*	*65+*
More spending	14	11	15	10	17	10
Same	39	44	46	45	41	47
Less spending	47	44	39	45	42	43

Private sector provision and attitudes to public spending

One of the factors which might influence individual attitudes towards public spending is whether the individual concerned is likely to benefit directly from the provision of the service. Individuals may fail to benefit directly from public services for at least two reasons. First, the service may not be available to the individuals. We would not, for example, expect those aged over 65 to derive very much direct benefit from more education spending. Second, although the service may be available, the individual may choose to use a private sector alternative. There are many examples of private alternatives to public sector provision such as private medical insurance, private schools and private pensions.

We will focus briefly on the impact which the take-up of private medical insurance may have on the demand for public expenditure on health care, borrowing from work by Besley, Hall and Preston (1996). The coverage of private medical insurance grew throughout the 1980s and after a period of stability in the early 1990s seems to have increased again recently. In 1994, 15.4 per cent of the BSA sample responded that they were covered by a private health insurance scheme such as those provided by BUPA and PPP, which allows them to obtain private medical treatment. Of these privately insured households just over half have bought the insurance policy themselves, while the rest have had most of the insurance premiums paid for by their employer.

Among all respondents taken together, we argued above that there was a broad consensus of support for higher public expenditure on the National Health Service, despite significant real increases in health expenditure throughout the 1980s and 1990s. One very interesting question for public policy is whether such high levels of support for public spending on health care can be sustained if a large number of individuals make alternative private arrangements. In other words, is the growth of the private sector likely to undermine support for the National Health Service?

Table 7.7, from Besley, Hall and Preston (1996), compares the percentage of respondents who support higher expenditure on health care between those individuals who have made alternative private arrangements and those who are solely reliant on the NHS.[2] The great majority of individuals, whether insured or not, would like to see public health spending increased. This is perhaps not surprising since the private sector typically only provides a limited range of services, even those individuals with private insurance rely on the NHS for the provision of some of their health care needs, such as accident and emergency

Table 7.7. Public spending attitudes to health spending: those with and without private insurance (%).

	More	*Same or less*
Uninsured	91.3	8.7
Insured	85.1	14.9

Table 7.8. Public spending priorities: those with and without private insurance (%).

	Regard health as top priority	*Same regard health as lesser priority*
Uninsured	54.2	45.8
Insured	47.6	52.4

treatment. In addition, those with private insurance are also likely to have friends or family whom they care about who rely on the NHS for medical treatment. Despite this, those respondents with private medical insurance do show a greater tendency than the uninsured to want no increase in health spending, and this difference is significant in a statistical sense.

We can obtain additional information on this issue by using a question in the British Social Attitudes survey which asks respondents to specify their top two priorities for public spending. Table 7.8 indicates that while there is not an enormous difference between the attitudes of those with and without private health insurance, those with private coverage are less likely to prioritize health spending as compared to alternative public spending programmes.

Conclusions

There appears to be a broad measure of support for higher levels of public expenditure on some of the core services of the Welfare State such as health, education and pensions expenditure, although the lack of a clear link in the question asked between increased spending and the personal tax consequences for the individual is a major cause for concern.

We have, however, identified large differences in the relative popularity of the various government spending programmes. Higher spending on some other programmes such as culture and the arts is far less popular and attitudes diverge between different groups of individuals. Different income, age, gender and political groups often have distinct attitudes towards individual spending programmes.

One additional source of divergence in individual attitudes towards health spending is whether the individual respondent is covered by private medical insurance. Those individuals with some form of private medical cover are less likely to prioritize health care spending, although the difference is not large.

This information poses new problems and questions for public expenditure policy. It is important that in analysing attitutes to public spending the information is disaggregated to try and understand exactly what is going on. In that way better decision making is likely to result.

Notes

1. This chapter draws on research funded by the Economic and Social Research Council under the Economic Beliefs and Behaviour Programme (grant no. L122521004). We are grateful to Social and Community Planning Research and to the ESRC Data Archive for access to British Social Attitudes survey data. The authors are also grateful to Mark Stanfield for research assistance.
2. Since this and Table 7.8 are calculated from different years of data to that used in the rest of this chapter the proportions do not match exactly those in other tables.

References

Besley, T., Hall, J. and Preston, I. (1996). *Private Health Insurance and the State of the NHS, Commentary No 52*. London: IFS.

Bosanquet, N. (1986). 'Interim report: Public spending and the welfare state'. In: Jowell, R., Witherspoon, S. and Brook, L. (eds), *British Social Attitudes: the 1986 Report*. Dartmouth: Aldershot.

Giles, C., Johnson, P., McCrae, J. and Taylor, J. (1996). *Living with the State: The Incomes and Work Incentives of Tenants in the Social Rented Sector*. London: IFS.

Lipsey, D. (1994). 'Do we really want more public spending?' In: Jowell, R., Curtice, J., Brook, L. and Arendt, D. (eds), *British Social Attitudes: the 11th Report*.

Taylor-Gooby, P. (1991). 'Attachment to the welfare state'. In: Jowell, R., Brook, L. and Taylor, B. (eds), *British Social Attitudes: the 8th Report*.

Taylor-Gooby, P. (1995). 'Comfortable, marginal and excluded: Who should pay higher taxes for a better welfare state?' In: Jowell, R., Curtice, J., Park, A., Brook, L. and Arendt, D. (eds), *British Social Attitudes: the 12th Report*.

8

Finding Out What People Want from Public Services

Martin Cave

Contents

The benefits generated by public spending depend, crucially, on matching the quality of the goods or services produced to need or demand. This is true both of a marketed sector such as transport, as well as of non-marketed services such as the bulk of education and health. Traditionally, however, debates about the nature or quality of the service have taken second place to how much should be produced and how it should be allocated. The nature of the service itself has usually been left to the supplier.

A similar situation prevailed in the utilities before privatization. Complaints about poor quality were rife, but managers were not much concerned since customers had little or no leverage. Much of this changed after privatization for a number of reasons. Customers became more demanding of unpopular and highly profitable investor-owned firms, some companies were subject to competition and regulators, aware that the form of price of control chosen gave firms an incentive to degrade quality, increasingly focused their efforts on the problem. As a result, quality of service generally improved (Rovizzi and Thompson, 1995). Moreover, some utilities discovered that certain improvements could be made relatively costlessly through better management and a clearer customer focus.

It has not proved easy to tackle issues of quality in the public sector. The present government has attempted to specify quality targets, and has published reports on their attainment through, for example, the Citizen's Charter. Critics of such charters claim that these have been captured by the suppliers, who set targets to suit themselves. Others argue that charters are simply a means of facilitating further cost reductions in the public sector. Objective analysis of the effects of the charters is too sparse for any conclusive judgements to be made.

But there can be no doubt that, explicitly or implicitly, choices have to be made about the quality of public sector output. In the case of non-marketed services such as health or education, quality decisions directly affect us all not least because we pay for them. Levels of quality of many of the marketed services, such as transport, also involve public considerations albeit different ones. For example, while passengers might be able to get a more comfortable seat by paying more, they experience the same timetable on a route as all other travellers. Some collective decision-taking process is needed here as well.

Here, we are concerned mainly with how standards of quality in the public sector should be set. This question has numerous dimensions and we focus on two. First, whose preferences should legitimately be taken into account in determining quality? Second, how can the views or preferences of the relevant parties be discovered so that rational choices on quality can be made? We shall argue that a clear and consistent approach to the choice of quality in the public sector, which takes account of the inevitable trade-offs between public and private spending and between quality and quantity, can yield considerable social benefits. Since quality (in its many dimensions) is an important element of any service, this is referred to as the 'quality' issue, even though other attributes of public services are also covered.

The first part of the chapter considers the question of whose preferences should count. We go on to describe methods used to gather views on quality that are based on consumer satisfaction surveys. An alternative method, the stated preferences approach, is now increasingly being used to elicit consumers' views and we describe its use and potential across a range of public services.

Whose preferences should count?

Even before 'stakeholding' entered the currency of general political debate, the term was widely used in relation to the assessment of standards of quality in the public sector. Here, there are two relevant questions: who should define quality, and who should assess it once it has been defined? (The discussion that follows draws heavily on the contribution by Pollitt to Cave *et al.* (1993)). Opinions as to who should be involved in the decision-making are subject both to shifts of fashion and to subtle changes in public and political opinion. The issue is unmistakably a normative one and is often very complex.

Nowadays, a frequent reply to both of the above questions is to say that all major stakeholders – defined as all those individuals or bodies inside or outside an organization who are directly affected by what the organization does – should have the opportunity of expressing their views. To be 'directly affected' means that one has an interest in the outcomes of the organization's activities.

While interests may be obvious to all concerned, they may sometimes be concealed or even suppressed. Williamson (1992) is one of several writers to have produced a classification of interests which expresses these possibilities. Thus, she distinguishes between:

- *apparent interests* which are readily apparent to service users and which are also consonant with the wishes of service providers;
- *'inapparent' interests* which may not be apparent to users, but are in the providers' interests to explain/bring to their attention;
- *oppressed interests* which, though apparent to service users, are inconvenient or threatening to providers, who either ignore or reject them (for example, waking times on hospital wards, where patients are all awoken at the same early hour, more for the convenience of ward staff than of many patients);
- *suppressed interests* which are not apparent to users and are not in providers' interests either. They are hard to get on anyone's agenda and may lie dormant for long periods of time.

Political theorists have been especially concerned with the notion of suppressed interests. A controversy has long raged as to whether it is acceptable for observers to claim to be able to identify interests of which the 'holders' are themselves unaware. An argument originally developed by Barry and elaborated by Dowding (1991) runs approximately as follows:

1. To have an interest means much more than to have a preference or desire for something. In order to satisfy our desires we may need certain prerequisites, but may not always be aware of these prerequisites (needs).
2. Many interests are dependent, not only on the consumers' desires, but also on factors that are external to the individual. Thus, once individuals' desires are known, others may be able to calculate what is in their interests as well, or even better, than the individuals themselves.
3. Even studying the behaviour of individuals ('revealed preferences') is not by itself sufficient to identify their interests, since behaviour is shaped by the choice available, as well as by desires and preferences.

There are at least four implications of the above for stakeholder analysis. First, citizens may have an interest in a particular public service without realizing it – in other words, services may have 'unconscious stakeholders'. Second, the expression (or lack of expression) of preferences/desires by consumers may provide vital data, but these cannot be assumed to indicate fully those consumers' interests. Third, there is a need to take close account of the circumstances under which preferences and trade-offs are elicited. Fourth, there are likely to be some circumstances where consumers' interests are difficult to discover, not only because these are not readily apparent to the consumers themselves, but providers may have little reason to search for them.

Despite these complications, most of the management literature, both public sector and private, seems to take a fairly brisk, no-nonsense approach to the identification of stakeholders. For the private firm, for example, the list usually begins with shareholders, employees, customers and suppliers. These are sometimes referred to as the primary stakeholders. Beyond these lie a more varied and shifting collection of secondary stakeholders, which may include government agencies, consumer groups, residents in the neighbourhood of a firm's factories and so on.

Similar lists have been produced for public sector organizations. They usually include actual or potential customers, indirect beneficiaries and others – citizens, taxpayers and so on. Neither the private sector nor the public sector literature has developed any specific technique or method for identifying stakeholders other than the very general procedure suggested above – in other words, to try to think of every group that has an identifiable interest in the service.

Even if it were to be decided, for the purpose of quality valuation, to take a narrow definition of stakeholders, and to confine attention to customers only, there would still be choices to be made in identifying the relevant population. In the case of most public services, there are at least four possible answers to the question 'who are our customers?':

- those who are actually receiving the service now;
- those who are known to be waiting for the service;
- those believed by professionals or others to need the service (in other words, in whose interests it would be to have the service) but who are not currently seeking it;
- those who might need the service in the future.

It is evident from this brief review that the identification of stakeholders inevitably entails judgements about the existence and relative strengths of the interests of what is potentially a large population of groups. There appears to be no technical shortcut. Indeed, there are strong reasons why stakeholder identification should itself be regarded as a complex and value-laden decision, appropriate to political and senior management levels. In approaching the issue, decision makers will need to consider the following:

- whether to pay attention only to articulated interests, or to try also to identify and take account of 'inapparent', oppressed and suppressed interests;
- whether to exclude 'secondary' interests;
- whether to exclude 'internal' interests;
- how extensive a definition of 'consumers' to adopt.

Everyone has his or her own views about how widely to cast the stakeholder net in connection with decisions on public services. In major issues, such as the overall level of public spending, the role of citizens and taxpayers is likely to be of key importance. However, as the decision narrows, the weight attached to such views should diminish, while the weight given to consumers increases. For example, the amount of subsidy to a public transport system is a decision which affects most people, including taxpayers as well as victims of traffic congestion and pollution. However, the details of the timetable can be left to the preferences of actual and potential users.

There still remains, however, the problem of information and misapprehension of interests. The former is likely to limit the range of issues in which consumers' preferences can be elicited. Thus, it would not be usual for patients to make judgements about appropriate medical interventions. The issue is complicated because even well-informed individuals may not fully understand their own interests. This argument is sometimes used in discussions of broadcasting, for example, where it is asserted that people's viewing helps form their tastes. As a result, what they like now does not matter, as their tastes could be changed by a different diet of programmes. Although this qualification may be appropriate in certain contexts, it is not a satisfactory reason why stated or revealed preferences should be ignored.

Preferences should count in relation to public sector output even though it is a complicated process. Furthermore, as the scope of the decision narrows, the weight attached to the potential users expands. In the inevitably detailed decisions about the quality of public services, there is a good basis for considering consumers' views (if they are willing to give them). We go on to consider how this might best be achieved.

Alternative methods of assessing quality

The private sector has developed a variety of market research methods for eliciting information about consumers' attitudes towards goods or services. At a general level, several of the techniques are concerned with identifying deficiencies in service quality, defined as the gap between customers' perceptions of performance and their expectations. An example of such a technique is an instrument known as SERVQUAL developed by Parasuraman and colleagues (1988). This is designed to be applicable across a broad range of service industries. The basic premise is that whatever the customer thinks is important, is important.

The notion of gaps between perceptions and expectations is also implicit in a technique widely used in the public sector. This seeks to classify quality attributes in two dimensions: importance (do the customers think that the attribute in question is important) and deficiency (do the customers think that performance is deficient in any respect?)

The Benefits Agency, for example, has conducted a national customer survey along those lines for several years. Users of benefits who have visited their local Benefits Agency office during the previous 12 months are asked how much they agree or disagree (on a five-point balance scale) with 19 statements that describe various aspects of the office and staff. Claimants are than asked to rate the importance of each of the statements. In the 1991 survey, only 31 per cent of respondents agreed that the office was pleasantly decorated, while only 23 per cent said that this was very important. On the other hand, 82 per cent asserted that it was important that staff seemed knowledgeable, and 71 per cent agreed that they were knowledgeable (Benefits Agency, 1992).

Similar surveys have been developed for the National Health Service. For example, a questionnaire developed by Thompson (1993) offers patients a choice of alternative responses that relate to particular aspects of their care. The responses are processed to provide a measure of satisfaction across a range of quality dimensions, chosen because they reflect what patients report are pertinent aspects of their care. The questionnaire for acute in-patients contained some 280 items for self-completion by recently discharged patients, leading respondents through a logical progression from pre-admission, admission, the residential phase, to discharge and after-care.

Studies of this kind have not escaped criticism. Carr-Hill (1992), after a review of some 300 patient satisfaction surveys, concluded that the majority are producer-led: 'Once the fieldwork is over, there is considerable temptation to forget that what are confidently described as respondents' views are only their replies to questions devised by the researcher and not necessarily the patient's own views and priorities. Thus it is commonplace to observe that health service policy has been steered by providers' perceptions and definitions of good practice' (p. 245).

Even if ways can be found to overcome these problems, it is a major defect of consumer satisfaction surveys that, while they are helpful in identifying gaps and in producing fairly crude measures of importance, they fail to provide comparative valuations of specified changes in quality attributes. The next section considers an alternative method which does provide such valuations.

The stated preference approach

This approach involves the use of hypothetical questions to elicit respondents' valuations from the statements, rather than from observed or revealed behaviour. The approach includes contingent valuation and the market research technique known as conjoint analysis. A number of stages are involved in the process, involving qualitative research, experimental and fieldwork design, fieldwork and analysis.

Qualitative research is undertaken to determine the most relevant attributes to be considered as part of the trade-off; to find the levels of those attributes which respondents are able to identify with, and to trade-off against levels of other attributes. The qualitative research usually involves in-depth interviews with a relatively small sample, and is undertaken by highly skilled interviewers.

Experimental and fieldwork design begins with the selection of the attributes to be traded and the number of levels for each attribute. This is followed by the choice of an experimental design, which determines the combinations of attributes and levels to be presented to ensure that the maximum information can be obtained from the trade-off decisions. Careful choice of experimental design and of the values to represent each level facilitates the investigation of issues such as interactions between attributes. If, for example, all interactions were thought likely to be significant in a case where we were considering three attributes each at three levels, it would be necessary to produce a design which involved $3 \times 3 \times 3 = 27$ different combinations. However, if the third order interactions and the second order interactions were not considered to be of real importance, it would be possible to produce a design in which only nine combinations need be considered. The choice of design and of values to represent each of the levels is usually tested, by means of simulation, to ensure that the anticipated range of trade-off valuations can be recovered in the analysis. Investigation of non-linearity requires the consideration of an increased number of levels for the attributes of interest.

Once the experimental design has been determined, the form of presentation must be decided. There are a number of different methods of presentation: choosing one of a pair, ranking between three and nine options, and rating (usually) up to four options, where the rating itself may be on either a semantic scale ('poor, satisfactory, good') or a numeric scale (1–5).

In addition to the experimental design, it will be necessary to prepare an appropriate questionnaire, with suitable introductory material and illustrations to ensure that respondents are able to understand the issues fully. It will also be necessary to design the fieldwork itself, in terms of defining the relevant population to be considered, the potential stratifications within that population, the sample to be drawn, efficient methods of contact and of interviewing, and finally the expansion process. In particular, the sample size must be identified, usually built up from the need for at least 50 respondents in each of the stratifications for which separate valuations are expected or are required. The precise sample size required per stratification is determined by the method of presentation, which determines the amount of information obtained from each individual.

The *fieldwork* itself can be conducted with paper questionnaires, often using cards to present the trade-off options. Increasingly, however, there is a move towards the use of computer-assisted personal interviewing (CAP), which provides the potential for the values presented to be customized to the individual respondent's circumstances. The computer-based approach may also be used to undertake adaptive stated preferences, in which the values to be considered in a trade-off are determined by the response to a previous trade-off, such that the process is able to 'home-in' on the respondent's valuations.

The analysis of the responses consists of the estimation of coefficients in a utility function, which represents the relative contributions of the individual attributes to the overall utility of the good of service considered. The precise method of analysis is determined, in part, by the method of presentation. The analysis may be undertaken either at the individual level, since the number of responses per respondent is usually sufficient to allow estimation of coefficients, albeit with limited accuracy, or by pooling the responses derived for a stratification of the sample.

This method has been used extensively by market researchers for a range of products. The areas that it has been used in the public services are transport (see MVA (1992) and Jakubiak *et al.* (1990)) and, more recently, the quality of service provided by public utilities. Market research has also been carried out over the past ten years for London Underground Ltd (LUL) into passengers' perceptions of stations, trains and general aspects of the service. The most robust estimates from this work have been summarized (LUL, 1992); they are based upon a series of stated preference questionnaires conducted over a number of years by LUL consultants.

Transport

Table 8.1, adapted from the reports, summarizes passengers' valuations of attributes relating to the experience of the train itself. The table shows the percentage increase in in-vehicle travel time which passengers would be willing to incur if the quality of service improved in the way indicated. Thus an improvement in internal cleanliness from very poor to very good is regarded as compensating for a 7.2 per cent increase in travel time. On a 20 minute journey this represents 1.44 minutes of passenger time or (given the estimated value of time) of 7.82 pence per minute per journey. If 20 million passenger journeys of this length are undertaken on a line each year, the total loss is £2.25 million.

The stated preference alternatives are often formulated in terms of trade-off between other quality attributes and travel time. The use of a conventional non-monetary numeraire may improve the intelligibility of the questions and produce more accurate responses in the valuation of politically sensitive services that are currently provided free of charge.

The proliferation of stated preference research in the transport field and the reported convergence of results suggests that the method has proved its potential, but still has scope for improvement. The MVA report noted above concludes:

Table 8.1. Valuation of changes in train characteristics.

	Very poor	*Poor*	*Fair*	*Good*	*Very good*
Improvement of existing equipment/service	1	2	3	4	5
Cleanliness (Internal)	7.2	5.4	3.6	1.8	0
Graffiti	3.6	2.7	1.8	0.9	0
Heating	6.7	5.0	3.3	1.6	0
Lighting	5.2	3.9	2.6	1.3	0
Noise	4.8	3.6	2.4	1.2	0
Seating comfort	8.3	6.2	4.1	2.0	0

Note: Units are percentages of the time cost of a journey.
Source: LUL (1992), p. 4.

> Stated preference methods have made good progress in the area of 'the quality of a journey'. We are conscious that much remains to be done in the area of presentation, realism and separation of effects. It appears most likely that further concentration on stated preference methods may enable such improvements to be made.

Other public utilities

Regulators in the energy, telecommunications and water sectors are obliged by law to set individual and overall standards of performance for quality of service. The specification of these standards has been the subject of public consultation in many industries. Quality is of particular importance in the water industry, where improvements in quality to meet rising environmental standards run the risk of imposing enormous additional costs on the water companies. For this reason, it is vital to link such standards to households' valuations of improvements.

In the 1994 water price control review, the water regulator, OFWAT, told the companies that it expected their business plans to contain provisions for gauging the strength of consumers' demand for higher standards, and some of them used contingent valuation methods. In addition, the water regulator OFWAT commissioned research into households' willingness to pay for an improvement in the taste of tap water, for reductions in the risk of a hosepipe ban and for reductions in the risk of their homes being flooded by sewage (Tunstall *et al.*, 1993). Analysis showed that willingness to pay was linked both to income and to policy views: those who disapproved of water privatization were prepared to pay less.

Health services

Judgements on the quality of health services may be divided into those relating to structure (the setting in which medical care takes place), process (medical procedure) and outcomes (for example, recovery rates and restoration of function). In recent years, evaluation of healthcare outcomes has relied extensively on a form of stated preference leading to estimation of 'quality adjusted life years' (QALYs). Expected life years from a treatment are adjusted for quality using respondents' valuations of the health states, variously described and classified, usually relative to death or to full or normal health. The relative values of health states are elicited through various techniques, including the standard gamble and time trade-off.

In the standard gamble approach, individuals are presented with a situation in which they must choose between a certain outcome or a gamble which might result in either a better or a worse outcome. The probabilities of the better and worse outcomes are then varied until the individual is indifferent between the certain outcome and the gamble. This probability is a measure of the utility of the certain outcome. With the time trade-off technique, individuals are presented with a comparison between living for a period in a specified but imperfect state versus having a healthier life for a shorter period. The shorter period is then varied until the respondent is indifferent between the alternatives. The utility score of the imperfect health state is then given by the ratio of the shorter to the longer periods.

The alternative willingness-to-pay method elicits information on valuations by pushing individuals to consider the maximum amount of money they are willing to pay for a given outcome. They are either asked directly, or shown a number of possible values on a card and asked to circle the amount which represents the maximum they would be willing to pay. Responses of this kind are, of course, likely to be income-related. They may also be coloured by the respondent's views on the appropriate financial structure for the delivery of health care and embody strategic responses.

More recently, greater attention has been paid to evaluating the process of delivering health care, or the quality of delivery. For example, Propper (1991, 1992) examined willingness to pay for an attribute of the delivery of a service, rather than the ultimate effectiveness of that service. The hypothetical context was specified as follows:

> The respondent was asked to imagine that he/she had a medical condition which required an operation. Prior to this operation (implicitly the only treatment possible) the respondent would not be able to perform his/her normal activities, would have to take a specified amount of time away from work or from household duties and would experience fairly constant pain. The condition would not deteriorate during a wait, but neither would it improve. Once the operation was performed, the respondent's health would return to normal. It was assumed that respondents would view this situation as associated with minimum anxiety over the possibility of deterioration of health status during the wait.
>
> (Propper, 1992, p. 13).

Each replication consisted of three variables: a cost (varying from £50 to £800), a waiting time (varying from two to 12 months) and uncertainty, which has a value of one if the exact admission date is not known and of zero otherwise.

The study was designed to investigate whether individual preferences exhibited a threshold effect – in particular, whether once high values of costs had been reached, alternatives were rated entirely in terms of their money values rather than all their attributes. Propper also asked so-called 'transfer price' questions. These involve asking the individual the amount by which the cost of one option would have to be varied to make an individual indifferent between it and another pre-defined option. Propper's study found that the average value to a demander of health care of a reduction of one month's time spent on a waiting list for a non-urgent medical intervention was of the order of £40 in 1987 prices.

More significantly, the Propper study provided some evidence of the usefulness of contingent valuation experiments to estimate the value of unpriced services in sensitive areas of the public sector such as health care where there is strong political belief in 'free' provision. She concludes

> . . . the results can perhaps provide some support for the use of contingent valuations. Respondents appeared able to make trade-offs between waiting time and cost . . . Some non-trading by certain respondents did occur. If this is essentially due to

> lack of income (the absolute values of costs being too high for low income respondents), it could be overcome by the use of different replications for respondents with different incomes . . . However, if the non-trading reflects a non-willingness to trade because of a political belief in 'free' health care, the problem must be tackled in another way.

Another recent study by Ryan and Farrar (1994) applied a similar technique to estimate marginal rates of substitution between delivery attributes without including price as one of the variables. This study dealt with preferences with regard to the location of treatment and waiting time in the provision of orthodontic services. Three attributes were the location of the first appointment, the location of subsequent appointments, and waiting time. The authors concluded that the location of the first appointment was not significant, while location of subsequent appointments was. Waiting time was also found to be significant. The researchers were able explicitly to calculate marginal rates of substitution among the attributes. Thus, it was estimated that individuals were willing to wait an extra six days to have their first appointment at a local clinic, and an extra 19 days to have their second appointment at a local clinic.

In a comprehensive review of the application of conjoint analysis to healthcare decision making, Ryan (1996) concluded that the stated preference approach used in relation to health care

> overcomes the limitations of the techniques that are currently used to elicit community values (opinion polls and satisfaction surveys) since it provides information on intensity of preferences . . ., can be designed to reflect specific choices facing health boards/authorities (via the design of the study), addresses realistic scales of change . . ., and involves the crucial notion of opportunity cost (via the discrete choice questions which are posed where individuals have to sacrifice one level of an attribute to achieve an increase in another).

Higher education

The stated preference approach could also be applied to higher education, where it would be possible to draw a distinction between the content of the curriculum and the manner of its delivery. Potential students are unlikely to be expert at judging the appropriate content, although past students are likely to have expertise in this regard, and are increasingly consulted some years after graduation on which parts of their education they have found particularly useful. However, current students are likely to be well placed to offer opinions about attributes of delivery. These are likely to include such variables as the experience of the lecturer, the number of students in seminar groups, the frequency of lectures and seminars, the speed with which work for assessment is returned, the availability of lecture notes or readers, and so on.

Moreover, it is comparatively simple, using a model of the costs of higher education provision, to establish the marginal costs of varying the form in which courses are delivered. It should be possible, within a given budget, to maximize the utility derived by students from the form of delivery of their courses. An exploratory study of this kind is in progress at Brunel University.

Conclusions

We have argued here that a relatively simple and direct method may enable us to improve the returns to expenditure on public services. Clearly, fundamental decisions about overall levels of expenditure on public services and the distribution of expenditure among major programmes will need to be made through the political process. These types of decisions will need to take into account the interests of all the relevant stakeholders. However, more detailed decisions on, for example, the way in which services are delivered, should take account of consumers' opinions. If there is to be continued support for publicly provided services, it will be essential to deliver the kinds of services that people value most highly.

As we discussed, a simple, questionnaire approach is useful in eliciting consumer satisfaction. However, questionnaires do not generate sufficiently detailed information about consumers' trade-off among quality attributes or between quality and quantity. Useful information of this kind can be provided by using the 'stated preference' approach. This is already in wide use in the transport sector and, increasingly, in health services. It could also be used with success for other public services.

The idea of 'learning from the people' in the field of public services should appeal to all political parties, including New Labour. Many of the public sector reforms of the past ten years have involved the use of quasi-markets, in which purchasers act as proxies for consumers when they deal with providers. The approach proposed here is fully consistent with quasi-markets, if information about consumer preferences is used by purchasers to help them in their decision-making. Information about consumer preferences could also be made available directly to providers. In this latter case, providers' autonomy would be affected, a problem which has to be faced. However, knowledge of consumers' trade-offs is a necessary, if not a sufficient, condition for rational decision-making in the public sector.

References

Benefits Agency (1992). *The Benefits Agency National Customer Survey*. London: HMSO.

Carr-Hill, R. (1992). 'The measurement of patient satisfaction', *Journal of Public Health Medicine*, **14**(3): 236–49.

Cave, M. *et al.* (1993). *Valuation of Changes in Quality in the Public Services*, Report to HM Treasury. London: HMSO.

Cave, M., Copley, G. and Hanney, S. (1995). 'Setting quality standards in the public sector: Some principles and an application', *Public Money and Management*, **15**(1): 19–34.

CEPPP (1992). *Considering Quality: An Analytical Guide to the Literature on Quality and Standards in the Public Services*. Uxbridge: Centre for the Evaluation of Public Policy and Practice, Brunel University.

Dowding, K. (1991). *Rational Choice and Political Power*. Aldershot: Edward Elgar.

Harwood, R., *et al.* (1994). 'Measuring handicap: the London handicap scale, a new outcome measure for chronic disease', *Quality in Health Care*, **3**: 11–16.

Jakubiak, S. *et al.* (1990). *Using Market Research to Improve Management of Transportation Systems*, Transportation Research Board, National Research Council, Washington DC.

London Underground Limited (1992). Passenger Preferences User Manual, Interim Report.

MVA (1992). *Quality of a Journey: Final Report for the Department of Transport*. The MVA Consultancy.

Parasuraman, S.A. *et al.* (1988). 'SERVQUAL: A Multiple Item Scale for Measuring Perceptions of Service Quality', *Journal of Retailing*, **64**: 12–40.

Propper, C. (1991). 'Contingent Valuation of Time Spent on NHS Waiting Lists', *Economic Journal*, **100**: 193–199.

Propper, C. (1992). *Valuing the Disutility of Time Spent on UK National Health Service Waiting Lists*, Mimeo, Bristol University.

Rovizzi, L. and Thompson, D. (1995). 'Regulation of Product Quality in the Public Utilities'. In: Bishop *et al.* (eds), *The Regulatory Challenge*, Oxford: Oxford University Press.

Ryan, M. (1996). Using Consumer Preferences in Health Care Decision Makings: The Application of Conjoint Analysis, Office of Health Economics, 12 Whitehall, London.

Ryan, M. and Farrar, S. (1994). *A Pilot Study Using Conjoint Analysis to Establish the Views of Users in the Provision of Orthodontic Services in Grampian*, Discussion Paper 07/94, Health Economics Research Unit, University of Aberdeen.

Thompson, A.G.H. (1993). 'Inpatients Opinions of the Quality of Acute Hospital Care: Discrimination as the Key to Measure Validity'. In Fitzpatrick, R. and Hopkins, A. (eds), *Measurement of Patients' Satisfaction with their Care*, RCP Publications, London.

Tunstall, S. *et al.* (1993). *Customer Preferences and Willingness to Pay for Selected Water and Sewerage Services*, Flood Hazard Research Centre, Middlesex University.

Williamson, C. (1992). *Whose Standards? Consumer and Professional Standards in Health Care*, Open University Press, Buckingham.

Part III
Ensuring We Get The Best Out Of Public Expenditure

9

Controlling Public Expenditure

David Heald

Contents

Introduction

Control is a word carrying a powerful resonance; it clearly sounds preferable that something is 'under control' rather than 'out of control'. Evaluation of a particular control system can be hampered by ambiguity as to what that control system is designed to achieve and by the fact that objectives themselves shift as a result of experience. True political objectives are not necessarily rendered explicit (Hood, 1994): for example, it is genuinely difficult to determine whether the motivations for the adoption of public management reforms are to sustain the public sector by rendering it more efficient and legitimate or to erode political support for its services.

It is a central argument of this chapter that those more philosophically well-disposed to public expenditure need to pay the greatest attention to the efficacy of control systems. Not least, any future government without a fashionable and/or accumulated distaste for the public sector will confront intense pressures for higher expenditure. We begin by looking at the overall Conservative record on control, in the two different senses in which the word is used. Next, we look in some detail at how the reforms in the public sector have affected the nature of public expenditure control. We then look more widely at the lessons to be drawn from the last 17 years, before looking forward to prospective developments in this area.

The Conservative record

There are two distinct senses in which the word control is regularly applied in public expenditure contexts. First, control is used in the sense of 'conformity to plan', meaning that out-turns are 'in line with' the expenditure which has previously been planned by the relevant political decision makers. Such a characteristic is essential whatever views are held on the appropriate level of the General Government Expenditure/Gross Domestic Product (GGE/GDP) ratio. Second, control is often used as a euphemism for containment or reduction of spending. On this interpretation, evidence would be sought that public expenditure had fallen, in cash or in real terms, or perhaps relative to GGE or to the experience of other OECD countries.

Thain and Wright (1995) displayed evident pleasure in showing how the Conservative Government after 1979 failed to deliver on its successive public expenditure objectives (absolute reductions; reductions in real terms; and reductions as a proportion of GDP). However, the picture looks different if UK developments over this period are compared with those in other European Union (EU) and OECD countries. Figure 9.1 plots general government outlays as a percentage of GDP, separately for: the United Kingdom; the EU (with various memberships); and the OECD. In 1979, the United Kingdom starts well below all three EU averages and further detaches itself, briefly falling below the OECD weighted average (in which the United States and Japan have a combined weight of 58.66 per cent) in 1988 and 1989. Particularly striking is that the relative fall in the UK ratio, which took place during the Lawson boom, has subsequently been sustained. From 1990, the five series track each other very closely.

The United Kingdom is probably the most deregulated economy in the EU. This means that public functions can less readily be executed through regulatory instruments that do not affect the budget. In theory, a more deregulated economy may have either a higher GGE/GDP ratio (public functions can only be achieved through public expenditure) *or* a lower ratio (there is a more sceptical view of which public functions are desirable).

Some have argued that public expenditure should be curbed much more drastically than has so far been the case. Clarke (1995) and Patten (1995) have set 40 per cent as the desirable GGE/GDP ratio while Skidelsky (1995, p. 190) and Duncan and Hobson (1995, p. 435) outbid them at 30 per cent and 15–20 per cent respectively. Part of this agenda involves greater self-provision of public services, perhaps encouraged by tax incentives, while another part explicitly involves mandated private expenditures such as compulsory health insurance and pension provision. It is possible to take the view that the United Kingdom is pioneering the way to public expenditure retrenchment, just as it

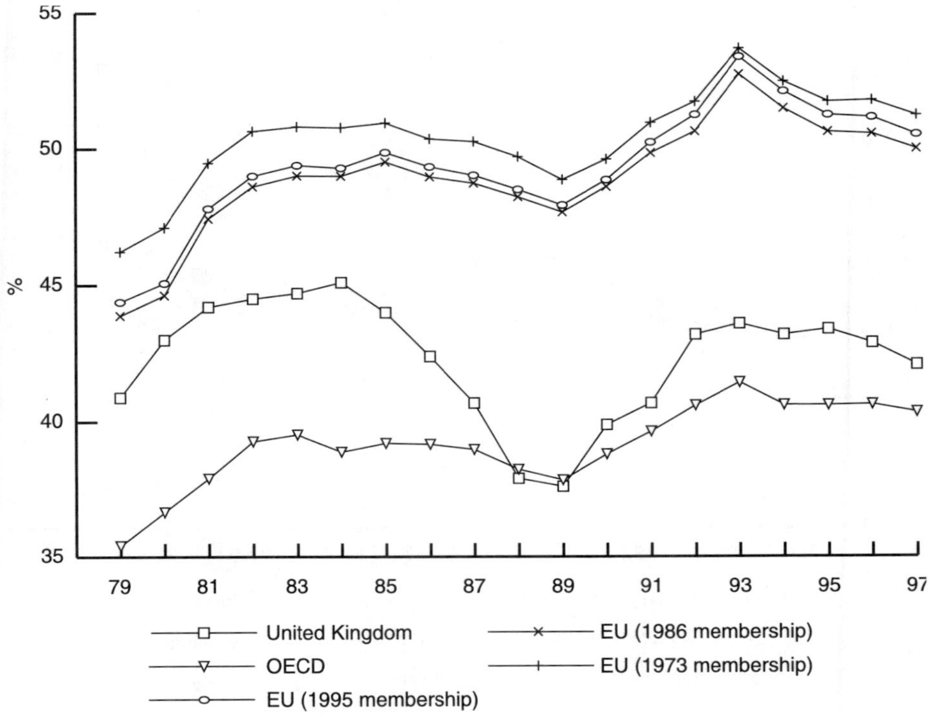

Figure 9.1. Comparative experience: general government outlays/GDP ratios (%).
Source: OECD (1996).
Notes: OECD and EU figures are weighted averages and exclude the UK. Data is missing for Luxembourg in the EU figures due to data non-availability. The following countries are excluded from the OECD figures for the same reasons: Iceland, Mexico, New Zealand and Turkey.

In order to calculate weighted figures for the EU and OECD, the GDP weights (based on 1991 Purchasing Power Parities, with the benchmark year being 1990) constructed by OECD (1996, p. 2) have been used.

did earlier on privatization. On this view, detachment from the EU constitutes an enormous policy success, some of the credit for which should be attributed to the control system. Indeed a somewhat smug attitude to the current fiscal problems of France and Germany can readily be detected.

Figure 9.2 provides insights into trends in the composition of UK public expenditure between 1978–79 and 1995–96 (estimated out-turn). Summary graphics have obvious limitations: interpretation must proceed on the understanding that client group sizes may have changed markedly and that relative price effects may differ across spending areas. This plot of indexes of real expenditure by function (cash expenditure adjusted to 1994–95 prices by the adjusted GDP deflator, then converted to an index with 1978–79=100) shows just how pronounced compositional changes have been over 17 years. The 'winning' programmes are undoubtedly law, order and protective services (+109 per cent), social security (+84 per cent) and health (+69 per cent). These can be compared

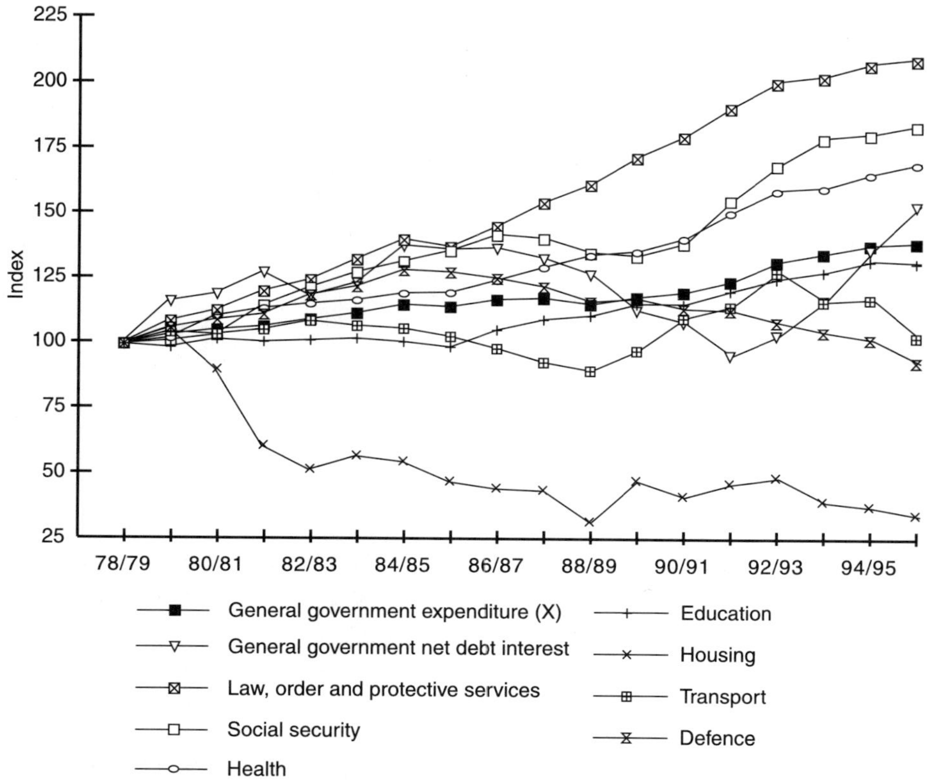

Figure 9.2. Real expenditure by function (1994–95 prices, indexed 1978–79 = 100). *Source*: Treasury (1996a), Table 1.3. The data for 1979–80 and 1980–81 were provided by the Treasury.

with the 39 per cent increase in GGE(X).[1] The 'losing' programmes shown in Figure 9.2 are housing (−65 per cent) and defence (−7 per cent). The profiles are also interesting. Defence peaked in 1984–85 (+28 per cent) before falling sharply, while education remained flat up to 1985–86 (−1 per cent) from which point it has grown quite steadily (+31 per cent by 1995–96). Transport shows an anti-cyclical path around an unchanged index. The strongly rising trend of general government net debt interest from 1991–92 carries a warning for the future. Further discussion of such trends has to take place at a more disaggregated level, for example, distinguishing between age groups within the education programme and with proper recognition of substitution effects (for example, housing's loss has been partially offset by the growth of housing benefit expenditure within social security). An obviously relevant question is whether or not such changes have reflected conscious political choices.

Figure 9.3 represents changes in functional composition in a different way, analysing programme contributions to changes in real GGE over the period 1978–79 to 1995–96 (estimated out-turn). This has the advantage over Figure

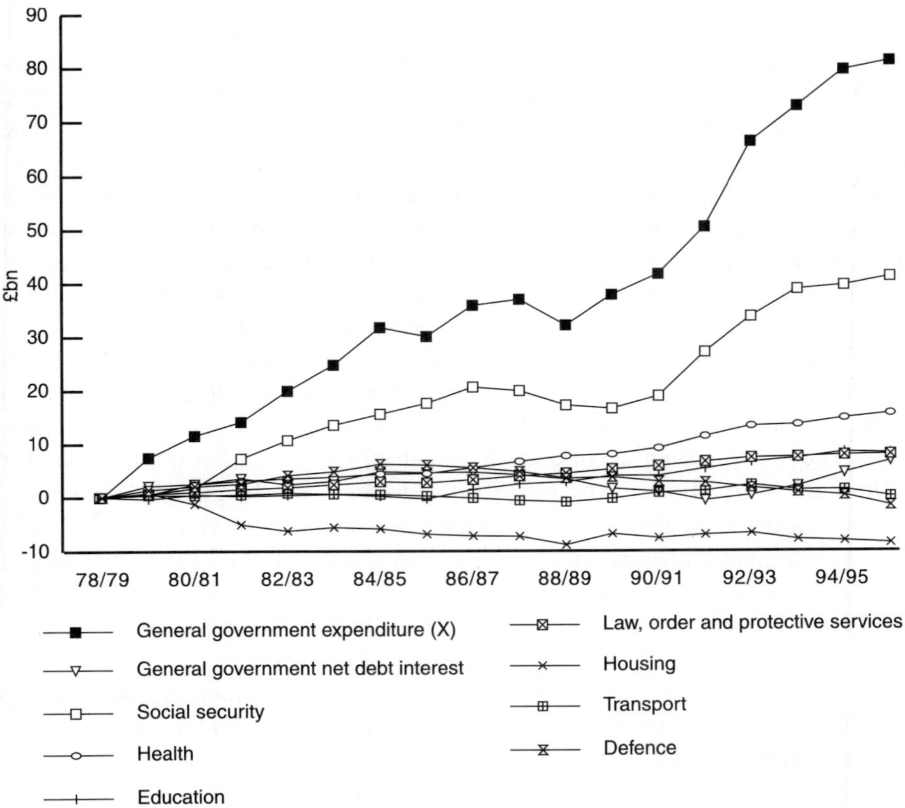

Figure 9.3. Real increase in programme expenditure since 1978–79 (change in expenditure £bn, 1994–95 prices).
Source: Treasury (1996a), Table 1.3. The data for 1979–80 and 1980–81 were provided by the Treasury.

9.2 of incorporating information about the relative size of different programmes. In terms of such contributions, social security has been a dominant force. Out of gross increases to real GGE totalling £96 billion between 1978–79 and 1995–96, social security accounted for 43.2 per cent.

Control in the 'new' public sector

Control is essentially an executive process, in which Parliament has little role. Within a parliamentary system such as that of the United Kingdom, the role of Parliament is best understood in terms of authorization. For example, the Treasury mechanically converts the first year of the Public Expenditure Survey plans into the necessary form for Estimates. These have traditionally differed in both coverage and measurement convention, though the introduction of the matrix-style simplified Estimates in 1996–97 (Treasury and Civil Service Committee, 1995; Treasury, 1996b) was intended to bring about some convergence. The Supply procedure has huge constitutional symbolism, being described by Elliott (1985) as the 'dignified element', in contrast to the Survey as the executive process (the 'efficient element'). In practice, however, Members of Parliament take remarkably little interest in the formal financial procedures of the House of Commons, and the limited discussion of public expenditure which does occur is conducted *ex ante* through the Treasury Committee and the departmental select committees and *ex post* by the Public Accounts Committee. This reality is unlikely to be changed either by procedural reforms or by injunctions from outsiders that Parliament should take these matters more seriously. This context, in which control is seen as an executive matter, has important implications for the flow of information about government finances into the public domain.

Those parts of the public sector which have not been privatized since 1979 have seen dramatic changes in organizational shape, external relationships and managerial culture (Flynn, 1993; Lovell, 1994; Russell and Sherer, 1994; Walsh, 1995; and Farnham and Horton, 1996). Cumulatively, the influence of the New Public Management (NPM) (Hood, 1991) has been pervasive.

This transformation is exceptionally difficult to characterize, particularly because of the tension between decentralization (devolving budgets and decision making) and centralization (establishing clearer lines of vertical accountability, often disrupting older collegiate or consensus models). Despite the rhetoric of decentralization, there have been successive waves of central initiatives. These include the Financial Management Initiative, the creation of agencies, market testing, management plans and running costs controls, the Private Finance Initiative (PFI) and Resource Accounting and Budgeting (RAB) (Treasury, 1995). This complex brew generates its own ambiguity about ultimate management responsibility and about where the line between political and managerial decision making lies. The greater recourse which is now made by ministers to the claim that 'operational matters' are for managers and not for them has led many outside government to suspect that this formula is being developed into a potent instrument for blame deflection.

The architects of NPM reforms believed that restructuring the public sector with smaller, more focused organizations, relating to each other via formula funding and quasi-markets, would deliver efficiency savings. There would be more output from the same input or, alternatively, the same output for less input. Although the pace has varied, the direction of reform in most OECD countries is similar (OECD, 1993; 1995a, b). Two questions therefore arise: whether the NPM reform programme has genuinely delivered efficiency savings; and what effect it has had on the controllability of public expenditure. The first question is discussed in Chapter 12 by Peter Jackson. The second is addressed here.

Is control now easier or harder?

Two distinct stories can be told. First, the package of reforms makes public service delivery units compete against each other, giving them incentives to secure cost reductions and quality improvements. Much greater attention is paid to service delivery, and to strengthening institutional management against both trade unions and professional groupings such as doctors. Such managers face the rigours of market and quasi-market mechanisms set in place by the central decision makers. Albeit in a garbled form, public choice ideas have certainly influenced the NPM reform agenda (Kraan, 1996).

This appears to be an optimistic story. Nevertheless, this optimism has to be qualified because of the huge gulf between the rhetoric about 'buying outputs to secure outcomes' (which ministers and civil servants have increasingly mastered) and the reality of output and outcome measurement where serious work within government seems to have been squeezed by a combination of lower running costs and a fundamental lack of interest in evaluation.

The second story is less optimistic. In the new structure, the public sector can be conceptualized as a set of planets (government departments), many with a set of moons, some of which have their own satellites. What is distinctive about this constellation is that the planets are often dwarfed in size by the moons and satellites. Such fragmentation may complicate the control of public expenditure aggregates in a number of ways, most notably if delivery units are able to mobilize political resources against the centre. One manifestation may be a refusal to surrender efficiency gains in the form of budget reductions and an insistence upon using them to expand output or quality in that particular programme area. In other words, the inter-programme flexibility enjoyed by central decision makers may be impaired. The system may become arthritic in the sense that public money can less readily be switched around as new priorities unfold.

Quasi-autonomous units may pursue their own narrowly focused agendas (where only specified outputs and their own costs matter) and may be able to sustain greater resistance to reductions (one obvious mechanism involves independent public relations activity which can be used to mobilize opposition). An interesting example relates to housing associations and their 'peak' organizations which operate with a measure of lobbying independence from the non-departmental public bodies (NDPBs) which fund them out of departmental programmes. During the 1980s and early 1990s they were able to exploit the hostility of Conservative ministers towards local authority housing to their own advantage.

Even more seriously, the complex network of quasi-contracts (purchaser/provider contracts in the NHS are not legally enforceable) and real contracts (emerging from market testing, contracting out and the PFI) may accentuate the difficulties of securing reasonably rational expenditure cuts if these are suddenly required for macroeconomic reasons. The capacity to implement top-down reductions may be seriously impaired. Moreover, through contracts, present decision makers may have greater ability to 'lock in' future decision makers. Some of the former might even relish the thought that engineering a fiscal crisis in which existing public provision becomes unaffordable is a tactical route to desirable but otherwise infeasible welfare state privatization.

The experience of the community charge shows just how difficult it can be to predict the long-term consequences when financial systems interact with political systems. The advocates of the community charge believed that local authorities would cut expenditure in response to high marginal tax costs. In fact local authorities increased expenditure, successfully transferring the blame to central government which then delivered more grant (Gibson, 1990).

It is difficult to make a judgement between the two stories: namely, competition between providers leads to efficiency enhancement and strengthens expenditure control *versus* fragmentation leads to a loss of control and flexibility. A possible synthesis of the two stories is that the new structure may produce genuine efficiency gains but at the cost of greater system instability and at more risk to aggregate public expenditure control.

Is central control illusory?

Jenkins's (1995) critique of quangocracy emphasized the illusory nature of the central control which appears to have been established. There are concerns relating to the organizations which supervise quasi-markets and to those that contract with them. Of immediate relevance is the current fashion for downsizing the centre of departments, most notably the Treasury itself. The idea seems to be that the adoption of NPM techniques renders the task of the centre easier.

Yet the counter-argument can readily be mobilized. Fundamental Expenditure Reviews (FERs) may be accentuating an inherent problem, by delayering, demanning and deskilling the Treasury and core departments, just as their workload changes but expands. The Treasury FER documents are eloquent about the need for the Treasury to adopt a more 'strategic' approach to public expenditure control (Southgate *et al.*, 1994; Treasury, 1994). Paradoxically, an authoritative study of the Treasury over the period 1976–93 casts the Treasury's 'expenditure controllers' (those Treasury officials who shadow spending departments) as the heroes of the control system, notably in the way in which they exploit knowledge and contacts in developing a relationship of constructive tension with 'their departments' (Thain and Wright, 1995). It is not yet clear what a strategic approach means in practice (Wright, 1995), especially when the 'devil' frequently resides in the 'detail'.

Heald and Scott (1996) drew attention to the weakness of the centre of the NHS financial system, characterizing the finance directorates of the four management executives (i.e. one for each country) as understaffed and overstretched. The fragmentation of delivery organizations which themselves had weak accounting and finance functions accentuated the vulnerability of financial control. Below Director of Finance level (where the 1990–92 recession rebounded to the NHS's advantage by making it more appealing to professional accounting staff), many NHS providers are thinly staffed. Quasi-markets naturally involve higher transactions costs than more hierarchical systems. The relevant test is whether the total costs of given output levels are reduced. Populist attacks on NHS managers and accountants may lead to the implementation of half-baked proposals to control management costs through central command, leaving financial control vulnerable and preventing savings in total costs from being reaped. The tone of a recent House of Commons debate on NHS bureaucracy (*Hansard*, 26 June 1996) vividly highlighted these risks.

What should worry the Treasury is that the Thain and Wright (1995) analysis seems to support the view that effective defence of global totals from political and other threats may require a high level of detailed intelligence about programmes. Without that, it is difficult to judge whether departments and subordinate provider units are engaging in shroud waving or whether there are real difficulties. Misjudgements may backfire in the form of higher expenditure, either because the shroud-waving story is believed or because a genuine case is resisted and later explodes. The final public expenditure cost of bovine spongiform encephalopathy (BSE), or 'mad cow disease', is as yet incalculable, but it seems at least possible that much of this cost could have been avoided had proper inspection and regulatory systems been in operation during the 1980s. Weak regulation has led to large unexpected public expenditure costs.

An aggressively tough attitude to expenditure reduction may lead to significant falls in real output, a particularly serious issue where output measurement is inherently difficult. Moreover, a rapid deterioration in the finances of public and quasi-public providers not only obscures public understanding but could also seriously undermine aggregate control. Alarms have recently been sounding about NHS trusts and about higher education institutions (HEIs). Although some of this is undoubtedly part of the bargaining game, there is the genuine point that reductions in the control aggregate may be achieved in ways which reduce the net worth of the public sector. They may also weaken the financial viability of the providers that actually deliver public services.

Incentives

The formula funding systems upon which central government increasingly relies can have unexpected and dysfunctional consequences (Heald and Geaughan, 1994). For example, the way in which the 1996 Research Assessment Exercise in the higher education sector stimulated the growth of a transfer market for researchers may have bid up unit costs just at the time when the HEIs needed to reduce unit costs to safeguard financial viability. Trends which are widely recognized as unsustainable at system level may be irresistible at institutional level: unilateral non-participation in such a transfer market might have led to serious reductions in research grant.

Because of risk pooling, the level of aggregation at which funding takes place may be vitally important. Excessive fragmentation may render the funding recipient vulnerable to random variation in, for example, patient needs. This will lead to a 'false' uniformity in expenditure levels where both under-provision and over-provision relative to need become prevalent. In turn, the exploitation of horror stories about service failures in the under-provided areas may lead to an upward drift in real funding or to a serious loss of public confidence.

Systems which involve more high-powered incentives may lead to the aggressive exploitation of micro-level incentives, without regard to system stability. Even when formula funding and quasi-markets lead to genuine cost reductions, the new arrangements will alter the balance between programme and running costs. Moreover, an admirable concern to secure cost reductions may lead to attempts to shift costs on to third parties; lower levels of cost internalization within organizations subject to unified management control accentuate this tendency. Naturally, the alignment of financial and opportunity costs becomes much more important in a system exhibiting managerial decentralization. In such a context, it is necessary to establish who is responsible for the broader range of costs and benefits which do not necessarily accrue to the decision makers, who are themselves under pressure to pay greater attention to financial variables. Transport is an excellent example (Maddison *et al.*, 1996).

Tougher questioning of the value-for-money of public expenditure programmes is undeniably a feature of NPM, notwithstanding doubts about the reliability of performance indicators and measurement systems. This insistence upon performance is taking place against a backcloth of profound social change whose implications for public expenditure growth reverberate upon control systems. It is useful to force a distinction between those factors which would generally be viewed as incidental to 'good news' and those incidental to 'bad news'.

For example, many public expenditure pressures in the health and welfare fields can be traced to a substantial lengthening of life expectancy, reflecting the benefits of improved living standards and public services. In such cases, policy makers ought to be pleased about the cause of the expenditure pressure. The expenditure consequences of 'success' do not disappear but present different problems, relating, for example, to the renegotiation of earlier commitments like care for the elderly, or to the response to new circumstances (e.g. student finance in the context of a mass higher education system).

In contrast, some expenditure pressures can be linked to policy failure. Higher rates of imprisonment because of rising crime and higher social security benefits because of long-term unemployment are good examples. Moreover, the 1980s and 1990s have witnessed a sharp increase in economic inequality in the United Kingdom, to a much more dramatic extent than has been seen in other EU countries (Atkinson *et al.*, 1995). There is considerable controversy as to the underlying causes (e.g. tax/benefit policy, deregulated labour markets and increasing returns to human capital as a result of economic globalization) and as to whether the UK experience represents the future for other EU countries.

The implications of increased inequality

The focus on value-for-money has also led to tougher questioning of the distributional consequences of public expenditure (van de Walle, 1995). This new scepticism about who the beneficiaries are should be welcomed. Nevertheless, it is essential that such evaluations focus upon long-term and system effects, not just first-round effects. For example, affluent-worker exit from council housing or middle-class exit from state education may temporarily improve distributional targeting but later diminish political support for continued expenditure. Whereas greater inequality emphasizes the importance to economic and social functioning of good public services, it also makes them more difficult to sustain politically.

When growing economic prosperity was broadly based and hence socially inclusive, it was possible for some authors such as Alan Peacock to envisage a future in which society 'grew out' of the welfare state and where individuals would make private provision for educational, health and welfare services in a way unforeseen when the welfare state was established (Wilson, 1985). Now that growing economic prosperity is much less inclusive, some authors have argued that the welfare state can no longer be afforded: the aspirations of the affluent for public services far outstrips what governments, nervous of taxpayer reaction and fearful for international competitiveness, are willing or able to provide. The key political judgement, of course, relates to whether those who have opted out of public services would remain willing to finance public services for those still dependent upon the state. The political dynamics of such a situation are difficult to predict: for example, a substantial minority of the population self-providing for health might set new benchmarks for service availability which governments would later find difficult to deny to NHS patients. Unexpected or unintended consequences can be pervasive in their effects. For example, the US healthcare system has become more aggressively competitive in the 1990s, a development which is helping to control costs but which is also exposing the extent to which the problem of the uninsured population had hitherto been dealt with through (no longer viable) cross-subsidies out of charges made to insured patients.

The problem is further aggravated by the probability that increasing inequality may damage the productive efficiency of some public services. It may be exceptionally expensive, or even impossible, to produce high-quality educational services in a crime-ridden, drug-affected inner city area or peripheral housing estate. This deterioration in production conditions is taking place in the context of moves from needs-based funding, where central government grants for health and local authority services delivered more money to under-performing areas, to more performance-based models. Fragmented structures may lead to coordination problems in terms of their impact on particular geographical areas, arising from the narrow aims of each body and the dysfunctional incentives of multiple funding systems. This echoes the argument frequently made by John Stewart (e.g. Jones and Stewart, 1983) in favour of multi-purpose local authorities, though the coordination problems existing within such organizations should not themselves be underestimated.

In a proper cybernetic sense, a system is under control when it is capable of being steered to a desired state. However, this discussion has thrown serious doubt upon such a claim for the current UK public expenditure control system. What lessons then can be derived from the experiences of 1979–96, and what modifications of the present system are suggested?

Lessons from the period of Conservative Government

Several lessons can be drawn from the period of the Conservative Government after 1979, a period remarkable in post-war terms for the sustained commitment to curtailing the resource demands of the public sector.

First, medium-term control over public expenditure aggregates is difficult. There have been powerful external pressures generating higher claims for expenditure: for example, notwithstanding the strong desire of Conservative ministers to curtail such expenditure, real GGE(X) grew by 38.8 per cent between 1978–79 and 1995–96, and the proportion of GGE(X) accounted for by social security increased from 23.5 to 31.2 per cent (Treasury, 1996a).[2] Indeed, public expenditures on goods and services have been crowded out by such growth of transfer payments: without such growth, real expenditure on, say, health and education would probably now be higher. The unexpected severity of both the 1979–81 recession, where seasonally adjusted real GDP at market prices fell by 6.0 per cent between 1979(Q2) and 1981(Q2) and the 1990–92 recession, with a fall of 3.6 per cent between 1990(Q2) and 1992(Q1), threatened medium-term public expenditure control. Moreover, even in retrospect, there has been considerable difficulty in disentangling cyclical from trend factors in expenditure growth (Virley and Hurst, 1995).

Complicating matters further, the political presentation of fiscal objectives has taken precedence over consistency. The meaning which Treasury ministers attach to the policy commitment of 'balancing the budget over the economic cycle' has changed markedly: from the sum of surpluses and deficits being zero over the cycle (November 1991) to the Public Sector Borrowing Requirement (PSBR) returning to zero at some point during the cycle (November 1992) (Heald, 1995). The projected PSBR for 1996–97 (revised upwards in July 1996 to 3.6 per cent of GDP) – a deeply disturbing figure for the fifth year of continuous real GDP growth – is attributable to revenue shortfalls rather than to expenditure overruns (Mowl, 1995).

The lesson here is that any specific commitment about the level of the PSBR might well be compromised by the apparent increase in fiscal instability – in part arising from more pronounced economic cycles – and by the fact that the economy seems to have become more resistant to generating tax revenue.

Second, there has been less constancy in the Conservative Government's approach to public expenditure than is typically projected or assumed (Thain and Wright, 1995). Periods of repressed growth store up future problems. An example is the pre-1988 controls over public sector pay. The effects of the political cycle can also be detected, most notably in the 1991–92 loss of control. There was ample contemporary evidence about the likely path of expenditure aggregates after the 1991 Autumn Statement (Heald, 1991b), but the issues were postponed until after the 1992 general election.

In their account of his premiership, two of John Major's then closest advisers have written:

> As one seasoned Treasury mandarin puts it, a five-year Parliament tends to be more expensive than a four-year, because two spending rounds take place under the pressure of an election. And if you have two Prime Ministers in this period, you double the pressure, since they will inevitably have different priorities. Margaret Thatcher had agreed to an enormous roads programme. John Major was to give more money to health.
>
> (Hogg and Hill, 1995, p. 119).

In contrast, surprisingly tough public expenditure control has been exercised in the run-up to the 1997 general election, undoubtedly assisted by sustained economic growth and low inflation. The lesson is that the public expenditure process is an intensely political one, rendering elusive medium-term stability in the pursuit of defined objectives.

Third, since 1988 much Treasury effort has been wasted on redefinitions of the control aggregate. The real motivation for the 1990 redefinition, by which the old planning total was replaced by the new planning total which excluded local authority self-financed expenditure, still remains obscure (Heald, 1991a). The 1992 switch to the Control Total, which mainly excluded cyclical social security spending, was essentially diversionary: 'There are circumstances when it appears easier to change systems than to admit to the real nature of problems . . . ' (Heald, 1995, p. 231). Such redefinitions, characterized by Thain and Wright (1990) as 'coping strategies', are resorted to by the Treasury in the face of failure to achieve public expenditure objectives. It is far from obvious what this process of successive redefinitions has achieved for the Treasury. The serious consequence is that the loss of data comparability renders public expenditure figures increasingly impenetrable to anyone other than technical specialists, further aggravating the 'switch-off' effect so evident in the parliamentary neglect of financial matters. In consequence:

> There has been a loss of information from the public domain, and of transparency about public expenditure. This conclusion is robust, whether this outcome is interpreted as deliberate obfuscation (an abuse of executive power by a government continuously in office for a long period of time and expecting to remain there) or as unintended (cumulative definitional change surpasses the Treasury's information processing capacities).
>
> (Heald, 1995, p. 234).

Two speculations are worth airing. One is that it might be necessary to distinguish between the 'official' and 'ministerial' Treasury. Chief Secretaries now come and go – there have been 10 in 17 years – and may have career agendas which rank higher in their priorities than a coherent public expenditure system. A Chief Secretary who is expected to and does run the term of a parliament has more to gain from a secure control system. The use of this post as a stepping stone at the bottom of the Cabinet promotion ladder has undoubted costs: greater longevity of office for John Biffen (Chief Secretary 1979–81), in the manner of Jack Diamond (1964–70) and Joel Barnett (1974–79), might have substantially affected how systems and expenditure developed. The other speculation is that, the rapid succession of incumbents in key posts in the Treasury (notably, the Grade 3 in charge of the Survey) may have encouraged new incumbents to seek kudos and hence further promotion in taking credit for new systems rather than in making existing systems work. The lesson here is that careful attention is required to staffing matters, both ministerial and official, to ensure that the correct signals are transmitted.

Fourth, systems of control which are geared to severe input restrictions must be supported by subtle and sophisticated monitoring on the output side. Gray and Jenkins (1990, 1993) have regretted the lack of integration in the United Kingdom between budgeting, auditing and evaluation. The quality of available output information has been thrust to the centre of the debate on RAB by the National Audit Office (1996), which has implied that audited performance information should be viewed by Parliament as a pre-condition for resource budgeting (RB). Extending the argument much further, Laughlin and Broadbent (1996) have remarked upon:

> . . . the growing call for the accountability of the Conservative Government of the UK for the range of far-reaching managerial changes which have been implemented in the public sector over the last fifteen years . . . the Government should be accountable for this investment of taxpayers' money but not in a way which simply justifies its actions to the body politic but rather in a way which goes beyond this to a complete critical evaluation of the merit and worth of the Reforms.

A lack of systematic evaluation is emerging as a characteristic of NPM reforms, the agenda often being moved on – perhaps, deliberately – too quickly for evaluation to secure adequate attention. Despite OECD rhetoric about New Zealand and the United Kingdom as model pupils, that organization has itself shown more interest in proselytizing than in careful evaluation. It is essential to recognize that outputs and outcomes are themselves problematic:

> . . . researchers have generally taken an uncritical view of what constitutes outcome. That is, they have taken the favoured concept of outcome as given. So – for example – in health care the received wisdom is that outcome relates to the enhancement of the quality and quantity of life. Yet it may well be that citizens value many other features of the health care *system*, such as the reduction of risk, the promotion of equity, and the reassurance of a culture of care.
>
> (Smith, 1996b, p. 3, italics in original).

The burst of enthusiasm for evaluation within the Treasury in the mid-1980s appears to have faded, with no published successors to Lewis (1986) and Durham (1987). Smith (1996a) noted the unevenness of work across public services in output measurement and the links to outcome. The United Kingdom is not represented in Pollock *et al.* (1994), the prestigious handbook on operational research in the public sector. Given the growth of academic work on Data Envelopment Analysis (Ganley and Cubbin, 1991), there has been a notable lack of published work from the Government Economic Service which enjoys privileged data access. Viewed from outside, it seems that the analytical capacity of the Treasury, notably in terms of microeconomics and operational research, has been allowed to degrade. Some of the work traditionally conducted in-house may now be subcontracted, though its nature may be affected by the renowned tendency of consultants to produce managerially or politically desired results.

The lesson here is not to be optimistic about the development of evaluation capacity within UK government. Leaving aside issues of cost and technical difficulty, evaluation is potentially threatening because of its uncontrollability. For example, it *might* generate unwelcome evidence of underfunding (e.g. in health) or conclusions which contradict ministerial policy beliefs (e.g. 'prison works'). The most effective way to secure better analysis conducted in and published by central government is to concentrate upon structuring external challenges.

Fifth, the published documents which derive from the Survey, the departmental reports and the Statistical Supplement, have become much less effective at communicating the Government's forward expenditure priorities. The Treasury cannot necessarily deliver a particular forward functional pattern, primarily because of to the multi-functional expenditure responsibilities of local authorities. However, messages about priorities are important, even if these are to be understood as indicative of central government wishes. Certainly, the claim that the figures traditionally published in earlier public expenditure White Papers were 'worthless' is unconvincing.

The disappearance of such forward figures has led to much greater public confusion about which functional expenditure areas are really receiving priority. Even public expenditure specialists cannot disentangle this. Moreover, there arises a considerable likelihood that the gains and losses of successive Surveys to some extent cancel each other out.

There are no publicly articulated medium- or long-term priorities. Though there have been internal updates, the Treasury has never published a sequel to its 1984 Green Paper on public expenditure prospects on a 10-year horizon (Treasury, 1984). The forward projections which have been published for particular programmes (e.g. Department of Social Security (1993)) have been viewed externally as softening-up exercises for entitlement reductions rather than as genuine attempts to stimulate public debate. In practice, the composition of expenditure appears to have been driven by a mixture of external factors (like continued social security growth, concerns about law and order and policy disasters such as BSE) and by the accretion of *ad hoc* commitments, the implications of which are not thought through. An example of the latter is the 1992 election commitment to maintain health expenditure in real terms, which has been interpreted to involve no adjustment for the transfer out of the health programme of certain responsibilities under community care.

This is not a complaint about the balance of programmes being determined politically rather than through a technocratic cost–benefit analysis. Rather, it is a complaint about the structuring of the agenda for political decisions. Those journalistic accounts which have benefited from access to insiders dwell excitedly but depressingly upon the role of personalities and of ephemeral political clout, with little sense of medium-term political priorities. For example, some ministers have refrained from fighting their corner and making bids in the expected way while other ministers have been ambushed by the presence of senior ministers whose experience and knowledge of departmental programmes has exceeded their own. Rapid ministerial turnover has been an aggravating factor (Bogdanor, 1996). Some of the compositional shifts in expenditure highlighted in Figure 9.2 may have their origins in such chance events: the lack of growth of education spending in the early 1980s seems to be such an example.

The lesson here is that reliance upon crude mechanisms of aggregate control can eliminate effective political choice. Where there are genuine ceilings on aggregates, trends in particular areas, like rising social security expenditure in the past and perhaps 'PFI costs' in the future, can severely constrain options. After any change of government, the new Chief Secretary would be well advised to expect to be told by the Treasury official running the Survey that binding commitments have more than exhausted the automatic release from the Reserve.

Sixth, media coverage of public expenditure has become dominated by leaks of various provenance, and there is no longer much serious coverage of the official documents. There are some technical reasons for this. The advent of the Autumn Statement in 1982, which gave the aggregate decisions on public expenditure down to departmental level, reduced the news value of the main documents published in February. The unified Budget has predictably further displaced coverage of public expenditure.

Nevertheless, the political reasons are much more important. Politicians increasingly respond to a tabloid agenda, a response which is believed necessary for political survival. Regarding the Survey itself, very little is known about its conduct and substance, though documentary accounts such as that of Thain and Wright (1995) afford valuable insights about earlier periods. While spin-doctoring and leaking are now pervasive, intelligent discussion of priorities between programmes is minimal. Insiders have formidable advantages over outsiders in terms of access to data and expertise, a situation becoming more pronounced in a political climate in which opposition parties hardly dare talk about expenditure options. More consistent data and greater openness are preconditions for higher quality debate.

One difficulty is that the United Kingdom lacks institutions with bite, such as the US Congressional Budget Office whose analysis fatally damaged the Clinton Administration's health reform package (Congressional Budget Office, 1994). Another is that the prevailing politically directed managerial culture forces civil servants to 'sell' existing policies rather than to 'speculate' about alternatives.

Those with political power derived from control over information flows will never willingly relinquish this. The Treasury's success in excluding the scrutiny of 'policy objectives' from the remit of the National Audit Office when it was established in 1983 (Jenkins, 1995) has reduced the effectiveness of its value-for-money work. The lesson here is that regular and systematic evaluation requires institutional innovation.

Improving control

Machinery of government

The 1990s have seen a crisis of confidence in British public life whose implications are far-reaching. The combined effect of the report *The Proper Conduct of Public Business* (Public Accounts Committee, 1994) and of the Nolan Committee (Nolan, 1995) has been to demonstrate both how standards of public behaviour have declined and how behavioural norms, previously thought to be deeply internalized, need to be rendered explicit. These events have undoubtedly generated a cynicism about elements of 'quango government', with potentially long-term consequences. However, reform is not straightforward. Any superimposing of decentralized political control over the managerial model of centre/purchaser-funder/provider may further complicate control over aggregates. For example, proposals to 'democratize' mono-functional quangos may accentuate the problem as they may acquire greater legitimacy and hence become more effective as spending lobbies.

The fundamental question is about where in the system political choices can be and are made. This question is wider than the control of public expenditure but its resolution is profoundly important for the design of control systems. Devolution, of the kind proposed for Scotland, will require new fiscal institutions, relating to data gathering for purposes of fiscal equalization and of fiscal coordination (Heald and Geaughan, 1996).

More generally, there are direct consequences from the diminution of the effective power of local authorities whose expenditure in 1995–96 still accounted for 24.7 per cent of GGE(X). A consequence of 'opting out' (for instance of schools) from local authority funding and control is that the expenditure-switching discretion of democratically elected local authorities is lost. A corrective mechanism is removed.

Once unleashed, the centralist potential of the UK system resists restraint. Paradoxically, greater centralism has been accompanied by greater pretence about local authority discretion, perhaps in recognition of how useful this fiction is in terms of blame transfer. A specific problem has been that, while immensely successful at winning national elections, the Conservative Party's defeats in local elections have provoked both a retreat from participation and a deeply ingrained contempt for local authorities. Stripped of functions and disabled by reorganization, local authorities have faced intensifying pressures to conform to central government expenditure assessments, not just on levels but also on the composition of spending. More intense political interest in the pattern of local authority expenditure (e.g. statements about schools expenditure in the November 1995 Budget) renders it more difficult to resist expectations of 'pass-through'.

The problem is that such centralism breeds more centralism, not only through the actions (legislative and financial) of central government but also through party control exerted by the Opposition front bench over Labour Groups on local authorities. Over time, the information content of variations in per capita expenditure is eroded, as these variations begin to reflect earlier formula allocations rather than local political choices in varying contexts.

Public expenditure management

Public expenditure is undoubtedly a technical area, though not as inaccessible as many politicians and opinion formers profess to believe. A number of technical changes, notably concerning definition and coverage, would make the nature of the available policy options more transparent, and that is healthy for political debate. However, an enthusiasm for transparency may not be universally shared.

First, a new government would be under pressure from spending lobbies to exploit perceived loopholes in control systems in order to achieve desired policy goals. Resisting such temptations would undoubtedly be difficult for a government more ideologically sympathetic to public expenditure.[3] There will be pressures to redefine particular items out of the totals that government seeks to control. Current examples include Hawksworth and Wilcox (1995) and Radcliffe *et al.* (1996) concerning local authority housing. A strong line should be taken against 'playing with the rules'.

In addition to these 'wheezes' at the margin, there will be proposals to quasi-privatize expenditure functions, by substituting mandated private expenditures for public expenditure (e.g. Field (1995) on social security, and Minford and Ashton (1995) on health). Such proposals ought to be evaluated on their specific merits in relation to public policy objectives and not in relation to their effect on the GGE/GDP ratio.

The efficiency of the economy is not synonymous with the containment of public expenditure. Some of the proposed methods would reduce overall efficiency. Tanzi (1995) described a number of ways in which developing country governments have reacted to public expenditure reductions by substituting inferior instruments. For example, they have used quasi-fiscal regulations such as rent controls in place of housing subsidies and quasi-fiscal activities such as differential exchange rates and interest rates.

This warning about fiscal gains being illusory if quasi-fiscal mechanisms are substituted for public expenditure is also relevant to OECD countries. For example, the United Kingdom has shifted some of the costs of statutory sick pay and statutory maternity pay from public expenditure to employers. This search for substitute mechanisms is one of the dysfunctional consequences of control. Alternatives are not necessarily inferior but inferior ones may be adopted in order to circumvent scoring systems. As with tax expenditures, such instruments tend not to be properly costed, for both opportunistic and technical reasons. Well before the advent of NPM it was recognized that definitional issues concerning the boundary of the public sector were both technically difficult and vulnerable to gaming (Gretschman, 1985).

Second, the Treasury should reinstate the pre-1990 practice of publishing forward projections of the functional and economic category compositions of public expenditure. Undoubtedly, these need to have health warnings attached, specifically relating to the considerations that out-turns will be affected by the decisions of separately elected local authorities and devolved Parliaments. The importance of understanding how the Treasury expects functional composition to evolve is even more important because of the growth in lottery-financed expenditure (where issues of additionality will figure prominently) and of the growth in PFI activity and costs. Quite apart from the value of such material to those outside the Survey process, Cabinet ministers themselves must be able to set one year's decisions within the proper context.

Third, there is a strong case for maintaining the present Control Total. This is not because it is entirely suitable but because the increasing instability of public finances makes it important to have a control aggregate whose behaviour can become reasonably well understood. Changes in the definition of the control aggregate both damage data continuity and hinder data interpretation. Provided that the Treasury is willing to devote the staff resources, it can provide a consistent series for a particular control aggregate for an earlier period and the Treasury have done this for the Control Total back to 1984–85 (Treasury, 1996a, Table 1.1). However, because a different control aggregate was in use until 1993–94, the earlier cyclical behaviour of the current definition is not necessarily a good guide to future cyclical behaviour. One advantage of the current Control Total from a Treasury perspective is that reductions in cyclical social security are not available for transfer to other programmes.

Fourth, several important changes coming on stream will affect the capital component of public expenditure and will have important consequences for control. The Treasury's RAB initiative will profoundly affect the treatment of capital. Assets will be valued and included in commercial-style balance sheets. Capital charging will be instituted across central government. Resource budgeting will involve the Survey being conducted, and Supply voted, on a resource accounting (RA) basis, which means that capital expenditure will be excluded from the Estimates unless there is dual voting of accruals and cash.

Despite the lack of attention that they have received, two other developments are likely to have significant impacts. Lottery-financed capital has implications for priority setting, not least because such grants can effectively commit future revenue expenditure (e.g. by making it too politically costly to resist requests for money to meet operating costs). The PFI raises a number of issues concerning expenditure control (see Chapters 2 and 14 by Sheila Watson and John

Flemming respectively) particularly because it 'posts' bills to the future and because information on future commitments may be denied to Parliament on the grounds of commercial confidentiality. Some progress has been made but this is limited. The departmental report of the Department of Transport, for instance, now separately identifies a PFI costs line as part of its future current expenditure, but without revealing information about the present value of future commitments.

The question of the guarantees extended by government to the moons and satellites has been highlighted by the application of the PFI to the NHS, leading to an untypical explicitness on the question of guarantees. If an NHS trust went bankrupt, its liabilities would be transferred either to another NHS body or to the Secretary of State (*National Health Service (Residual Liabilities) Act 1996*). This is exactly the kind of contingent liability which the Estimates will describe as 'unquantifiable'. Such arrangements have implications for the extent of risk transfer to the private sector and render the centre vulnerable to long-term contracts signed either carelessly or with regard to self-preservation.

Traditionally, the Survey has been criticized for treating capital as the 'swing' item, which could be turned on and off at will. If PFI commitments were to acquire considerable magnitude, the situation would change drastically. Moreover, the present emphasis on the PFI runs counter to one of the central motivations of capital charging, namely to bring home to decision makers the full opportunity costs of capital. Ministers greatly enjoy announcing and later opening new facilities. The enjoyment may be even greater when, if PFI-financed, new prisons and new roads do not score against budgets at that juncture (Heald, 1996).

In all these areas, the clear need is for the accounts to be transparent in terms of what commitments have been entered into and what they imply for public expenditure in the future.

Fifth, new machinery for the evaluation of public expenditure programmes should be introduced. It needs to have a medium-term agenda as well as a capacity to provide authoritative costings of policy proposals for select committees and for Members of Parliament. The existence of such a facility would significantly undermine the information monopoly which currently protects departments and disables opposition parties. As well as a remit to evaluate departmental performance and output and outcome indicators, the new machinery should address two troubling issues. One is whether the concern to cut running costs ('wasteful bureaucracy') may in practice diminish the effectiveness of much larger programme expenditure. The other is the examination of trade-offs between expenditures which fall on different programmes (e.g. social security versus employment; social security versus housing), and the analysis of spillovers between programmes. If an unsatisfactory mix of expenditures is currently leading to waste, that creates the possibility of releasing resources. It seems likely that external consultants would play a considerable role in such machinery, though recent experience of their extended use in government has emphasized that the location of control over the commissioning budget for such work must be carefully considered.

Sixth, there are several outstanding issues on the road to full RAB. Resource budgeting entails conducting the Survey on an accruals basis and Estimates being voted on an accruals basis. There needs to be clarification about the relationship between the proposed Resource Control Total and cash totals. There is also the question of how accounting policies will be determined, especially as choices between alternative treatments may impact sharply on 'key' numbers. Accruals accounting is more judgmental than cash accounting and there will be issues which are both technically difficult and politically sensitive. In New Zealand, which has pioneered government accounting reforms, an unspoken motive on the part of reformers has been to restrict the opportunities for politicians to manipulate the numbers. If, in the United Kingdom, the Treasury were to dominate standard-setting, such reforms might on the contrary confer greater discretion on politicians (Jones, 1996). The work of the (independent) Financial Reporting Advisory Board, established by the Treasury in response to parliamentary pressure, will be important as a safeguard.

Finally, there is the question of how to express a new government's medium-term public expenditure objective, and the level at which this would be set (e.g. a target GGE/GDP ratio or one relative to some EU average). There are genuine dilemmas here. If an aggregate target is set but there is no clear forward view of the desired composition of expenditure, it is likely that the control system, heavily concentrating on aggregates, will by default deliver a composition far removed from that which would consciously have been chosen.

The binding constraint is likely to be externally imposed, namely conformity to the obligations entered into under the Maastricht Treaty. It should never be forgotten, however, that control systems are more sustainable if there is comprehension of their relevance to policy objectives and acceptance of their legitimacy. When they are considered to be arbitrary and irrational, they become viewed as legitimate targets for circumvention.

Conclusion

We have seen that public expenditure control is inherently difficult and that it shapes decision making at all levels. Yet the Survey, as the core system, is conducted in a private world, with many of the glimpses offered to others being fragmented or simply manipulative. The message of this chapter is that control of public expenditure, in its proper sense of steering towards chosen objectives, is essential if wider policy objectives are to be achieved. A failure of control in terms of aggregates will lead to deep and ill-directed retrenchment. During the past 17 years, in which containing aggregates has received great priority, there has been a drift in composition towards one which is favoured neither by advocates of high or low public expenditure.

The best way to contain aggregate pressures is to build greater transparency into the process, a task which will require both technical ingenuity (e.g. providing documentation which is intelligible) and political resolve (e.g. those within the private world will resist intrusion). There is no reason for panic about affordability because the UK's position in terms of aggregates is superior to that of many other EU countries (e.g. in terms of the public debt/GDP ratio and of unfunded public sector pension liabilities). Nevertheless, it is sensible to have a somewhat crude aggregate target to act as a hard budget constraint but this must be accompanied at programme level by sophistication about objectives, outputs and outcomes. Clearly, the aggregate target should itself be subject to periodic review. What must be resisted are attempts to circumvent that target by means of wheezes such as reclassifying items outside the control aggregate and adopting substitute instruments such as mandated private expenditures. When there is much talk about the desirable size of government, it needs to be remembered that a GGE/GDP ratio of 40 per cent may be too low if health and education are entirely public but too high if both are fully private.

Notes

1. In June 1995, the Chancellor of the Exchequer substituted GGE(X) for GGE excluding privatization proceeds as the Government's public expenditure objective, the aggregate which is judged relevant to the Government's medium-term objective that public expenditure should take a declining share of GDP. GGE(X) differs from GGE in (a) excluding privatization proceeds; (b) excluding lottery-financed spending; and (c) measuring debt interest net of interest and dividends from public corporations and the private sector.
2. Such comparisons through time are not exact because of the changing form of programmes: for example, housing benefit expenditure (part of social security) has been substituted for housing expenditure.
3. Barnett (1982, pp. 124–5) explains Harold Lever's 'ripping wheeze' for financing the Housing Corporation outside the PSBR, using a private limited company as the vehicle. There is a sting in the tale: 'Unfortunately the company later lost money, mainly because the variable interest rates it had to pay were higher than the fixed interest on its long-term loans to Housing Associations. So this particular "ripping wheeze" ended with a private company becoming a wholly owned subsidiary of the Housing Corporation, eventually to be wound up' (p. 125).

References

Atkinson, A.B., Rainwater, L. and Smeeding, T.M. (1995). *Income Distribution in OECD Countries: Evidence from the Luxembourg Income Study*. Paris: OECD.

Barnett, J. (1982). *Inside the Treasury*. London: André Deutsch.

Bogdanor, V. (1996). 'Ministerial chairs'. *Guardian*, 23 July.

Clarke, K. (1995). *The Future of Conservatism*. Speech to the Conservative Political Centre at St Stephen's Constitutional Club, 1 March. Conservative Party News Release 76/95.

Congressional Budget Office (1994). *An Analysis of the Administration's Health Proposal*. Washington DC: Congressional Budget Office.

Department of Social Security (1993). *The Growth of Social Security*. London: HMSO.

Duncan, A. and Hobson, D. (1995). *Saturn's Children: How the State Devours Liberty, Prosperity and Virtue*, London: Sinclair-Stevenson

Durham, P. (ed) (1987). *Output and Performance Measurement in Central Government: Some Practical Achievements*, Treasury Working Paper No. 45, London: HM Treasury.

Elliott, M. (1985). 'The control of public expenditure'. In: Jowell, J. and Oliver, D. (eds), *The Changing Constitution*, Oxford: Clarendon Press, pp. 149–73.

Farnham, D. and Horton, S. (eds) (1996). *Managing the New Public Services*, 2nd edn. Basingstoke: Macmillan.

Field, F. (1995). *Making Welfare Work: Reconstructing Welfare for the Millennium*, London: Institute of Community Studies.

Flynn, N. (1993). *Public Sector Management* 2nd edn. Hemel Hempstead: Harvester Wheatsheaf.

Ganley, J.A. and Cubbin, J.S. (1991). *Public Sector Efficiency Measurement: Applications of Data Envelopment Analysis*. Amsterdam: Elsevier Science.

Gibson, J. (1990). *The Politics and Economics of the Poll Tax: Mrs Thatcher's Downfall*. Warley: EMAS.

Gray, A. and Jenkins, B. (1990). Policy evaluation in British government: from idealism to realism? In *Program Evaluation and the Management of Government: Patterns & Prospects across Eight Nations*, (ed) R. Rist, New Brunswick: Transaction Publishers, pp. 53–70.

Gray, A. and Jenkins, B. (1993). Separate developments: budgeting, auditing, and evaluation in the United Kingdom. In *Budgeting, Auditing & Evaluation: Functions & Integration in Seven Governments*, (eds) A. Gray and B. Jenkins, New Brunswick: Transaction Publishers, pp. 41–64.

Gretschman, K. (1985). Measuring the public sector: a contestable issue. In *Guidance, Control, and Evaluation in the Public Sector*, (eds) F.X. Kaufman, G. Majone and V. Ostrom, Berlin: de Gruyter, pp. 139–58.

Hansard (1996). 26 July, cols. 359–440.

Hawksworth, J. and Wilcox, S. (1995). *Challenging the Conventions: Public Borrowing Rules and Housing Investment*. Coventry: Chartered Institute of Housing.

Heald, D.A. (1991a). The political implications of redefining public expenditure in the United Kingdom. *Political Studies*, **39**: 75–99

Heald, D.A. (1991b). The Public Expenditure Survey in a state of crisis. In: *The 1991 Autumn Statement*, Treasury and Civil Service Committee, London: HMSO, HC 58 of Session 1991–92, Appendix 8, pp. 99–115.

Heald, D.A. (1995). Steering public expenditure with defective maps. *Public Administration*, **73**: 213–40.

Heald, D.A. (1996). The Private Finance Initiative: value for money and public expenditure control. In *The Private Finance Initiative*, Treasury Committee, London: HMSO, HC 146 of Session 1995–96, pp. 160–71.

Heald, D.A. and Geaughan, N. (1994). Formula funding of UK higher education: rationales, design and probable consequences. *Financial Accountability & Management*, **10**: 267–89.

Heald, D.A. and Geaughan, N. (1996). Financing a Scottish Parliament. In *The State and the Nation: The Politics of Devolution*, (ed) S. Tindale, London: IPPR, pp. 167–83.

Heald, D.A and Scott, D.A. (1996). Lessons from capital charging in the UK National Health Service. *International Association of Management Journal*, **8**(2): 29–45.

Hogg, S. and Hill, J. (1995). *Too Close to Call: Power and Politics – John Major in No. 10*. London: Little, Brown and Co.

Hood, C. (1991). A public management for all seasons. *Public Administration*, **69**: 3–20.

Hood, C. (1994). *Explaining Economic Policy Reversals*. Buckingham: Open University Press.

Jenkins, S. (1995). *Accountable to None: The Tory Nationalization of Britain*. London: Hamish Hamilton.

Jones, G.W. (1996). Resource Accounting and Budgeting: another false trail? *Public Finance Foundation Review*, No. 10: 7–9.

Jones, G.W. and Stewart, J. (1983). *The Case for Local Government*. London: George Allen & Unwin.

Kraan, D.-J. (1996). *Budgetary Decisions: A Public Choice Approach*. Cambridge: Cambridge University Press.

Laughlin, R. and Broadbent, J. (1996). *Redesigning Fourth Generation Evaluation: An Evaluation Model for the Public Sector Reforms in the UK?* Working Paper 96/07, Department of Accounting and Financial Management, University of Essex, Colchester.

Lewis, S. (ed) (1986). *Output and Performance Measurement in Central Government: Progress in Departments*. Treasury Working Paper No. 38, London: HM Treasury.

Lovell, R. (ed) (1994). *Managing Change in the New Public Sector*. Harlow: Longman.

Maddison, D., Pearce, D., Johansson, O. *et al.* (1996). *The True Cost of Road Transport*. London: Earthscan.

Minford, P. and Ashton, P. (1995). *Public Spending: A Twenty Year Plan for Reform*. London: Centre for Policy Studies.

Mowl, C. (1995). 'Oral evidence'. In: *The 1995 Budget*, Treasury Committee, London: HMSO, HC 79 of Session 1995–96, Qs. 176–80.

National Audit Office (1996). *Resource Accounting and Budgeting in Government: The White Paper Proposals*, HC 334 of Session 1995–96, London: HMSO.

National Health Service (Residual Liabilities) Act 1996, Chapter 15, London: HMSO.

Nolan, Lord (1995). (chair) *Standards in Public Life*, First Report of the Committee on Standards in Public Life, Cm 2850–I,II, London: HMSO.

OECD (1993). *Managing with Market-type Mechanisms*. Paris: OECD.

OECD (1995a). *Governance in Transition: Public Management Reforms in OECD Countries*. Paris: OECD.

OECD (1995b). *Budgeting for Results: Perspectives on Public Expenditure Management*. Paris: OECD.

OECD (1996). *OECD Economic Outlook*, No. 60, Paris: OECD.

Patten, C. (1995). *Britain, Asia and Europe – A Conservative View*, Lecture to the Conservative Political Centre, London, 24 October.

Pollock, S.M., Rothkopf, M.H. and Barnett, A. (eds) (1994). *Operations Research and the Public Sector*. Amsterdam: Elsevier.

Public Accounts Committee (1994). *The Proper Conduct of Public Business*, Eighth Report of Session 1993–94, HC 154, London: HMSO.

Radcliffe, R., Hawksworth, J. and Glanville, J. (1996). *Consensus for Change: Public Borrowing Rules, Housing Investment and the City*, Report by Coopers & Lybrand. Coventry: Chartered Institute of Housing.

Russell, P. and Sherer, M. (1994). *Managerialism in the Public Sector: Recent Developments in Accounting and Management Control*. London: Research Board of the Institute of Chartered Accountants in England.

Skidelsky, R. (1995). *The World After Communism*. London: Macmillan

Smith, P. (ed) (1996a). *Measuring Outcome in the Public Sector*. London: Taylor & Francis.

Smith, P. (1996b). *Outcome Measurement: Progress and Prospects*, mimeo.

Southgate, Sir Colin, Heywood, J., Thomas, R. and Cook, S. (1994). *Fundamental Review of HM Treasury's Running Costs*. London: Treasury.

Tanzi, V. (1995). *Government Role and the Efficiency of Policy Instruments*. Paper presented to 51st Congress of the International Institute of Public Finance (The Changing Role of the Public Sector: Transitions in the 1990s), 21–24 August, Lisbon, Portugal.

Thain, C. and Wright, M. (1990). Coping with difficulty: the Treasury and public expenditure, 1976–89. *Policy and Politics*, **18**: 1–15.

Thain, C. and Wright, M. (1995). *The Treasury and Whitehall: The Planning and Control of Public Expenditure*. Oxford: Clarendon Press.
Treasury (1984). *The Next Ten Years: Public Expenditure and Taxation into the 1990s*. Cmnd 9189, London: HMSO.
Treasury (1994). *Improving the Treasury: Initial Decisions on the Fundamental Review of Treasury Running Costs*. London: Treasury.
Treasury (1995). *Better Accounting for the Taxpayer's Money: The Government's Proposals*. Cm 2929, London: HMSO.
Treasury (1996a). *Public Expenditure: Statistical Analysis 1996–97*. Cm 3201, London: HMSO.
Treasury (1996b). *Supply Estimates 1996–97: Main Estimates*. HC 261 of Session 1995–96, London: HMSO.
Treasury and Civil Service Committee (1995). *Simplified Estimates and Resource Accounting*. Fourth Report of Session 1994–95, HC 212, London: HMSO.
van de Walle, D. (1995). *Public Spending and the Poor: What We Know, What We Need to Know*. Policy Research Working Paper 1476, World Bank: Washington DC.
Virley, S. and Hurst, M. (1995). *Public Finances and the Cycle*, Treasury Occasional Paper No. 4, London: HM Treasury.
Walsh, K. (1995). *Public Services and Market Mechanisms: Competition, Contracting and the New Public Management*. Basingstoke: Macmillan.
Wilson, T. (1985). The unwithered welfare state, in *Public Choice, Public Finance and Public Policy*, (eds) D. Greenaway and G.K. Shaw, Oxford: Basil Blackwell, pp. 78–93.
Wright, M. (1995). Resource Budgeting and the PES system. *Public Administration*, **73**: 580–90.

10

Getting the Most Out of Public Expenditure: Some Micro Appraisal and Evaluation Issues

Geoff White

Contents

Introduction

It is clearly important that we get the most out of public spending whatever views are held about its appropriate level in total. The fact that the delivery of many policies and programmes has been decentralized in recent years means that it is even more important to appraise expenditure proposals at the microeconomic level consistently and well. This chapter will focus on one example of this decentralization, namely the way in which programmes in support of regional and local economic development are now delivered. These include grants for regional assistance (for example, to attract inward investors), the support provided for training and enterprise by the Training and Enterprise Councils (and the Local Enterprise Companies in Scotland), and the range of assistance provided by local authorities and regional development agencies.

The chapter will be concerned with the guidance provided by the Treasury in its 'Green Book' and other publications, and whether this is appropriate for appraising decentralized programmes and projects. It will first consider whether the current guidelines deliver appropriate control and management incentives and whether they accord with sound economic principles. By way of illustration it will look at one much-criticized aspect of the current criteria – the presumption against the use of shadow wages, even during a period of sustained high unemployment. It will then go on to consider, more generally, how the Treasury's guidance on strategic appraisal and output and performance measurement of local economic development programmes could be improved.

Microeconomic appraisal

At the microeconomic level, a vast array of decisions are made involving public expenditure. These range from a local authority considering the purchase of information technology equipment to a central department's assessment of a major investment, e.g. in a road building programme. Decisions such as these require the application of consistent criteria and procedures for assessing which of the available options represents the best use of limited funds and resources. This is the *appraisal* process. Whatever decision is taken as a result of an appraisal, we usually want to assess at some later date whether it was the right one. This is the process of *evaluation*.

Central government lays down rules and procedures for the appraisal and evaluation of all decisions that involve public expenditure. These are contained in two Treasury publications. The first, *Economic Appraisal in Central Government* (HMT, 1984 and 1991), is more commonly known as 'The Green Book'. More specific guidance on evaluating local economic development programmes is contained in *A Framework for the Evaluation of Regeneration Projects and Programmes* (HMT, 1995).

Both documents are designed to exercise a powerful influence on the way in which microeconomic appraisals and evaluations are carried out. They contain a number of key messages which are, in effect, different types of control mechanisms. These are set out below (paraphrased from the relevant Treasury source) under headings which indicate the type of control being sought by the Treasury, as follows:

- organizational controls and management incentives;
- valuation using market prices;
- macroeconomic constraints on microeconomic appraisal.

Organizational controls and management incentives

- The delegation of responsibilities for ensuring effective appraisal procedures should be confined in the main to the finance or policy divisions of central government departments. Although appraisals are carried out by operational staff, this is within the centrally determined framework of rules and procedures (HMT, 1991, p. 9).

- The same expenditure should often be appraised at successive levels – at a business planning level, as a programme or major investment decision, at project level within a programme, and even at sub-project level (e.g. a small equipment purchase). Although the detail of appraisal might vary between these levels, the decision rules should be based on the appraisal principles set out in the guidance (HMT, 1991, p. 10).
- Public expenditure planning and control systems are generally designed to minimize conflicts between economic costs (i.e. opportunity costs to the whole economy) and budgetary costs to the spending authority (HMT, 1991, p. 10). However, while the guidance qualifies this general proposition, it is clear that it would only exceptionally be the case that appraisal would use economic rather than budgetary costs (where they were different).

Valuation using market prices

In general, market prices are the best measure of opportunity costs (i.e. the value of a resource in its best alternative use) and only where specific Treasury guidance is issued should 'shadow' prices be used instead of market prices to measure opportunity costs (HMT, 1991, pp. 18–19).

Macroeconomic constraints

- Increases in national income will derive from publicly funded projects to the extent that they strengthen the supply side of the economy, in particular by removing obstacles to the proper working of markets. Indeed, at the national UK level, in the absence of supply side improvements, spatial cross-subsidies will tend to decrease *national* income and employment (HMT, 1995, pp. 10–11).
- Tax flowbacks, savings in benefit payments (from reduced unemployment), and balance of payments gains should not be counted as project benefits. The case for a project must depend on its microeconomic impact not on its influence on macroeconomic variables *which would be affected by any alternative use of the public expenditure in broadly equivalent ways* (HMT, 1991, p. 20).

There are undoubtedly some controversial messages here. However, it would be wrong to assume that these paraphrased extracts from the Treasury's guidelines reflected a slavish (and, perhaps, politically determined) adherence to the principles of the free market and to take issue with them on those grounds alone. It is the proper role of the Treasury to exercise control over public expenditure and to ensure its most effective use. This means that it has to adopt simplified appraisal rules and procedures so that they stand the best chance of being transmitted to, as well as understood and adopted by, those working in all the tiers of government administration. These simplified rules must, nevertheless, satisfy two questions:

- Do the guidelines deliver appropriate operational control and management incentives with regard to the use of public spending?
- Do they accord with sound economic principles?

These questions are considered next in the specific context of the guidelines' treatment of shadow wages and, then, in the general context of the guidelines themselves.

Use of shadow wages

Where shadow wages are proposed for use in project appraisal this is usually taken to mean shadow wages less than market wages (although, in principle, they could be higher). One argument for this is that where labour would otherwise be unemployed, its 'opportunity cost' is lower than the wage suggests (see Appendix for fuller explanation). The use of shadow wages requires that the appraiser makes a downward adjustment to the market wage component in the UK project options being considered. The cost of labour is lowered, with the effect, all else being equal, of making the labour intensive and/or the UK project option the preferred one for the decision maker.

One carefully crafted clause in the 1984 version of the Green Book rejected the general case for the use of shadow wages: 'in the appraisal of individual expenditure proposals, unless there is specific Treasury guidance to the contrary, labour should be costed at its full wage rate even when unemployment is high' (HMT, 1984, p. 8). The formulation was changed in the 1991 version, both to make it more general and to make the macroeconomic dimension more explicit. This left open the possibility that there might be specific guidance on the use of shadow pricing, although no such guidance has ever been issued.

According to the 1991 Treasury guidance: '. . . shadow prices in the UK economy based on macroeconomic arguments about, for example, international trade or employment, should not be used unless there is specific Treasury guidance to the contrary' (HMT, 1991, p. 19). '. . . The usual assumption . . . is that market prices generally reflect opportunity costs, so that there is no need for shadow prices for such [macroeconomic] effects' (HMT, 1991, p. 20).

On this formulation of the guidance, it looks as if it is drawn from the model of perfect competition in which all markets clear and market prices are equal to the opportunity costs of resources – i.e. their full value in the best alternative use to which they could be put.

The Treasury does not do itself any favours in this formulation. First of all, it invites criticism for adopting the other-worldly assumptions of perfect competition. As an old colleague of mine once declared, the only thing certain about the invisible hand of perfect competition is that it has two fingers firmly extended.

There are a number of well-established circumstances in which market prices will not equate with opportunity costs. Back in 1968 Prest and Turvey summarized the main reasons for the divergence (see Box 10.1).

Secondly, the Treasury's guidance on the use of shadow prices does not, in fact, rest upon an assumption of perfect competition but on whether it is the appropriate policy response to imperfect competition and market failures. Shadow prices may be an inappropriate response to the presence of market failure for a variety of reasons, some of which are set out in Box 10.2.

The counter-arguments set out in Box 10.2 suggest that the use of shadow

Market prices and opportunity costs may diverge in circumstances where:

- market prices are distorted through imperfections in the market such as will be induced by the existence of monopolistic elements;
- market prices cannot be used to value benefits (or costs) where they are not capable of being marketed (e.g. what are called externalities such as pollution);
- there are public sector induced constraints (e.g. trade agreements with other states or international bodies) and imperfections such as taxes and tariffs;
- the investment or project in question is large enough to affect market prices (i.e. it becomes a non-marginal decision).

Box 10.1. Why market prices can diverge from opportunity costs.

Shadow prices may be an inappropriate response to market failures because:

- it may be better to tackle the market failures directly;
- if the market failures cannot be tackled directly, the preferred second best option might be to introduce subsidies to adjust market prices generally;
- shadow prices introduce a distortion by being confined to public sector decisions with implications for the tax burden on the rest of the economy;
- there are bound to be difficulties in defining the level and duration of the shadow prices and, hence, confusion in the decision rules and the danger of their being abused;
- public sector management may be burdened with opaque decision rules and costly information requirements in using shadow prices when the use of market prices would be easier and approximately correct.

Box 10.2. When shadow prices should not be used.

pricing could result in imperfect targeting, less than clear management incentives, and higher taxation. In the Appendix to this chapter I consider the case for using shadow pricing in the labour market – both the case for a general shadow wage and for a shadow wage specific to certain labour market conditions (e.g. the long-term unemployed).

The excursion in the Appendix into the world of shadow wages is designed to test, with an illustration, whether the Treasury's simplified appraisal rules deliver the appropriate control procedures and management incentives and are consistent with sound economic principles. My conclusion is that, on the latter, the Treasury message passes the test.

However, what will be apparent from the interplay of argument presented in the Appendix is that the Treasury position requires rather more advocacy than a simplistic appeal to the 'usual assumption . . . that market prices generally reflect opportunity costs' (HMT, 1991, p. 20). Such simplistic appeals do little to advance debate and, in fact, can be quite counterproductive in terms of getting the most out of public expenditure. This proposition is explained more generally in the next section.

The Green Book and other Treasury guidance

The Green Book is intended by the Treasury as the embodiment of guidance which should influence the way all programmes and projects involving public expenditure are appraised. If it is the bible for economic appraisal in government, then the Treasury is the priesthood – delivering the word and its correct interpretation.

The Treasury's public expenditure administrators and microeconomic advisers are the custodians of the Green Book and its application to economic appraisal throughout government. They seek to ensure that the finance and economics divisions of departments understand it and impart its lessons to departmental decision-makers. They can check that this is the case by inspection of the projects being presented for approval which exceed departmental delegated authority limits or which for other reasons are high-profile decisions.

But that is essentially it – the Green Book itself and the small body of the priesthood resident in the Treasury and in the finance and economics divisions of departments and some of the major agencies. There has been little attempt to develop user-friendly versions of the Green Book and to open it up for debate.

This gives the Green Book almost mystical status. I have seen terms of reference from public sector clients for project appraisals and evaluations that make the requirement that the work to be done must be consistent with the Treasury 'model'. The implication is obvious – the Treasury has a view of the world, a model, which has to be complied with whatever the rights or wrongs of the matter.

This presumably is not totally unattractive to the Treasury since it limits discretion and helps keep the lid on public expenditure. However it might not be helpful in making the best use of public expenditure when the guidance is not understood properly or if it is incomplete. Certainly in the area of local economic development I have encountered circumstances where the Green Book is not known or is misinterpreted.

The brevity and cryptic nature of some of the wording in the Green Book has contributed to this misinterpretation. Moreover, in the case of spending on local economic development, there are a number of important omissions. 'Additionality' is briefly mentioned in the 1991 version, while 'displacement' is not mentioned at all (although 'crowding out' in the macroeconomic sense is discussed). These concepts are, however, central to the assessment of the effects of intervention on local economic development. Additionality refers to the extent to which an intervention actually makes a difference relative to what otherwise might have happened. (Where public spending makes no difference in this sense, it is sometimes known as 'deadweight' expenditure.) Displacement refers to the extent to which any additional output from one project leads to less output from other sources. For instance, one firm being set up with help from government might lead to another losing business or closing down.

More significantly, the Green Book only pays cursory attention to a number of key concepts, including strategies, outputs and impacts (although much attention is paid to inputs and costs). These deficiencies have been remedied somewhat in subsequent Treasury guidance – *A Framework for the Evaluation of Regeneration Projects and Programmes* (HMT, 1995). This does define gross and final outputs and acknowledges that the difference between the two is the result of, among other factors, deadweight and displacement effects. However, even this inadequately thinks through and explains the central concepts of strategic rationale, outputs and impacts and the relationship between them.

The strategic rationale for a programme or a project defines its underlying principles, its primary purpose, and the way in which it should be implemented. Strategies provide the context in which projects should be appraised. It could be argued, therefore, that the development and appraisal of strategies is more important than project appraisal. Focus on the latter is like examining an elephant with a microscope. Area economic development strategies require assessment of whether elephants or camels are needed (or, to use real-life examples, light rapid transit systems or housing investments). Only then is it appropriate to carry out an appraisal of, say, the transit types and routes. There is a need for advice on credible methods of developing and appraising strategies particularly in the context of delivery mechanisms based – largely at Government's insistence – on partnerships between different regional and local interests.

As for output and impact measures, the 1995 Treasury framework gives a number of examples of intermediate and final outputs (and appropriate indicators). However, there are a number of inconsistencies, for example:

- Activities and outputs are confused (for example, the number of training places provided and the numbers who have completed training are both

described as intermediate outputs, whereas the first is a measure of the intervention activity and the second an output from that activity).
- The distinction between intermediate and final outputs is similarly fudged (e.g. the reduction in the percentage of firms going out of business is presented as a measure of final output from a business development intervention whereas this seems more appropriate as an intermediate output measure leading to the final output of, say, increased employment generation).
- Final output measures are often vaguely defined and are very disparate (for example, market rents in one case and school staying-on rates in another) such that it is difficult to see how interventions could be compared on any common basis.

There is, thus, a confusion of terminology and the lack of a clear framework which establishes relationships between expenditure and activities, outputs and impacts within a well-specified strategic context.

These deficiencies are also present in the Department of the Environment's guidance on the Single Regeneration Budget Challenge Fund (1995). This provides a selection of so-called output measures which fail to distinguish between activities, outputs and impacts. For example, the number of new childcare places provided (an activity measure), the number of those trained who have obtained qualifications (an intermediate output measure), and the number of jobs created/safeguarded (a final output or impact measure) are all given equal status as 'output measures'.

This confusion in the available guidance on the treatment of strategies and outputs is likely to be particularly unhelpful where delivery of economic development programmes has been decentralized. In these circumstances, those making decisions about the use of public money at the decentralized level need to understand and apply the appropriate appraisal rules and procedures. Otherwise, there is the danger of ineffective and wasteful use of public expenditure.

Decentralized delivery of economic development programmes

During the 1980s there was increasing interest in local, as distinct from regional, economic development. A number of agencies, both public and private, began to develop programmes and activities to assist the process. Because this happened in a rather piecemeal way, by the end of the decade a large number of local organizations were either supporting or funding various forms of economic development activities. In addition, central government multiplied the number of awareness and advisory schemes in support of business development. At the same time, the European Commission introduced Integrated Development Operations Programmes or Community Initiatives for the delivery of Structural Funds assistance at sub-regional level.

The late 1980s and early 1990s saw a number of government initiatives to rationalize the mechanisms for local economic development and regeneration support. The aim was to encourage programme design and delivery to meet local needs through partnerships between local interests. This was done by bringing together training and business development support and assigning responsibility for its delivery in England and Wales to the Training and Enterprise Councils (TECs) and in Scotland to Scottish Enterprise (SE) and Highlands and Islands Enterprise (HIE) each of which established a number of Local Enterprise Companies (LECs). The business development advisory and consultancy services were also rationalized by providing local one-stop shops, again through local partnerships in which the TECs and LECs were expected to exercise a leading role.

As a result of this rationalization, as many as 82 TECs were established in England and Wales and 22 LECs in Scotland. Regional development agencies continued to function in some areas – SE and HIE in Scotland, the Welsh Development Agency and the Development Board for Rural Wales in Wales, and regional development organizations in some, but not all, English regions (the North East, the North West, Yorkshire and Humberside, the West Midlands, and Devon and Cornwall). The offices of central government departments in the regions were combined and became the location for the monitoring committees and secretariats responsible for the management of European Union Objective 1, 2, and 5(b) assistance under the Structural Funds and of the Single Regeneration Budgets. In addition, and most recently, local government has been reorganized into unitary authorities.

One result of all these changes is that there is now increased delivery of economic development programmes at a local level, alongside centralized funding. Local democratic accountability has been diluted by weakening local authority influence and, although regional structures were retained, they did not strengthen regional control and influence.

All these institutional changes have taken place over a relatively short period of time – some five years. In that same period the capacity for effective central control of the public funding associated with regional and local economic development was weakened by the rationalization at the Treasury which involved major reductions in the staffing complement for public expenditure administration and microeconomic advice. Consequently, since the Green Book was published in 1991, there has been such a degree of decentralization in delivery that it is even more likely that the Treasury's appraisal rules and procedures will not be fully understood or, indeed, deliberately misunderstood or ignored.

The Green Book emphasized that 'responsibilities and procedures for initiating, carrying out and vetting appraisals need to be clear within each organization', that 'responsibility for carrying out appraisals normally lies in the executive or policy divisions' and that 'responsibility for procedures, departmental guidance and vetting generally lies with finance divisions'.

When the Treasury provided these guidelines in 1991 it may have been able to claim that they were broadly adhered to. At that time, the traditional, fairly tight hierarchy of control was still in place. However, by 1996 it seems likely that there has been a loss of clarity in the allocation of responsibilities and procedures for the conduct of appraisals and for output and performance measurement. This is likely to have happened both within and between the different bodies that are responsible for designing, delivering and monitoring economic development programmes.

My own impression is of fragmentation in this allocation of responsibilities such that there is no clear and consistent definition of roles between central government departments, their regional offices, regional development agencies, and the TECs and LECs. The weaknesses of the Green Book and in other guidance, particularly with regard to output measurement in the economic development context, mean that there is lack of clarity from this source as well. In such a situation either control will be exercised inadequately within budget locations or it will be imposed in a somewhat arbitrary fashion for accountability purposes. The demands of the latter have led to increasing use of targets and performance measures for planning and monitoring which, given the confusion in central guidance, has resulted in a system based on controlling what can be measured rather than seeking to measure what needs to be controlled. As a result, it must be assumed that public expenditure is not being used as effectively as it could be.

This raises the question of the extent to which decentralized delivery of economic development programmes needs to be accompanied by increased autonomy of control and funding for local or regional agencies and by a stronger element of local and regional democratic accountability. Certainly, the emphasis that should be given to developing a strategic context for project appraisal at local and/or regional level would suggest an important role for all substantial stakeholders. At the very least, there is a case for revised guidance on project appraisal and output measurement, for open discussion and dissemination of the guidelines and for clearer allocation of responsibilities for monitoring how the guidelines are applied.

Towards revised guidance

Content

A revised Green Book needs to contain a fuller discussion of strategy appraisal, outputs and impacts, and of how the latter should be appropriately incorporated into microeconomic appraisals. On the treatment of output measures, generic definitions should be provided which both distinguish between intervention activities, outputs and impacts and explain their interrelationships. In my own work on appraisals and performance measurement for local economic development I have found it helpful to distinguish between activities, outputs and impacts. These terms are defined in Figure 10.1 and discussed in Box 10.3 and are roughly equivalent to the terminology used in the Treasury and other

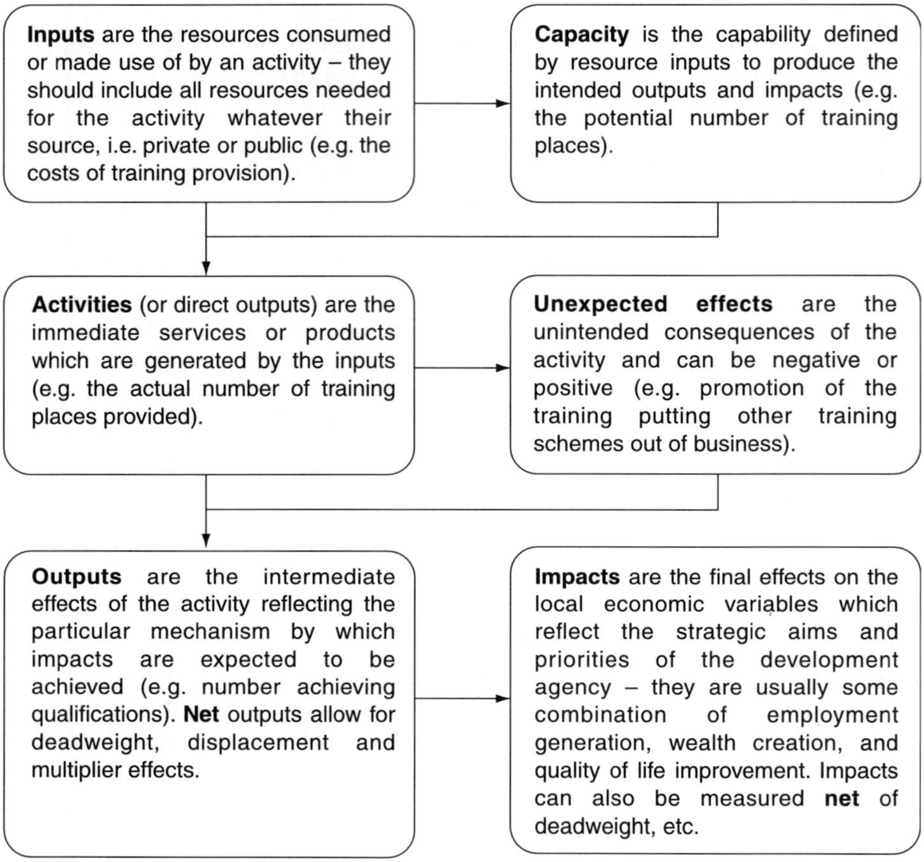

Figure 10.1. The causal chain from expenditure to impacts.

The planning and reporting process will be facilitated where there is a clear depiction of the casual chain between a development agency's intervention (its *expenditure and activities*), the intermediate effects of its intervention (the *outputs*), and the final consequences for the economic development components which the agency is seeking to influence (the *impacts*). At the outset – during the planning and appraisal stage – the agency will not necessarily be sure about the nature and scale of the links in the causal chain. Moreover, it may be that the intervention will generate unexpected side-effects (either adverse of beneficial). These uncertainties make it all the more important to specify the expected links in the causal chain at the planning stage and then monitor and evaluate the outcomes as programmes and projects are implemented.

Box 10.3. The importance of specifying the causal chain.

Whitehall documentation – inputs, intermediate outputs and final outputs. It is important, in devising appropriate output and performance measures, to be clear about the expected stages in the causal chain from expenditure to final outputs (or impacts) and the distinction between them.

The causal chain will vary, depending on which type of market failure prompts the intervention. Thus, a property market intervention (for example, subsidizing the building of a managed workspace) will be associated with activities and outputs which are distinct from a labour market intervention (e.g. a training programme) even where the impacts sought are the same. Plotting the distinct route in the appraisal of a proposed intervention will help in the identification of the appropriate measures of activities and outputs which can then be targeted for project monitoring.

Although I have been concerned here with appraisal and evaluation in the context of local economic development, the definitions offered above, and the principles which underpin them, could be applied to all types of microeconomic public sector funding. It may be difficult for a revised Green Book to be comprehensively detailed in its treatment of activities, outputs and impacts, but it would not have to be. Its main purpose would be to set up a framework of principles and illustrate its application in different circumstances.

On the treatment of appraisal, the revised Green Book should devote particular attention to the derivation and use of cost-effectiveness ratios. The current version recognizes the importance of cost-effectiveness analysis but emphasizes the model of project appraisal in which benefit streams can be given value and net present values (where future benefits are taken into account after an appropriate discounting) can be generated. This model has its place and, indeed, should be applied and extended (e.g. to business development as well as property development interventions), but there are a wide variety of circumstances in which it has severe limitations because of the nature of the outputs and impacts being generated. For example, programmes and projects devoted to improving the access of the disadvantaged to labour and housing markets are best appraised using cost-effectiveness measures.

Advances in the use of cost-effectiveness measures will require work to be done in two main areas. First, there will need to be the development of a consensus on the core measures of outputs and impacts (on the definitions above) which should be used for measuring cost-effectiveness in different categories of intervention. Second, there must be effort devoted to the collation of the results of monitoring and evaluation work which can then provide a source for benchmarks against which appraisal estimates can be compared.

Open and consultative process

The centralized hierarchical control model implicit in the Green Book no longer applies to the extent that it once did. This means that new guidance cannot be developed as if that model of control still applies, i.e. in closed discussions between the Treasury and central government departments. The issues discussed here are sufficiently important to justify a much more open and consultative process. With this in mind, there are at least three options for developing new Treasury guidance.

First, there is a more consultative and open version of the previous hierarchical model. Here, the Treasury might be expected to take the lead using the hierarchy of central government departments to canvas for best practice and to collect views on changes required in the existing guidance. With this approach, resolution of differences and the development of consensus on revisions would probably take place in an inter-departmental committee. At various points in this process, the debate could be widened through conferences, seminars and workshops.

Second, there is what could be described as the technocratic model along European Commission lines. This would involve setting up a technical assistance programme in which specialists are recruited through competitive tendering to advise on the appropriate appraisal procedures and practice, to produce guidance material, and to recommend the methods by which it should be disseminated and its application monitored. The commissioning authority could be an inter-departmental committee, but the hierarchical element this would retain could be weakened by requiring the technical specialists in their independent capacity to engage the interests and views of the regional and local organizations.

A third and more decentralized approach would directly involve regional and local interests – for example, the central government offices in the English regions and the development authorities in Wales, Scotland and Northern Ireland.

The three approaches are not mutually exclusive and it seems likely that some optimum combination could be found. The central hierarchical model should not be totally rejected, mainly for reasons of potential inter-regional and inter-local displacement. However, it should be deployed with both technical assistance and the direct engagement of the regional authorities.

The needs of users

The current Green Book and other Treasury guidance are often unnecessarily written in the language of neo-classical economics. This means that they are not always easy to read by those who are trying to apply the guidelines at a local level. This suggests, first, that any new guidance should be prepared with technical advice taken on its format, presentation style and dissemination.

Second, the guidance should be 'owned' by those who use it. It should be seen as a management tool which will help organizations to develop programmes and projects that meet their strategic goals in cost-effective ways. This means that there may need to be a 'portfolio of guidance' based around a core Green Book, to comprise guidance notes and illustrations specific to certain categories of microeconomic programmes and projects and/or to certain regions of the country. This suggests that, even with a hierarchical model for the development of the guidance, its application and dissemination should be managed in a decentralized way.

Finally, greater attention needs to be paid to the education and training needs of those involved in decision-making – particularly investment appraisal techniques – in the public sector (along the lines of that already provided to private sector managers). It is only relatively recently that initiatives have been taken to establish academic qualifications in local economic development. The presumption – which still runs through much of the UK's attitude to training – is that learning on the job is the most effective way of developing the necessary techniques to support local economic development. It is time for central government departments to give serious thought to the education and training needs of those involved in the appraisal of macroeconomic policies, programmes and projects that use public expenditure. The subject is too important to be left to the Treasury and too large to be contained within a single Green Book.

Appendix: the use of shadow wages in the appraisal of publicly funded projects

A general shadow wage

A general or economy-wide shadow wage implies that, in the economy as a whole, prevailing market wages do not properly reflect the social opportunity cost of employing more people. This is distinct from the argument for specific shadow wages based on market failures in the supply and demand for particular categories of labour.

At times of sustained high aggregate unemployment, it is sometimes argued that a general shadow wage should be used to give special weight to increased employment and reduced unemployment in public sector expenditure decisions.

The argument runs something like this. Many of the unemployed are looking for work and are willing to take jobs at existing wages. However, they are still unable to find jobs. Since the unemployed produce no output, the opportunity cost of employing them is zero (in other words, they would be doing nothing else otherwise). Consequently, using market wages distorts public sector expenditure decisions about whether to undertake or fund a particular activity and about the choice of implementation method (i.e. its labour intensity). On this argument, a public sector decision based on using shadow wages would yield the same benefits as other options but would employ more people – somebody gains and nobody loses. (There is a variant on this argument which is based on adjustment time in the labour market and, here, the case becomes one for a temporary, general shadow wage.)

There are some qualifications needed to this argument but they are not totally damaging to it. Thus, even in its own terms, the argument should be for a shadow wage that is greater than zero but one that is less than the going market rate. For example, the private costs of unemployment are not equal to the market wage foregone. They also need to take into account unemployment benefits and the costs of working – for example, travel to work costs.

The counter-argument to the case for a non-zero shadow wage less than market rates has three strands – macroeconomic, microeconomic and managerial.

Macroeconomic case

The introduction of a general shadow wage would be equivalent to changing employers' national insurance contributions for all employees or altering the marginal cost of labour (e.g. by a recruitment subsidy). As such, this would disturb the balance that the government of the day had already sought to establish (through its monetary, fiscal and supply-side policies) between price stability and output. Consequently, its introduction would require some offsetting policy adjustments elsewhere in order to restore the balance. All governments are likely to adopt this position, whatever the balance between outputs and prices they wish to see in the short term and whatever their view about the relationship between them in the longer term.

It is important to be clear about what is being said in making this macroeconomic response. It is not an argument against shadow wages as such; it simply states that the introduction of a shadow wage on macroeconomic grounds will necessitate adjustments elsewhere if the government of the day is content with the balance it is seeking to strike between prices and outputs in the economy as a whole. Prest and Turvey (1968) noted some 30 years ago, and hence couched it in somewhat old-fashioned terms, that 'in most cases it is best for unemployment policy to be left to the central government and for the agencies responsible for public works to confine their corrections of market prices on account of under-employment (i.e. overpricing) to divergences which are local or which relate to some specialised factor of production'.

Microeconomic case

As Prest and Turvey recognized, the case for shadow wages must, therefore, be found in the microeconomic arena. But there are counter-arguments here as well. First, the impact of shadow wages would tend to be confined to the public sector, since only the public authorities would be pricing labour in this way. Labour would be bid away from the private sector even where it had a higher marginal product there. Second, its introduction would put upward pressure on public expenditure and expand public sector provision – more projects would yield a positive present value in those areas where the outcome was traded or otherwise could be given a monetary value. Third, its impact as a counter-cyclical device (i.e. a temporary shadow wage) would be limited, since major public sector projects tend to have long gestation periods.

To sum up: the main argument against a general shadow wage on microeconomic grounds is that the market failures or other factors which apparently justify the use of shadows are likely to be better dealt with by other policy instruments which act on them directly and seek to eliminate them. A general shadow wage would tend to perpetuate underlying market failures while, at the same time, putting upward pressure on taxation.

Managerial case

Practical managerial drawbacks to the use of shadow wages include the following:

- The use of shadow wages in public sector appraisal will tend to depress the financial returns of trading bodies, making their performance more difficult to assess, and possibly de-motivating managers.
- Shadow wages could introduce further distinctions in project appraisal between 'resource' costs and the budgetary costs which fall on departments – this could reduce managerial efficiency because it confuses the optimization process.
- The information requirements for project appraisal and implementation would be increased. It is argued that a shadow wage is one that is set at a level we cannot estimate in circumstances we can never know. This means that there would be potential for misleading and confusing signals.

Specific shadow wages

The Treasury guidance admits the possibility of shadow wages in specific circumstances. While the Green Book does not say so explicitly, the case derives from segmentation in the labour market, either in terms of spatial areas (e.g. inner cities) or categories of the unemployed (e.g. the long-term unemployed). At the heart of the case is the possibility that some groups in the labour market (e.g. the long-term unemployed) have only a limited impact on wage pressure and, hence their increased employment will not have the same impact on the average output-price trade-off as would the increased employment of other groups.

However, even here the case for specific shadow wages is not clear and raises a number of questions. For example, how can they be set and targeted? Why are alternative policies not available or preferred? How will financial discipline and motivation be maintained where the use of shadows justifies projects with low financial returns? How can the temporary nature of any shadow be assured? What safeguards can be put in place to ensure that shadow wage setting is not simply being used for protectionist and subsidization purposes?

To sum up: a theoretical case for specific shadow wages can be made. In practice, however, it is doubtful whether they would be effective. They will need to be argued for on a case-by-case basis with a general presumption against them.

References

HMSO (1996). *Government Response to the Environment Committee First Report into the Single Regeneration Budget*. Secretary of State for the Environment, London: HMSO.

HMT (1984). *Investment Appraisal in the Public Sector*. HM Treasury, London: HMSO.

HMT (1991). *Economic Appraisal in Central Government*. HM Treasury, London: HMSO.

HMT (1995). *A Framework for the Evaluation of Regeneration Projects and Programmes*. HM Treasury, London: HMSO.

Prest, A.R. and Turvey, R. (1968). *Cost benefit analysis: a survey*. In: Surveys of Economic Theory, Volume III, Resource Allocation. London: Macmillan.

11

Public Sector Pay

Chris Trinder

Contents

Public sector pay accounts for two thirds of all government current expenditure on goods and services and one third of the general government planning total (which also includes transfers and capital expenditure). What happens to public sector pay is therefore a major determinant of what happens to public spending: if public sector pay increases get out of control or are not properly budgeted for, the consequences for non-pay items can be severe. This chapter therefore focuses on several aspects of the pay issue.

First, it considers in more detail why public sector pay matters in terms of public expenditure and what has been happening to it over time. Second, we look at whether it can be cut back and what happens if one tries this. Next, we look at how different groups of public servants have fared relative to one another, to those in other countries and compared to private sector workers. Following this, we focus on an important development of the last decade or so, that of the decentralization of public sector pay. How far has it happened and to what effect? Finally, the chapter looks to the future and what a new government might do in this area.

Public sector paybills

The public sector paybill is a product of the scale of employment; the structure of employment – as it divides up into occupations, grades and part-timers versus full-timers; the way that payment is calculated, for instance whether it is worked out on an individual basis or across the board; government policies on basic wage rates and gross earnings; general policies on things like pension contribu-

Table 11.1. Public sector paybills and paybill changes adjusted for inflation 1961–95.

Year	*Public sector paybill (£ bn)*	*Paybill change adjusted for inflation (%)*
1961	4.57	
1962	4.85	1.9
1963	5.14	4
1964	5.47	3.1
1965	5.93	3.6
1966	6.36	3.4
1967	6.87	5.5
1968	7.44	3.6
1969	7.89	0.6
1970	8.92	6.7
1971	10.22	5.2
1972	11.8	7.9
1973	13.4	4.4
1974	16.83	9.5
1975	23.32	14.4
1976	26.46	−3
1977	28.64	−7.6
1978	32.35	4.7
1979	37.08	1.2
1980	46.14	14.5
1981	51.61	0
1982	55	−2
1983	58.8	2.3
1984	60.33	−2.4
1985	61.13	−4.8
1986	65.79	4.2
1987	67.51	−1.6
1988	71.41	0.9
1989	75.79	−1.6
1990	80.71	−3.1
1991	85.24	0.5
1992	92.81	4.4
1993	93.95	−0.3
1994	94.34	−2.0
1995	95.79	−2.0

Source: Office for National Statistics (1996a, b), July.

tions, income tax and national insurance contributions; and the policies of the government towards the increases in public sector pay that it will allow. We will look at each of these aspects. However, it is clear that the dominant factor will be the scale of employment.

The public sector employs approximately one fifth of the workforce of the whole economy and its paybill makes up 22 per cent of the total income that people receive from employment and self-employment. The public sector paybill is now about £100 billion a year, in a Gross National Income of just over £600 billion, and planned total general government expenditure of around £300 billion. So simply, in terms of size, pay is an issue of great importance.

Table 11.1 sets out the total public sector paybill in each year since 1961 and the real percentage change in the paybill (i.e. after adjusting for inflation) in successive years. It shows clearly that the movements in the public sector paybill over time are erratic: and these oscillations are still visible after allowing for inflation. Sometimes it is hard to see what is driving the changes; at other times there are clues. For instance, there was a big catch-up in 1980 and 1981 following the Clegg Commission findings. And in 1992, in the run-up to a general election, the paybill rose from £85.2 billion to £92.8 billion, 4.4 per cent more than inflation.

While the paybill has many influences going into it – as we have seen – the fact is that whether we focus on the paybill or other measures of pay, the public sector is characterized by large pay fluctuations. These large oscillations in public sector pay are damaging and unhelpful particularly because they take it out of step with private sector pay. Figure 11.1 shows the difference between annual public and private sector pay increases differences – in terms of changes in gross average earnings per head.

The cycles in relative public–private pay usually last for a considerable time and involve rather more than just a slight falling behind in one year and a catching up in the next. Certain years, notably 1974–75 and 1980–81 and, more recently, 1991–92 were relative high points for the public sector. In general, there is a pattern of prolonged falls in relative pay, and sometimes absolute pay, followed by a large and expensive 'catching up' process, usually via particular awards following 'Inquiries' or Pay Review Body reports. In contrast, average private sector pay follows a much smoother course.

Public sector pay policies

In truth, governments have made some efforts to try and avoid these oscillations. Focusing on civil service pay, the pay determination system set up in 1956 involved a pay research review once every five years for each group of staff to try to avoid things getting too far out of line. The Megaw Inquiry into civil service pay in 1982 said a weakness of this system, which set pay for 1956 to 1981, was that in practice there were always delays in adjusting pay.

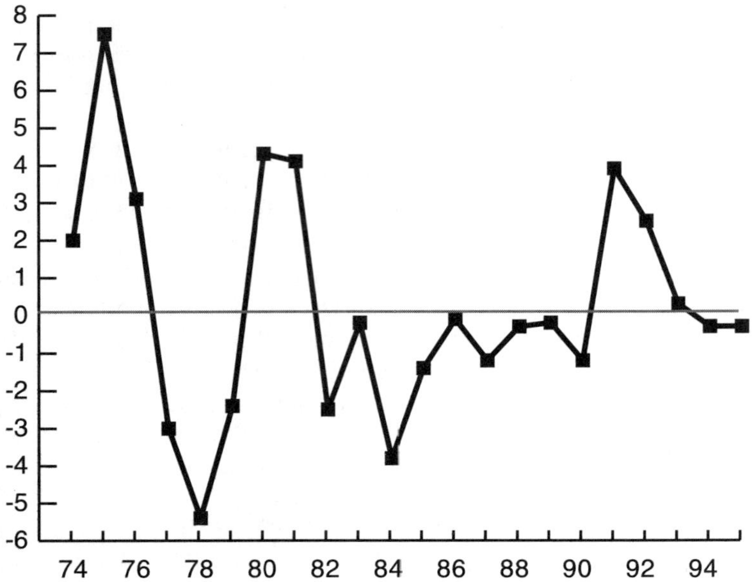

Figure 11.1. The relative size of public and private sector pay increases 1974–95
% difference between annual public and private sector pay increases (positive number means public increase exceeded private).
Source: Department of Employment, (1974–95).

When the trend in private sector pay settlements was downward the government was reluctant to permit a civil service pay settlement on the basis of the earlier higher rate. When the trend was upward, civil service pay rises usually lagged behind them. At times of large fluctuations in pay trends and high inflation, these lags caused staff difficulties and were de-motivating even if in the long run they were ironed out by one-off comparability inquiries or by other means. Moreover, such cycles can have a most unjust effect upon those who retire during the period before 'catch up'. They can become the permanent victims of a policy which merely has temporary disadvantages for those continuing in the service. As we have seen from the paybill figures, the pattern of increased pay followed by a gradual slippage in the pay league is not confined to the civil service.

In assessing why the existing machinery had been unable to maintain the position repeatedly accorded to civil servants by independent inquiries, arbitration and pay research, Megaw concluded that when the government finds itself obliged to give priority to national economic policy over the maintenance of civil service pay levels in a particular year, there is difficulty in taking a longer-term view. The government has often made it clear that at times of tight constraints in public expenditure it cannot agree to arbitration on the total cost of civil service pay settlements. Thus political expediency interferes with attempts to rationalize pay systems. The worry is both with the total cost of public sector pay, and also with being seen to set a 'going' rate for private sector pay increases that may then influence the behaviour of wages in the economy, with consequences for unit labour costs, inflation and so on.

In oral evidence to Megaw, the government said that it did not seek year after year to pitch civil service settlements below market rates in the private sector. It agreed that pay cycles were not desirable and that industrial unrest and catching-up increases would surely follow as they had in the past.

There are ways of avoiding such problems. The government can build realistic assumptions for pay into its cash limits, based on what is happening in the private sector. But despite its statements that it wished to avoid the problems, the actions of government have not followed this logic. Instead, in recent years the government has put its policy for restraint of public sector pay right at the centre of its spending programme and way above any kind of desire to deal with pay in an orderly way.

In the 1992 Autumn Statement the Chancellor said: 'As far as the public spending side of things is concerned, our plans depend on pay restraint. I wished to control public expenditure and I did not wish to add to the PSBR, which I believe is uncomfortably high.'

To achieve this, in November 1992 the government announced public expenditure plans for the financial year 1993–94 in which civil service pay settlements and other public sector groups were restricted to a maximum of 1.5 per cent. The pay restraint aimed to release sums of the order of £1.5 billions in 1993–94 in order to allow for increased capital expenditure. The government stressed that it was not an incomes policy and would not be imposed on the private sector but was a decision by a major employer – the government – to control its costs.

> Only by exercising restraint on current expenditure, of which pay forms so large a part, can the inescapable pressure elsewhere in spending programmes be accommodated, and capital spending in particular be given the emphasis widely urged, while keeping to our published plan for public spending, as a whole.

The government stressed it was seeking to restrict Civil Service and other public sector settlements to 1.5 per cent or less for one year only (due to exceptional circumstances), but would not allow a series of catching-up settlements in the following years so the financial savings by this policy in 1993–94 would lead to 'similar effects on the paybill in future years'. In fact there has been a paybill freeze policy for the last couple of years, one that is currently scheduled to go on until at least 1998.

The 1990s pay policy can be characterized, in the main, as a central government funding assumption for the paybill with little regard for any other role that pay may play. It is similar to the approach adopted unsuccessfully in the early 1980s and dropped in 1985.

The main criticism which is levelled at restrictions on public sector pay of this kind is that they simply represent a means of postponing expenditure, because any pay restraint in the short term will necessitate increased pay settlements in future years. Such policies also came into conflict with paying a rate necessary to recruit, motivate and retain staff and to introduce more decentralized, performance-related pay.

It is well worth pointing out that despite the severe restriction on the paybill, actual pay increases for staff have been quite reasonable over this period. This reflects the fact that the paybill constraint had often been managed by reducing the numbers of those employed – or by shifting to cheaper forms of employment like part-timers and temporary staff. In this sense, surviving public sector workers have not done too badly. However, such reductions in numbers have implications for the ability to deliver decent services in the longer run. A pay policy cannot be made without due regard to the policy on public sector employment.

In any case, while average increases have been reasonable in recent years, the falling behind in the 1980s has never been made up. The continuing squeeze on the paybill is therefore storing up potential trouble. The large pay awards granted to MPs in the summer of 1996 are fuelling demands for similar treatment by other public sector workers and there has been unrest among postal workers, transport staff and civil servants and signs of it among nurses and other health staff.

The changing size and composition of the public sector

Size

For a long time, the public sector only carried out core activities. Employees were supposed to be reasonably paid, so that they would resist opportunities to supplement their income by abusing their power. Public service was a secure job, providing you were of the 'calibre' to gain entry.

This changed over time, as we can see from the evolution of the civil service. The early service was small and limited in scope but over time its remit was widened, for instance, after welfare reforms, and so the numbers employed increased. The total workforce remained small until the Second World War, rose dramatically during it, and then shrank to a level which remained stable until the mid-1970s. Figure 11.2 shows that since 1979 the total number of public sector workers has fallen steadily.

To some extent definitional changes have influenced this. For instance, former polytechnics, further education and sixth-form colleges and grant-maintained schools are now counted as in the private sector (ONS (1996b), August 1996 p. 376) whereas most would think of them as still being in the public sector. But this does not explain most of the changes.

One implication of a smaller public sector is of course a smaller paybill; this is now a smaller proportion of the whole economy paybill than any time since 1960. It is still large, however, at close to £100 billion, and it is certain that it will be clamped down on still more, as the public sector borrowing requirement continues to cause concern. Hardly a month passes without functions being

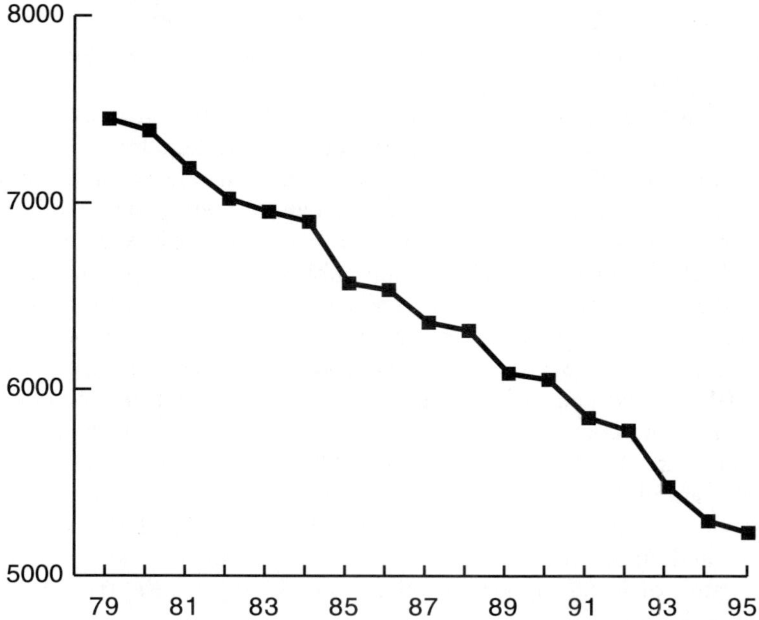

Figure 11.2. Public sector employment 1979–95 (thousands).
Source: ONS (1996c), Economic Trends, February.

discontinued, streamlined or privatized. New technology can save on the paybill by increasing staff efficiency. For example, the Benefits Agency aims to deliver a service at its present level with only 75 per cent of the staff by the year 2000. But often fewer staff means less of a service. Many public sector activities are very labour intensive and if the pay bill is excessively reduced the service will suffer.

Composition

This overall stability 1950–75 concealed changes in composition. In this period, blue-collar jobs were lost and the number of white-collar jobs increased. In the post-1979 period the manual workforce has continued to bear the brunt of the reductions.

The experience of the civil service (10 per cent of all public sector employees) is representative of what has happened to the public sector as a whole. The parts of the public sector which have already been shed, have been mainly blue-collar, male-dominated, capital-intensive parts such as electricity, gas, water, telephones, steel, car manufacture, and most recently, British Rail. Remaining in the public sector are parts which are difficult to sell because they do not offer ready profits or which are deemed inappropriate for sale. Schools and hospitals fit into this latter category, and employ large numbers of workers, mainly female, and often part-time. Even where sell-off has not been carried out, there have been reductions in numbers. The armed forces, for instance, now employ half the workers they did 35 years ago.

These changes have brought about a shift in the types of employees in the public sector, from a domination by male, full-time workers towards female and part-time. In mid-1979, there were 4.2 million men and 3.3 million women employed in the public sector. By mid-1995 there were just 2.2 million men but still 3 million women. Employment of women has thus been relatively stable in a period when 50 per cent of the male public sector employees have gone.

Half of the women work part-time; whereas only 155000 men do. That means that compared to 1985, when 24 per cent were part-time, 33 per cent are now part-time. This clearly means that the headcount is no longer a good guide to the number of hours worked or the total paybill. In terms of full-time equivalents (where part-timers count for less than a full-timer) the current numbers in the public sector are 4362000 – around 900000 less than the headcount (ONS, 1996c). In addition, while almost all these people are employees – self-employment remains rare – increasingly temporary and casual staff are employed, and fixed-term contracts are being introduced more widely. This shows the start of what might be another major change in the types of workers in the public sector.

At the latest count of the 5.25 million people working in the public sector, 1.5 million are town hall staff, 1 million are in the health service, nearly 1.2 million are in education (of which half a million are teachers), half a million are civil servants, and a quarter of a million workers are in each of the armed forces, the Post Office and the police. The rest are to be found in a wide variety of jobs.

Information on employment in the public sector comes from a variety of sources using different definitions. Information on public sector employment from administrative sources shows that for the first quarter of 1996 the average figure for the 1995–96 financial year was 40000 lower than 1994–95. On a headcount basis the total was only 18000 lower so there is still substantial substitution of part-time for full-time staff taking place in the public sector at the present time.

Comparison with other countries

There has been a structural change over the last quarter of a century in the composition of public sector employment in most developed countries. This has involved a rise in the proportion of highly trained employees and a decline in the unskilled and less well qualified categories (ILO, 1989). But aside from this the evolution of the UK public sector has been different from that in most countries.

Figure 11.3 shows that the UK level of public sector employment is higher than the OECD average and indeed higher than Germany, Italy and Spain, although it is now below that of France. Part of this difference reflects differences in what the public sector does in different countries, rather than things like

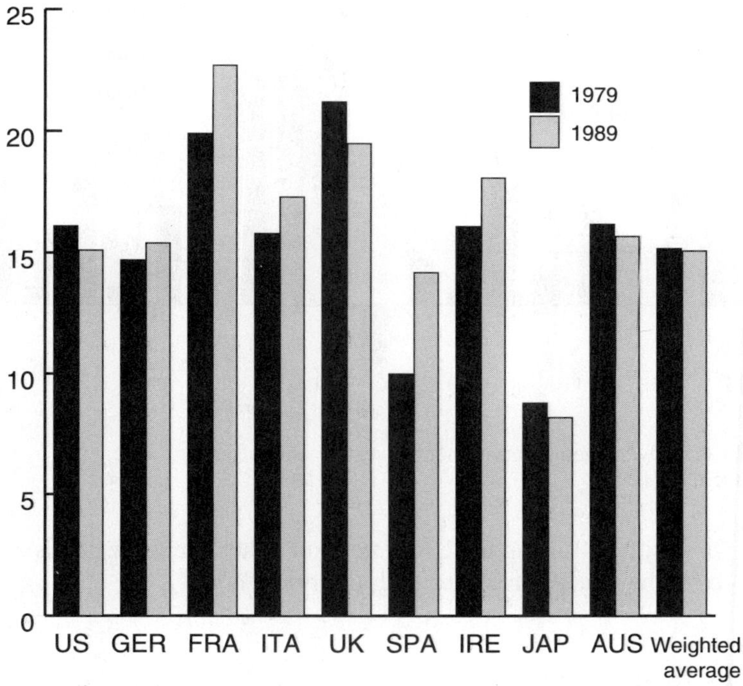

Figure 11.3. Government employment as share of total employment in various countries. *Source*: Oxley *et al.* (1990).

efficiency. For instance, defence accounts for a much higher proportion of spending in the UK than in most other countries while in the USA most health expenditure is in the private sector.

But Figure 11.3 also shows that public sector employment in the UK has fallen at a time when in other countries in the OECD as a whole it has remained roughly constant, and in most other major European countries it has been rising. This trend is shown more clearly in Figure 11.4.

One well-known area where the UK has clearly pressed on more rapidly than other countries is with its privatization programme for what were previously public corporations. In addition, public service employment has a long history of providing a stabilizing influence on cyclical fluctuations in private sector employment in most major developed countries (Stevenson, 1992) and in most of them this role is continuing. In the UK however, this normal 'safety valve' function performed by the public sector has been abandoned.

Government employment has continued to rise in absolute terms in all three of our major European partner countries, i.e. France, Germany and Italy, during 1979–92, albeit at a slower pace than employment growth in the private sector. Even over the latest two years for which data are available, a period of recession in most countries, the OECD average shows government employment up 0.9 per cent per annum 1990–92 compared to a reduction of –1.0 per cent per annum in

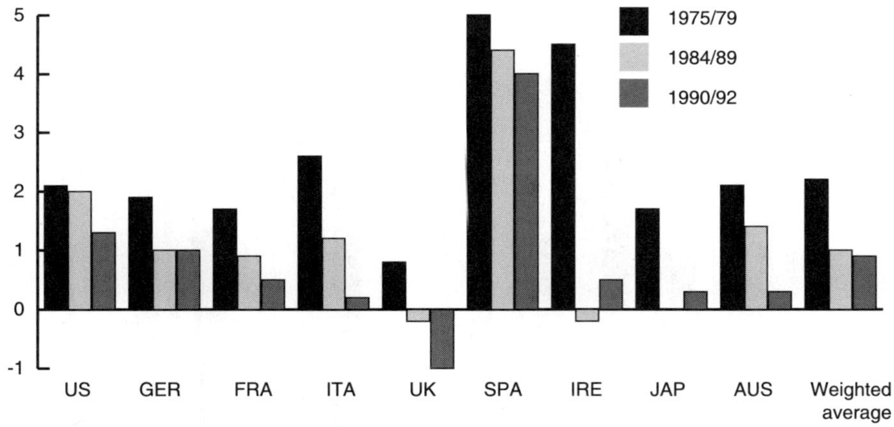

Figure 11.4. Government employment: average annual growth rate.
Source: OECD (1993).

the UK. Countries following the UK pattern on either cycles or trends can clearly be seen to be the exception rather than the rule.

Changes in pay relativities

Within the public sector

After the Clegg comparability awards in May 1980 the civil service national pay structure for administrative assistants (the bottom layer of the administrative grades) consisted of a scale running from £3075 to £3775. The top point for the next rung up, an administrative officer, was £4740; the executive officer scale ran from £4900 to £6745. At that time, a police constable earned a similar maximum of £6741, as did a nursing sister at the top of her scale at £6807. A fairly senior civil servant at Grade 5 (assistant secretary) was earning between £16650 and £19500 while a brigadier in the armed forces earned £18250, as did the highest-paid head teacher.

By 1994 a great deal had changed. The abandonment of comparability criteria in the civil service in 1981 has meant that these national civil service scales have fallen well behind those of other public sector groups which have either retained comparability (e.g. the armed forces), had indexing formulas (e.g. the police) or have independent pay review bodies recommending what their national pay scales should be (e.g. nurses and teachers). Thus the pay for a Grade 5 civil servant in 1994 was £36019 to £47921, while the highest-paid head teacher was paid £50682 and a brigadier £53600. A nursing sister had a maximum of £23040 and a police constable £21266, but the civil service executive officer scale had a ceiling of just £15520.

The numerically largest civil service category is the administrative staff, administrative assistants and officers. The scales for these in 1996 are now £6928 to £12174. This means that the bottom of the scale has increased by 125 per cent since 1980 and the top by 157 per cent. When compared with the 215 per cent increase in police salaries, the 194 per cent increase in armed forces pay and the 177 per cent increase for teachers over the same period, the magnitude of the gap that has opened up over the past decade and a half is clear. This has led to the description of the public service in Britain as being a two-tier system, with the civil servants being in the lower (or undeserving) category and police, army, nurses and teachers being in the upper (or more deserving) group. Over the period 1988–93 civil service national pay rates rose on average by 39 per cent, local government by 41 per cent and police, armed forces, health and education all by approximately 50 per cent.

There are, of course, several potential explanations for these divergent trends. One is that the nature of the jobs have changed, with people like head teachers taking on more duties (e.g. financial management under local management of schools) and administrative staff becoming de-skilled with the coming of new technology. But although this may be true in some cases, it is hard to argue across the board. Executive officers, for instance, are now far more likely to be university graduates than they were at the beginning of the 1980s.

Another is that there have been differing degrees of difficulty with recruitment and retention so that the emerging differentials simply reflect supply and demand forces. Again there have been periods when teachers, soldiers and nurses have been hard to recruit, especially in boom times and when demographic facts mean there are shortages of certain types of people (e.g. young women). But pay is also important in motivation. There will always be people coming forward to be executive officers (EOs) in the civil service, but if their pay drops, market theory suggests that so too will the quality and the morale of those working as EOs.

Finally, the argument is that government has responded to political pressures and advantage, rewarding what the public see as front-line services in the areas they care most about, while making savings from the 'backroom' staff. While this may be in a sense legitimate, it misses the point that the front-line staff can only be effective if the bureaucracy is working well. We may hate paper pushers, but we also need them to make the machine run smoothly.

Compared to the private sector

Even though civil service national scale rates have fallen well behind those of comparable occupations in both other parts of the public sector and the economy at large, gross earnings could still have moved in line because of the great increases in flexibility of civil service pay. But whereas the gross earnings information shows that civil service pay kept broadly in line with earnings elsewhere between 1956 and 1981 (Megaw, 1982), since 1981 civil servants have fallen behind in terms of gross earnings too.

In the economy as a whole, earnings for non-manual men, for example, rose by 156 per cent between 1981–93, but for administrative civil servants the rise was only 123 per cent (middle and higher grades) and 134 per cent (clerical grades) over the same period. Only for professional, technical and scientific civil service staff was the rise noticeably faster, with an increase in average gross earnings 1981–93 of 146 per cent. But even here this increase is still 10 points below that seen in the private sector. For local government workers a similar story applies, with there being a clear shortfall compared to the private sector in the 1980s and 1990s.

Professional groups such as nurses and teachers and others such as the armed forces and police have had trend pay rises closer to the private sector average. But there are legitimate grievances in some of these occupations as well. The predominantly female nursing and teaching professions argue strongly for a rise up the earnings league to reflect past discrimination against women's occupations and the increased demands being placed upon them.

Decentralization

At the start of 1991 there was a single employer in the health service, the NHS. This role has now been divided between 700 NHS trusts. Each of these takes responsibility for the pay and conditions of its staff, selling their output to central government. Similarly, most of the tasks formerly delivered by a lone civil service are now carried out by 200 executive agencies. This fragmentation has become the norm, and is planned to eventually embrace the entire public sector.

The process usually starts with control over budgets being delegated to local managers, with pay continuing to be influenced, if not determined, by bargaining at national level, or by pay review bodies or indexing, where these are in place. This is similar to the situation in central government outlined above. However, in the longer term more power over pay becomes decentralized both locally and by different occupations and grades. Parts of the public sector with a longer history of decentralized control already set pay at the local level.

In the 700 NHS trusts, in the medium term, local pay will become more prevalent and involve more groups. The education sector is being similarly fragmented, with local management of schools (LMS), and more decentralization may occur as developments in the rest of the public sector are monitored and evaluated and the lessons learned and transferred. The decentralization of pay setting may allow flexibility with more fine-tuning, which the current arrangements do not. Then we might see a change towards a pay structure which recognizes individual strengths, and rewards accordingly.

This market-orientated solution to public sector pay seems the one most favoured by the present government. But will it work to reduce the problems of recruitment, motivation and retention, to avoid the problems of public sector pay cycles, and to help the government keep more control over public sector pay?

In theory decentralization could ease the problems of public sector pay in a number of ways. First, pay can be set in response to local recruitment and retention difficulties, without having to up the going rate in areas where there are no problems. Second, decentralization may weaken the power of trade unions to force up wages. Third, to the extent that it leads to efficiency gains, staff numbers may be reduced, or their structure changed. One should note, however, that some of the reductions in staff costs can be rather illusory. For instance, if it is decided to contract out something previously done in-house, the accounts show less public money going on wages. But in fact the bill that the public sector pays to the private sector provider will include substantial amounts for wages.

These are early days and it is difficult to judge exactly what is happening but, so far, not much of this seems to be coming through. There certainly have been – as we have seen – reductions in full-time equivalent numbers but this is likely to have been as much a result of centrally determined cash limits on running costs as from decentralization.

The aim of making pay rises more flexible and reactive to local circumstances and to individual performance does not seem to have been accomplished so far. Teachers' pay rises in the last three years have been across-the-board increases of the same percentage value for the whole profession. This is also true for many other groups, such as police and doctors. This type of rise fails to reward high achievers. It is an expensive way of setting pay. In the private sector much use is made of bonuses and one-off benefits but this type of payment is yet to make an impact in the public sector.

It may be that the decentralization has the potential for moving in this direction in the future but this has not happened to date. This may partly be because money has been tight. There is an argument that if the economy grows faster and money becomes available, then it will be easier to start differentiating by area and occupation, given that everyone gets at least a reasonable increase as a baseline. In difficult times it appears that governments find it easier to treat everyone the same.

Indeed, an important reservation about allowing local pay to diverge from national agreements on pay in the absence of coordination or control is that it could lead to the practice of leapfrogging as employers outbid each other in order to attract scarce personnel. A 'going rate' emerges from a process of competitive leapfrogging, with one person's wage increase becoming another person's price increase. In a loose labour market, this may not be much of an issue, but it may well surface if and when shortages of labour start to emerge.

It is also too early to see if decentralization has led to lowering of pay particularly at the bottom. Certainly, and relative to the private sector, this has not been the trend in general. In 1971, the earnings distribution for full-time males in the public and private sectors was identical – the bottom 10 per cent got £20 per week, and the highest decile £48. In 1995, 24 years later, the corresponding figures are £202 in the public sector and £178 in the private sector; and £569 in the public sector, £616 in the private sector. Thus, the lowest paid do better in the public sector (one reason that a minimum wage would have less impact on the public sector than is sometimes supposed (Trinder, 1995)), but for high earners, the private sector is the place to be.

Of course there is an issue as to whether the lower-skilled public sector workers should be treated better than their private sector counterparts (many of whom are doing part-time jobs in companies with contracts with the public sector). But following similar logic, it is unclear why the top end of the skill spectrum should be discriminated against. Indeed as the public sector becomes less likely to give secure jobs for life, pressure to increase the pay in these higher jobs is likely to become more intense.

The low paid tend to do better in the public sector partly because public sector union negotiators traditionally favour the low paid, often opting for uniform flat rate rises which reduce differentials. In the private sector, there is a longer history of local pay bargaining and there has been a conscious effort to maintain, and indeed widen, differentials by management.

The future

In trying to predict the future of public sector pay, we must assimilate a wide variety of considerations. The government is both a major employer and is in the unique position of managing the economy that it is an employer within. It has, in the past, also had a vision of itself as an employer who sets an example of fairness and accountability to others. In some areas, the government is a monopoly employer and to some extent has a duty to treat staff in these areas fairly. All these aims inevitably conflict at times.

Public sector pay is paid for from taxation, not from profits or trading, so there is no commercial indicator as to what is an affordable or justifiable increase. The government is keen that taxpayers do not feel they are 'paying over the odds'. However, if increases are too limited or too arbitrary, effective use of the taxpayers' money is prejudiced. The impact that such policies have on management's time – if recruitment and retention and motivation become an issue – add up to avoidable inefficiencies. The costs of advertising, interviewing and recruiting is large in relation to a basic salary cost. Loss of trained staff and training their replacements also increases costs. Even more important than recruitment and retention, however, is both the quality of recruitment if pay policies are perceived to be 'unfair' and the impact on morale of those in post. This is a very costly effect although one that is almost impossible to measure, especially in areas where output indicators are non-existent or poorly related to ultimate outcomes.

The government's current mechanisms for determining pay and for planning for expenditure on pay do not seem to be rational, and give insufficient weight to the need to help recruit, motivate and retain high-quality staff. The key ingredients of a new, effective strategy should include:

- It must be medium-term: short-term policies can so easily be short-sighted. Any attempt to sort everything out at once is bound to fail. The need is to focus first on sorting out where differentials have become untenable and work on ways to solve these over time. Second, to design ways of making the whole system work better in the long run. This means thinking of ways to stop public sector pay falling behind private sector pay such that a difficult catch-up becomes needed, and also of trying to introduce more elements of pay that fairly reward good performance and effort without having to raise the pay for everyone.
- The strategy must build on existing institutions, starting from where we are, not where we might like to be. There are strengths in the current public sector which could be preserved. At the same time, there have been changes which mean that some of the old-fashioned characteristics and values of the public sector are gone for good, for better or worse. Any policy must recognize, for example, the reality of the fragmentation which has taken place and has become effectively irreversible. Similarly, the typical public sector worker is now more likely to be female and – increasingly – part-time.
- The approach must be holistic, taking a wide perspective. The government's unique position means that what it might save on public sector wages, it will have to pay for in terms of increased social security bills; unlike a private sector employer, a sacked worker on the dole is not cost-free to the government. Any policy must make sense overall in public expenditure terms.

A new government in 1997 will face the build-up of pressures described in this chapter. A future Labour government with a positive attitude toward unions could utilize the larger union structures to bring coherence to public sector pay: they offer economies of scale, and could be useful in dissemination of accurate information, helping with monitoring and evaluation. However, Labour would have to be tough with the unions. It is no good trying to make up for any unfairness and inefficiencies overnight, whatever the unions might desire. Labour should make clear how it intends to tackle these issues over the medium term and then hold fast to this policy.

In local government in particular, both management and unions feel, with some justification, that successive Conservative administrations have singled out their employees (especially white-collar workers) for particularly harsh treatment. This sector may argue very hard for an ample 'bounce back' for their workers. One approach to these problems would be to extend the pay review body – and indexing approaches – as mechanisms to act to remove unfairness over time. This approach could be made available to the entire public sector.

This extension would allow anomalies to be revealed and removed. This would not mean the levelling *up* of all the public sector – leading to an outcry from the impoverished private sector employee. Some groups who have done very well will lose a bit. By way of illustration, the comparability criteria enjoyed by the armed forces in determining pay might well be extended to other areas, but the fact that this currently also extends to armed forces' pensions would not be extended and would be withdrawn for the armed forces as well. Similarly, employment practices for groups like ancillary workers in the NHS would be brought more into line with practices for other groups, like teachers and nurses. The results would be constrained not to be more expensive overall, but this process would once again unify the public services.

For the past 15 years we have had a two-tier public sector, with some groups, such as the police, doing very nicely and other groups, such as town hall staff, falling behind. The changes suggested here would be fairer and more efficient and offer the prospect of a public sector workforce that is affordable and fairly treated.

References

Department of Employment (1974–95, annually) New Earnings Survey.
ILO (1989). *Structural Adjustment and Public Service Employment*, World Labour Report.
Layard, R. (1990). *How to End Pay Leapfrogging*. Employment Institute.
Megaw, J. (1982). *Inquiry into Civil Service Pay*. London: HMSO.
New Earnings Survey (annually). *Part A: Streamlined and Summary Analysis*, Department of Employment, London: HMSO, October.
OECD (1992). *Structural Change and the Public Sector*. Paris: OECD.
OECD (1993). *Pay Flexibility in the Public Sector*. Paris: OECD.
ONS (Office for National Statistics) (1996a). United Kingdom National Accounts, HMSO.
ONS (Office for National Statistics) (1996b). Labour Market Trends (monthly), HMSO.
ONS (Office for National Statistics) (1996). Employment in the public and private sectors, *Economic Trends*, February. HMSO.
Oxley, H. *et al.* (1990). *The Public Sector: Issues for the 1990s*. Paris: OECD.
Stevenson, G. (1992). *How Public Sector Pay and Employment Affect Labour Markets*. World Bank.
Trinder, C. (1995). What about the public sector? *New Economy* (Special Issue on Minimum Wages), **2**, (4).

Part IV
Allocating Public Expenditure Sensibly

12

Planning, Control and the Contract State

Peter M. Jackson

Contents

In an attempt to improve the management and control of public expenditure, successive governments have introduced a number of structural and cultural changes to the public sector over the past 15 years. Competitive tendering was introduced to blue-collar services in local authorities and hospitals; executive agencies were set up and quasi or internal markets were created in the NHS and local government. A mixed economy of care was introduced into social services, with the public, voluntary and private sectors competing against one another to supply services such as domiciliary care for the aged.

This exposure to greater competition and internal markets has produced what may be termed the 'contract state', in which the public sector acts increasingly as an 'enabler' or 'facilitator'. The new structures challenge traditional bureaucratic and professional public service values and have shifted power from local to central government and from professionals to managers. One result is that there now exists a 'tangled web' of relationships, some purposefully designed and others which emerged as the reforms were implemented. This web of relationships involves the separation of purchasers from providers; new committee structures to deal with purchasing and the letting of contracts; agency relationships between the public and private sectors.

Planning public expenditure – in other words, keeping spending within certain targets – is fundamental to both management and control. How, then, have reforms such as competitive tendering, executive agencies and value-for-money auditing helped in the planning process? We consider, first, whether government has been able to exercise greater control over overall spending; second, what the results of the reforms with regard to cost savings and greater efficiency/effectiveness have been; and finally, whether the public sector now gives greater value for money.

Planning the overall amount of public expenditure

The control of public spending has been one of the central planks of economic and social policy over the past 20 years. The budgetary procedures that were in place during the 1960s and 1970s were based upon volume planning and had resulted in unplanned expansions in public spending. This was especially true during periods of rapid inflation, as during the early 1970s. Cash limits on selected items of public spending were introduced in 1976. These were later extended to cash planning of public spending generally.

Successive Conservative governments put forward a number of arguments to justify control of the public expenditure total. One of the most commonly argued was that if both tax rates and tax as percentage of gross domestic product (GDP) were to be reduced so as to create favourable incentives to stimulate the supply side of the economy, public spending could not be allowed to grow faster than real GDP. However, despite the tightening of the control regime, the government was largely unsuccessful in achieving these objectives. Public expenditure often breached the control targets; and taxation as a proportion of GDP did not fall (for a more detailed discussion see Chapter 3 by Corry and Gray).

The control of total public expenditure is a formidable task. It is the outcome of a myriad of decisions made by different agencies. Moreover, many items of public expenditure, such as the social security budget, are responsive to events which are outside public sector managers' control, for example unemployment levels. In 1984 provision was made for such uncertainty by increasing the size of the contingency reserve within the control total. This is an amount of money budgeted for but not allocated to any particular use.

The larger contingency reserve, by making provision for a greater amount of unallocated public spending within the planning total, acted like a buffer absorbing uncertainty and shocks when they arose. Greater emphasis was placed upon controlling rather than planning public spending. The shape of public spending became more dependent upon unpredictable events (either actual ones or changes in ministers' preferences) and the persuasive powers of individual spending ministers.

However, increasing the size of the contingency reserve did not result in improved control over public spending. As Table 12.1 shows, the out-turn for public spending still often exceeded the plan. Too often, the bilateral negotiations between departments and the Chief Secretary for resources from the contingency reserve to fund new and existing programmes had a built-in upward

Table 12.1. Public expenditure planning total against out-turn.

	Plan (£ bn)	*Out-turn (£ bn)*	*Difference (£ bn)*	*%*
1983/84	119.3	120.3	+0.95	+0.8
1984/85	126.5	129.8	+3.3	+2.6
1985/86	132.1	133.7	+1.6	+1.2
1986/87	139.1	139.2	+0.1	+0.7
1987/88	148.6	145.7	−2.9	−2.0
1988/89	156.9	149.6	−7.3	−4.6
1989/90	161.9	162.9	+1.0	+0.6
1990/91	179.0	180.1	+1.1	+0.6
1991/92	200.3	203.5	+3.2	+1.6
1992/93	226.6	226.1	−0.5	−0.2
1993/94	244.7	241.4	−3.3	−1.3

NB: Plans set in November of each year.
Source: Thain, C. and Wright, M. (1995). *The Treasury and Whitehall*. Oxford: Clarendon Press, p. 490.

bias on public spending. Departments relaxed their controls, knowing that they could always appeal for money from the contingency reserve.

From 1992 a new control total was introduced. This meant that if a department wanted to introduce a new programme or expand an existing one it had to find savings elsewhere within its budget. This implied that the size of the contingency reserve could be reduced. Moreover, with low and stable inflation from 1992, the size of the reserve which is required is much smaller.

As recent history shows, even a government with a strong ideological commitment to control public expenditure has found this a difficult task. Gaps in the planning total left by adventitious savings obtained from favourable downturns in cyclical factors, such as unemployment benefits, are rapidly filled by other claims. The change to the control total in 1992 to exclude 'cyclical social security' means it is easier to see if control totals are being achieved and harder for 'adventitious savings' to be filled by other claims, but does not solve the problem completely.

Over time, the presentation of the notion of public expenditure control has changed. It has moved from being thought of as representing a reduction in the absolute size of public expenditure to a reduction in the ratio of public expenditure to GDP.

There are, however, inherent problems in planning spending to hit a target for the ratio of public spending to GDP. On the one hand are uncertainties about the future path of GDP. On the other are the problems of controlling the amount of spending. The 'relative price effect' is a particular problem here. Accounting conventions for public services mean that expenditure on inputs rather than outputs are recorded. This is equivalent to assuming a zero rate of productivity growth. Therefore, even modest increases in public sector wages, that lag behind those of the private sector, will push up the ratio of public spending to GDP. This also means that reductions in the absolute real volume of public spending could also result in an increase in the recorded ratio of public spending to GDP (at current prices).[1]

This illustrates how the planning and control of public expenditure requires a deep understanding of what is really going on. Indicators such as the ratio of public spending to GDP are crude and, therefore, need to be presented and interpreted with intelligence.

Planning for efficiency: the new public sector management

A new wave of managerialism swept through all parts of the private sector during the 1980s. The rationale lying behind such reforms as competitive tendering, executive agencies and value-for-money audits was the search for improvements in the efficient use of resources. These efficiency gains were to result in budget savings which could be used either to reduce public spending or reallocated to other parts of the service. The claim from public choice economists on the New Right was that, in the absence of competition and the discipline of the market place, public services would always be produced inefficiently. There were also suggestions that Adam Smith's 'invisible hand' of market forces was a better coordinating mechanism for deciding upon the level and mix of public services than the professional public sector bureaucracy. Efficiency would be improved by ensuring that public services would conform more closely to the needs of those who used them, rather than the interests of those who provided them.

What has, in fact, been achieved by these reforms?

Competitive tendering

It is difficult to place a monetary value on the results of competitive tendering. How, for example, does one assess how much of any budgetary change should be attributed to competitive tendering rather than to restraints upon public sector expenditure and wages, or the use of new management techniques? However, a number of studies have attempted to measure the financial savings. The National Audit Office (NAO, 1987), for example, found savings of up to 20 per cent when NHS domestic catering and laundry services were contracted out. Domberger *et al.* (1987) found that the contracting out of NHS laundry services resulted in cost savings of 34 per cent.

Cost savings have also been confirmed in other studies, though the amounts vary considerably (Milne, 1987; Milne and McGee, 1992). The Audit Commission (1991) found cost savings of 14 per cent in the contracting out of highway services. Domberger *et al.* (1986,1988) also found cost savings in local authority services that had been contracted out, as did Cubbin *et al.* (1987) and Walsh and Davis (1993).

Overall, then, competitive tendering appears to have resulted in some savings, although these are not as large as the wild claims made by some. Carefully conducted micro-level studies carried out by Walsh and Davis (1993) put the figure at about 7 per cent. This is, moreover, a gross figure, before netting off the management costs of acquiring the cost savings. Cost savings are also highly variable and some studies suggest that savings tend to disappear over the longer term (Szymanski and Wilkins, 1992; McMaster, 1995). Evidence from the US confirms that the long-term benefits of competitive tendering could be very small or even zero (Smith and Lipsky, 1993; Kettl, 1993).

Furthermore, any cost benefits may be lost in higher management costs (or in greater use of the service). In particular, there are the transaction costs of designing, writing, administering and monitoring contracts. Only when the service that is being contracted out is simple and involves repetitive routine tasks, such as refuse collection or grass cutting, will contracts be simple and relatively costless to administer and enforce. However, even in the case of a simple service, important choices have to be made if the contract is not to create adverse incentives. For example, a contract for grass cutting can specify that the grass be cut once a week during certain times of the year or that the grass be cut when it reaches a height of one inch. The first contract involves unnecessary activity and expense during dry weather and will, therefore, be more expensive.

Another source of difficulty arises when a contract to supply services has to be written for all contingencies. This is virtually impossible and if it was to be attempted would be very costly. The result is that the contracts which have been written have tended to be incomplete in their specification.

Agencies

The notion of Next Steps Agencies was set out in a report produced by the Efficiency Unit (1988). This change in the organization of government devolved non-strategic decisions to operational agencies. The rationale of Next Steps was to improve the management of public service organizations by separating the management of policy, which was the responsibility of central government departments, from operational management, which was to be the responsibility of the agencies.

It is difficult to assess whether agencies such as the Child Support or Benefits Agency have achieved their aims of improvements in efficiency and effectiveness. While agencies are obliged to provide a number of key performance indicators, these are seldom related to the objectives of their business planning document. Moreover, agencies tend to change the types of indicators they produce from one year to the next. It is also difficult to assess from the way in which their accounts are presented whether agencies have released resources through efficiency gains.

As the government's own Efficiency Unit (1995) noted (with regard to both central government departments and agencies): 'more than a decade after the launch of the Financial Management Initiative many departments still did not have in place the full [planning and monitoring] systems to manage effectively' (para 3.3) . . . 'even though systems might be in place, they were not necessarily regarded as being of use to managers or "owned" by them' (para 3.4). The Efficiency Unit also found that only 6 per cent of departments and 18 per cent of agencies had made any attempt to cost their objectives.

It is certainly difficult to find resource savings following the introduction of the Financial Management Initiative, the Resource Management Initiative or executive agencies (Jackson, 1995).

Value-for-money audits

The main emphasis in the Financial Management Initiative was on value for money (VFM). As developed and implemented by the National Audit Office and the Audit Commission, VFM was defined in terms of *economy*, doing things at lowest cost; *efficiency*, doing things the right way; and *effectiveness*, doing the right thing.

Central government departments had to demonstrate to the Treasury that they had in place a VFM framework. A range of performance indicators were introduced to reflect economy, efficiency and effectiveness. The rationale was that performance indicators would enable managers to find resource savings while, at the same time, improving the quality of public services.

There were too many indicators, however, and many were meaningless. Managers could not distinguish between those indicators that were useful and those that were not. Most of the indicators only covered areas that were easily measured and they covered inputs and throughputs rather than outputs and outcomes. The result was that most of the indicators concentrated on economy, few gave an indication of efficiency and virtually none measured effectiveness.

It is easy to introduce a new management information system which generates performance indicators. The challenge, however, is to use that information to improve the planning and management of public services and achieve more efficiency and effectiveness in resource use. The most recent research (see, for example, Jackson, 1995) suggests that performance indicators helped to promote a change in the general culture of public sector management. Overall, the sector became more 'customer' focused. However, the VFM framework has also made more transparent the difficulties and problems which public sector managers face. Trade-offs have to be made between efficiency and effectiveness. Take, for example, the Benefits Agency, where good adjudication (effectiveness) may be a slow process, but comes into conflict with the time it takes to deal with a case (efficiency).

One major difficulty which confronted those who were trying to implement VFM was that it was carried out in a climate of public expenditure control and reduction. This had the effect of making public sector employees suspicious and threatened by the whole exercise. In many cases, managers found it difficult to gain their confidence, enthusiasm and cooperation. Public service organizations played a game in which they were seen to be cooperating by producing performance indicators. Behind this ritualistic symbolism, however, there was great deal of cynicism.

Performance indicators were also used as an extension of the classical management 'command and control' atmosphere which permeated the public sector. Indicators were used as league tables, often without appreciating the inherent difficulties of interpreting the data they contained in the league tables; the injustices that would result if the information in the league tables were acted upon and the disincentives that this harsh climate would produce.

There is no doubt that performance indicators have a vital role to play in the effective management of public services. If managers are to learn how to improve the quality and the efficiency of the services that they deliver, indicators are needed to show them how well they are doing compared to target. Indicators, however, need to be meaningful and relevant and they need to be trusted by those who provide the information and by those who use them. They also need to be used in a positive learning context rather than in a negative command and control climate. The full potential of performance indicators in the public sector remains unrealized. As the private sector discovered many years ago, they are essential to the strategic management of services but they must be used sensitively.

Implications for planning and responsibility

The discussion above has raised a number of questions. In the case of incomplete contracts, for example, how has the public sector coped with the subsequent planning uncertainty? Like all organizations in a similar situation, recourse is made to trust. Charlesworth *et al.* (1996) found that purchasers of personal social services tended to continue to use long-standing providers – those that were to be trusted because of their reputation. Similar findings were reported by Bennett and Ferlie (1996) in their study of HIV/AIDS services, where contracts were not awarded simply on the basis of least cost. Other important considerations, such as reliability of supply and quality, were also taken into account.

Frequently it has been the in-house supplier that has been chosen since their reputation is well known (and the sheer threat of competition from alternative sources of supply has forced them to compete on price as well as quality). This is despite the fact that, unlike the private sector, the public sector supplier is obliged to achieve at least a 5 per cent rate of return on capital employed and that some private sector firms have used the public sector contract as a loss leader in an attempt to gain entry into that market (and if they see off the in-house competition they can raise prices when the contract comes up for renegotiation).

To be efficient and effective the contract state requires an enormous amount of information. Not only is information required to design and monitor contracts – and this is expensive – it has been estimated that about £1 billion has been spent hiring management consultants and IT specialists and to install new management information sytems to make the NHS internal market work – it is also required to set prices. One of the lessons of the past few years is that local authorities and health authorities do not possess the finely detailed management accounting information that will enable contract managers to price treatments such as a coronary bypass.

The transparency of contracts should mean that ministers can be held accountable for the details of implementation. In reality, ministers have tended not to accept responsibility and have distanced themselves from implementation matters. Any failures are blamed on the chief executive of an executive agency. For example, the head of the Prison Service, Derek Lewis, was sacked by the Home Secretary when the policy he was carrying out was set by the minister himself.

In the highly centralized state that the UK has now become, there has been a growth in the number of non-elected bodies. What Stewart (1993) has referred to as the 'new magistracy' includes training and education councils (TECs), hospital trusts, city technology colleges, the Further Education Council and urban development corporations. The management of these organizations are accountable to central government though the impact of their policies is highly localized. There is no locally elected voice represented in their management boards. Their budgets are tied to performance criteria that are centrally determined and there is a general belief that the chairmen who are appointed by central government are usually in sympathy with the policies of central government.

One result of the above is that the decision-making processes and accountability have become obscure: 'public accountability, if it exists at all, is through a long and uncertain line . . . to the Minister who appointed them or who appointed the people who appointed them' (Davis and Stewart, 1994, p. 8). In fact, questions of accountability become problematic within the contract state.

In the case of contracting-out, while there is greater local responsibility for managing resources at the point of delivery, control over policy and strategy is now highly centralized. Centralized controls exist in the form of a national curriculum; national testing and framework documents. This means that local providers are less likely to identify local solutions to local problems. Furthermore, as Charlesworth *et al.* (1996) found, the voluntary sector has become more formal, with less variety of service provision, because of the need to comply with contract specifications.

Conclusions

The reforms of public expenditure planning and control introduced over the past 15 years have resulted in new relationships within the public sector and between that sector and its external environment. Power has been shifted from local to central government and from professionals to managers. The paradox is that this increased centralization has been promoted by successive governments whose own ideology has been based upon improving freedom and choice.

Too often, public expenditure reforms have been based on blind faith in the power of markets to deliver efficiency savings and to promote the interests of those using the services. Little recognition has been given to the costs of managing complex and sophisticated services which cannot readily be written into contracts. The problems arising from imperfect information and uncertainty, which constrain the efficiency of market outcomes, appear not to have been given sufficient weight. It is not, therefore, surprising that such solutions to complex problems have, in many respects, failed.

Does the contract state better represent the preferences and demands of the electorate and service users? On balance, the answer would appear to be no. Need assessment and valuation is the outcome of a complex interplay of professional, political and managerial calculation. Assessments are required for the writing of contracts. Increasingly, however, it is contract managers who are defining needs and it is budgetary demands that are shaping these definitions. Professionals are becoming marginalized and in some cases are not even consulted. At the same time, the system is now better focused and there is the potential for gains in some public services. However, there will need to be continuing appraisal and evaluation, otherwise there is a danger that there will be a decline in both the quality of services and value for money.

Another consequence of the reforms, however, is the extent to which the systematic planning of public spending has been seriously dented. When all decisions were taken by central government, there was at least the possibility of making overall plans and trying to achieve them. It may be, of course, that this does not matter so long as services are being delivered efficiently and are what people want. The worry, however, is that the contract state may be getting its priorities out of line with what citizens and government want. More than ever, there is a need for greater transparency. In particular, the centre needs to know more about the activities of the decentralized providers. This calls for a reform of the current system, with its poor accounts, opaque PFI and less than satisfactory output and outcome measures.

Note

1. One should recognize that there is a real problem in the long run if the relative price effect does drive up the share of GDP that an activity takes up (especially in sectors where productivity gains are hard to achieve). It is not just an accounting point.

References

Audit Commission (1991). *The Impact of Competitive Tendering on Highways Maintenance*. London: HMSO.

Bennett, C. and Ferlie, E. (1996). 'Contracting in theory and in practice: some evidence from the NHS', *Public Administration*, **74** (Spring): 49–66.

Charlesworth, J., Clarke, J. and Cochrane, A. (1996). 'Tangled webs? Managing local mixed economies of care', *Public Administration*, **74** (Spring): 67–88.

Cubbin, J., Domberger, S. and Meadowcroft, S. (1987). 'Competitive tendering, tendering and refuse collection: Identifying the sources of efficiency gains', *Fiscal Studies*, **8**(3): 49–58.

Davis, H. and Stewart, J. (1994). *The Growth of Government by Appointment: The Implications for Local Democracy*. Luton, Local Government Management Board.

Domberger, S., Meadowcroft, S. and Thompson, D. (1986). 'Competitive tendering and efficiency: The case of refuse collection' *Fiscal Studies*, **7**(4): 69–87.

Domberger, S., Meadowcroft, S. and Thompson, D. (1987). 'The impact of competitive tendering on the costs of hospital domestic services', *Fiscal Studies*, **8**(4): 39–54.

Domberger, S., Meadowcroft, S. and Thompson, D. (1988). 'Competition and efficiency gains in refuse collection: a reply', *Fiscal Studies*, **9**(7): 86–90.

Efficiency Unit (1988). '*Improving Management in Government*' (The Ibbs Report). London: HMSO.

Efficiency Unit (1995). '*Resource Management Systems*', London: HMSO.

Jackson, P.M. (ed.) (1995a). *Measures for Success in the Public Sector*, London: Public Finance Foundation.

Jackson, P.M. (1995b). 'The new public sector management: surrogate competition and contracting out'. In: Jackson, P.M. and Price, C.M. (eds) *Privatisation and Regulation*, Longmans.

Kettl, D.F. (1993). *Sharing Power: Public Governance and Private Markets*, Washington DC, Brookings Institution.

McMaster, R. (1995). 'Competitive Tendering in UK Health and Local Authorities. What Happens to the Quality of Service?' *Scottish Journal of Political Economy*, **42**(2): 407–27.

Milne, R.G. (1987). 'Competitive Tendering in the National Health Service: An Economic Analysis of the Early Implementation of HC (83)18' *Public Administration*, **65**(2), 145–60.

Milne, R.G. and McGee, M. (1992). 'Competitive Tendering in the NHS: A New Look at Some Old Estimates', *Fiscal Studies*, **13**(1): 96–111.

National Audit Office (1987). *Competitive Tendering for Support Services in the National Health Service*, London: HMSO.

Smith, S.R. and Lipsky (1993). *Non Profits for Hire: The Welfare State in the Age of Contracting*. London: Harvard University Press.

Stewart, J. (1993). *The New Magistracy*. London: European Policy Forum.

Szymanski, S. and Wilkins, S. (1992). *Cheap Rubbish? Competitive Tendering and Contracting Out – 1981/88*. London: London Business School, Centre for Business Strategy.

Walsh, K., and Davis, H. (1993). *Competition and Service: The Impact of the Local Government Act 1988*, London: HMSO.

13

What Difference Does Resource Accounting Make? The Case of New Zealand

June Pallot and Ian Ball

Contents

New Zealand appears to be the first national government to have placed all its appropriations, budgets and financial statements on a full accruals (or resource accounting) basis. These accounting changes form an integral part of a much wider series of reforms designed to improve the performance of the public sector, including the effectiveness and efficiency of its expenditure (for reviews see Boston *et al.*, 1991; 1996). This chapter describes the new financial management regime in New Zealand, discusses its impact on decision making at departmental, ministerial and whole-of-government levels, and identifies some lessons for other countries.

New Zealand's financial management system

As in many other countries, the early 1980s saw New Zealand attempt a variety of managerialist, but largely piecemeal, reforms in the management of central government departments. These included sporadic efforts at corporate planning, loosening input controls, keeping asset registers and measuring non-financial performance (Pallot, 1991). Radical reform of the core public sector began in 1986 with the corporatization of a number of state trading activities (McKinlay, 1987; Mascarenhas, 1991; Duncan and Bollard, 1992; Kelsey, 1993). Drawing its theoretical foundations from public choice, agency theory and transactions cost analysis (Scott *et al.*, 1990), the new model for state enterprises had several key components. These included a clear identification and separation between the roles of ministers and those of boards and managers, and the reporting of actual performance against prior specification of objectives. Furthermore, while the government's interest in state enterprises was primarily as an *owner* seeking the highest possible return on investment, it was acknowledged that the government would frequently also have a role as regulator, and could, in some circumstances, have a different interest as *purchaser* of non-commercial goods and services. If the government wished a state owned enterprise (SOE) to undertake unprofitable activities for social reasons, it was to make specific payments to the SOE for these.

The principles underlying the State-owned Enterprises Act had a significant influence on the subsequent redesign of the core public sector, including changes to the machinery of government, human resource management and financial management. Two mutually reinforcing pieces of legislation – the State Sector Act 1988 and the Public Finance Act 1989 – underpinned the reforms. The State Sector Act was designed to promote more efficient, responsible and accountable management of public agencies. It brought significant changes to the process of appointing departmental chief executives and ushered in a new era of devolved human resource management (Walsh, 1991). To strengthen the rewards and sanctions available to ministers, chief executives ceased to have permanent employment but were placed instead on renewable performance-based contracts of terms not exceeding five years. Chief executives gained unprecedented flexibility in their powers to hire and fire staff and to determine their remuneration. The Public Finance Act (PFA) redefined the appropriation process, shifting the emphasis from inputs to outputs, and established departmental and whole of government ('Crown') reporting requirements. It also removed many centralized controls over day-to-day administration, gave departments their own bank accounts to manage and made chief executives responsible for departmental financial management.

Central to the redesign of the appropriations and reporting requirements under the PFA was a new framework for thinking about performance, linked to the performance agreements between ministers and chief executives established under the State Sector Act. Building on the distinction between the ownership and purchase interests of government, the nature of the purchase interest was fleshed out in more detail (see Pallot, 1991; McCulloch and Ball, 1992). The government's purchase interest was described in terms of the quality, quantity and cost of *outputs*; that is, the goods and services produced by governmental and non-governmental bodies (e.g. policy advice, administration of regulations, payment of welfare benefits, police patrolling). While the ultimate objectives of the government (and the public at large) are *outcomes* (the impact of the government's activities on the community), it was not considered feasible to hold departmental chief executives accountable for them since they were affected by many factors beyond their control. Instead, they would be held accountable for delivering the specified quantity, quality and cost of outputs, but be subject to incentives designed to encourage them to produce outputs of value to ministers in achieving their outcome objectives. The public would hold the government as a whole accountable for outcomes and the selection of outputs to achieve those outcomes. While the terminology of outputs and outcomes has been used elsewhere (e.g. Ramanathan, 1985; GASB, 1994), the way these notions were linked to the newly defined roles and performance expectations of the government and departments is distinctive to New Zealand.

Under the PFA, appropriations were redesigned as a series of purchases, investments or transfers. It is in light of the purchase and ownership interests involved in the assessment of chief executive performance and the appropriation process that the significance of accrual-based information is to be appreciated. Such information is essential if parliament and ministers are to know the full costs of outputs to be purchased and if relevant comparisons are to be made with private sector suppliers. Information on assets and liabilities, which accrual accounting provides, is needed to monitor aspects of the ownership interest such as financial viability, return on investment, and maintenance of capital.

Whole of government accounting and budgeting

By July 1991 all government departments were accounting, budgeting and receiving appropriations on a full accruals basis. This facilitated the production of combined financial statements, covering departments, offices of Parliament and the Reserve Bank, on a full accruals basis in 1992. In 1993, the Crown reporting entity was extended to include all entities owned by the Crown. These number nearly 3000, ranging from large state enterprises to small primary schools. Accrual-based Crown financial statements are now produced monthly (as required by the PFA Amendment Act 1994). Financial statements at all levels in the New Zealand government are described as being on a 'modified historic cost basis' although effectively they are close to being on a current cost basis. For example, all fixed assets, including infrastructure and heritage assets, are revalued at least every three years. The New Zealand government has therefore moved further towards current cost accounting than most organizations in the private sector in New Zealand.

The Fiscal Responsibility Act 1994 (FRA) was the next major development in resource accounting and budgeting (RAB). The FRA requires governments to state their fiscal objectives and report progress towards achieving those objectives. It does not set mandatory fiscal targets, which overseas experience suggested might merely result in window dressing or disputes about reporting rules. Instead it establishes five principles of responsible fiscal management. Any departure from these principles must be both transparent and temporary. The principles are:

1. Reducing Crown debt to prudent levels by achieving operating surpluses every year until a prudent level of debt has been attained. The legislation

does not define or prescribe what is meant by a 'prudent level of debt'. Rather, it is left to each government to determine, and justify to the public, what it considers 'prudent' and 'reasonable'.

2. Maintaining total Crown debt at a prudent level by ensuring that, on average, operating expenses of the Crown do not exceed operating revenue.
3. Achieving and maintaining levels of Crown net worth that provide a buffer against adverse future events.
4. Prudent management of the fiscal risks facing the Crown.
5. The pursuit of policies consistent with a reasonable degree of predictability about the level and stability of tax rates for the future.

The FRA requires a series of accrual-based financial reports, including:

- A *budget policy statement*, setting out long-term objectives for fiscal policy, broad strategic priorities for the Budget and fiscal intentions. The government must assess whether these are consistent with the principles of responsible fiscal management and previous budget policy statements, disclosing and explaining any departure from them. The budget policy statement must be published by 31 March. That means it must be produced prior to the resolution of the detailed budget allocations.
- *Economic and fiscal updates*, containing economic and fiscal forecasts for the current year and each of the following two financial years. Each economic and fiscal update must be accompanied by a statement of responsibility signed by the Minister of Finance and the Secretary to the Treasury. Economic information provided includes forecasts of movements in GDP, consumer prices, the current account position of the balance of payments and a description of all significant underlying assumptions. The fiscal updates comprise forecast Crown financial statements, in the same format as the ex post statements, together with details of all significant underlying assumptions. They must be produced at the time the Budget is prepared and in December and March of each year. An economic and fiscal update must also be produced between 42 and 28 days in advance of a general election.
- A *fiscal strategy report*, containing projections of total revenue, expenditure, debt and net worth over at least the next 10 years, and assessing whether the trends and updates are consistent with the budget policy statement.

The introduction of a formal strategic phase, culminating in the production and publication of a budget policy statement prior to the drawing up of the budget itself, is an important initiative in whole of government priority setting. It has been complemented by a new framework for strategic decision making which requires ministers, individually and collectively, to be explicit about their priorities and to translate the government's broad vision statements[1] into specific strategies to be pursued by the public service in major areas of policy (economic growth, enterprise and innovation, education, community security, social assistance, protecting the environment). These Strategic Result Areas (SRAs) are linked to the Key Result Areas (KRAs) specified in the performance agreements between chief executives of departments and ministers. They therefore cease to be vague political statements and become an integral part of the accountability system and, hence, the way that departments actually operate. The SRAs for the following three to five years are established in discussions between ministers and officials and agreed to by the Cabinet as a whole at a full-day strategic planning retreat held about three months into the financial year. Finalized SRAs are released to the public at the same time as the budget policy statement, the first such occasion having been in March 1995. The SRA/KRA framework attempts to provide not only vertical integration between ministers and officials but also horizontal integration across ministers and departments. The SRA approach is currently at an early stage and is expected to evolve over time (for a discussion see Boston and Pallot, 1997).

Effect on decisions

RAB can contribute to improved performance of government in two interrelated ways. First, because it presents different data from that previously available, it may alter the decisions made at each level within government. These are the departmental or managerial level (in particular, choices about inputs); the ministerial level (mainly choices about outputs); and the public level (where choices about outcomes are made). Second, RAB may enhance the operation of incentives for good performance by improving transparency and accountability or by supplying information essential for the operation of those incentives (e.g. information on assets is necessary if a capital charge incentive is to be used). The effects that RAB has had at managerial, ministerial and whole-of-government levels in New Zealand are described below. It should be noted, however, that it is not that sensible to evaluate RAB independently of the whole model since the system was designed as an integrated whole.

Management decision making

The PFA has meant a shift from detailed centralized *controls* over *inputs* to ministerial *control* over *outputs*. Performance is now viewed in terms of results rather than cash spending. With improved control over *what* departments do, ministers can feel relaxed in giving departments freedom to decide *how* they do it. (Ministers, with advice from Treasury, do however retain control over borrowing and departments are not permitted to borrow.)

Having discretion over the choice of inputs contributes to better performance because decisions such as whether to acquire, replace or dispose of assets can be made by people with first-hand knowledge of the assets. Being freed from centralized input controls has had beneficial effects on motivation and helped to attract good managers from the private sector who had hitherto been discouraged by the extent of detailed administrative controls. In relation to control over outputs produced, and benefits received, by parties *other* than departments, the Audit Office has detected some concern about the adequacy of contracting, monitoring and accountability arrangements, given that these payments represent a large and increasing proportion of Parliament's appropriations (Audit Office, 1994).

Accrual accounting, in conjunction with the capital charge detailed below, means that departments must record assets and that their ongoing costs include both depreciation and the opportunity cost of capital. Under the previous cash accounting regime, assets once acquired were viewed as a free good (or forgotten altogether) with the result that there was no incentive to utilize them efficiently or dispose of idle assets (Ball, 1981). While departments were encouraged in the early 1980s to keep asset registers, the extent to which they did so varied enormously. Since appropriations are now on an accrual basis, the associated shift to accrual accounting meant that all departments established asset registers and were forced to manage their assets properly.

With balance sheets in place, the new regime has been able to introduce incentives for better asset management. Under the old regime, if a department sold off some of its assets, the proceeds went straight back to the centre – to the consolidated fund. Further, if the asset was being sold only to update, say, the vehicle fleet, the acquisition of new vehicles required separate appropriation. This placed significant hurdles in front of a department attempting sensible asset management. Now a manager can sell the asset, retain the proceeds and acquire a replacement asset without reference to the minister or parliament as long as the new assets can be acquired within the department's existing balance sheet.[2] If the department requires an increase in capital, it has to make a business case in a similar manner to a private sector firm. If the case is successful, there is an appropriation injecting the additional capital into the department's balance sheet.

One of the most important financial management incentives has been the introduction of a capital charge. The aims of the capital charge regime are, first, ensuring comparability of costs between departmental and external producers of goods and services and, second, assisting departmental managers in making decisions about trade-offs between alternative types of resources or the disposal of surplus assets (McCulloch, 1992). The capital charge is calculated by multiplying the government's investment in a department by the capital charge rate. The latter is based on the weighted average costs of debt and equity capital and expected future growth for private sector counterparts, with this rate representing the opportunity cost of the funds to taxpayers. Where there are no private sector comparators, a standard rate is set by the government. Once balance sheet valuations had been established, all departments were given an appropriation to cover the capital charge. If the asset base is reduced, the charge is correspondingly reduced but not the appropriation, thus providing an incentive to dispose of unproductive assets.

A 1993 survey found that departments had better control of working capital, undertook more rigorous reviews of surplus assets, investigated rent versus buy options, and had an improved understanding of risks and investment analysis

(Price Waterhouse, 1993). However, the extent to which this has been prompted by the capital charging regime, as distinct from other financial management changes, is unclear; a desire to fund new asset purchases may have been a more important incentive to sell existing assets than the capital charge *per se* (Audit Office, 1993a, p. 41). It is possible that a capital charge regime could result in leasing or disposal decisions which meet short-term departmental objectives but which are less than optimal in the longer term. This would be most likely if the cost of capital implicit in the lease cost is less than the capital charge rate. There is, however, no indication that this has been a widespread practice in New Zealand.

Various reviews have seen scope for enhancing the effectiveness of the regime. The Audit Office (1994) has identified the need for greater awareness of the capital charge outside head offices if it is to have an incentive effect on the managers who actually use many of the assets. Another issue is how the charge is to be passed on to third-party clients. Some government departments provide services to low-income clients who may not be able to pay the increased charges. How the government is to address this matter requires further attention, though presumably the answer is not to misrepresent the cost of the services. The options open to the government range from full user charging without compensation, effectively denying the service to some users, through to the government continuing to provide the service at the present rate of charge, thereby accepting that the charge is for less than the full cost of the service.

Decentralization of accounting systems and the shift to accrual accounting have also improved the information available to departments for the management of debtors and creditors. Savings from improved cash management (including better accounting for, and use of, supplier credit and improved debt collection) were some of the earliest benefits to be realized from the reforms. Morris (1995) identifies a range of benefits including improved understanding of departmental business, savings of around $31 million a year in interest costs through the use of supplier credit and improved utilization of cash, and unquantified savings in bank fees from more efficient transaction processing (Deloitte Ross Tohmatsu, 1990).

Public expenditure is difficult to measure and interpret at the best of times. While a significant reduction in spending by administrative government departments appears to have taken place, it is virtually impossible to determine how much of this is due to better decisions on the part of managers amid radical restructuring – including privatization and shifting of activities from departments to Crown entities – and how much to changes to the bases of measurement. Further, it is not easy to disentangle the effects of accrual accounting from those related to restructuring, reallocation of responsibilities and human resource management. This should come as no surprise since RAB was never intended to be adopted in isolation (McCulloch and Ball, 1992). Nonetheless, anecdotal evidence, as well as more formal evaluations (e.g. Logan, 1991; Price Waterhouse, 1993; Audit Office, 1994) suggest that managers are accomplishing more with fewer resources, that poor decisions such as those involving year-end spending are increasingly rare and that there is, on the part of departmental managers, a positive preference for the extent and nature of the information now available to them. A study of managers' perceptions of the reforms has accrual accounting described as 'an unqualified success' (Norman, 1995) .

Ministerial decision making

Under RAB, ministers believe that they are able to make more informed choices about outputs. Likewise, Parliamentary select committees feel able to ask questions more relevant to what departments and ministers are trying to achieve. Ministers are now in a better position to target their expenditure. Also, there is less tendency to think of expenditure in terms of existing organizational structures. Ministers have commented to the authors that they no longer need to employ 'across-the-board' expenditure cuts which may have unfairly disadvantaged departments, or sections of departments, which had been efficient and had less 'fat' initially. Departments with a disproportionate amount of unavoidable costs in an area, and facing higher-than-average cost increases, also tended to be disadvantaged in the past by across-the-board cuts. For example, libraries might have been particularly sensitive to increased costs of foreign currency. Likewise, increases in expenditure on, say, education can now be targeted to specific deliverables rather than 'education' in general.

While ministers felt they had better control over the mix of outputs to be purchased, some departments claimed initially that improved specification decreased managerial flexibility and increased the chances of appropriations being cut (Logan, 1991, p. 99). In practice, however, central agencies tended to treat areas where specification was poor more severely. It is not clear whether this reflected the central agency's assessment that the department was unreasonably attempting to avoid clear specification, or whether the central agencies factored in the inherent difficulty of specification of some outputs. It should also be pointed out that, while fiscal restraint (most obvious in the National Party's 1991 budget) has probably contributed to New Zealand's economic recovery, the emphasis (and the political rhetoric) has been on improved performance rather than on cutting government expenditure *per se*. The emphasis in RAB on results rather than the cash cost of inputs is consistent with this emphasis on performance rather than expenditure cuts.

That ministers feel better informed than before does not mean that there is not considerable scope for further improvement, however. One of the most difficult problems in the early days of output budgeting was the allocation of costs to output classes. The Audit Office had to qualify the financial statements of a number of departments because of inadequate cost allocation systems (Audit Office, 1992). While there has been a significant improvement since (Audit Office, 1993b) most departments are continuing to refine their cost allocation systems. Purchase decisions by ministers are also highly dependent on good information about the *quality* of outputs. While specification of quality is never simple, it is less intractable in relation to outputs than it is in the case of outcomes. The Treasury has provided examples of quality measures for the whole range of governmental activities in its 1995 guidelines on purchase agreements. The experience in New Zealand has been that it has been possible to find private sector outputs very similar, though not identical, to most of those produced by governmental agencies. In the wake of the Total Quality Management movement in the private sector, sophistication in quality measurement can be expected to increase.

Particular attention has been paid in the New Zealand central government to assessing the quality of policy advice. In 1992 the State Services Commission produced criteria for good quality policy advice. These included whether the assumptions behind the advice are explicit, the argument is logical and supported by facts, all options have been assessed, interested parties have been adequately consulted, problems of implementation have been addressed and the reports have been well written. If these criteria are followed, there can be greater confidence (although no guarantee) that policy advice about the link between outputs and outcomes – needed to make output purchase decisions – is sound. Just as judgements are made about the quality of professional services in the private sector, so ministers make judgements about the quality of policy advice. Indeed, ministerial satisfaction is one of the quality measures used.

In the case of non-policy outputs purchased by ministers but delivered to other parties, there is some scope for gathering more information about quality as perceived by those other parties rather than relying on perceptions of ministers and the relevant government department (Wyse, 1996). A related issue is the extent to which ministers require purchase advice independent of the advice received from departments. Some ministers are beginning to use independent purchase advisors but most depend on departments for purchase advice: in some instances the same departments that deliver the outputs being purchased. These are not, however, issues on which accrual accounting itself can have a direct impact.

Ministers, under the new regime, make a quite different set of decisions. A very significant volume of routine decisions is now delegated to chief executives. Ministers focus on key decisions such as major investment decisions (but not individual, small, capital expenditure decisions) and choices about the introduction or discontinuance of outputs. They will also, normally, be involved in ownership decisions with significant political implications, even though such decisions may be formally the responsibility of the chief executive. An example would be major redundancies.

The effect of the extensive delegation to chief executives is that they implicitly accept responsibility for the political impact of routine operating decisions. One example of a decision taken by a chief executive where political consequences were considered by the minister to have been poorly handled led to the resignation of the chief executive (Boston, 1994). There remains, however, an expectation among citizens that ministers will take steps to remedy systemic deficiencies in policies and procedures. When a forest park viewing platform collapsed in 1995 killing 14 people, public pressure eventually resulted in the resignation of the minister from his Conservation portfolio.

Collective decision making

While most of the whole-government initiatives are too recent to enable an assessment of their impact over the longer term, there are a number of reasons to expect that they will change and, hopefully improve, decisions involving public expenditure.

The Crown financial statements include much more than the operating statement, statement of financial position (balance sheet) and statement of cashflows produced by private sector companies. They also contain more detailed information about actual and potential liabilities in the form of a statement of borrowings, a statement of commitments and a statement of contingent liabilities (both quantifiable and non-quantifiable). The publication of monthly Crown financial statements ensures that continuous attention is paid to the fiscal position. Under RAB, it is no longer possible to hide the costs of decisions that have medium- to long-term financial implications such as superannuation, defence contracts, accident compensation payments or settlement of Treaty of Waitangi claims. Thus the politicians who make financial decisions are fully aware of the cost associated with those decisions.

Such reporting should also militate against financial arrangements driven by inappropriate measurement rules. For example, there would be little incentive to move financing to the private sector if, in order to make a project viable to investors, the government has to create a liability to provide services in roughly equivalent amount.

Consider, for example, the position of Cabinet ministers contemplating the settlement of some claim against the government. Under a cash accounting system, ministers might have considered that if the other party were content with a payment spread over a number of years, they could afford to be somewhat more generous with taxpayers' funds. In terms of political visibility a cost of $10 million per annum over 10 years is a far more attractive option than $100 million right now (or even than the present value equivalent of $10 million per year). The immediate impact on the cash deficit would be only $10 million; furthermore, much of the cost would be incurred after the next election. In short, the effect of the decision would be deferred for up to 10 years and therefore heavily discounted. Under RAB, the accrual result would be decreased by $100 million immediately, irrespective of how the cash payments were spread. Neither could the costs be deferred until after the next election; with Crown financial statements prepared on a monthly basis, the settlement would show up within about eight weeks at most. This changes the incentives on the Crown, encouraging settlement at a level less than is likely to occur under a cash basis of accounting. Conversely, on the asset side, RAB is likely to remove the bias against capital investment which might have existed under cash accounting because it would have appeared as an expenditure of the immediate period.

Requiring governments to state their fiscal objectives and report progress towards achieving those objectives is expected to 'encourage the Government to take a longer term perspective to fiscal management' (Treasury, 1994, p. 5). Furthermore, the improved information should allow better and more focused debate about fiscal policy. The idea is that a government will find deviations from good fiscal management more difficult if it has to report, explain and justify any such deviations. This will be important in the event that loosely bound governments elected under mixed member proportional representation (*MMP*) find it more difficult to resist temptation to adopt short-term fiscal strategies which are inconsistent with longer-term goals (Richardson, 1994).

Both forecast information and subsequent reporting must be in accordance with generally accepted accounting practice (GAAP) established by an independent body under the Financial Reporting Act 1993. In most countries the government is reluctant to give away the power to choose its own accounting rules. The New Zealand government, by contrast, saw value in committing itself and future governments to a regime in which their fiscal plans were as transparent as possible. Transparency would be diminished, however, if governments could manipulate accounting policies. Those politicians who had worked hard to bring public expenditure under control, in particular Ruth Richardson, Minister of Finance 1990–93, were naturally keen to prevent the gains achieved being eroded by their successors.

The new strategic management framework can also be expected to have a significant impact on decisions concerning public expenditure. The process has provided forums for discussion among ministers, between ministers and officials and across departmental boundaries, thus improving both vertical and horizontal coordination and helping to prevent unnecessary duplication or unintended oversights. The new framework has also had implications for the budget which can now be developed within a more clearly articulated set of priorities and through a more stable process. Whereas in the past, strategy emerged as a consequence of developing the budget, and often in conditions of secrecy and haste, there is now a formal strategic phase prior to determining micro-level budget allocations. SRAs are used to guide the initial determination of budgetary parameters and priorities. As Fancy and Matheson (1995, p. 5) put it:

> These new strategic management processes are designed to ensure that wider policy issues are more consciously reflected in the formation of the budget and in appropriation decisions. It is an attempt to enrich the budget process and create incentives for more strategic thoughtfulness amongst both politicians and public servants. The present Government gives strong emphasis to the annual 'Premier House' retreat to allow ministers to more deliberately set the budget parameters and their strategic objectives within them.

New Zealand's overall economic performance had improved significantly by the mid-1990s with growth rates in the 4–5 per cent range, low inflation and falling unemployment. Public expenditure fell as a proportion of GDP from over 40 per cent to around 35 per cent in 1995. The country is running fiscal surpluses for the first time in decades. There have been successive upgradings of its credit ratings and tax cuts have been announced. Against this, there has been criticism about the widening gap between rich and poor and the associated social problems this may produce (Kelsey, 1996).

It is very difficult, however, to isolate the effects of RAB in all this from the effects, positive or negative, of wider economic reforms such as deregulation, the removal of subsidies and tariffs, and tax reforms. Much of the deficit reduction can be attributed to improved private sector productivity, and hence higher tax revenue, plus reduced interest costs. While new systems of financial management in government may have made some positive contribution to deficit reduction by constraining expenditure, it is impossible to demonstrate any causal link to wider economic consequences.

Lessons for other countries

Differences in constitutional structures and conventions, size, political culture, administrative ethos and available technology or skills all make the transfer of systems and ideas anything but straightforward. Not all countries are likely to have the commitment to openness and transparency apparent in the New Zealand government. Nonetheless, there are some lessons learned in New Zealand which may be worth sharing with other countries.

First, New Zealand found it very helpful to have a coherent framework of ideas to guide system design. Its earlier experiences of *ad hoc* tinkering with financial management systems in central government led, for the most part, to incomplete or inconsistent changes. A coherent framework helped to integrate the various aspects of the reforms – restructuring, performance agreements, incentives, budgeting, human resource management, industrial relations and collective strategizing, as well as accrual accounting, budgeting and reporting – in a mutually reinforcing manner. It also helped in quickly addressing new issues as they arose and in ensuring consistency, where appropriate, across the public sector. The introduction of strategic management should enable new ideas to emerge and keep the framework responsive to changing circumstances.

Second, appropriating and budgeting by outputs, rather than by aims, objectives or programmes enables a more transparent targeting of expenditure. The principal advantage of budgeting by outputs is that it enables resources consumed to be related to services produced; that is, there is a relationship between outputs and costs. Where the particular department is responsible for producing a range of services, each with different cost structures, the budget for the department ought to be determined by reference to output production. If budgeting does not relate to outputs, it is difficult to establish a relationship between the result of the expenditure and the level of expenditure. While it is possible, though not necessarily straightforward, to assign input costs to outputs, it is normally impossible to assign output costs to outcomes. For example, the cost of running an anti-smoking campaign cannot be meaningfully allocated to outcomes like reduced infant mortality, air pollution or lung disease.

Third, the cost involved in reporting, particularly for smaller departments, needs to be considered carefully. Initially, some chief executives felt that the monitoring functions of central agencies had an excessive impact on departments, with information being requested without regard for the costs involved (though it appears that the level of concern diminished with experience in the new system). As a result, the 1992 amendment to the PFA removed the requirement for half-yearly audit, the Treasury modified its reporting requirements for small departments and some duplication of information was eliminated (for example, by ceasing to require published corporate plans as well as the Estimates and purchase agreements). In 1994 a working party set up to review accountability requirements developed a list of protocols which it thought the central agencies and the Audit Office should observe. These were:

1. The purpose of, and justification for, the information should be made clear.
2. The purpose should be consistent with the responsibilities and accountabilities of ministers, chief executives and the central agencies.
3. The information processes to be used should be the most efficient and effective way to achieve that purpose.
4. Issues of materiality and risk should be properly addressed.
5. Duplication and overlap should be minimized.
6. Reasonable assurance should be given that benefits exceed costs, and/or that overall costs are minimized.

Fourth, much can be learned, and much progress can be made, simply by embarking on the process. As other chapters have noted, the measurement of public expenditure poses many theoretical and practical problems. Likewise, some accounting issues were particularly difficult to deal with as there was virtually nothing in the way of established practice for accrual accounting by sovereign governments (for a discussion see Audit Office 1993c; Pallot 1994). This included the valuation of infrastructure and heritage assets, the reporting of future liabilities for welfare payments, and the timing for recognition of taxation revenues. While further work on these issues continues, the experience in New Zealand was that more progress was possible by making a start than by trying to solve all theoretical problems in advance. Operationally useful financial statements, even if theoretically less than ideal, have long been accepted in the private sector.

Finally, explicit attention needs to be given to mechanisms for collective strategizing. There is no guarantee that the introduction of RAB in individual departments will improve inter-departmental coordination and cooperation; in some instances it may even run counter to it. In the early stages of implementing the requirements of PFA, the focus was on clarifying relationships between individual ministers and their departments primarily in terms of the purchase interest rather than the ownership interest. Consequently, insufficient attention may have been paid to longer-term and cross-sectoral issues or to accountability of the government as a whole. The RAB initiatives at the whole-of-government level provide information for a more open and transparent budget process in which greater attention can be paid to both strategic purchases and managing ownership risks in the longer term. Particularly useful has been the introduction of a strategic phase prior to, and separate from, the process of drawing up the budget in detail. This process of agreeing strategic result areas and developing a budget policy statement means that the budget ceases to be the de facto driver of strategy, and key decisions are no longer made in secrecy and haste.

Conclusion

Although a number of countries are introducing accrual accounting, some distinctive features in New Zealand can be identified. First, accounting has not been viewed as a technical issue in isolation but as an integral part of, firstly, public management reforms and, secondly, wider economic reforms of the 1980s. The overriding objective of the reforms has been improved *performance* with less emphasis on *cutting* expenditure per se, and more on control through *targeting* expenditure. Budgeting has been linked to outputs rather than 'programmes' or 'objectives'. There has been a commitment to transparency and open decision making processes among both bureaucrats and politicians. Accounting standards for government are set independently of government, and the same generally accepted accounting practice is applied to both the public and private sectors. Finally, RAB cannot strictly be labelled 'managerialist' in that it addresses longer-term and collective interests as well as the micro-management of departments.

There has been a significant improvement in New Zealand's overall economic position: ministers say that they are able to make more informed decisions under the new system, and parliamentarians are able to ask more meaningful questions about government expenditure. Despite this there are a number of difficulties in obtaining 'hard' evidence on the success, or otherwise, of RAB in New Zealand.

First, for some of the changes (such as the Fiscal Responsibility Act and the SRA framework) which are very recent and are intended to address the longer term, it is simply too early to evaluate their impact.

Second, it is impossible to obtain consistent trend data on public expenditure amid radical restructuring and changes to the bases of measurement; indeed one of the objectives of RAB is to overcome deficiencies in information previously available. In many cases there is no clear benchmark or counterfactual against which the policies can be assessed. But the costs of *not* changing the accounting and budgeting system may be as relevant a question as the net benefits of changing to RAB.

Third, RAB formed part of a much wider public management reform. Most departments have been restructured, have different responsibilities and operate in a radically different personnel and industrial relations environment. Thus improvements in the efficiency and effectiveness of departments, even if they could be measured, cannot be attributed to RAB alone.

While some matters requiring further work have been identified, the relevant question is not whether the system is ideal but whether it is an improvement on the prior regime. The authors have detected no desire at any level – even if it were administratively feasible – for a return to cash accounting and input controls.

Notes

1. The first of these vision statements was a document published prior to the 1993 election titled *Path to 2010*. It has been succeeded by annual follow-up statements titled *The Next Three Years* [1994], *Investing in Our Future* [1995] and *New Opportunities* [1996].
2. Each department has a balance sheet with all of the assets and liabilities under the department's control listed. Assets and liabilities are defined in a conventional fashion, i.e. in conformance with Generally Accepted Accounting Practice in New Zealand. Each department – and the Crown as a whole – also produces a separate statement of contingent liabilities and a statement of commitments.

References

Audit Office (1992). 'Cost allocation systems'. In: *Report of the Controller and Auditor General: on the Audit of the Crown and Government Departments for the Year Ended 30 June 1992*. Wellington: Audit Office.

Audit Office (1993a). 'Management of physical assets'. In: *Report of the Controller and Auditor General: Second Report for 1993*. Wellington: Audit Office.

Audit Office (1993b). 'Cost allocation systems'. In: *Report of the Controller and Auditor General: Second Report for 1993*. Wellington: Audit Office.

Audit Office (1993c). 'Commentary on crown accounting policies'. In: *Report of the Controller and Auditor General: Second Report for 1993*. Wellington: Audit Office.

Audit Office (1994). 'Financial management reforms'. In: *Report of the Controller and Auditor General: Fourth Report for 1994*. Wellington: Audit Office.

Ball, I. (1981). *Measuring the Cost of Government Services*. Wellington: New Zealand Planning Council.

Boston, J. (1994). 'On the sharp edge of the State Sector Act: the resignation of Perry Cameron', *Public Sector*, **16**(2): 12–14.

Boston, J., Martin, J., Pallot, J. and Walsh, P. (eds) (1991). *Reshaping the State: New Zealand's Bureaucratic Revolution*. Auckland: Oxford University Press.

Boston, J., Martin, J., Pallot, J. and Walsh, P. (eds) (1996). *Public Management: The New Zealand Model*. Auckland: Oxford University Press.

Boston, J. and Pallot, J. (1997). 'Linking strategy and performance: Developments in the New Zealand public sector'. *Journal of Policy Analysis and Management,* forthcoming.

Deloitte Ross Tohmatsu (1990). Extracts from Post-Implementation Review of Cash Management Reform, November 1990.

Duncan, I. and Bollard, A. (1992). *Corporatization and Privatization: Lessons from New Zealand*. Auckland, Oxford University Press.

Fancy, H. and Matheson, A. (1995). *Future Directions in Public Management in New*

Zealand: Towards Strategic Management. Paper presented at the New Zealand Society of Accountants Public Sector Convention, Wellington, 5–8 November 1995.

Governmental Accounting Standards Board (1994). *Concepts Statement No. 2: Concepts Related to Service Efforts and Accomplishments Reporting*. Stamford, Connecticut: GASB

Kelsey, J. (1993). *Rolling Back the State: Privatisation of Power in Aotearoa/New Zealand*. Auckland: Bridget Williams Books.

Kelsey, J. (1996). *The New Zealand Experiment: A World Model for Structural Adjustment*. Auckland: Bridget Williams Books.

Logan, B. (1991). *Review of State Sector Reforms*. Report of the Steering Group on the Review of State Sector Reforms, Wellington.

Mascarenhas, R. (1991). 'State-owned enterprises'. In: Boston, J., Martin, J., Pallot, J. and Walsh, P. (eds), *Reshaping the State: New Zealand's Bureaucratic Revolution*. Auckland: Oxford University Press.

McCulloch, B. (1992). 'A charge for government departments: What is it all about?' *The Accountants Journal*, **70**(9): 21–23.

McCulloch, B. and Ball, I. (1992). 'Accounting in the context of financial management reform'. *Financial Accountability and Management*, **8**(1): 7–12.

McKinlay, P. (1987). *Corporatisation: The Solution for State Owned Enterprise?* Wellington: Victoria University Press/Institute of Policy Studies.

Morris, R. (1995). *Public Sector Management – Looking Back and Looking Forwards*. Paper presented to the Institute for International Research conference on Public Sector Financial Accounting and Management, Wellington.

Norman, R. (1995). 'New Zealand's re-invented government: Experiences of public sector managers'. *Public Sector*, **18**(2): 22–25.

Pallot, J. (1991). 'Financial management reform' and 'Accounting, auditing and accountability'. In: J. Boston, J. Martin, J. Pallot and P. Walsh, *Reshaping the State: New Zealand's Bureaucratic Revolution*, 166–197. Auckland: Oxford University Press.

Pallot, J. (1994). 'The development of accrual-based accounts for the Government of New Zealand'. *Advances in International Accounting*, 7: 287–308.

Price Waterhouse (1993). *Capital Charging Regime for Government Departments – Survey of Benefits and Current Issues*. Wellington, Price Waterhouse Management Consultants.

Ramanathan, K. (1985). 'A proposed framework for designing management control systems in not-for-profit organizations'. *Financial Accountability and Management* **1**: 75–92.

Richardson, R. (1994). 'Opening and balancing the books: The New Zealand experience'. *The Parliamentarian*, October: 244–246.

Scott, G., Bushnell, P. and Sallee, N. (1990). 'Reform of the core public sector: New Zealand experience'. *Governance*, **3**: 138–167.

State Services Commission (1994). *Review of Accounting Requirements: Report of the Working Party to the Advisory Group*, Wellington.

Treasury (1994). '*Fiscal responsibility act: Brief overview*'. FM Report, 8. Wellington: Treasury.

Walsh, P. (1991). 'The State Sector Act 1988'. In: J. Boston, J. Martin, J. Pallot and P. Walsh (eds), op. cit.

Wyse, N. (1996). *Quality Outputs: But Whose Quality?* Master of Public Policy Research Paper. Wellington: Victoria University of Wellington.

14

Integrating Microeconomic and Macroeconomic Approaches to Public Expenditure and its Control

John Flemming

Contents

Public expenditure is incurred to provide public sector infrastructure and services in support of economic and social objectives. There are two broad areas of concern with respect to the use of public expenditure. First, there is the microeconomic problem of making sure that this expenditure is efficiently planned and implemented. Second, there is a macroeconomic concern with the scale of public spending.

Because it accounts for a large proportion of total expenditure, public spending has always loomed large in Keynesian analyses of aggregate demand since it can be used as a regulator of total demand and hence employment. Since the mid-1970s, macroeconomic policy has focused more on the control of inflation than employment, largely within a monetarist framework. Nevertheless, public expenditure has continued to be a macroeconomic concern and has been subject to constraints, such as that on the size of PSBR, derived from macroeconomic concerns.

The fact that public expenditure must meet certain microeconomic objectives gives rise to a certain tension in its planning and control. This chapter highlights a number of contradictions or paradoxes in the Conservative government's public expenditure policies particularly as they relate to infrastructure projects. We look particularly at their preference for private finance to fund these projects. We find that the present approach is deeply flawed and incoherent. We then suggest some more sensible ways ahead.

The microeconomic approach

Public expenditure, like private expenditure, is undertaken to satisfy users, clients or customers. Its allocation cannot, however, be left to the market because most of the products of public expenditure are not sold. One way round this might be to give public sector suppliers notional, or 'shadow', prices for their products and to tell them to maximize 'profits', as their private-sector counterparts would do, but calculated at the shadow prices.

This is not, however, very practical. The contributions of social services departments, hospitals and roads are not very easily divided up into homogeneous categories to which unique prices can reasonably be assigned. While arguments about the valuations to be used might be healthy, the arrangements to monitor quantities would be very difficult and costly. In any case, the market test of efficiency would be entirely hypothetical unless there was real competition for the contracts to supply. One would therefore not escape the problem that what must inevitably be primarily administrative arrangements, can mean that the decision makers charged with achieving public goals fail to suppress their personal and sectional interests as suppliers.

Dealing with contracting out

Both of these arguments point to the difficulty of mimicking market mechanisms. There may be no halfway house between traditional public service approaches and privatization, or at least, contracting-out, or 'internal market' arrangements (as in the NHS). In either case possible public sector investment and expenditure needs to be appraised with a view to ensuring that the option that offers best value for money is chosen. Cost benefit analysis (CBA) can play a role here since it provides a systematic framework for structuring the decision making process.

One of the key issues surrounding the decision on whether to contract out or not revolves around its impact on investment. Investment by contractors or franchise holders will be extremely sensitive to the terms of their contracts and the life and specificity of the assets in question. If low-cost operation requires investment in long-lived assets with little or no alternative use, it will not be achieved by contracting-out unless the contracts are equally long.

Satisfactory long-term contracts are difficult to write since a great number of relevant conditions are likely to change in ways that need to be covered by the terms of the contract. An alternative answer to this problem is to have the contractors' staff operating publicly equipped facilities. In this way shorter contracts can be used and the investment decisions are kept in the public sector.

What becomes clear is that if one is to consider a range of contractual arrangements of this kind it is important to develop an appropriate method for comparing their costs. If, for instance, a long-term contract by the public sector to buy the services of a private prison does not count as a capitalized liability, then it is costing less in initial public expenditure and contributing less to the Public Sector Borrowing Requirement (PSBR) than the more traditional option. In this case decisions may be taken that represent, in effect, very high-cost borrowing indeed and therefore do not meet the microeconomic goal of value for money.

Macro and microeconomic reasons for distinguishing capital from current expenditure

'Monetarism' is a convenient label for a bundle of ideas and doctrines that relate primarily to the role of monetary growth in determining the rate of inflation, but that also encompass views about the determinants of other aspects of economic behaviour. One of the valid 'monetarist' criticisms of UK public expenditure systems of the 1960s and 1970s was an inadequate distinction between capital and current expenditure.

There are two reasons, at least, for drawing such a distinction, both of which also apply in the private sector. The cost of providing a given service in a given year should include the cost of committing and using relevant capital goods and equipment (real interest and depreciation charges) but not the cost of acquiring those assets, which may fall disproportionately heavily in some years and lightly in others (cf. Pallot and Ball, Chapter 13).

Of course the full cost of acquisition must be recognized over the asset's lifetime. The asset's remaining value is an element in the balance sheet list of capital assets and liabilities.

There had, traditionally, been a 'line' drawn between current and capital public expenditure in the public accounts which was dropped in 1970 on the 'Keynesian' grounds that both contributed equally to aggregate demand. Full employment was then the principal objective of policy: public expenditure, whether capital or current, was an instrument for its achievement.

Monetarist theory places more weight on the balance sheets and portfolios of economic agents than the Keynesian analysis of the circular flow of expenditure, which treated capital only as the sum of past (net) investment (excluding land and natural resources).

But in practice the 'monetarist' approach did little to restore the capital/current distinction as focus shifted from the demand-expansionary implications to the inflationary potential of fiscal deficits – to which all forms of expenditure were again seen as contributing equally. Attention was focused on the PSBR initially at the suggestion of the IMF in the crisis of 1976, but subsequently embraced by both Labour and Conservative governments.

The PSBR and the golden rule of borrowing for public investment

Although an element in the analysis of monetary expansion, the PSBR does not, of itself, have any particularly potent inflationary capacity. Indeed if one takes a long view it is clear that borrowing to finance investment involves a prospective addition to the capacity to supply, as well as a current increase in demand. It is therefore likely to have a different, and smaller, impact on the price level than borrowing to finance current expenditure.

This insight lies behind the so-called 'golden rule' that the German authorities were said to favour – that borrowing for investment is allowable; it is only borrowing for recurrent expenditure that is reprehensible. This 'rule' is subject to at least two qualifications. The first is that investment expenditure is only as good as the assets acquired. Holes in the ground might represent investment (in that they were durable), but unless there was a use for them they would be indistinguishable from the litter remaining after recurrent expenditure.

Second, the link of borrowing to capital formation is related to the idea that the stock of debt is backed by the stock of assets. Much investment is replacement investment needed to maintain rather than increase the stock of assets and the maintenance of the asset stock does not warrant more than maintaining the real stock of debt. This gives rise to many complexities.

The notion of asset-backing for the debt has two aspects. It might be possible to sell the assets to redeem the debt[1] or it may be possible to generate a sufficient surplus from the operation of the assets to service the debt without resort to general taxation. This is a more demanding condition than that the assets be 'useful'. A beautiful hole in the ground might possibly enhance the quality of a park but it might not, even then, have any revenue raising potential.

Fiscal sustainability and balancing the budget over the cycle

The renewed emphasis on balance sheets, including those of the public sector, is important. A private enterprise is insolvent if it does not have assets in excess of its liabilities. It therefore needs to monitor the development of their relationship in order to ensure that it is pursuing sustainable policies.

Sustainability is also an issue in public finance. If the stock of debt is rising persistently, relative to public capital and national income, then either public expenditure must stop rising or revenue must rise, either by explicit taxation or by implicit inflationary taxation, or some other form of default will ensue (Sargent and Wallace 1981).

One way of ensuring sustainability is to balance the government budget year by year, or to constrain the total deficit (including the real interest costs) to a percentage of GDP that keeps the debt constant as a share of GDP (for instance, if the debt is to be stabilized at 50 per cent of GDP a deficit of 1 per cent of GDP is called for if GDP itself is growing at 2 per cent per annum). But this is excessively strict. It makes no allowance for the revenue potential of some quasi-commercial debt-financed public projects, or for the fluctuation of revenue over the business cycle. If such a rule generates wide swings in tax rates it will impose unnecessarily high costs on the economy, leading to a reduction in overall welfare.

For instance, if public expenditure does not fall in recessions, a rule requiring the budget to be balanced at all times would require tax rates to rise yet further. This would not be efficient even if it did not depress the economy further in a Keynesian manner and cause unemployment to rise further.

The deadweight burden of tax distortions rises more than proportionately with the rate of (marginal) taxation. Thus a steady tax at 25 per cent would cause less damage (and raise more revenue) than one fluctuating (symmetrically) between 20 per cent and 30 per cent (Barro 1979, Flemming 1988). Borrowing may be used to smooth tax rates and reduce the welfare costs of financing a given level of public expenditure. Keynesian arguments might increase the *scale* of borrowing appropriate in recession – but there is a compelling case for doing some borrowing anyway.

It may be possible to smooth some definition of 'public expenditure' itself by varying the mix between capital purchases and the renting of privately financed buildings (as seems to be being proposed by the Labour Party for rehabilitating schools). But this is really just a specific and rather inflexible form of borrowing to finance a somewhat lumpy expenditure profile.

Overall, then, it is clear that it does not make sense to control public expenditure at a macro level in a way that leads to decisions that are very far from optimal in micro terms. In practice however, the 'PSBR' constraint has been a very important influence on public expenditure policy.

The PSBR constraint in British practice

In Britain the level of the PSBR has acted as a very important constraint on Government behaviour. However, it has contributed little, if anything to the two key macroeconomic concerns surrounding public expenditure, namely its implications for inflationary and fiscal sustainability.

It has only offered protection against inflationary expenditure by stifling public projects even where it was clear that they would have been unobjectionable if undertaken in the private sector. This is worrying. The resource utilization and inflationary implications of the project are essentially the same in both cases inasmuch as both need the same amount of finance.

It is possible that the use of private finance will leave the government paying less on its own debt since it has less to issue. Technically this depends on the extent that public and private debt instruments are imperfect substitutes. But if the reason for keeping government borrowing costs down is that higher interest rates raise the cost of capital to the private sector, the argument is perverse. The private borrowing will tend to raise the cost of private finance relative to that of the public sector.

The PSBR constraint gave raise in the 1980s to limitations on each of the nationalized industries ability to borrow; this took the form of an External Financing Limit (EFL). Claims were made that this control was frustrating worthwhile public sector infrastructure projects such as the renewal of 19th-century sewers. This was denied by the government of the time and not clearly established by the coalition of public enterprises and civil engineering contractors who wished to see a higher level of such activity. Nevertheless, considerable ingenuity was employed in trying to structure leasing or other arrangements with private sector bodies designed to reduce the immediate cash call on the commissioning public sector body. If such an arrangement could be achieved, the investment by the private sector partner would not count either against the EFL or the PSBR. Only the payment by the public sector partner would.

These attempts to reduce the impact of EFL and PSBR constraints led to increasingly thorough Treasury scrutiny of the borderline between the two sectors. The official position on this was spelled out in the Ryrie rules drawn up for the Treasury by Sir William Ryrie. As originally specified, these took a hard line, ruling out most devices designed to circumvent the PSBR/EFL constraints on the grounds that leasing, or equivalent, arrangements left the risks inherent in the operation with the public sector partner. Such arrangements were therefore to be classified as relating to the private supply of *finance* rather than of services. Such schemes did not reduce the scale of the public sector and therefore were not allowed to be used as a way of departments increasing their budgets.

The private finance initiative of 1992 and the superiority of private sector project management

In response to increasing pressure, particularly from interested would-be contractors, the rules surrounding the use of private finance and the way it affects the public accounts have been progressively relaxed. The government's Private Finance Initiative (PFI) involves the government itself in setting targets for the quantity of hybrid finance to be mobilized – targets which the Treasury Select Committee has recently said are unlikely to be met (*Financial Times*, 3.4.96; see also *Financial Times* 17.4.96). The question is whether this is a sensible policy.

There is certainly evidence to suggest that major private investment projects in Britain, such as opening up new mines, are at least as well and probably better managed, in terms of cost and time overruns and achieving projected returns, than most major public sector projects. This raises questions about the way public sector projects should be organized. Since these have nearly always used private contractors it suggests that the problems concern the efficiency of public sector project management for one reason or another.

A distinctive feature of the PFI is its concentration on private *finance*. But as we know, this invariably comes at a higher cost than that at which the government can borrow in its own name. The ideal would seem to be to combine cheap public *finance* for such projects with the rigour of private sector project *management*. It may however be that this combination is unachievable.

A key feature of private management relates to the incentives, and hence motivation, of the managers themselves. This may be difficult to replicate within a public sector context. Thus there may be a good case for attempting to involve private enterprise more fully in traditional public sector projects – and this may involve bringing in private finance. But the reason for doing so is that it is required by the incentive structures: in itself private finance is more costly.

Implications of higher cost of capital and 'cheaper' labour in the private sector

This cost difference is borne out by the studies underlying various changes that have been made to the Central Government Discount Rate (CGDR) prescribed by the Treasury for use in the appraisal of proposed public sector projects. Even when the logic for arriving at the CGDR has given weight to the possibility that public projects displace profitable private investment, the CGDR has always been below 10 per cent (in real terms) though the private sector has always used hurdle rates above 10 per cent.[2]

A substantial increase in the role of private finance in formerly public projects, whether through contracting-out, privatization or hybrid schemes, will lead to significant changes in the scale and shape of projects as the cost of capital is increased and, very often, labour costs are reduced (e.g. in NHS contracting-out arrangements). Thus one should expect to see a fall in the capital intensity of the relevant operations and perhaps in the durability of the associated facilities – at least unless contracts put high values on ensuring that durability and maintainability are designed into the infrastructure.

Risks specific to private provision of public services

The complexity of the contracts involved in hybrid financing and ownership of facilities also raises the level of risk taken on by the investors. If private investors bear the risks, as required, the return they seek on a 'public' project is liable to be above the normal cost of capital to the private sector.

Consider a private enterprise contemplating building a prison. Clearly if the building were simply leased to the government for its life of, say, 50 years, the builder would face risks only of cost overrun and completion delays. The government's rental agreement would be a bond which could be sold, or otherwise hedged, on the capital market. It is the fact that such leases are equivalent to borrowing to finance the purchase of facilities that underlies their exclusion under the Ryrie rules.

Suppose now that the private enterprise is also going to operate the prison and instead of a fixed rental it will be paid a service fee depending on the number, category and treatment of prisoners. Risks are inherent in the 'natural' fluctuations of such things. But, in addition, sentencing policy may change, as may required standards of treatment or those for staff qualifications and training. To some extent these risks may be covered by contingent elements in the contract – but a manageable contract will inevitably be incomplete and unable to cover all possible eventualities.

In the case of the privatized utilities, prices are set by regulators who are obliged to ensure that investors can, on average, earn a fair return. If environmental or safety standards are raised, the costs necessarily incurred in meeting the new standards are allowed to be passed on to consumers. No such guarantee, which in practice has offered limited comfort anyway, applies to those providing private finance to one-off public projects in the face of a possible change of government. In theory the price attached by the capital market to such risks should depend on their correlation with risks already allocated through the market. For this reason it may initially be priced relatively cheaply, especially if the programme is not expected to grow very much in the lifetime of the first projects. However, it is not clear that the markets work this way in practice and risks associated with a change of government also affect financial claims on the private sector.

There is an analogy here with the domestic housing market. Landlords impose conditions on what their tenants can do. Prospective occupiers who are not quite sure what they want to do should buy rather than rent if it is costly for tenants to move or if the initial contract specification is non-standard. This argument applies more strongly in the public sector, where electoral uncertainties impinge directly on future requirements, than in the private sector, where the impact is less direct and more general.

The discount rate, decentralization of investment decisions, and capital rationing

Reference has already been made to the idea that public sector projects might, like those of the private sector, be those someone thought 'profitable' at a set of prices given either by the market or by the Treasury (such as the discount rate or shadow cost of capital). Such an approach would extend to the public sector the decentralizing role of market prices in the private sector and, in principle, allow decisions to be delegated to local decision makers.

No serious attempt has ever been made to implement such a scheme, probably for two reasons. The first relates to the problems of holding the managers of the relevant units appropriately accountable for their use of resources. What kind of incentive contract should they be under? Would the managers still be in place when the truth or falsity of their projections and the quality of their investments became known?

A second reason relates to the need for central budgeting and macroeconomic control of the total amount of investment. Typically in the private sector the managers of business units are told what return they must earn on any use they make of central funds – but they are not told that they can have as much capital as they like at that 'price'. Rather they have to apply to the centre for permission to undertake specific, costed, investments which they know have to promise the required return (or offer some equivalent strategic advantage).

Capital rationing, in the sense that subordinate units are subject to quantitative constraints is, then, endemic in the private sector and we should not be surprised that it is the norm also in the public sector. Nonetheless the Treasury has always claimed, even in the period of EFLs, that capital was being controlled by price rather than quantitative rationing.

One of the problems of purely quantitive capital rationing is that it radically alters the framework of inter-temporal decision taking. In its absence such decisions are in principle simply taken on the basis of the present value of future cash flows and non-cash benefits. Where there is capital rationing, investment decisions are more complicated. The relevant information now also includes the size and determinants of future capital budgets. This means that the nature of future options is not adequately described by prices alone.

Whether a project should be deferred or carried out now depends, under capital rationing, partly on whether the shadow price of rationed funds (i.e. their availability and scarcity) is expected to be higher or lower at the future date.

The complexity deepens if any funds earned on one project are added to those available for subsequent investment by the managers of the same business unit, as increasingly happens with the coming of agencies and other elements of marketization of the public sector. In this case the (cash) returns on projects as well as their inputs have to be valued at the shadow price of rationed funds in each successive accounting period.

There is also an increased 'politicization' and scope for game-playing in the budget setting process – especially if agencies are seeking capital budgets to spend at their discretion rather than approval for each and every project. A presentation will be sought in which it is suggested that the project thought to be most appealing to the higher authority is at risk unless the agency is given the funds it seeks.

If leasing and other such potentially off-balance-sheet financing arrangements are to be considered fairly alongside up-front purchase and ownership, it is very important that the accounting and appraisal of such schemes be placed on a consistent footing. This is not with a view to applying some arbitrary cut-off, to classify activities, facilities or their financing as being either public or private. It is simply in order to compare the costs to the taxpayer of the range, possibly a very full one, of alternatives under consideration.

The inevitability of quantitative limits on the annual totals of infrastructure investment should be recognized, but if alternative ownership and financing arrangements are to be considered it is important that the choice between them be made on the basis of their cost – not as a way of circumventing a constraint. This means either that the constraints apply both to current and capital expenditure (suitably weighted) or, more plausibly, that they apply to additions to the capital stock *used* by the relevant agencies whether publicly owned or not. In this way the constraint would apply more to the (national) resources committed to the provision of infrastructure than to the public (or private) provision of finance for it.

If the infrastructure in question is exclusively for public use it will have to be paid for eventually by taxpayers and any deferral of that payment constitutes borrowing. As has already been said, the choice of financing, to the extent that it can be separated from project management, should be determined by considerations of cost. It is just possible that there might be an independent constraint on private borrowing arising from market perceptions or, perhaps, from the application of arbitrarily defined external constraints arising, for instance, from the Maastricht convergence conditions for a single European currency. But the PSBR cash flow concept is virtually unknown on the Continent where attention focuses rather on the PSFD (Public Sector Financial Deficit) or, more often, on the GGFD (General Government Financial Deficit).

The Financial Deficit differs from the Borrowing Requirement in being an accrual rather than a cash flow concept which charges depreciation (or capital consumption) rather than actual capital expenditure. General Government differs from the Public Sector in consisting of central and local government and excluding public corporations. Most of the finagling to circumvent a PSBR constraint would have been irrelevant under a GGFD constraint, though it would, of course, have done nothing to relieve the pressure of demands for assistance from the public purse.

Externally imposed constraints would set up a game between UK and EU (or IMF) authorities which would present opportunities for playing a variety of strategies if the constraints and definitions were at all loosely articulated or if they differed from the consistent framework of domestic controls sketched above.

The way ahead: concentrate on resources used – and their cost

We have identified two major inconsistencies in recent policies in this area. The first is the belief that there is any relevant macroeconomic, as opposed to managerial, constraint that is eased by the substitution of private for public finance of social infrastructure projects. The second inconsistency is that doctrines of decentralizable market prices have been annunciated for several decades when in fact, and probably inevitably, capital rationing has prevailed but not been consistently allowed for in appraisal procedures.

The managerial arguments of accountability and motivation, referred to above, may point to the appropriateness of genuine privatization (subject if necessary to specific regulation) and to contracting-out, when this can be done by arms' length competition. In order to reconcile these requirements with the assurances needed to invest in long-lasting infrastructure facilities it may, however, be necessary to retain the latter in public ownership when the conditions for public sector leasing do not apply or are costly.

How should the UK government's capital budget relate to such things as the economic situation, including employment and inflation, the debt/income ratio and the cost of capital? And how should this regime relate to that for regular taxation?

In these areas the requirement of stability must carry considerable weight. So too should the comparison of the returns to such investment, properly monitored and measured on an *ex post* basis, with the average returns on private investment over a run of years. If the return on public infrastructure exceeds that on private investment, the size of the infrastructure investment budget should grow as a proportion of trend GDP.

Taxes should be levied at rates sufficient to cover, over an economic cycle, recurrent expenditure, depreciation and the servicing, in real terms, of all outstanding debt including that implicit in any private or hybrid financing arrangement used for previous infrastructure investment. This approach could be operated in such a way as to allow the national debt to grow at a similar trend rate as GDP (e.g. by having a deficit of 1 per cent of GDP in the example cited above).

If the return on infrastructure investment is relatively high it should be expected to grow as a proportion of GDP, as proposed above. This would mean setting tax rates above those otherwise necessary in order to provide for the non-revenue-generating elements of the growing investment programme.

There are a number of statistical techniques which could be used to monitor the cyclicality of GDP and the way it is changing, and thus the number of years over which its trends should be calculated as well as the likely duration of downturns or recoveries. It is to be hoped that it would never be necessary to raise taxes or cut infrastructure investment because of a recession. In fact anything to which the word 'recession' is properly applied is surely temporary and should not be aggravated by cuts in public investment programmes or rises in tax rates.

Recent recessions have, however, typically been policy-induced in response to a perceived inflationary threat. Does public expenditure, and particularly infrastructure investment, have a part to play in maintaining price stability?

It is hard to deny that they should play some role but it is almost certain that it should be a small one. Inflation control is primarily a matter for monetary policy, while the rules proposed above for public expenditure, infrastructure investments and their financing are exclusively real. To the extent that fighting inflation raises real interest rates, as it usually does, our approach would involve some moderation of the growth of infrastructure investment for the duration.

To sum up, we have found that there are numerous ways in which the simultaneous pursuit of the macroeconomic role of public expenditure and the need for sensible microeconomic decision making create tension and often conflict. Many of these are inevitable and need to be managed sensibly. But there are a number of areas, particularly the use of private finance where it is not the best option, in which current policy needs revising to ensure that public expenditure is used to mobilize national resources in the best way.

Notes

1. Privatization proceeds used in this way do not, however, strengthen the public sector balance sheet if the assets have been sold at a discount – the public sector's assets then fall more than do its liabilities.
2. These figures may not in fact be strictly comparable as the two sectors may differ in the consistency of their inflation adjustments and in the ways in which they allow for the risk that project out-turns may fall short of those projected at that time of the decision to implement them.

References

Barro, R.J. (1979). 'On the determination of the public debt', *Journal of Political Economy*.
Flemming, J. (1988). 'Debt and taxes', *Scottish Journal of Political Economy*, **3**(4).
Sargent, T. and Wallace, N. (1981). 'Some unpleasant monetarist arithmetic', Federal Reserve Bank of Minneapolis, Quarterly Review, pp. 1–17.

Part V
Improving The Machinery of Public Expenditure

15

The Relationship Between the Treasury and Spending Departments

Jon Stern

Contents

In the UK, traditionally, the Treasury has had a great deal of control over the allocation of resources down to quite a detailed micro level. There is, however, a case that while allocations overall should be decided at this level, more freedom should be given to departments to allocate the money they are given themselves. Indeed some recent changes to the relationship between the Treasury and departments are pushing this way. But what are the pros and cons of each option?

In this chapter we analyse this issue by using a stylized model of the process of taking public expenditure decisions. The model is intended to focus on the relative roles of a central coordinating ministry and of spending ministries. In the UK case, the former is, in effect, the public expenditure divisions of the Treasury.

What kind of decentralization?

The aim is to compare and contrast a regime in which the central body has the responsibility of jointly agreeing bids for new expenditure with spending ministries with the alternative model in which the spending ministries are free to decide their own expenditure projects, provided they stay within financial limits. The former model is intended to capture the essential features of the traditional public expenditure decision-making system in the UK; the latter is intended to represent the main features of an alternative, decentralized model.

Decentralization could take several forms. One example is a model where there is a 'market' for public expenditure bids so that departments bid for funds or are even responsible for financing their own expenditures. However, unlike private sector companies, the revenue flow and hence the income stream received by government departments from their activities is almost always very much less than the costs of provision and so this model is quite unrealistic even in economic terms. In addition, it could reasonably be argued that the idea of a single 'government' entity comprising a set of departments has effectively disappeared in a framework of this type. Partly for these reasons the decentralized model for public expenditure that we consider here corresponds broadly to the way a multi-divisional private sector company operates, where the controls over the divisions work purely through financial indicators.

As we shall see, the questions of low direct income streams to departments and the point at which the idea of a 'government' as an integrated entity are important in the corporate model as well. Indeed, we will argue not only that these issues set limits to the degree of decentralization that is feasible for spending departments but that these limits are much narrower than those that exist in private sector companies.

A comparison of the Treasury–spending department relationship with those in a multi-dimensional company is particularly important, given the calls by many observers for increased use of commercial and managerial techniques in government. The model of the private sector conglomerate appears to have been influential in much of the discussion of the Whitehall reforms, including further use of agencies and trusts and the current restructuring of ministries, including the Treasury. This gives the analysis practical relevance as well as theoretical interest.

Perhaps the clearest statement of this trend was contained in the Fundamental Review of the Treasury (1994), in which the basis of the Review appeared to be that the Treasury should dramatically reduce the degree to which it 'second-guessed' departmental spending proposals. This led to a series of recommendations for considerably contracting Treasury staff numbers on the Treasury public expenditure side. The proposals, which have now been implemented, not only cut back staff numbers but also involved a reorganization under which most economists on the microeconomic side were incorporated ('bedded-out') into spending divisions, leaving only a small microeconomics specialist unit.

Of course, it can be argued that there has not, in practice, been much of a switch. Rather, there has merely been some move along the spectrum towards more decentralization, reflecting changes in circumstances. That may well be true but it leaves the question of whether there is the potential for more radical moves in this direction.

The two models

There are essentially two ways in which governments and large companies can organize expenditure control. These are:

1. Requiring all important spending decisions to be discussed and agreed with a central coordinating department; and
2. Allowing units the freedom to decide on spending provided that they remain within centrally determined financial guidelines.

The former corresponds broadly to the traditional system of public expenditure control as it operates under the Public Expenditure Survey (PES), where spending departments have been obliged to discuss and agree proposals for new spending with the Treasury. The latter is intended to correspond more to the way in which large private sector companies, particularly conglomerates, seem to run their businesses, with profit centres reporting to a lean HQ. It is apparently leading to a serious attempt to make government operate in a decentralized way.

The two questions, then, are how far it is (a) feasible and (b) desirable for governments to plan and control public expenditure simply through financial controls on ministries and agencies. The question raises some fundamental issues concerning the nature of government as well as many technical questions of public expenditure control.

The framework set out above is couched in terms of bids for new expenditure ('marginal' public expenditures) and does not cover existing programmes ('average' public expenditures) which make up the overwhelming bulk of public expenditure. Expenditure levels for the latter are driven primarily by history and controlled through the PES and estimates process. This has been supplemented by periodic attempts at reviewing the need for existing programmes such as Programme Analysis Reviews (PARs) and zero budgeting in the past and, more recently, Fundamental Expenditure Reviews (FERs). It may therefore be argued that the framework of the model proposed in this paper (and the posed dichotomy) is unrealistic and misses the main point.

This argument is incorrect. Firstly, it underestimates the degree to which successive new public expenditure programmes increase public expenditure totals. Secondly, it greatly underplays the role of *ex post* evaluation and its potential use in the PES process. The key point at issue is not just the role of Treasury *ex ante* appraisal of new public expenditure bids as a method of controlling public expenditure, but the integrative role of the Treasury in appraisal, monitoring and evaluation of programmes as a contribution to this process. Can this be achieved merely by the issuing of Treasury guidelines and guidance of investment appraisals and so on (as in the 'Green Books'), or does it actually require active and continuing Treasury involvement in public expenditure decisions – marginal and average? For a private sector conglomerate, HQ guidelines plus financial controls may be sufficient; for governments, they are likely not to be.

The stylized models presented here are intended to address these issues.

The feasibility of controlling public expenditure through financial controls alone

In a multi-divisional company, it is typically possible for the company to be organized with the divisions as separate profit centres with separate internal accounts and separate management groups with a managing director or equivalent, each directly accountable to the company managing director and board of directors. In many cases, the profit centres are constituted as separate companies, for example as wholly-owned subsidiaries in a holding company structure.

In a company of this type, central management can decentralize, to a very considerable extent, expenditure and investment decisions within a framework of financial targets for each profit centre. However, even within this framework it would be normal for the sub-units to have very limited borrowing powers on their own account and for the central management to agree borrowing proposals of any magnitude.

There are various features of such companies that allow for financial decentralization that do not apply within government. These include the following:

The sub-units have separate accounts

As yet, government departments do not have separate accounts for capital. This should change with the progressive introduction of resource accounting and budgeting (RAB), but for some years to come, separate accounting within government will only exist for operating costs.

In addition, the absence of a full accounting framework creates serious problems for the centre (the Treasury) in ensuring that the cost and financial information provided by ministries and agencies is full and fair. The information asymmetry problem has emerged as a major issue in the economic regulation of privatized utilities and one might well expect it to be even more serious between the Treasury and spending departments.

Central management can reduce the operating levels and output of units failing to meet their financial targets

Non-performing sub-companies can be required to contract or close and they can also be sold to competing companies or to the management. This happens frequently in the private sector.

The position is very different in the public sector as shown in the health sector and more widely where the running out of funds during a financial year triggers (tightly controlled and monitored) infusions of funds rather than the stopping of operations and/or closure. In the longer run, public sector units can be contracted out for commercial or non-commercial reasons, but one cannot readily imagine (say) the DTI being closed because for several years it had failed to meet its financial targets. Similarly, governments cannot sell off financially non-performing departments to new owners.

These points are unsurprising to the point of being banal. However, they illustrate how much harder it is to enforce genuinely hard budget constraints within the public sector than within the private sector. If activities are exclusively or very largely commercial, then efficiency considerations suggest that they be carried out in the private sector in a commercial way with hard budget constraints being imposed by internal and external capital markets.

The problem with attempting to rely on credible financial control procedures with hard budget constraints in the public sector is that the activities of public sector agencies and ministries are primarily non-commercial in their justifications. Hence, the arguments against the privatization of British Rail or the financial management of hospitals rest heavily on the grounds that these activities should not be treated as if they were commercial activities like making cars or shirts and hence should not have their level of activity rationed by the internal financial position of the provider.

The company sub-units and their management are explicitly subordinate to the overall company's central management, managing director and board of directors

In a company, the managers of any sub-unit are appointed by and their continuation in office is dependent on approval of their performance by the company board. This is very different from the position of spending ministers relative to Chancellors and Chief Secretaries or the departmental officials.

It might be argued that the Prime Minister and Cabinet Office provide the equivalent and that the importance of financial spending controls is an important reason for a good relationship between the Prime Minister and the Chancellor as being fundamental to good government. Nevertheless, government in general and the planning and control of public expenditure in particular are essentially collegiate and cooperative tasks which do not fit well into a hierarchic structure with clearly defined boundaries that would encourage management of investment by decentralized financial targets.

This section has suggested some reasons why the model of a multi-divisional corporation may be a poor guide to the relationship between the Treasury and spending agencies within government. These points raise doubts about how far the Treasury will, in practice, be able to restructure the control of public expenditure by financial decentralization so that it is not involved in discussions and approval of departmental options. We will return to this issue in the last section. In the next section we discuss the desirability of such changes even if they were feasible.

The desirability of controlling public expenditure through decentralized financial controls

Many people believe that the Treasury's public expenditure control power is exercised by saying yea or nay to all emerging public expenditure proposals. This is not true. First, the number of Treasury officials involved in this area has never been more than a few hundred in total. Second, public expenditure decisions are agreed between departments and ministers, the Treasury does not have a veto.

Of course, Treasury powers depend on their ability to refuse agreement to spending proposals on a bilateral basis requiring spending departments to seek approval in Cabinet Committee or Cabinet. Therefore, for the Treasury to take that route involves political calculation on whether or not it would win in the wider forum. Given the numbers of decisions and the need to maintain the flow of affairs, these disputed cases are the exception rather than the rule. In practice, Treasury public expenditure control powers have in the past effectively rested primarily on its ability to provide clear frameworks for the justification of, the assessment of and the evaluation of public expenditures.

For both spending departments (and their finance departments) as well as the Treasury public expenditure divisions, it is essential to know what spending proposals are likely to be acceptable and on what grounds. In addition, it is important that no spending ministry (or minister) could reasonably argue that they had been dealt with unfairly by the Treasury. These pressures led to the development of frameworks for policy appraisal, costing and evaluation as well as the promulgation of sets of rules such as the Ryrie rules on the use of private finance (currently evolving into the private finance initiative).

These frameworks provided a mechanism by which:

- departments could structure and consider potential bids (and the Treasury do likewise for cuts proposals);
- routine and uncontentious decisions could be taken without requiring major examination;
- more difficult cases could be classified and handled; and
- potential anomalies in existing frameworks could be identified, discussed and rectified if necessary.

The ultimate foundation of this framework was the notion that public expenditure had to be justified on the basis of the needs of the country, citizens and consumers that could not be met adequately by market-based economic activity in the absence of government intervention and expenditure. This broad 'market failure' definition encompasses foreign policy and defence issues on the one hand and education, health, and welfare policies on the other. It corresponds to a position where tax revenue is relatively scarce.

The definition does not of course attempt to give any objective economic criterion for the *scale* of public sector involvement in the relevant areas. Many economic criteria are likely to be relevant in helping judge a proposal. Ultimately, however, the activities involve public good or other inevitably political elements where decisions rely on a balance of judgements between economic and non-economic criteria.

All of this discussion may seem a long way from whether or not public expenditure should be planned and controlled by decentralized financial guidelines. However, it is at the heart of the issue.

The more that the Treasury's public expenditure involvement is confined to setting financial limits for spending departments, the more that each department has to carry out these integrative functions for itself. In other words, the Treasury downloads the expenditure programme appraisal, monitoring and evaluation responsibilities to individual ministries and their finance divisions. But, how then is common treatment of environmental costs and benefits or the treatment of risk to be achieved across departments? Shouldn't one expect appraisal and evaluation criteria to diverge considerably across departments? If so, is the emerging pattern consistent with a view of 'government' as an integrated entity with the Cabinet of Ministers at its apex?

In this perspective, the Treasury could easily lose effective influence over the frameworks for planning public expenditure. One way in which this could happen is that Treasury officials could lose the practical basis for the progressive updating of the frameworks unless they are actively involved in the approval basis for major and/or difficult public expenditure decisions. More radically, the scenario outlined above could lead to an evolution of very different frameworks to suit the interests of different departments. Spending ministers would certainly have an incentive to create special-case justifications for their pet schemes.

Thus, it can be argued that requiring all important spending decisions to be discussed and agreed with the Treasury is an essential integrative function of government. Not only does it force departments to justify their bids and provide protection against over-cosy relations with producer pressure groups, but it also helps ensure that as far as possible the same considerations affect the case for, the scale and the method of provision of, public and related goods across the whole of government.

Eliminating the Treasury capability to carry out its previous responsibilities in this area is to mistake governmental coordination and integration for second-guessing and functional redundancy. Thus, even if controlling public expenditure by decentralized financial targets alone were feasible, there is a strong case for arguing that it was not desirable.

Will the Treasury decentralize?

There are thus strong reasons for doubting whether the public expenditure process can in practice be radically decentralized using financial guidelines and eliminating the role of the Treasury in the discussion and agreement of major and/or problematical public expenditure decisions. We have also suggested that there could be serious problems in maintaining coordinated government in an integrated fashion. Instead, spending departments, agencies and lower-level units might become increasingly divergent in their objectives, criteria and procedures.

This raises the question of whether such decentralization as potentially indicated in the Treasury Fundamental Review will actually happen. Are we merely attacking a straw man? I think not, because there is a strong lobby for such change. In any event, it is useful to consider the longer-term implications of an approach which appeals to those who believe that government should be organized on the basis of modern corporate management techniques. This, I would argue, is to misunderstand what markets can and cannot do as well as to misunderstand the nature of government and the role of public expenditure.

So, will radical financial decentralization actually happen? Will the Treasury observe a self-denying ordinance and refrain from second-guessing departments? I think not and there is no evidence that they are doing so.

The pressures on the Treasury are such that they will always and inevitably be actively involved in approving public expenditure bids as well as in setting financial guidelines such as cash limits and required rates of return. Although I would argue that the Treasury inevitably has to be responsible for this work, this does not mean that it has to be done by Treasury staff in Treasury offices. There seems no obvious reason in principle why parts, potentially large parts, of public expenditure control could not be contracted out. The main impediment would seem to be the UK culture of secrecy. It would seem very odd for these difficult, sometimes politically contentious and commercially sensitive issues to be put into a quasi-public domain without a major cultural shift in favour of governmental openness and perhaps a Freedom of Information Act. This, however, raises issues that go way beyond the scope of this paper.

But whatever the mechanism, the Treasury will continue to play a major role in this area and it is right that they shall do so. As before, the responsibility will remain as much in framework setting as in casework, as shown in the very active involvement of the Treasury in pursuing the private finance initiative. The problem in the short term is whether, after the staff reductions they still have the capability to do so.

16

The Need for a Strong Treasury, and How to Make it Work

Nick Monck

Contents

Gentlemen: Whilst marching to Portugal to a position which commands the approach to Madrid and the French forces, my officers have been diligently complying with your requests . . . We have enumerated our saddles, bridles, tents and tent poles and all manner of sundry items for which HMG hold me accountable. I have dispatched reports on the character, wit and spleen of every officer.

Each item and every farthing has been accounted for with two regrettable exceptions for which I beg your indulgence. Unfortunately . . . one shilling and ninepence remains unaccounted for in one infantry battalion's petty cash and there has been hideous confusion as to the number of jars of raspberry jam issued to one cavalry regiment during the sandstorm in Western Spain. This reprehensible carelessness may be related to the pressure of circumstances since we are at war with France, a fact which may come as a bit of a surprise to you gentlemen of Whitehall. This brings me to my present purpose, which is to request elucidation of my instructions . . . so that I may better understand why I am dragging an army over these barren plains. I construe that perforce it must be one of two alternative duties . . . I shall pursue either one . . . but I cannot do both:

1. to train an army of uniformed British clerks in Spain for the benefit of the British accountants and copyboys in London, or perchance
2. to see to it that the forces of Napoleon are driven out of Spain.

Wellington (Attributed)

> [Comparing Treasury control to conventional morality] There is a great deal of it rather tiresome and absurd once you . . . look into it . . . nevertheless it is an essential bulwark against overwhelming wickedness.
>
> Keynes

The Treasury is very often blamed for everything that goes wrong in the UK. Therefore there are often calls for it to be weakened. This chapter argues that this would be a mistaken policy. There are timeless reasons why a strong Treasury is needed, which apply in most countries most of the time. These are compelling enough on their own. On top of those, special reasons would apply on the arrival of a new Labour government.

The chapter first looks at the case for a 'strong Treasury' both timeless and at a change of government. Next it looks at what it means and what pre-conditions are needed for it to play this role. This is especially true if a new Labour government is to use public expenditure efficiently. It then looks at tools and techniques for managing public expenditure and keeping it tight. It shows that efficiency gains are being made and argues that they can be made in the future.

Timeless reasons for a strong Treasury

Any country with a state that spends taxpayers' money needs political and administrative arrangements capable of tackling several tasks:

- taking decisions on total spending levels;
- deciding how much to borrow;
- trading off public spending against taxes;
- allocating spending between different purposes and programmes;
- getting good value from public spending, in terms of current welfare and of investment in human and physical capacity;
- delivering these decisions and accounting for the results.

These tasks are familiar and sound basic. But they are also intensely political and extremely difficult to carry out successfully in countries at all stages of development. As a *Financial Times* editorial in January 1996 said: 'The US has one, Europeans have one, and now even Japan has one. What do they all have? A serious fiscal problem. This is the theme of the decade.' It pointed out that in industrial countries:

> the overall ratio of Government spending to GDP . . . stabilised in the early 1980s. It did so, however, at levels that individual governments were unable or unwilling to cover by taxation . . . The resulting fiscal deficits . . . increased the ratio of gross public debt to GDP from 41% in 1980 to 72% in 1995. Unfunded pension promises ensure there is worse to come almost everywhere.

Though it cannot guarantee success, a strong Treasury (or at least a strong Bureau of the Budget) is a necessary part of doing better at these basic tasks.

The difficulties governments face in tackling these tasks are great, various and interrelated. First, there are political difficulties. There is an array of powerful pressures, whether self-interested or altruistic, which favour more public spending but oppose higher taxes. Some of the pressures are strengthened by social and demographic changes at national level and by international economic forces which individual governments cannot control. The choice about where to yield and where to resist can and should be made better by objective analysis. But it cannot be based on any single calculus.

Second, there is the 'economic' difficulty that a higher level of unemployment appears to accompany the achievement of low inflation than was the case in the early post-war decades. This puts upward pressure on spending and reduces revenue growth.

Third, and at a more technical level, macroeconomic instability and uncertainty about 'cyclical adjustments' make it genuinely difficult to interpret borrowing, revenue and spending figures. This tempts governments to mislead themselves and their electorates about the fiscal position and prospect.

There is often *some* chance that optimism is justified. Treasury economists have estimated that a one per cent increase in output relative to trend will reduce the PSBR/GDP ratio after two years by about three-quarters of a percentage point or about £6 billion. But advice expressed in terms of probabilities or opinions can be set aside without blatant irresponsibility. It is notorious, for example, that the Treasury's forecast of the PSBR at the time of the negotiations with the IMF in 1976 proved to be far too high.

Pressures on a Labour government

Any incoming government faces several additional problems. First, it will want to change priorities. Second, it will be watched very closely by outside observers including the financial markets. Third, the civil service will not be familiar with the assumptions and aims of the new administration.

These problems will be more intense for a new government that is under strong pressure to increase expenditure, which might well be the case for a new Labour government elected in 1997. Many of its supporters and some of its members would have a long list of cases of Conservative 'under-funding' which they would expect the new government to correct. Some will wonder what the Labour government is for if it doesn't do so. Examples come easily to mind in health, education, law and order, help for the long-term unemployed and welfare to work, the regime for local authorities and public sector pay.

The difficulty of the task for a Labour government is put into perspective by the fact that the series of Conservative administrations since 1979 in fact achieved no more than partial success in reducing public expenditure, if that is measured against their original aims. They failed to reduce the level of spending in real terms or even to freeze it. But they did achieve a modest trend reduction in the share of GDP devoted to public expenditure and kept the share well below the European Union average (see Figure 16.1). The UK share is still

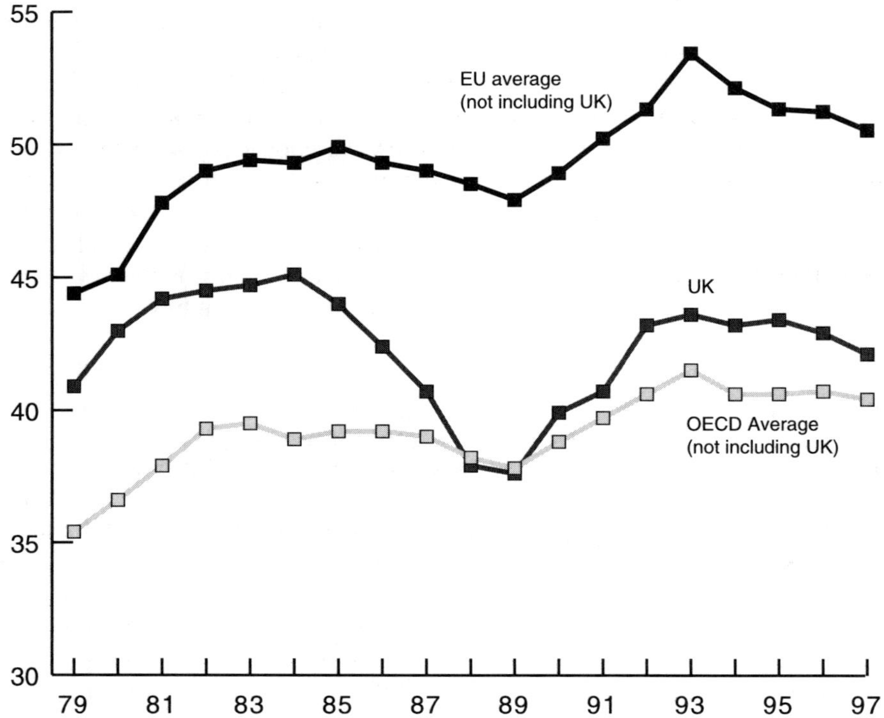

Figure 16.1. General government outlays as % of GDP (weighted).
Source: Treasury.

above the OECD average, which is pulled down by the figures for the USA, Canada and Japan, but the gap is much smaller now than in the early 1980s.

There are alternative explanations of the Tory record on public spending since 1979. It can be seen as a story of an irresolute approach, or mistaken policies (see Chapter 12 by Jackson). Alternatively, it shows how hard it is to reduce the growth of spending below that of the GDP. I think the second is right.

It would on the face of it be open to a new government to raise the share of GDP devoted to public spending towards the EU average by a few percentage points (each one per cent equal to about £8 billion). It could defend this approach by pointing to the long run success of some EU economies even though they spend more than the UK.

But as part of its commitment to macroeconomic stability, Labour has endorsed the 'golden rule' for fiscal policy. This rule means that over the economic cycle as a whole revenue should match current expenditure; and borrowing should not exceed net capital investment. This is much stricter than the UK's actual performance over the last 40 years.

The Red Book for the 1995 Budget projected a downward trend for the PSBR as a percentage of GDP, reaching overall balance by 1999–2000 (assuming that

GDP grows at nearly 3 per cent a year over the period). For most of the years between now and then the PSBR was forecast to be larger than net capital spending.

If a Labour government sticks strictly to the golden rule (i.e. that borrowing should only be for investment), it would find it had little or no room for raising current spending without raising taxes. There would be flexibility on capital spending. But key programmes, such as education, training, employment measures and health consist largely of expenditure normally defined as current.

These commitments on borrowing, combined with a reluctance to raise taxes other than the windfall tax on utilities, will put a premium on identifying expenditure savings to finance new current spending without adding to the total.

If this outline of Labour policy aims proves to be broadly correct, a strong Treasury will certainly be needed to make it happen. The rest of this chapter describes the conditions necessary for a strong Treasury and some of the approaches it might use.

Pre-conditions for a strong Treasury

A 'strong Treasury' is useful shorthand for many attitudes, arrangements and approaches at ministerial and official level, which go much wider than the Treasury itself. They need to prevail also in spending departments and to apply throughout the year, not just during the annual public expenditure (PES) round.

The primary pre-condition for the Treasury to play a strong and effective role is that there should be broad agreement between the Prime Minister and Treasury ministers – and enough other ministers – about the desirable level of public expenditure (or at least about the direction in which the share of GDP devoted to public spending should be moving over the medium term). This agreement need not be about the allocation or the level of individual programmes but does need to cover *total* spending, a more plausible subject for agreement.

If this broad agreement is absent, a 'strong Treasury' in the narrow sense will not prevail. The situation has not changed since Keynes observed it 70 years ago:

> . . . no Chancellor of the Exchequer can in the long run enforce a policy which is opposite to the prevailing current in the Cabinet or contrary to the temperament of an autocratic Prime Minister [Lloyd George].

Views about total spending should be related to views about the tolerable level of taxation and borrowing in relation to GDP. Such views will probably be partly political and partly economic. They are likely to be based on observation and hunch rather than any sophisticated economic theory. But it is helpful if they reflect some wariness about the ability of financial markets to penalize governments which spend on a scale that leads to high borrowing.

Views about spending should also be based on a cautious estimate of the economy's likely growth rate. Any new economic policies will have only a delayed effect on the growth of the economy's capacity. Spending plans, particularly for the first term of a new government, should not be based on any more optimistic assumptions.

Setting ceilings first

If the primary pre-condition of broad agreement on the right level for total spending is met, several others should also be attainable. A key one is that the Cabinet should agree on ceilings for total public expenditure, preferably for three years ahead, *before* serious negotiations begin between Treasury and spending ministers in the annual spending round on the allocations to individual departments and programmes. It should also be possible, at the end of the round, to publish medium-term plans for spending which become ceilings for future years. (The ceilings settled in this way in the last four years have applied to the 'new control total' which is defined to exclude some large elements in total expenditure, notably debt interest and cyclical social security.)

Setting ceilings before the round begins may sound obvious. But by the 1992 election this was no longer the practice in central government. Each July the Cabinet ritually endorsed weasel words about the aim of the Survey – roughly to stick as closely as possible to the plans published the year before. But in practice in the early 1990s the new plans were not constrained by the totals published a year earlier (which, admittedly, had sometimes been unrealistic). Instead they were the aggregate result of a series of lengthy bilateral negotiations between the Chief Secretary and individual spending ministers.

Hardly surprisingly the totals reached under this procedure tended to be higher than the previous plans. This was only partly due to changes in unemployment or inflation that had genuinely not been foreseen a year earlier. The control total grew in real terms by 3.5 per cent and 4.5 per cent in 1991–92 and 1992–93; General Government Expenditure or GGE(X), the Government's aggregate for overall public spending grew by 3.5 per cent and 6 per cent.

How should the expenditure ceilings be arrived at? There are many possible answers and what makes sense will vary with the circumstances. At one extreme, when the post-1992 system is working properly, the ceilings for the first two years come from last year's plans, and the third year's can be derived from a projection of some kind.

However, a new government may not want to fly blind in this way and may want to consider, at least in broad terms, whether its highest priority spending commitments can be fitted within the ceilings which the Cabinet is asked by Treasury ministers to endorse before the government's first expenditure round. A Cabinet paper discussing this could not be at all detailed without making the ceilings proposed too conditional (i.e. weak) to be an effective constraint on the expenditure round. But, as an illustration of the level of discussion, the paper might argue that after making a realistic allowance for demand-determined expenditure on social security, the proposed ceiling might include a significant increase on the inherited plans in either education or health but not both. Ideally such priorities would be agreed before the election. History suggests this is unlikely.

On the other hand, if a new government arrives with a clear commitment on borrowing (the golden rule) and a belief that taxes cannot be raised significantly without jeopardizing the chance of re-election, the level of expenditure ceilings will have been largely determined. Settling them, at least for current expenditure, would then be quicker and simpler than a wholly new start and would be more like deriving ceilings from previous plans.

Resolving disagreements

An equally important requirement in the management of public expenditure is an effective mechanism for resolving disagreements between the Treasury minister in charge of expenditure (that is, the Chief Secretary to the Treasury) and spending ministers and for deciding on the allocation of spending between different purposes and departments within the agreed totals.

Under the pre-1992 arrangements – and after Lord Whitelaw's departure from the Cabinet brought an end to the 'Star Chamber', a Cabinet committee which had settled disputed expenditure programmes – tenacity and political status had too much influence on the outcome of bilateral negotiations. This led to excessive totals as well as to the endorsement of spending of low merit. The allocation process will always be imperfect and will be influenced by personalities and prejudices. But it should clearly be informed so far as possible by thorough information and analysis of the benefits actually produced by different programmes.

There are two broad alternatives to 'bilaterals' between spending and Treasury ministers for resolving disputes about the size of individual programmes. One is close collaboration between Treasury ministers and the Prime Minister. The other is some wider sub-committee of the Cabinet, consisting of senior ministers, which can judge whether a proposed allocation within the ceiling expresses the government's priorities acceptably. Such a Cabinet committee can be chaired by a figure like Lord Whitelaw (i.e. a fixer acting on behalf of the Prime Minister), the Prime Minister in person, or the Chancellor of the Exchequer.

Since 1992 the UK has adopted a version of the second option, with the Chancellor in the chair of a committee known as EDX. This option is very time-consuming for EDX members but it saves the Prime Minister's time (though the Prime Minister can of course arrange to be kept in touch closely), reduces the risk that the PM's and Chancellor's favourite programmes escape rigorous scrutiny, and widens the consensus built up by the time final proposals go to Cabinet. It also leaves the Prime Minister formally uncommitted and in that sense better able to chair the Cabinet discussion of the proposals EDX puts to it.

Any of these options could work and different Prime Ministers and administrations will have their own preferences. The important thing is that one of these options should be clearly chosen for a new government's first expenditure round.

The pattern chosen in the first and probably crucial year can be varied later on if need be.

Splitting the Treasury?

Although these preconditions for effective fiscal policy and expenditure control are necessary, they will not stop expenditure rounds from being experienced as rough, bruising, undiscriminating and even random and irrational. This reflects the wide range of values and purposes embodied in spending proposals, the impossibility of ranking them all in any objective way that commands assent, the sheer number of decisions to be taken, and the extent of evidence that is available and relevant.

Many participants and observers feel there must be a better and more 'rational' way to do things. This leads to various proposals for institutional change. One is having the Prime Minister as chairman of EDX; more frequently heard is the call to split up the Treasury, which is often said to be 'too strong'. The UK Treasury is unusual compared to other countries in that it has two Cabinet Ministers and combines the responsibilities of Ministry of Finance, Bureau of the Budget and Economics Ministry. Some therefore propose dividing the expenditure side from the fiscal policy side to remove the bias against public spending, or separating spending, tax and borrowing policy from the rest.

The recent reorganization of the Treasury can be seen as a variant of this. Three different directorates have partly overlapping responsibilities. One advises on the aim and path for borrowing; another on the implications for spending and taxes and on delivering results in the budget; and a third contains the 13 spending teams dealing with individual departments and responsible, with a longer-term focus, for making expenditure as effective as possible in economic terms within an affordable total.

There are advantages in the broad span of the UK Treasury since it increases the chance that the fiscal functions will be informed by knowledge about the economy and will not be at odds with monetary policy. But in any case, such a reorganization would not reduce the difficulty of deciding and delivering fiscal policy and public expenditure control.

Useful approaches to controlling and managing public expenditure

Many components contribute to success in the planning, control and management of public expenditure. Some involve ministers, though in many the main activity is carried out by officials in the Treasury and in spending departments. These include: timely statistics about expenditure; realistic forecasts – especially of social security expenditure; a good flow of information and analysis about the intended and actual results of different programmes; and a culture that ensures cash limits and financial control generally are taken seriously.

Most of these depend partly on the accounting officer responsibilities of permanent secretaries (the heads of departments) and others. These people need to pride themselves not only on financial control but on running effective departments. They should be looking to increase value for money through clarity about objectives, regular information about how far they are being achieved, and arrangements for improving performance through changes in the design, funding or management of programmes. They should be ready to identify areas where close working with other departments is required and be willing to make it happen. An important stimulus is auditing and scrutiny by the National Audit Office, backed up by the Public Accounts Committee of the House of Commons (both of which look at central government expenditure), and by the Audit Commission (which deals mainly with local government). All of these need to be maintained by a new Administration. They all go wider than the Treasury alone, which can probe and initiate but needs help from departments to make real progress.

Several less traditional approaches, developed during the last 15 years or so, are also available to help a new Labour government combine tight overall control of public expenditure with changed priorities and getting more out of the available resources.

Using the private sector

Structural transfers of responsibilities to the private sector are one example. Classic privatization may no longer offer sizeable opportunities even if it were attractive. But a further transfer of pensions to funded private sector schemes may eventually play a useful part.

The Private Finance Initiative (PFI) also tends to appear under this heading. This reflects the fact that conventional public investment is accounted for at present with a lumpy impact in the year the investment is made, whereas the cost of investment under the PFI is spread over the years in which the capital produces services and the private sector investors are remunerated. When resource accounting and budgeting is introduced into all programmes, all investment will be scored in the same way with the cost spread over the period of capital consumption. This will help to remove the bias against capital in the present survey and also to strengthen the value for money test applied to PFI projects.

The PFI has some risks as it can be used as a way of cutting investment or of shifting expenditure off balance sheet in the short term. But it also offers potential value-for-money (VFM) gains through involving the provider of capital goods in operating them and in accepting risk transfer from the public sector. Strict management is needed to ensure that the VFM gains outweigh the higher cost of capital to the private sector which eventually falls on taxpayers or, more rarely, customers.

Reviews and reallocation between programmes

Fundamental Expenditure Reviews (FERs), introduced in 1992, can make a useful contribution not only to identifying savings within a department but also to improving value for money and service quality. Recent FERs of defence, social security and health have illustrated this.

FERs have varied in quality and sometimes been dismissed as 'no more than cuts exercises'. But their zero-based approach, which tackles the whole programme and not just proposed additions, reaches expenditure that may be missed by the annual round. Savings which do not damage the quantity or quality of a desired output will be welcome to most governments: the health FER certainly found ways of improving quality.

Analytical work of this kind could be relaunched by a new government, aiming to cover all major programmes in the first parliament. This would ensure that the aims and values of new ministers are brought to bear effectively. Since Labour may want to reallocate public expenditure between programmes, and this is certainly something the Conservatives have done between 1990–91 and 1996–97. Table 16.1 (p. 285) shows that over this period one group of programmes rose on average by about 25 per cent in real terms; another group fell by the same amount; and a third group including local authority spending has been held more or less constant. This suggests that the approach since 1990 has not been mechanical or across the board but highly selective, reflecting political judgements as well as analysis by officials. It also shows that a Government can shift the balance of spending over a fairly short period.

Governments should demand rigorous analysis of VFM by officials. Officials, as Alan Bailey argues in Chapter 17, cannot rank projects across programmes objectively in the way that, say, road projects can be ranked against each other. But analysis which shows, for instance, that only a low proportion of a particular programme produces an additional benefit of the kind intended can and clearly should influence ministers' judgement on priorities. EDX can make use of such information provided officials make sure it is obtained in the first place and then communicate it to ministers in formal papers or in briefing.

Management techniques

Lastly there is a whole range of management techniques that have been progressively introduced into government and other parts of the public sector, improving efficiency and quality of service. These include:

- Defining objectives, setting and publishing quantified targets, and monitoring and publishing performance. The Citizens' Charter has reinforced these approaches.
- Altering organizations to match their particular tasks, notably by setting up

Table 16.1. Re-allocating public expenditure (big changes in real terms from 1990–91 to 1996–97).

	1994–1995 prices (£bn)		*Change*
	1990–91	*1996–97*	*(%)*
Falling			
Defence Trade & industry incl. NIs Housing Transport Revenue & other Treasury departments	48	35.5	−26
Rising			
Social security (non-cyclical) Education and employment (largely excl. schools) Health Scotland, Wales, N. Ireland Home Office & Legal	123	155	+25
Flat (or very small)			
Other	53	54	+2
of which local authorities (largely incl. schools)*	(42)	(42)	(neg)
Control total	224	246	+10
(GGE-X)	(252)	(290)	(+15)

* Excluding specific grants from departments other than DOE.
Source: Derived from Table 6A.4, p. 142, November 1995, Budget Red Book.

executive agencies; and finding ways of reconciling financial control with more organizational flexibility.

- Using the purchaser/provider distinction and competition between suppliers to achieve efficiency or quality improvements, often both together.
- Squeezing administration and overheads, sometimes crudely as in running cost cuts and sometimes more analytically as in senior management reviews. The aim of both is to leave more room within a given total for expenditure on services, though the relative size of running costs limits the scope for this.

Acting on the belief that continuous improvement in efficiency and quality can be achieved in public services is a recent development. It should be taken further by any new government that sets itself difficult targets and wants a second-term. If efficiency and other gains can win the race against rising expectations (or at least keep pace), the politics of expenditure control can be transformed or at least made more tractable.

Can efficiency be improved?

There is no convincing overall measure of changes in efficiency or quality in the public sector. But disaggregated information about big components of it, such as education, health, defence and the largest agencies, suggests that improvements have been large enough in aggregate to make public expenditure control a little less difficult. It has also helped to undermine the reflex view that inadequate quality must mean there is 'underfunding'. Below we give some examples of how efficiency may be improving, which also give some grounds for hoping for more. The areas covered – education, hospitals, defence and the four largest 'next steps' organizations (Employment Service, the Benefits Agency, and the two Revenue Departments) – account for around two thirds of General Government Expenditure on services. So the encouraging performance described here seems likely to be reasonably representative.

Some of the measures quoted below are of inputs or throughput but wherever possible information about output quantity or quality is used.

Although serious problems in *education* remain, there has been a sizeable cumulative improvement in the percentage of pupils getting A/AS level passes in secondary schools and FE colleges over the last ten years:

Passes	*1984–85*	*1994–95 (provisional)*
1+	19.5	33.8
2+	15.4	29.0
3+	10.6	21.9

Even if there were some truth in the claim that examination standards have slipped, it would probably only partially offset this steep rise.

Between 1989–90 and 1992–93 there was a large increase in productivity and a reduction in real costs per student of 20 per cent in higher education and 10 per cent in further education. So far there has been relatively little evidence of damaging results. For example there has been little growth in the UK drop-out rate which continues to be low compared with other countries. Quality too is said to have remained generally high despite the rapid growth in the number of HE students, although some capacity shortages are now beginning to show up.

In *health* Hospital and Community Health Services (HCHS) activity is estimated to have risen by 28 per cent over the latest 10 years available (1983–84 to 1993–94). About 15 per cent of this can be attributed to efficiency gains. The annual gain in efficiency has risen from less than 2 per cent, first to over 2 per cent and then to over 3 per cent. Although there are well-known problems in health, the Fundamental Expenditure Review has shown that great scope for further gains in efficiency and service quality remains through reducing the gap between low and high cost areas and by making use of 'evidence-based medicine' to stop or reduce procedures that are either useless or positively harmful to health.

In *defence* efficiency savings achieved each year have risen from £260m in 1989–90 to over £500m in 1994–95. These are to be sustained to the end of the century under the banner of Front Line First.

In the *agency* field the latest Next Steps Review expresses some concern about the proportion of agency targets set below last year's target or even last year's performance, although only about a third of them can be directly compared in this way. Nonetheless the detailed information the Review provides about the performance of the largest agencies over the last three years is on the whole impressive and suggests that on average agencies have made steady improvements in efficiency and/or service.

The *Employment Service* has increased the number of people it places in jobs and the proportion of placements going to the long-term unemployed (up from a target of 19 per cent in 1992–93, which was exceeded, to a target and out-turn of over 29 per cent in 1994–95 and 1995–96) at the same time as achieving rising efficiency savings. The *Benefits Agency* raised output per staff member by over 25 per cent between 1990–91 and 1994–95, and made increasing savings of various kinds. The two *Revenue Departments* collected increasing revenue while reducing their combined staff from over 90 000 in 1992–93 to under 8000 in 1995–96.

Conclusions

Successful performance of the basic fiscal tasks of any state is extremely difficult and requires a 'strong Treasury' in the wide sense described above. A new Labour government would face special pressures for more public expenditure on top of the timeless arguments for a strong Treasury, particularly given the stringency on public finance that it now espouses.

A broad consensus between the Prime Minister and the Cabinet about the desirable level of public expenditure in total is a necessary pre-condition for a strong Treasury and for effective fiscal policies. Ceilings for the control total should be agreed in advance of serious exchanges between Treasury and spending ministers in the public expenditure round.

A choice should be made between two broad mechanisms for allocations between programmes and spending ministers within the agreed totals: close collaboration between the Chancellor and the Prime Minister; or a Cabinet Committee on the lines of the post-1992 EDX, probably but not necessarily chaired by the Chancellor.

Further efforts should be made to inject information and analysis about the intended and actual effects of different programmes into the allocation process. But the process cannot be wholly objective and it will still be contentious, time-consuming and rough.

There are many components in effective management of public spending issues, some primarily for ministers, others for officials. Some traditional arrangements and disciplines, which are more fragile than they may seem, need to be maintained.

But there are also some more recently developed approaches which may help a Labour administration. These include transfers to the private sector; Fundamental Expenditure Reviews and re-allocation between programmes to bring the new government's priorities to bear; new management techniques, particularly the use of public targets and performance against them, which have had a major impact on efficiency and service quality.

All these can help but will not of course remove the difficulty of public expenditure choices, which are not just about stopping useless or wasteful spending but also involve judgements between competing proposals, many of which typically have something to be said for them.

17

The Spending Department Perspective

Alan Bailey

Contents

Introduction

While no one questions the need for central control of public spending, opinions differ as to how that would best be achieved. One's point of view depends on whether one is on the side of the Treasury or a spending department. I have some claim to have seen the argument from both perspectives, having been in charge of public expenditure in the Treasury for three years in the early 1980s and Permanent Secretary in the Department of Transport between 1986 and 1991. It was a common observation among Permanent Secretaries that the fiercest critics of excessive intervention by the Treasury tend to be those with previous Treasury experience.

Clearly, the Treasury is a key player in the control of public expenditure and the first part of this chapter defines that role. In recent years, however, the Treasury has become more involved in areas (including microeconomic decisions) that have, traditionally, been the responsibility of spending departments. Against this background, what lessons might an incoming government draw? In particular, how should it set about reversing what many believe to be an excessive centralization of power and bring the Treasury back to its proper role in controlling public expenditure?

Role of the Treasury

At one level, the role of the Treasury is easy to define. Its job is to help ministers, collectively, to reach decisions, at the margin, between rival spending priorities and between the totals of expenditure and taxation. The Chancellor and Chief Secretary have, respectively, key responsibilities for the balance of tax and spending, and the public expenditure function. However, the public expenditure side of the Treasury can be seen as an expanded 'secretariat' for the Cabinet as a whole.

In practice such issues may be settled on behalf of the Cabinet by the Prime Minister as 'First Lord of the Treasury', the Chancellor and/or the Chief Secretary, and whatever 'spending' ministers are directly involved. The Cabinet may choose to delegate the time-consuming task of setting public expenditure totals to a group of 'wise men'/non-spending Ministers (the EDX Cabinet Committee being the latest manifestation).

The Treasury has two important powers which stem from its 'secretariat' role, and because of the role of Treasury ministers in looking after taxpayers' interests. First, agreement from the Treasury is needed before a department enters into any new policy commitment that has expenditure implications. Within individual departments, the formal responsibility for ensuring Treasury approval lies with the accounting officer and principal finance officer. Second, the Treasury's agreement is needed before any policy paper goes to Cabinet or a Cabinet committee, or to the Prime Minister or an informal ministerial group chaired by the Prime Minister. This latter is used increasingly, hence the importance of the traditionally strong Treasury presence in 10 Downing Street.

All this means that a great deal of work has to go on at official level in support of this function, not least in terms of Treasury expenditure divisions deciding what can be cleared at official level and what needs to be referred to ministers. A Treasury official, like any other civil servant on policy work, ought to advise ministers in accordance with what ministers themselves would decide if they had all the time and facts to make a decision. To do this properly, those working in expenditure divisions need to learn about their 'client' departments, and get to know the key people, especially in finance branches. Hence their right to ask questions, often to the fury of 'client' officials who suspect foot-dragging as a way of holding back expenditure.

Avoiding pitfalls

In assessing a department's real priorities, and what it can most easily afford to give up at the margin, Treasury officials need to guard against two distortions which are, in effect, two sides of the same coin.

First, there is what may be termed 'bleeding stumps'. This is when a spending department claims that conspicuous and politically embarrassing consequences will follow if the Treasury fails to agree more funds. The Treasury may, however, try to call the department's bluff, decide to leave the control total unchanged and challenge the department to make the threatened cut. In this event, the department may well find that it is able to identify some lower-priority programme which it can cut (to the embarrassment of the finance branch).

A second distortion results from bureaucratic inertia. If there is insufficient pressure from the Treasury (or managerial ministers and macho senior officials), spending programmes can continue to exist, even where they are no longer justified. This involves waste of public money, especially on running costs. Here, again, the Treasury's role is to draw attention to the waste of public money. This involves having enough knowledge to probe into the issue, using the department's finance officers as allies (there is nothing more useful than a finance officer in a department telling his eager troops that 'the Treasury won't agree . . . ').

Role of personalities

What have been described above are all features of a familiar game played between the Treasury and spending departments. It would be easy to conclude that the outcome is mainly determined by the relative political and personal strengths of Treasury ministers and the various spending ministers. There is undoubtedly some truth in this. As with all human decisions, public expenditure decision making is often the result of a mixture of factors, including rational long-term priorities, short-term vote-winning and personal game-playing and machismo.

This cynicism about personal and short-term factors should not, however, be exaggerated. It is true, of course, that strong ministers make the best of a good spending case. However, ministers can also make their reputations from cost-cutting and increasing efficiency. In my experience there is little in the theory that bureaucrats try to build up the size of their departments so as to enhance their own status and salaries; even before the present wave of 'down-sizing', good civil service managers knew that building or keeping staff numbers beyond what the volume and quality of work required would be bad for morale, for staff retention and for their own reputations. While personal and short-term factors will always be important, serious long-term discussion of public-interest considerations, both within government and in the public domain generally, is the best way of containing and counteracting them.

The temptation to take short-cuts

It is tempting for the Treasury to try to cut through all this complexity by setting fairly arbitrary control totals and letting departments manage within them. This sounds like good business management. However, applying arbitrary across-the-board formulae such as fixed totals, percentage uplifts and 'equal misery' cuts negates collective ministerial choices on priorities, and, hence, the Treasury's proper role. Control totals may be useful as a starting-point for debate or as a way to cut short disputes in a crisis or in the public spending round 'end game'. But such methods will leave ministers and departments dissatisfied if they have not had their cases for spending priorities ('additional bids') properly weighed. By definition, some other priority (unexamined continuing spending programme, or tax cut) may have got through at the expense of a new high-priority claim on resources which ministers would have preferred if they had been allowed to address it.

Jon Stern (see Chapter 15) reaches the same conclusion on the related grounds that Treasury-imposed 'appraisal and evaluation criteria' would tend to diverge across Whitehall if over-ridden by arbitrary expenditure ceilings. Having advocated cost-benefit analysis at various stages of my Treasury and Transport career, I would not want to discount that argument. But the truth is that while cost-benefit analysis is sometimes effective in ranking similar projects within programmes, it has little or not impact in evaluating priorities across programmes. The recent sharp cuts in the road construction programme were not the result of changing 'appraisal and evaluation criteria'. It is still the case that, on the most thorough quantitative analysis of economic and environmental factors, the benefits of road schemes are still likely to be two or three times their costs. What has changed is the 'political value judgement' that the environmental damage caused by such schemes should be given greater weight, or, put more crudely, that new roads lose votes.

Recent expansion of Treasury's role

The Treasury's power has extended over the years way beyond its role in controlling cash Estimates and in macroeconomic management. This extension came about for good historical reasons.

The Plowden Report followed the 1960s' fashion for 'indicative planning' by setting up a five-year expenditure planning and control system in 'volume' terms. There were good reasons for this, given the five-year (or longer) timescale for investment projects, in defence and elsewhere; and public-sector managers have always appealed for greater certainty in their expenditure allocations for future years. But planning quickly went out of fashion. Economic crises required short-term measures which invalidated the five-year programme, and it was always difficult to persuade ministers to focus seriously on decisions for forward years well beyond the horizon of the next election. So the nominal planning cycle was cut successively to four years and then to three.

Following this attempt at 'volume' planning, the 1970s saw a return, under IMF pressure, to the basics of public expenditure control – cash planning, cash limits, controls on manpower numbers, external financing limits as control totals for the nationalized industries, all to be strictly enforced with full Cabinet backing. The 1980s then developed in a different direction, towards 'scientific' or business management aimed at more systematic assessment of 'value for money'.

Recent reforms, including the Financial Management Initiative (FMI), greater emphasis on control of running costs, executive agencies, privatization and the Private Finance Initiative (PFI) have all had the effect of extending the role of the Treasury into microeconomic decision making.

Financial Management Initiative (FMI)

The FMI involves setting objectives, measuring outputs and managing according to defined targets. The application of what was standard private-sector practice has been useful (although one ought to remain sceptical about the possiblity of any complete or adequate measurement of socio-political 'values'). The overall result, however, has been a whole new range of interventions by central departments (in practice, the Treasury expenditure division) in the outputs, targeting and management of spending departments.

Control of running costs

This was an improvement on control of manpower numbers (under which a clerical officer or cook could be saved to make room for an extra deputy secretary). It was the best mechanism available if ministers wanted to put a differential squeeze on the costs of public administration, and it fairly reflected the fact that if a department was free to switch spending from 'programmes' into extra staff, it would be incurring obligations for the future which needed some form of central control.

But there was the opposite risk, that departments could no longer manage their programmes adequately or use their capital assets effectively because their administrative resources were squeezed. Indeed, I believe that one of the origins of agencies, well before the Next Steps Report, was Nicholas Ridley's insistence on being able to recruit extra driving examiners to meet growing demand for tests, on a net cost basis outside running costs control. There were also large problems in defining running costs (pensions, redundancy costs, a whole range of 'administrative capital' items) which left scope for creative accounting. To guard against this required another tranche of detailed Treasury intervention.

Agencies

The setting up of executive agencies followed the recommendations of the Next Steps Report. Their importance, however, has been somewhat exaggerated. There have always been distinct sub-departments with executive heads who reported direct to Ministers (HMSO, the Royal Mint and, in effect, the Revenue Departments). The result of the recent reform is a clearer structure, allowing greater freedom of management over a wider range of civil service executive activities. However, management freedom has had to be balanced by more explicit financial and 'quality' objectives. Approving these objectives means that the Treasury is now closely involved in areas where, previously, it had not been much concerned.

Privatization and other examples of the Treasury going too far

The sale of publicly owned assets was the biggest microeconomic initiative of the 1980s. It is ironic, however, that while the nationalized industries were being sold to the private sector, the executive agencies were being transformed along lines recommended for the nationalized sector in the 1981 report by the CPRS (headed by Sir Robin Ibbs, who was also the author of the Next Steps Report).

The Treasury played a key role throughout the process of selling publicly owned assets. It ensured propriety and 'value for money' and disseminated best practice as experience of the sales built up. Successive Financial Secretaries took this on as their main responsibility, and were supported by a key Treasury division. My contention is that, in this important area of government activity, value-for-money (VFM) considerations and wider microeconomic policy issues became confused. It is one thing for the Treasury to insist on its primacy in policy decisions where it is arguing for maximization of proceeds, or for propriety in the sale of public assets (selection of financial advisers, claw-back on realization of asset values, etc.). It is another, however, for the Treasury to insist on its primacy regarding decisions on the structure of industries such as transport and energy which will continue to be the responsibility of departmental ministers.

There have been a number of other recent examples of the Treasury taking its public expenditure powers too far. In the case of rail privatization, Treasury officials appear to have gone further than putting forward the arguments for maximizing the sale proceeds. They have advocated a particular form of restructuring of an industry which would remain heavily dependent on public sector regulation and subsidy and, therefore, would continue to be the central responsibility of a departmental minister. The issue is not whether the Treasury's views were right or wrong, but whether they were given undue weight because of its wider public expenditure role.

On a major public investment project such as Crossrail, it is, of course, legitimate for the Treasury to produce counter-arguments and to brief its ministers before a collective ministerial decision is taken. But even after a collective decision in favour of the project was announced, it was suggested in the press that the Treasury has continued to fight a rearguard action. An essential element of good Cabinet government is that once ministers have taken a decision, officials in all departments must accept and work towards that decision. The only exception to that unwritten rule is when a minister decides that circumstances or policies have changed enough to call the decision into question, and persuades his or her colleagues of that view.

It has also been reported that the Treasury has intervened in senior appointments, for example in public corporations. For Treasury officials to have a veto on appointments to jobs where relations with ministers and officials in a department will be crucial to success, and where the department is accountable for failure, seems an excessive and unreasonable extension of Treasury powers.

Private Finance Initiative (PFI)

Again, the importance of the PFI has been somewhat exaggerated. Projects such as the Dartford Bridge, the Channel Tunnel and the Second Severn Crossing were either completed or well in train before the PFI was announced in 1991. Nevertheless, the existence of the PFI has changed the Treasury's role. In practice, the Treasury can intervene on any significant capital project in the public sector, not simply to ensure that standard investment-appraisal criteria have been applied, but to insist that the project must, in the first instance, be set up as a privately financed project. The (unquantifiable) transfer of risk to the private sector must be judged against the extra cost (also hard to quantify) of this form of finance. This involves the Treasury at every stage, slows down projects and, again, tends to confuse responsibilities.

To sum up: the move towards centralization has probably swung too far. There is now a proliferation of central units (including a unit to monitor the Citizen's Charter, the Efficiency Unit to monitor the FMI, the unit to promote Next Steps agancies and the PFI unit within the Treasury). One result is that the decision-making process has become over-complicated, making the job of spending departments and their ministers more difficult. A new government would do well to consider whether all these units should be disbanded.

Redefining the Treasury's role

There have been many changes in recent years in the way that public expenditure control is carried out. The annual spending round process, where options for additional spending and cuts required detailed negotiations between the chief secretary and spending ministers, has been replaced by 'top-down' imposition of control totals by the EDX Committee of senior ministers. It is generally agreed, however, that the previous system gave full weight to spending pressures and, it could be argued, made it harder for Treasury ministers to hold the line against tax increases. (The advice given to a former Chief Secretary by one of his predecessors was: 'You must learn to say simply "No!" – if you start saying "No because . . . ", you're lost!'.)

Recent reorganization within the Treasury means that new spending teams have responsibility 'for promoting policies and public expenditure priorities which improve the use of resources and the efficiency of markets within an affordable total'. This seems to assume a 'top-down', pre-ordained total (with no weighing-up of costs and benefits), and confuses value for public money with microeconomic efficiency. The reality is that these are two different concepts and that they sometimes are in conflict with each other.

It is generally accepted that the Treasury is now stronger than it once was. Partly, this is because John Major is the first Prime Minister since Harold Macmillan to have been a recent former Chancellor. Indeed, apart from Jim Callaghan, no other recent Prime Minister has had Treasury experience. It also stems from political perception that tax cuts merit a higher priority than public spending. This poses a dilemma for a new government in defining a role for the Treasury. The shadow Chancellor, Gordon Brown, has already indicated that Labour would give the Treasury a more positive remit to promote economic growth. It could be argued, however, that this aspect of policy would best be kept apart from public expenditure control (along the lines of Labour's separate Treasury division to promote its 'industrial strategy' in the 1970s).

One of the top priorities for a new government will be to avoid the mistakes of the 1970s. Essentially, it will need to reassure the markets (and the taxpayer) that public expenditure remains firmly under control. Here, the Treasury has played and will continue to play a key role. As the discussion above indicates, there are good reasons why a new government might consider returning to the former, more flexible system of public expenditure control. This would mean that the Treasury team would need to satisfy 'spending' colleagues that their priorities were being properly weighed against those of other departments. As a result the Treasury would have less 'top-down' power than at present, and its expenditure divisions would probably need to be reinforced to enable them to cope with the workload involved in supporting the Chief Secretary and arguing cases on their merits.

There will need to be clarification of where the Treasury's proper responsibility for the control of public expenditure should begin and end. As discussed, the Treasury enjoys special powers and privileges to enable it to carry out that role.

Treasury officials are accountable to the Chief Secretary and Chancellor, but in no real sense (in their public expenditure role) to parliament, the Public Accounts Committee or the public. At ministerial level, the conventions of collective Cabinet responsibility mean that departmental ministers have to defend their own projects and programmes, including 'cuts' and failures to spend, without blaming these on Treasury colleagues. This reflects the Treasury's essential role as a kind of extended secretariat for decisions on spending totals taken or endorsed by Cabinet collectively.

If the Chief Secretary were called on to defend publicly all the decisions where he had prevented colleagues getting their own way, his job would be impossible. Even as it is, if he has to tackle every major proposal for new expenditure in a 'spending' government his task can be very demanding indeed. But it is difficult for people working in the Treasury to realize how sheltered they are from the constant pressures of public accountability to which those in spending departments are exposed.

The danger is that these powers and privileges are carried across into policy discussions which are not (or not mainly) about public expenditure, but about all kinds of microeconomic issues. This gives Treasury officials too much power to block other departments' proposals, without they or their ministers having any need to defend the consequences.

Of course the Chancellor and Chief Secretary, as key economic ministers, may well wish to express a view, and will, therefore, need briefing for collective discussion in Cabinet, a Cabinet Committee or at No. 10. This, however, is no different from the role of, for example, the President of the Board of Trade, who relies on ordinary interdepartmental processes backed by the Cabinet Office to give him and his officials a say, without any special blocking powers.

Conclusions

There are two main conclusions that an incoming government might draw from the discussion above. First, the control of public expenditure will be both crucial and difficult. Strong Treasury ministers, with firm backing from the Prime Minister, will always be the key to success. The Treasury expenditure divisions, which have been cut back, will need to be reinforced by bringing in more people who understand the system and can assess departments' strengths and weaknesses.

There are, however, no short-cuts to controlling public expenditure. The Treasury will want to maintain fixed forward-control totals, and probably a senior ministerial committee on the lines of the present EDX to help impose these. 'Flexibility' is not a favoured word in the Treasury's vocabulary. But a new government will need to assess and re-assess its priorities, and here there is no substitute for evaluating options for additional and reduced spending at the margin in each programme.

Second, given that the balance of power appears to have shifted in the Treasury's direction, there will need to be a deliberate decision at Cabinet level to redress this balance. Essentially, the Treasury will need to be refocused on its 'core business' of public expenditure control. To this end, a clear distinction will need to be drawn between those issues which have a direct bearing on public expenditure (including value-for-money questions) and those issues where Treasury officials are simply briefing their ministers, as in any other department, without any special rights of consultation and veto. Such a distinction would be an effective step towards reversing the excessive centralization of recent years and bringing the Treasury back to its proper and crucial role of controlling public expenditure.

18

Watch the Wood Not the Trees: What the Treasury Should Be Doing

Pamela Meadows

Contents

It is remarkable to consider that even after a decade and a half of Conservative government, the fundamental problem of public expenditure, its tendency to spiral out of control, has yet to be tackled, and our institutions for controlling it are scarcely more capable of doing so than those of the 19th century.

This points the finger at the guardian of the public purse, the Treasury. In this chapter we look at why the public sector has been getting things wrong. Some are inherently difficult problems. Others stem from poor control and evaluation mechanisms. In either case they should form far more of the Treasury's agenda than they do now.

The Budget constraint

The challenge of public expenditure control is often presented as analogous to that confronting every household or company in the land. A family must, like Mr Micawber, live within its available resources. Furthermore, within its total envelope of cash it must balance competing demands: for rent, food, fuel, clothes, toys, cars, books, CDs, beer, holidays and so on. The Chancellor, in popular imagination (the Chief Secretary and the public expenditure divisions of the Treasury in reality), is likened to a frugal and prudent housewife.

But the analogy is bogus in two respects. In the first place most households have only a little control over their income. It is true that only the minority of households, dependent in the long term on state benefits, do not have any form of control. Other households have the choice at the margin of working extra hours, taking casual work, having an additional family member take a job, or of changing jobs. The Treasury, by contrast, has the power to tax.

In the second place, households that are having trouble making ends meet are generally prepared to take quite radical steps to eliminate unnecessary expenditure. They often sell their cars, stop eating meat, share bath water, or heat only one room. What they do not do is try and trim across the board. They certainly do not attach priority to maintaining their baseline expenditure in each area, and it would not occur to them to attempt to follow the Treasury approach of aiming to cut five per cent off expenditure in each area.

An analogy between the Treasury and companies also only gets us a little way. In a company, each set of costs is reviewed regularly for its contribution to output. If the product changes or the technology for producing it changes, then the expenditure on raw materials, equipment and people will inevitably be adjusted. Nothing has the right to continue unchallenged in existence, even in large and profitable organizations such as oil companies.

In the public sector these processes simply do not happen. The Treasury claims that the much trumpeted fundamental review process addresses this problem. That is either disingenuous or mistaken. Departments treat the fundamental review as a sporting contest. The Treasury is the opposing team. The strategy is to ensure that it scores as few goals as possible, while at the same time demonstrating the home team's essential sportsmanship and fair play.

Treasury impotence

This may best be illustrated by way of an example. All the evaluation evidence on government training schemes for the unemployed suggests that their impact is at best marginal in developing skills, improving participants' chances of getting a job or increasing their earnings. This has been consistently found to be the case for some time, and is widely recognized by those who are concerned with improving the level of skills available in the economy. Most of the debate about training and education therefore treats such schemes as an irrelevance. Yet when the then Department of Employment underwent its fundamental review there was no question of recognizing reality and abandoning such schemes altogether. True, provision was cut, but in a rational world a dead parrot would be recognized for what it actually is.

The problem is that within any spending department, officials' careers are bound up with delivering effectively the policy that ministers have decided to follow. It is possible to give up areas of expenditure that are not dear to ministers' hearts, however effectively and efficiently they contribute towards their objectives. The Enterprise Allowance Scheme, which encouraged the unemployed to start up in self-employment is an example of this. However, areas of expenditure where ministers have made claims and staked political capital are not susceptible to a process of open discussion. The only opportunity for such action comes with a change of minister since new ministers can more readily distance themselves from the pronouncements of their predecessors, and can therefore contemplate with relative equanimity the prospect of abandoning a particular programme or policy. The Treasury is relatively powerless in the face of a powerful and well-connected minister.

The main exception to this rule is the manifesto commitment. Anyone reviewing manifestos ten years after they were written will find a large number of forgotten and abandoned pledges. But some manage to achieve enormous significance. The Conservative party's commitment to child benefit has meant that alone of all the major welfare benefits, there has been no major debate about its distribution and level since 1979, until the recent suggestion from the Labour Party that it might be withdrawn from those over 16.

The only real hope for sensible examination of policies seems to lie with the National Audit Office (NAO). The old Exchequer and Audit Department concentrated on straightforward audit: what was paid to whom and why. The NAO also looks at value for money issues. This means that it is willing to consider challenging sacred cows if they do not seem to represent the most efficient or effective way of delivering a particular objective. While the NAO cannot challenge policy decisions as such, it can point out to taxpayers how much they are paying for the privilege of indulging the particular whims of politicians. This tends to lead to uncomfortable questions.

Producer control

In the public sector the market-driven disciplines that apply to households and companies simply do not exist. If an activity was undertaken last year there is at the very least an implicit assumption that it will continue this year, next year and every year into the foreseeable future. If a service has been delivered in a particular way, there is no automatic mechanism to challenge the method of providing the service, let alone its right to continued existence. There is no reward for improving efficiency, and therefore no incentive for anyone to attempt to do so. And the status of individual managers is related to the size of the budgets under their control.

The very suggestion that there might be some sort of challenge is greeted with cries of 'Cuts!'. This is a phrase that has a sort of totemic significance, particularly on the political left. In the early 1980s, when the first serious attempts were made to reduce some areas of expenditure, it was notable that the campaigns against the cuts sought to protect jobs and services in that order. There are times when the public sector resembles nothing more than a sheltered employment scheme for a significant share of the nation's relatively well-educated middle classes. The ethos is not so much about pride in providing high-quality services to a deserving public at a reasonable price: a laudable ethos that many diverse private sector companies such as Marks and Spencer or IBM would share. Rather the ethos is one of producer control. The high-minded people who run our public services know what services we should get and how we should get them. And we should never be expected to have less of any one of them, even if we have more of others.

There is a myth that the public sector has suffered major reductions in employment because of 'cuts'. In fact, the reduction in public sector employment has been minuscule compared with what has happened in manufacturing. Much of it has come about because of the transfer of activities into the private sector under contracting out. Moreover, the staff cuts that there have been have been concentrated on relatively low-paid manual workers (home helps, school dinner ladies, park keepers, street sweepers and the like). The armies of white-collar workers in our town halls and government offices have emerged virtually unscathed: indeed in local authorities they have grown. In our hospitals they have exploded in number to the point that even Conservative government ministers recognize that there is cause for alarm.

Practices that to the private sector seem merely quaint survive in the public sector. In much of the private sector, for example, developments in technology have led to the establishment of small teams of secretaries working in support of a group of managers. The one thing these secretaries rarely do is type, except for documents drafted on their own initiative. The managers themselves type much of their own material. In the public sector the traditional one-to-one (or one-to-two) relationship is more likely to persist. Indeed, it is quite likely that there are places where the typing pool still exists.

When I first joined the civil service in 1974, I was a reasonably competent touch typist and was used to drafting at least part of my work directly onto the keyboard. I therefore asked those responsible for office equipment for a typewriter. I was refused one on the grounds that only typists were allowed to type, and that by having the temerity to refuse to draft in longhand and wait five days for it to be returned, I was wickedly attempting to put those worthy and deserving typists out of a job. I would not want to claim that extreme examples such as this persist today, but the ethos that underlies it is still alive, and this is the challenge that has to be confronted.

Taxpayers' money and demand-led expenditure

Those responsible for the stewardship of public sector resources should be reminded at regular intervals that income tax is payable on earnings of less than £100 a week; that VAT is payable on a wide range of essentials; that some families are driven into debt to pay their council tax. Public expenditure is paid for by the poor as well as by the well-off and by companies. Indeed, the contribution by the poor to public expenditure is likely to make a greater difference to their standard of living than the far larger contribution made by those on higher incomes. A family paying £5 a week in tax may have a less nutritious diet, or dress its children only from charity shops as a result. A family paying £500 in tax may need to cut back only on the third holiday or car.

It is ironic that the emphasis in the public sector is on being careful with the expenditure of taxpayers' money, without recognizing that the two most important elements of public expenditure are transfer payments (mainly social security benefits) and wages and salaries. Great care is devoted, in theory at least, to the stewardship of the third item: expenditure on goods and services. But at times this reaches ludicrous proportions. The cost of managing and overseeing relatively small amounts of money is often disproportionate. This is readily apparent to anyone who has been on the receiving end of government research funding or many forms of DTI support to small businesses. The amount of time it consumes means that often public sector funding is too expensive for the potential recipients to take.

Demand-led expenditure

Social security expenditure is, of course, inherently difficult to control, since it is demand led. Demographic influences are powerful, and changes in rules to try and limit demand have a habit of encouraging people to qualify under another category. Given their importance in overall spending it is surprising that the Treasury rarely considers evidence other than that derived from economic modelling in its considerations. Evidence from psychology and sociology, particularly qualitative work, tends to demonstrate that administrative obstacles and procedures are as important as the qualifying rules in determining who will claim which benefits under which circumstances. Given that quite small changes in behaviour can have large expenditure implications, such evidence should be considered more carefully.

There is an inherent tension between policy decisions and expenditure decisions. The political game is to get political backing for the policy – be it the growth in the prison population or the installation of road humps. The pressure is then on the Treasury or the local authority finance department to find the resources. Yet policy decisions ought to be challenged on expenditure grounds. Long prison sentences are not a very cost-effective way of reducing crime. Road humps do slow traffic down, but they also slow down emergency service vehicles and can lead to the diversion of bus routes, to the disadvantage of the elderly and parents with young children who are more dependent on public transport than other groups. It is hard, however, to challenge expenditure on policies like this under the present institutional arrangements.

There are areas of public expenditure that we all know are a complete waste of money. My own local authority had a plan not so long ago to deploy council staff hiding behind trees to catch adults cycling on the pavements. Fortunately they had the sense to scrap the plan once it had been exposed to public ridicule. But that ridicule only came about because the council proudly announced the plan to the local press. A neighbour in his nineties was denied an elderly person's travel permit because he could not prove that he was over 60 at his first visit, even though he had an expired permit, was known to the social services department and it would have been difficult to mistake him for a man in his sixties. Everyone has their own stories.

The Treasury does not have the information to pinpoint where these kinds of waste occur and probably never could. This suggests that much stronger internal control mechanisms are needed. There can never be effective central control of all items in £300 billion worth of public expenditure. Instead of recognizing that and trying to take account of it, the Treasury tries to exercise excessive control over those items of expenditure that it knows about. Until the recent cuts in Treasury staffing, departments had to go to the Treasury for approval of some very small sums (sometimes less than £10000) even where the expenditure was covered by voted funds and was clearly being incurred for an appropriate reason. These levels of delegated authority, which varied across departments and across types of expenditure, gave the Treasury some semblance of being in charge but the decisions were invariably taken by junior officials, more or less on the nod. Those officials' salaries were a classic example of public sector waste.

Every proposal for new expenditure, however small, is scrutinized in great detail. Existing expenditure is simply not challenged in the same way, especially if it has persisted for 30 years or more, and particularly if it is large. Nobody says 'Do we need an army?'; they ask whether we should buy one type of tank or another, or even one type of shell or another. Encouragingly the question is now being asked as to whether we need the current level of expenditure on military music, but that is still a minor part of the whole operation.

I have to confess to being an admirer of the British army. It is well trained and professional, and every time it is seen on operational duties with counterparts from other countries, as in the former Yugoslavia, it is clear that it can and does deliver effectively. Whether we actually need such an institution, however, ought to be discussed. Perhaps we should be more like the Swiss and have a citizens' army, or the Israelis and rely on reservists. Within the army do we need all the ranks and trades that we currently have? In other walks of life flatter command structures with fewer middle management levels, which give greater autonomy and initiative to those in the front line, are proving to be very effective. They may not be right for the army, but the question does not even appear to have been raised. If cuts are made, they are of divisions or battalions, not the removal of majors or lance-corporals from the command structure.

The one area where there does appear to have been genuine progress towards challenging what is provided and how, is the much maligned National Health Service. The current system is certainly not perfect. There are clearly problems with accident and emergency services and with intensive-care bed availability. But the move to evidence-based medicine and the purchaser–provider split, including GP fundholding, are providing an inbuilt challenge mechanism. Ironically the new incentive structure may have introduced some inefficiencies. The air ambulance in London belongs to one hospital and as a result only takes patients there, even where there is a fully equipped accident and emergency department with a helicopter landing pad closer at hand. This is nonsense and endangers the lives of seriously injured patients unnecessarily. If there is a need for an air ambulance then it should be part of the ambulance service as it is in other parts of the country, and patients who merit the use of such a service should be taken to the nearest hospital equipped to deal with them.

But the remainder of the public sector continues to function in the old way, and this is why the company or household analogy simply does not wash. As children grow, households discard cots, prams and tricycles and move into video games, replica football kit and Sindy dolls. Changes in tastes and needs are adapted to naturally. In the public sector it is likely that there will be inertia in the provision of prams and tricycles. The trike and pram producers have good jobs. Their managers like being responsible for trikes and prams. They like the traditions and the sense of social worth. And after all, budgetary allocation has been made for trikes and prams since time immemorial.

There are absolutely no brownie points but potentially a good deal of grief from pointing out that public demand for trikes and prams seems to be falling off somewhat. The persistent failure in most local education authorities to eliminate surplus school places except after years of dithering is a case in point. Public sector managers are naturally reluctant to abolish the jobs of their own staff, and staff are, of course, the most important element of public expenditure. They do not have the excuse that because there is no longer a market for them there is no longer a need to produce winklepickers or hula hoops. In the market sector, changes in customer tastes and shifts in demand take the responsibility for making the challenge out of managers' hands. Unfortunately in the public sector it is patently in their hands. Their responsibility to distant taxpayers (however poor) rates less highly than their responsibility for their known colleagues (however well paid). This is why producer capture remains a very real problem in the public sector. Its roots lie in sociable human behaviour, and there are no countervailing forces.

This means that while the trike and pram division is continuing with its quiet and satisfying way of life the demand for replica football kit is going through the roof. The front-line workers in that area are cracking under the pressure. The consumers of the service are bombarding their councillors, their MPs and the press with their complaints about the inadequacy of the provision. Politicians quite rightly respond to that pressure and seek resources for the new services. But, unlike the household, they are also persisting in spending on a service for which demand has collapsed. Their traditions, culture and decision-making mechanisms do not make the abolition of somebody else's patch an appropriate solution to offer.

Boundary issues

This leads on to the general issue of turf. To a normal human being it is obvious that at times expenditure in one area is a direct consequence of failure to spend in another. It makes sense to spend money on education and social support mechanisms such as the youth service if that expenditure makes it less likely that young people will become involved in criminal activity, either now or in the future. However, there is no incentive at all for any public sector manager to incur expenditure which will yield savings for somebody else's budget, particularly if those savings will take 10 years or more to become apparent, and there is no mechanism within the Treasury to try and make those trade-offs more explicit. The old Programme Analysis and Reviews did recognize that sometimes trade-offs had to be made, but they were always approached by departments in a defensive way, and there was little eagerness to offer up serious problems for consideration.

Conclusion

Essentially nobody in the public sector believes that their budget constraint is genuinely binding. First, everyone knows that when it comes to the crunch the department or the council or the health authority has a reserve tucked away to deal with unexpected overruns. Second, other than in cases of flagrant disregard, it is relatively rare for a public sector manager to be disciplined or even reprimanded for the kind of budget overruns that in the private sector could lead to dismissal. Third, it is always possible to raise more money from anonymous taxpayers. Unlike households or private companies, the public sector has the power to confiscate money from law-abiding citizens, rich and poor alike. And it is not just the Treasury. Every local authority in the land, from the smallest parish council to the giant county of Hampshire, has the same power of extortion. So do all police authorities, the London Fire and Civil Defence Authority and related quangos.

If households or companies chose to rob their fellow citizens to pay for services that are provided unnecessarily, or unnecessarily expensively, but which provide them with a reasonable income, there would be an outcry and they would probably end up in prison. Yet this is what the public sector does every day. Until we find a way of challenging the expenditure of every pound – *really* attempting to implement zero base budgeting – any government is failing to exercise proper accountability to its citizens. It is this agenda that the Treasury should be applying its mind to seriously.

Index

Note page references in **bold** refer to figures, tables and boxes